NEW PERSPECTIVES ON
Margaret Laurence

Recent Titles in
Contributions in Women's Studies

Nineteenth-Century American Women Theatre Managers
Jane Kathleen Curry

Textual Escap(e)ades: Mobility, Maternity, and Textuality in Contemporary Fiction by Women
Lindsey Tucker

The Repair of the World: The Novels of Marge Piercy
Kerstin W. Shands

Clara Barton: In the Service of Humanity
David H. Burton

International Women's Writing: New Landscapes of Identity
Anne E. Brown and Marjanne Goozé, editors

"Some Appointed Work To Do": Women and Vocation in the Fiction of Elizabeth Gaskell
Robin B. Colby

Women, Politics, and the United Nations
Anne Winslow, editor

Envisioning the New Adam: Empathic Portraits of Men by American Women Writers
Patricia Ellen Martin Daly, editor

Before Equal Suffrage: Women in Partisan Politics from Colonial Times to 1920
Robert J. Dinkin

"Nobody Wants to Hear Our Truth": Homeless Women and Theories of the Welfare State
Meredith L. Ralston

Spanish Women in the Golden Age: Images and Realities
Magdalena S. Sánchez and Alain Saint-Saëns

Russian Women in Politics and Society
Wilma Rule and Norma Noonan, editors

NEW PERSPECTIVES ON
Margaret Laurence

Poetic Narrative, Multiculturalism, and Feminism

EDITED BY
Greta M. K. McCormick Coger

Contributions in Women's Studies, Number 154

GREENWOOD PRESS
Westport, Connecticut • London

Library of Congress Cataloging-in-Publication Data

New perspectives on Margaret Laurence : poetic narrative,
  multiculturalism, and feminism / edited by Greta M. K. McCormick
  Coger.
    p.   cm.—(Contributions in women's studies, ISSN 0147–104X ;
  no. 154)
    Includes bibliographical references (p.   ) and index.
    ISBN 0–313–29042–3 (alk. paper)
    1. Laurence, Margaret—Criticism and interpretation.   2. Feminism
  and literature—Canada—History—20th century.   3. Women and
  literature—Canada—History—20th century.   4. Pluralism (Social
  sciences) in literature.   5. Canada—In literature.   6. Narration
  (Rhetoric)   7. Poetics.   I. Coger, Greta M. (Greta Margaret)
  II. Series.
  PR9199.3.L33Z8   1996
  813'.54—dc20   95–35711

British Library Cataloguing in Publication Data is available.

Copyright © 1996 by Greta M. K. McCormick Coger

All rights reserved. No portion of this book may be
reproduced, by any process or technique, without the
express written consent of the publisher.

Library of Congress Catalog Card Number: 95–35711
ISBN: 0–313–29042–3
ISSN: 0147–104X

First published in 1996

Greenwood Press, 88 Post Road West, Westport, CT 06881
An imprint of Greenwood Publishing Group, Inc.

Printed in the United States of America

The paper used in this book complies with the
Permanent Paper Standard issued by the National
Information Standards Organization (Z39.48–1984).

10 9 8 7 6 5 4 3 2 1

Copyright Acknowledgments

The editor and publisher gratefully acknowledge permission to reprint the following material:

Excerpts from B. V. Andrzejewski and I. M. Lewis, *Somali Poetry: An Introduction*. Oxford: Clarendon Press, 1964. Used by permission of Oxford University Press.

Extract from Nuruddin Farah, *Close Sesame*. St. Paul, Minn.: Graywolf Press, 1992. Copyright 1992 by Nuruddin Farah. Reprinted from *Close Sesame* with the permission of Graywolf Press, Saint Paul, Minnesota.

From Karen Horney, *Our Inner Conflicts*. New York: W. W. Norton, 1945. Copyright © 1945 W. W. Norton. Used by permission of W. W. Norton.

From Karen Horney, *Self Analysis*. New York: W. W. Norton, 1942. Copyright © 1942 W. W. Norton. Used by permission of W. W. Norton.

Excerpts from *The Stone Angel*. U.S. edition: University of Chicago Press Edition, 1993. Copyright New End Inc. Permission courtesy of New End Inc.

Excerpts from *The Diviners*. U.S. edition: University of Chicago Press Edition, 1993. Copyright New End Inc. Permission courtesy of New End Inc.

Excerpts from *A Jest of God*. U.S. edition: University of Chicago Press Edition, 1993. Copyright New End Inc. Permission courtesy of New End Inc.

Excerpts from *The Fire-Dwellers*. U.S. edition: University of Chicago Press Edition, 1993. Copyright New End Inc. Permission courtesy of New End Inc.

Excerpts from *A Bird in the House*. U.S. edition: University of Chicago Press Edition, 1993. Copyright New End Inc. Permission courtesy of New End Inc.

Excerpts from *This Side Jordan*. © Margaret Laurence. Reprinted with the permission of the Estate of Margaret Laurence.

Excerpts from *The Tomorrow-Tamer*. © Margaret Laurence. Reprinted with the permission of the Estate of Margaret Laurence.

Excerpts from *The Prophet's Camel Bell*. © Margaret Laurence. Reprinted with the permission of the Estate of Margaret Laurence.

Excerpts from *A Tree for Poverty*. ©Margaret Laurence. Reprinted with the permission of the Estate of Margaret Laurence.

Excerpts from *Dance on the Earth*. © Margaret Laurence. Reprinted with the permission of the Estate of Margaret Laurence.

From *Dance on the Earth* by Margaret Laurence. Used by permission of the Canadian Publishers, McClelland & Stewart, Toronto.

From *The Diviners* by Margaret Laurence. Used by permission of the Canadian Publishers, McClelland & Stewart, Toronto.

From *The Prophet's Camel Bell* by Margaret Laurence. Used by permission of the Canadian Publishers, McClelland & Stewart, Toronto.

From *The Fire-Dwellers* by Margaret Laurence. Used by permission of the Canadian Publishers, McClelland & Stewart, Toronto.

From *The Tomorrow-Tamer* by Margaret Laurence. Used by permission of the Canadian Publishers, McClelland & Stewart, Toronto.

From *A Jest of God* by Margaret Laurence. Used by permission of the Canadian Publishers, McClelland & Stewart, Toronto.

From *A Bird in the House* by Margaret Laurence. Used by permission of the Canadian Publishers, McClelland & Stewart, Toronto.

From *This Side Jordan* by Margaret Laurence. Used by permission of the Canadian Publishers, McClelland & Stewart, Toronto.

From *The Stone Angel* by Margaret Laurence. Used by permission of the Canadian Publishers, McClelland & Stewart, Toronto.

Excerpts from *A Tree for Poverty* by Margaret Laurence. Copyright © The Estate of Margaret Laurence, McMaster University Library Press, and ECW Press, 1993. Used with permission of ECW Press, McMaster University Library Press, and the Estate of Margaret Laurence.

Extracts from *The Stone Angel* by Margaret Laurence are reprinted by kind permissions of the publisher, Virago Press.

Extracts from *The Diviners* by Margaret Laurence are reprinted by kind permission of the publisher, Virago Press.

Extracts from *A Bird in the House* by Margaret Laurence. Used by permission of A.P. Watt Ltd on behalf of New End Inc.

Extracts from *The Tomorrow-Tamer* by Margaret Laurence. Used by permission of A.P. Watt on behalf of New End. Inc.

Extracts from *The Prophet's Camel Bell* by Margaret Laurence. Used by permission of A. P. Watt on behalf of New End Inc.

Extracts from *This Side Jordan* by Margaret Laurence. Used by permission of A. P. Watt on behalf of New End Inc.

Extracts from *A Jest of God* by Margaret Laurence. Used by permission of A. P. Watt on behalf of New End Inc.

Extracts from *Dance on the Earth* by Margaret Laurence. Used by permission of A. P. Watt on behalf of New End Inc.

Extracts from *The Fire-Dwellers* by Margaret Laurence. Used by permission of A. P. Watt on behalf of New End Inc.

Extracts from *A Tree for Poverty* by Margaret Laurence. Used by permission of A. P. Watt on behalf of New End Inc.

"The Angel and the Living Water: Metaphorical Networks and Structural Opposition in *The Stone Angel* " by Michel Fabre. Translated into English by Marie Bell-Salter and edited by Raymonde Neil. Reprinted in *Etudes Anglaises* (Paris) 35.1 (1985): 57–70. Used by permission of Didier Erudition.

Every reasonable effort has been made to trace the owners of copyright materials in this book, but in some instances this has proven impossible. The editor and publisher will be glad to receive information leading to more complete acknowledgments in subsequent printings of the book and in the meantime extend their apologies for any omissions.

To the members of the Margaret Laurence Society

Contents

Preface   xiii

Introduction   xvii

PART I: LANGUAGE, THEME, AND IMAGE IN LAURENCE

1. Margaret Laurence: Novelist-as-Poet   3
 Walter E. Swayze
2. The Angel and the Living Water: Metaphorical Networks
 and Structural Opposition in *The Stone Angel*   17
 Michel Fabre
3. Stacey Cameron MacAindra: The Fire *This* Time   29
 Lyall H. Powers
4. A World Divided, A World Divined: Two North American Fictions   41
 Neil Besner

PART II: NARRATIVE STRUCTURE IN LAURENCE

5. Hagar Shipley's Rage for Life: Narrative Technique in *The Stone Angel*   51
 Alice Bell
6. "Sisters Under Their Skins": *A Jest of God* and *The Fire-Dwellers*   63
 Nora Foster Stovel
7. Coherence in *A Bird in the House*   81
 Bruce Stovel
8. Dividing *The Diviners*   97
 Ken McLean

PART III: MULTICULTURALISM IN LAURENCE

9. War in the Manawaka Novels as Macrocosm, Fictionalized
   Biography, and Imaginative History 115
   Greta M. K. McCormick Coger
10. Margaret Laurence of Hargeisa: A Discussion of *A Tree for Poverty* 129
    Fiona Sparrow
11. Margaret Laurence and the Ancestral Tradition 137
    Cecil Abrahams
12. "It Was Like the Book Says, But It Wasn't": Oral Folk History
    in Laurence's *The Diviners* 143
    Lynn Pifer

PART IV: FEMINIST PERSPECTIVES IN LAURENCE

13. Self-alienation of the Elderly in Margaret Laurence's Fiction 153
    Rosalie Murphy Baum
14. Coming to Terms with the Image of the Mother in *The Stone Angel* 161
    Cynthia Taylor
15. The Subversive Voice in *The Fire-Dwellers* 173
    Mitzi Hamovitch
16. Morag Gunn in Fictional Context: The Career Woman Theme
    in *The Diviners* 179
    Susan Ward
17. Wordsmith and Woman: Morag Gunn's Triumph Through Language 187
    Laurie Lindberg
18. Writing a Woman's Life: Celebration, Sorrow, and Pathos
    in Margaret Laurence's Memoir *Dance on the Earth* 203
    Alexandra Pett

Selected Bibliography 217

Index 221

About the Editor and Contributors 231

Preface

Coming to the South to teach in Senatobia near Oxford, Mississippi, I learned how Southern writers are highly prized: for instance, Eudora Welty, William Faulkner, and Tennessee Williams are celebrated in yearly symposia; Elizabeth Spencer, Walker Percy, Stark Young, Richard Wright, and Alice Walker have lived in and written about Mississippi. John Grisham became a popular culture literary phenomena who supports the annual Book Festival and *The Oxford American*. Furthermore, the American local color tale is a major indigenous literary mode. I compared its themes to Canadian regional and Leacock humor, Scottish reductive idiom, and African oral tradition. Margaret Laurence makes use of all three. The transition of American local color tradition to sophisticated narratives has a Canadian parallel in Margaret Laurence's creative narrative techniques: some of these are sayings; slogans; radio news lines; newspaper headlines; "Memorybank Movies"; tales (revised when retold) mythologizing ordinary, personable, and historical people; and dramatizations of past and present. The Southern attachment to land, as shown in William Faulkner's literary creation of Yoknapatawpha is as strong as the Scots-Canadian attachment to land, which Margaret Laurence shows in her "Manawaka" novels. Margaret Laurence vividly creates Manawaka as "a place to stand on."

All of this prompted me to compare Margaret Laurence's literary region of Manawaka based on a prairie town similar to Neepawa, Manitoba, and to explore the Scottish migrations in the nineteenth century to Mississippi and Manitoba. Margaret Laurence lived in more than one country--Canada, Somalia, Ghana, Britain. Her odyssey was similar to my own: I lived west of Neepawa, went to United College, and studied and taught in Scotland and West Africa. In Sierra Leone, I first read Margaret Laurence's African writings. When I came to Mississippi to teach, after completing my doctoral studies at the University of Colorado, I noted the literary industry of William Faulkner. I began to compare Margaret Laurence and her literary region to Faulkner and his and to Elizabeth Spencer whose odyssey took her from teaching at my college (where John Grisham was a student) in Senatobia (Mississippi) to Rome (Italy),

Montreal (Quebec), and back to the South in Durham (North Carolina). I observed that students comparing Margaret Laurence's *A Bird in the House, The Diviners,* and *The Stone Angel,* Eudora Welty's and Elizabeth Spencer's Mississippi stories, Camara Laye's *The African Child,* and some of Wole Soyinka's dramas saw more similarity between warm, wet Mississippi--extended family and oral culture emphasis with acceptance of the Gothic elements--and the tropical West African fecund environment --extended family and oral tradition--than with the cold northern climate and inward-looking, dour, cautious, Calvinistic Scots-Canadian characters.

Origins of this collection of essays began after I conducted ten interviews with Margaret Laurence's relatives, neighbors, classmates, teachers, and friends when asked to speak in honor of teachers at Cardale in my home municipality of Blanshard in Manitoba. Then in response to my notice for a Modern Language Association Special Session, I received several papers for what became "Margaret Laurence: A Tribute" which I chaired at the December MLA meeting in San Francisco in 1987. Rosalie Murphy Baum, Ken McLean, Alice Bell, and Cecil Abrahams presented essays to which Gayle Greene responded by placing Margaret Laurence's writings about aging and death in the context of many contemporary women authors.

Nearly all in the crowded room signed up to form a Margaret Laurence Society which they continue to support. Several--Alexandra Pett, Tracy Ware, Rosalie Murphy Baum, Ken McLean (associate editor), Gayle Greene, Lyall H. Powers (treasurer), myself (president and editor), Ann Barnard--were again present when the board was elected at Brandon University, August 8-11, 1988, at the "Margaret Laurence: Her Life and Work Conference." Over a hundred attended. Most became members: the first life members were Dorothy Campbell Henderson and Walter E. Swayze (honorary president); others were Nora Foster Stovel, Fiona Sparrow, Tracy Ware, Anita Skeen, Joy Kuropatwa, Henry Carr Phelps, Jo-Anne Elder, Lynn Pifer, Charlene Diehl-Jones, John Blaikie (member-at-large), Bruce Stovel, Susan Ward, Neil Besner (secretary), Christl Verduyn, Shawn Hayes, Elizabeth van Berkel, Wendy Olmstead, Theresia Quigley, Karen Macfarlane, Melissa Kaplan, Carolyn Hlus Redl, Helen Buss (vice-president), Barbara Powell, Marian Markham, Toshiko Tsutsumi (member-at-large), and Akai Asai. The last two introduced scholarship in Japan about Margaret Laurence --how her women characters are different from those portrayed by Japanese authors. More papers were placed in this collection; many other papers and tributes have been published in the *Margaret Laurence Review* and *Margaret Laurence Newsletter* (Northwest Mississippi), *Obirin Studies in English Language and Literature* (Tokyo), and *The American Review of Canadian Studies* (Washington, D.C.); also see Buss, Godard, and Verduyn in the Selected Bibliography.

Students and scholars sent papers and requested materials, some through the thirty-two national associations of Canadian Studies of the International Council of Canadian Studies. Nearly a hundred proposals received for the Margaret Laurence Symposium held at the University of Ottawa, April 29 to May 1 (1994), could not be scheduled; included here is Alexandra Pett's essay on Margaret Laurence's *Dance on the Earth: A Memoir*. The word count limit for this book did not permit the inclusion of papers from India, Spain, Japan, Germany, China, and America. The *Margaret Laurence Review* is the venue for these and other essays from Margaret Laurence Conferences.

In the preparation of this manuscript, I appreciate the editorial assistance of Nora Foster Stovel (Alberta), Laurie Lindberg (Pikeville College), Lucille Johnson (Pacific Lutheran University), Rosalie Murphy Baum (South Florida), Ken McLean (Bishop's), Carolyn Hlus Redl (Keyano College, Fort McMurray, Alberta), Helen M. Buss (Calgary), Bruce Stovel (Alberta), Lyall H. Powers (Michigan), Donez Xiques (City College), Gayle Greene (Scripps), Beth Bunce, Dale Davis, and Judy Vernon (Northwest Mississippi). Encouragement came from many--at Northwest Mississippi from Carson Holloman, Jean Moore, Dean Marilyn Comer, Joanne Reid, Linda Hogan, Pam Darnell, Erline Cocke, Charlotte Johnston, librarians Mae Belle Fly, Carolyn Ainsworth, Marvelen McCullar, Caroline L. Brownlee, Catherine S. Warren, and Betty Sykes Green--and at the University of Memphis from Rita Broadway, Jane Qualls, Dr. Pam Palmer, and Professor Leo Connolly. I especially thank my husband, Professor Dalvan M. Coger, who was preparing his own book manuscript at the same time.

Introduction

MARGARET LAURENCE'S LIFE AND LITERARY ACHIEVEMENT

When Margaret Laurence died on January 5, 1987, she had published sixteen books--five African books based on Somalia, Ghana, and Nigeria; five Manawaka novels modeled after her childhood hometown of Neepawa and other prairie towns; four children's books; one book of essays; and a memoir--besides innumerable poems; addresses; and articles in journals, magazines, and newspapers. Margaret Laurence was writer-in-residence at four universities. She was presented with the Governor-General's Award in 1967 and again in 1975. In 1971, she received the highest award available to a citizen when she was made a Companion of the Order of Canada. From 1981-1983, she was Chancellor of Trent University, Peterborough, Ontario. Interim chairman of the committee set up to found the Writers' Union of Canada, Laurence received eleven honorary degrees between 1970-1981 and refused many others. She was nominated for the Nobel Prize in Literature in 1982.

Laurence had roots in Canada and its Scottish tradition for her paternal forebears came from Fife and Edinburgh and her Scots-Irish maternal great-grandparents came to Canada from Country Tyrone, Northern Ireland. Robert Wemyss, a partner in his father's law firm in Neepawa, married Verna Simpson in 1922. Jean Margaret Wemyss, their daughter, was born on July 18, 1926. When she was four, her mother died. Her mother's sister, a teacher of English, became Laurence's stepmother. With her, Margaret Laurence began her literary career. They read many books and talked, especially about Canadian literature, long before it was a subject taught in Canadian universities and schools. "Peggy" and her friends made up "let's pretend" games; she wrote many stories in her notebooks. Conscious of her vocation to be a writer since she was fourteen, Margaret was editor of the high-school yearbook, *Black and Gold*. Of her contributions to *Vox* at United College in 1944, a line in one poem presented the author's own sensibly perceived experience of "A world which gave me my own lifework to do." She graduated with a Bachelor of Arts degree in Honors English in 1947 and became a journalist for the *Winnipeg Citizen*. In 1948, she married Jack Laurence, an engineer.

In England and then Somalia (1950-1952) Margaret kept journals, which became the bases, ten years later for her memoir/travelogue *The Prophet's Camel Bell* (1963), known in America as *A New Wind in a Dry Land*. Her first book *A Tree for Poverty* was innovative because she wrote, and did so poetically, the first translations of two Somali oral literature forms into another language. It was published by the British Protectorate of Somaliland Government (Nairobi, 1954), reprinted by Irish (Dublin, Ireland) and McMaster (Hamilton, Canada) University Presses (1970), and again reprinted with an introduction by ECW Press (Toronto, Canada, 1993). International scholars--for example, Fiona Sparrow in *Into Africa with Margaret Laurence* (Toronto: ECW, 1992) and B. W. Andrzejewski in *An Anthology of Somali Poetry* (Bloomington: Indiana University Press, 1993)--and Somali scholars and novelist, Nuruddin Farah--still applaud her artistically creative translations, which are true to the original Somali meanings, and still refer to her valid critical assessment.

Between 1952 and 1957 she bore two children, Jocelyn and David, while living in Ghana. While there Margaret Laurence wrote short stories published in Canadian journals (1957 to 1962) and collected in *The Tomorrow-Tamer and Other Stories* (1963). Before the widespread use of the term postcolonialism, Laurence earned the respect of African critics who consider these as the first writings by Westerners to portray African characters without imperial condescension. Ghana is the setting for her first novel, *This Side Jordan* (1960), one of the earliest to portray African and British cultures together. She was again innovative because she wrote the first book-length critique of literature in English by Nigerians, *Long Drums and Cannons* (1968). This viable literary assessment is still included in selected bibliographies.

In writing these five books and many newspaper reviews and articles Laurence matured her literary techniques. She then turned to the Canadian venue for what became her Manawaka novels. In Vancouver, where she returned in 1957, she wrote the first drafts in 1961 and 1962 of *The Stone Angel*. The final draft was written in Britain, her home for ten years. *The Stone Angel* was published in 1964. Her next Manawaka novels were *A Jest of God,* published in 1966, and *The Fire-Dwellers,* published in 1969. From 1962-1969, she also published the stories which were collected in *A Bird in the House* (1970). Because she wanted her daughter and son to be educated in Canada, between 1969 and 1974 she accepted positions as writer-in-residence at Massey Graduate College, University of Toronto, and at two other Ontario universities. *The Diviners* (1974) was written mostly in Canada at Lakefield, Ontario, where she purchased a house, and at a cottage on the Otonabee River. McMaster University Archives is the repository of these five Manawaka manuscripts. Several articles were republished in *Heart of a Stranger* (1976). Films were made of her life and of some novels. Near her death in 1987, she wrote a memoir, *Dance on the Earth* (1989), which highlights her relationship with and influence of her mother, stepmother, and mother-in-law. This modest woman with her love of writing and receiving letters corresponded with many and wrote about twenty-five hundred letters a year, now in York University Archives, Toronto. John Lennox edited the Margaret Laurence-Al Purdy correspondence of twenty years, from December 1966 to December 1986 in *Margaret Laurence-Al Purdy: A Friendship in Letters* (Toronto: McClelland and Stewart, 1993).

The literary achievement of Laurence places her as a leading major contemporary postmodern author. She shows her impressive range, variety, richness, and innovation in several ways. She chose women protagonists, of older ages, up to ninety years, who, moving forward in present time, can look back and evaluate / re-vision up to six generations. Though she was one of the first women writers to have themes of old age and death in women's experience, astonishingly, she was not near the age of her protagonists. She was only in her midthirties when she wrote *The Stone Angel;* its protagonist was in her nineties. Until this novel was published in 1954, very few writers had depicted old age in women or men. Also, Laurence's work has a major focus on the importance of accepting the fact of death. In this she can be compared to William Faulkner and Tolstoy; similar to the latter's *The Death of Ivan Ilyich*, Hagar has a compulsion to hold on to life while retreating to smaller spaces. Another major theme of her work is the mother-child bond. Furthermore, the theme of multiculturalism (sometimes called "conflict of cultures"), which one of her teachers, Wes McAmmond, said Margaret Laurence invented, appears in her early writing, for example, in *This Side Jordan*. She portrays new ethnic combinations as a result of marriage, and she portrayed cultures besides those of Africa and Britain, such as Canada where Scottish, French, Indian, Ukrainian, Jewish, and English heritage could be presented affirming life while working through various stages of resolution. She created a continuity of cultural heritages by integrating her thorough biblical knowledge (see *Old Testament Women in Western Literature* edited by Jan Wojcik and Raymond-Jean Frontain, Purdue University Press, 1989) to build up narrative and poetic image associations in contemporary parallels. That she was an innovator of styles shows in her newly created narrative structures to reveal more fully the characters' development. She chose to portray the inner point of view in the five Manawaka novels. Rachel Cameron's story could only be told through the first-person to reveal her awareness of herself and others. This viewpoint shows sensitivity as well as strength with self-criticism. Negative comments do not signal failure but recognition which leads to maturer action. Hagar is another protagonist whose negative comments are evidence not of failure but of her growing concern for others and relationships. Even in *The Fire-Dwellers* where Stacey's thoughts are set forth in third person, the perspective is her inward thoughts as she looks out on her world. Its four levels of consciousness are interwoven: outer reality, thoughts, memories, and reveries or fantasies. The modes for each level proliferate and vary in each Manawaka novel. Laurence also created new combinations of oral methods: memories and thoughts interspersed with news; both Western and African storytellers' methods. The variety and richness of Laurence's work led to a need for this book of eighteen essays.

New Perspectives on Margaret Laurence is a comprehensive collection of predominantly American scholarship. Furthermore, the American academic community can more easily obtain this book. Several books on Margaret Laurence's writing (by Canadians and a Scot) are published outside of America: for instance, *Margaret Laurence: The Long Journey Home* by Patricia Morley (reprint, with an Afterword, Montreal and Kingston: McGill-Queen's, [1981] 1991), *Critical Approaches to the Fiction of Margaret Laurence* edited by Colin Nicholson (London: Macmillan; Vancouver: University of British Columbia Press, 1990), and the

Proceedings of the Margaret Laurence Symposium, University of Ottawa, April 29-May 1, 1994, edited by David Staines, which focuses on her place in the Canadian literary canon. Only a few American university presses have published books on Laurence, such as Gayle Greene's *Changing the Story* (Indiana University Press, 1991) and Lorna Irvine's *Critical Spaces: Margaret Laurence and Janet Frame* (Columbia, South Carolina: Camden House, 1995). Greene assesses Laurence as seminal to the feminist movement. Irvine compares Laurence's decolonization experience to Janet Frame's in New Zealand.

Margaret Laurence is well-known to Americans because three novels were published simultaneously, two novels were Book-of-the-Month Club selections, one was made into the movie (*Rachel, Rachel*), *The Diviners* is widely read and taught in women's studies and literature courses in American universities, and the University of Chicago Press has issued all five Manawaka novels. Margaret Laurence's stories are included in anthologies used by several American colleges. In fact, letters in Princeton University library indicate that her first fictional African short story "Uncertain Flowering" (1951) was published in an American anthology (1953) by Whit and Hallie Burnett "to open volume four of their New York series *Story*" (Sparrow, *Into Africa* 83).

American readers have been attracted to the strength of Laurence's literary portrayals and her connections to the American tradition. In the Manawaka novels, Americans can identify with the Scots-Irish, the Slavic, the French, and even Indian associations since the United States has a similar cultural heritage. Students are drawn to Margaret Laurence's books because of the portrayal of her female subjects--not just feminine alone but of human beings becoming more aware of their places in the world, in family life with its matriarchal and patriarchal elements, and in the small-town person who eventually moves to the city and abroad--all of which Laurence has in common with American writers of the nineteenth and twentieth centuries. Laurence has an international place in contemporary literature.

Laurence is grouped with diverse writers, such as Carson McCullers--both have their places on the continuum that reaches from self-definition to social criticism--and J. D. Salinger--in the working out of inner life towards the outer. Gubar and Gilbert place Laurence with "Third World or Commonwealth" women writers for they have an "especially urgent" "search for the roots of selfhood" (*Anthology* 1677). These writers are attempting to define a woman's life, focusing attention on women's feelings towards men, raising children, daily living, and career. Yet, these details considered to be feminine concerns are really human concerns.

More innovation and expertise show in Laurence's portraying a wide range of protagonists: a ninety-year-old finishing-school graduate turned farmer's wife and housekeeper Hagar Currie Shipley; teacher Rachel Cameron in her thirties; Vanessa MacLeod up to her forties; high-school drop-out Stacey MacAindra in her forties; and writer Morag Gunn in her fifties. Margaret Laurence delineates their experiences as women in several roles--daughters, unmarried women, wives, mothers, grandmothers--and in their occupations. Characterization includes the love interests; one of these women--Morag--is virtually the first Venus figure in Canadian Literature (see Lindberg's 1976 review in *Branching Out* and Helen M. Buss's remarkable elaboration of this idea in her 1986 essay).

American students of Canadian literature studies have known that Margaret Laurence is a major author in the strong tradition of women writers found in Canada and England--considerably stronger than in the United States. Most outstanding of all, Laurence is a literary writer with a sureness learned from a long consideration of literature since childhood and an international perspective gained early in her writing career.

This collection clarifies Margaret Laurence's accomplishments. The Manawaka novels and other writings were the fruit of an early apprenticeship encouraged by her English-teacher stepmother, a college education in literature, a variety of journalistic writings during and after university, challenges in multiculturalism in Somalia and Ghana which led her to re-examine her Canadian and British experiences, and, finally, craftsmanship enabling her to write each book she felt was "given" to her. What she wrote embodies her words in her memoir, *Dance on the Earth*: "The writer's first, and perhaps only, responsibility is to be true to her or his own characters, human individuals that the writer cares about very deeply."

CRITICAL ATTENTION TO MARGARET LAURENCE IN THE UNITED STATES

Margaret Laurence has been largely neglected by American critics despite the fact that she is anthologized and read. The most significant book is Gayle Greene's *Changing the Story* (1991), in which she claims Margaret Laurence as one of the four major contemporary women writers--Doris Lessing, Margaret Drabble, Margaret Atwood--whom she considers as initiators of the feminist movement, focusing on a special form of feminist fiction--feminist metafiction. Feminist metafiction is "self-conscious fiction . . . that explores women's efforts at liberation in relation to problems of narrative form, fiction that destabilizes the conventions of realism in a project of psychic and social transformation" (1). For Laurence's feminist *Kunstlerroman*, Greene's "interpretative strategy" is "gender difference in intertextuality" in *The Diviners*. Angelika Maeser Lemieux's review of *The Diviners* points out:

Basically, Greene discusses *The Diviners* in terms of Laurence's revisioning of three "central myths of Western culture": "the 'fortunate fall,' paradise, and the idea of the artist" (149). In so doing, Laurence engages in an intertextual dialogue with three giants of the male literary tradition: Shakespeare (*The Tempest*), Joyce (*A Portrait of the Artist as a Young Man*), and Eliot (*The Waste Land*). Greene examines "the ways in which Laurence's metafictional strategy subverts and challenges the patriarchal power paradigm and, moreover, 'establishes a new genealogy' (149) which is 'antipatriarchal and delegitimizing.'"

Greene also draws attention to Laurence's preoccupation with the interaction of the past, present, and future--to the uses of memory--in order to achieve an imaginative reconstruction of experience that is, ultimately, liberating and empowering for woman. (*Margaret Laurence Review* 2 [1992] and 3 [1993]: 32)

Another American critic, Sue Leslie Kimball of Methodist College, North Carolina, includes Margaret Laurence in her bibliography of fictional and dramatic works about professional women who are portrayed with positive endings rather than defeat as in madness and death.

Critical insights came through my students as I perceived that the Scots who came in the nineteenth century to Mississippi appeared to have less in common now with the Scots who went to Manitoba than with non-Scots in warm climates, such as West and South Africa. Scots in the South evolved somewhat from the Calvinistic inwardness and attachment to the faraway old land which Canadian Scots mythologize in their cultural history telling of the importance of clans rising after the Battle of Culloden in 1746. The latter Margaret Laurence portrayed in the Manawaka novels, most elaborately in *The Diviners* with its myth of identity from the Macpherson pseudo-Ossianic tales upon which Christie Logan based his tales of Piper Gunn. I gradually realized that the emigrants to Upper and Lower Canada (Ontario and Quebec respectively) and the American north of upper New York settlements portrayed in John Galt's writings in the first decades of the nineteenth century were quite similar to Margaret Laurence's characters and mythologized historical references in her Manawaka novels. In the South, connections with Scotland are more tenuous. Mississippian Scots have undergone more language and attitude changes, for they responded more ebulliently to the warmth and fecundity of the region and the abundance in the environment. Indeed, several scholars attribute the cracker and redneck volatility of Southern character to Southerners' residual Scottish background. This emotional feature appears to be an outgoing social response. Southerners have strong clannishness in the extended family and oral communal culture. The Southern Scot talks it out keeping Gothic elements and the magnolia image present at the same time. Also, the warm environment has influenced a cavalier and carpe diem attitude more akin to that seen in other warm climates, such as sub-Saharan Africa.

During the summer of 1969, as I was preparing for life in the tropics, David Godfrey at Victoria University suggested I talk to Margaret Laurence at Massey College. My interview with her left me with warm respect for this author and a readiness to go for what turned into five years of teaching and studying at the University of Sierra Leone in Freetown, West Africa. While studying African oral and written literatures, I encountered Margaret Laurence's African books for the first time. Even though in Canada I had taken Canadian literature in the mid-1960s (an upper-division survey course at Queen's University and a Canadian poetry graduate course at the University of Toronto), I was not aware of her Manawaka novels. This mental colonization moved to postcolonial awareness not while I taught and earned a M. Litt. degree during three years in Scotland but in Sierra Leone. As I studied African literature and literary criticism of it, I found that Margaret Laurence had made a significant contribution in translations of oral literature, criticism, short stories, a travelogue / memoir, and a novel. In Mississippi, I began reading and teaching Laurence's Canadian novels and stories and Southern writers (Eudora Welty, Elizabeth Spencer, Flannery O'Connor, Katherine Anne Porter). When I put these with Wole Soyinka's plays, Camara Laye's *The African Child*, and John Galt's *The Provost* and *Annals of the Parish*, I found that Southerners had outgoingness, in common with Africans, the Scottish reductive idiom, and several residual Scottish words. However, they do not have the extent of dourness or Calvinistic guilt frequently found in

Scottish-Canadians. While students fully appreciate the family life in *A Bird in the House* and *The Stone Angel*, yet they would not consider most older Southern family heads as Victorian in patriarchal dominance; more often, the student regards his or her mother and father as his or her best friends.

Because the Civil War is pivotal to the South and military participation is above the average for the nation in proportion to the population, I found further correspondences between Canada, Scotland, and the U. S. South, particularly about the importance of war. The Battle of Culloden in 1746 is still a pivotal date in the Scottish character. Robert Burns and others like Hugh MacDiarmid provide the cultural continuity even if official political control was lost because of Culloden; with the oil boom, Scots have a partial restoration of their Scottish parliament in the council held on their own soil. The defeat at Culloden led to the subsequent migrations of clans to Canada, which led to Scots-Métis confrontations in the nineteenth century, culminating in the Riel Rebellions of 1870 and 1885, and in the twentieth century to deep involvement as Scottish regiments in World War I and World War II. War is important in the Canadian psyche, especially across the prairies where long lists abound on cenotaphs; similarly, the South has its own focus on war, not just the American Civil War, but in their continuing pervasive and strong "sense of duty."

I compared Margaret Laurence with other writers, such as the Southern writer Peter Taylor of Tennessee. Both have a special interest in the family--Peter Taylor's in the patriarchal heritage, Margaret Laurence's in the matriarchal. (Writers Anne Tyler's, Pat Conroy's, and Reynolds Price's interests are in both.) For Peter Taylor, the interaction of the generations who profess love and concern for children is more nearly obstruction of development of the other family member. His protagonist in *A Summons to Memphis* eventually finds out how his sisters and father interfered with his marriage plans; he also realizes that his sisters received advice from their dad to set up their own business. One can compare these revelations late in the protagonist's life with Laurence's ninety-year-old Hagar who, only on her deathbed, can tell her older son that she loved him and that he was the better of her two sons.

As my critical perceptions grew out of my international experiences and considerable study of international literatures and criticism, I realized the academic worth of my insights and became more aware of how innovations and different combinations of literary modes can convey one's most heartfelt perceptions. I could assess that Margaret Laurence, writing more and more about Canada's ethnic divisions, was helped by her observations overseas of ethnicity or economic status. Having been raised with the western Canadian mosaic idea, having knowledge firsthand of the Scottish and English differences (though little acquaintance of indigenous or Métis Canadians), and having an understanding of African peoples firsthand in West Africa and in fifteen other African countries since, I perceived racial changes in the American South differently. In the American South, reaction is reserved if a novelist portrays interracial "marriage" as Laurence does in her resolution in *The Diviners*--between Scots-Canadian Morag and Métis Jules. Their daughter Pique embodies the three basic Canadian ethnic identities of the Scot, French, and Indian into a new positive creative Canadian identity. Unacceptance of this identity by some readers probably was the root of some discussions over language in *The Diviners*.

Compare this Laurence novel to Judy Vernon's *Cousins* (Memphis: St. Luke's, 1984; New York: Dell, 1987) with its ironic mixings of Mississippi Indian, black, and white characters in various intermarriages since the arrival of Europeans; she concludes with the controversial "Elvis Presley" character, Trinity, who has a heritage of all of the three main Southern identities. In actuality, interracial marriages are lived out usually in urban centers or in the dominant cultural ethos. Paradoxically, Southern novelists Reynolds Price and Pat Conroy weave intricate family histories which show divergences from occasional interracial connections.

ESSAYS IN THIS COLLECTION

Scholars will welcome these eighteen essays--nine American, one British, one French translated into English, and seven Canadian--because they discuss topics related to all or each of the Manawaka novels and some of the African books. Walter Swayze looks at the poetry in most of Laurence's novels. Recent criticism of metafiction is discussed in relation to *The Diviners* which has the greatest number of essays: Susan Ward's analysis of the career woman unquestionably admits Laurence into the company of great women writers of various times. Bruce Stovel wrote a detailed essay on *A Bird in the House*. Lyall Powers, Nora Foster Stovel, and Mitzi Hamovitch offer three different perspectives of *The Fire-Dwellers*; Nora Foster Stovel relates Stacey to her sister Rachel, the central character in *A Jest of God*.

The major thesis of this book of essays is that Margaret Laurence is a novelist-as-poet, which is apparent in the richness of her imagery and the ever-present concreteness in her language. In the novels as in her essays on peace, she speaks of the future not in abstract terms but in terms of children in their environment. Image patterns reoccur throughout her narrative structures. She published poems first--in college and her first book *A Tree for Poverty*--and last--the dozen poems mainly to women--in the Afterword of her memoir, *Dance on the Earth*. Laurence exhibits the essential quality of a poet: the attempt to make harmonies out of disparate elements in human experience. Laurence exemplifies this in her consistent theme of characters' affirmation of life instead of portrayal of them as victims. A major part of her poetic richness arises from the biblical resonances throughout her writing. Several essays refer to Laurence's biblical imagery. Her characters have biblical names and their actions are consistent with the biblical stories. Morag, for example, is the Gaelic for Sarah who founded a new dynasty; this biblical association is congruent with Morag's conscious choice to have a child with Jules Tonnerre; in doing so she contributes to a new kind of Canadian dynasty which harmonizes separate ethnic (Scots-Métis) cultures.

This book is comprised of four parts. Page references to novels refer to the in-print editions of McClelland and Stewart, New Canadian Library, and the University of Chicago Press. In the text these are designated as "NCL" and "UC" respectively unless paginations are the same for both in-print editions. Part I shows use of language, theme, and image in Laurence's Manawaka novels. The novelist-as-poet is significant to Walter E. Swayze, as he extensively illustrates, and to Michel Fabre, who analyzes

The Stone Angel. Available for the first time in English, his essay discusses in great detail the contrasting images, such as water and stone, associated with Hagar in her long maturing process. Alice Bell's essay shows how images give unity to the narrative structure of *The Stone Angel*, and Bruce Stovel elucidates how a cluster of images unifies each chapter in *A Bird in the House*.

Lyall H. Powers sees Margaret Laurence's fiction as similar to William Faulkner's in the recognition "that a healthy life depends upon the frank . . . facing of the fact of death." In Laurence's obsessive concern with aging, she uses the metaphor of fire, internally and externally, for the force of life and of destruction in *The Fire-Dwellers*.

Neil Besner's "A World Divided, A World Divined" compares Laurence's *The Diviners* published in Canada to Irving's *The World According to Garp* published in the same year in America. More essays comparing works by Laurence to other writers are in the Selected Bibliography.

Part II focuses on the narrative structure in Laurence's novels. Alice Bell examines the narrative modes portraying one significant aspect of Laurence's fiction, the subject of age. Laurence's treatment of age is from within whereby she reveals Hagar's strengths. She has carefully arranged details--the pictures in Hagar's home, images--especially the animal imagery, episodes--the dead baby, the eggs at the dump, and the plaid shawl--and the point of view in order to portray a strong but sensitive woman possessed of a lust for life and survival and a corresponding disgust for those who are weak or who acquiesce to death. Hagar is telling her own story; consequently, negative comments she makes about herself are evidence of her concern for others and their relationships--not documentation of her failures. Bell delineates the complexity of Hagar's character, a complexity suggested by the image of the "stone angel"; she is, as her son Marvin calls her, a "holy terror."

Nora Foster Stovel demonstrates that *A Jest of God* and *The Fire-Dwellers* are sister novels in artistic and structural as well as personal and familial terms. The titles, epitaphs, nursery rhymes, names and settings are all clues to the connections between the two Cameron sisters, generating parallel themes and motifs in both novels. Laurence interweaves structural and symbolic technique to dramatize the sisters' identity crises, manipulating narrative method to delineate the divisions between the characters' inner and outer lives, subjective and objective realities. "Sisters under their skins," these two estranged siblings, by the end of both novels, will be *en route* to reunion.

Bruce Stovel argues convincingly for coherence in *A Bird in the House*. He perceptively critiques selected details of the characters as seen by Vanessa from age ten to forty. Themes treated include ancestors, freedom, self-knowledge, love, communication, and the differences between childhood and adult awareness. He skillfully traces the changes in the structure which enact the changes in Vanessa's awareness.

Updated by an extensive Supplement, Ken McLean assesses the relevance of critical theories to *The Diviners*. "Memory, Myth, and History in *The Diviners*" looks at the centrifugal tendencies. Laurence's novels are remarkable in regard to the subject of age as mythologized history and narrative structure. He reads the novel in terms of dialogizing, decentering, and indeterminacy. He convincingly demonstrates, as does

Gayle Greene, that *The Diviners* is a "genuinely writerly text."

Part III focuses on multiculturalism. According to her teacher, Wes McAmmond, Margaret Laurence invented "multiculturalism." The essays show how Laurence absorbed not just Scottish history but an understanding of its impetus in the formation of English Canada where it encountered Métis of Indian and French history. She also assimilated African storytelling into her methods of portraying characters coping with cultural values--Scottish, Métis (French and Indian), Ukrainian, Jewish, and English. Her interest came not only as a reporter for the *Winnipeg Citizen* and as a resident of Canada, Britain, Somalia, and Ghana but also from reconsidering various ethnic groups in Africa and Canada after reading Franz Fanon. She saw similarities between the Somalis and the Métis as both succumbed to stronger technology. Laurence was committed to racial equality, emphasized the biblical kind of exodus, and the struggles of the outsider. She said that one grows more humble and "Faith is . . . a reaching out to others." Even her children's book, *Jason's Quest*, is a parable on cultural exchange. She agreed with Michel Fabre about the evils of nationalism as restricting multicultural appreciation.

My overview essay traces Laurence's use of wars to evoke human depths in characterization of both women and men. Wars came from the lack of recognition of different cultures. Three major wars form and shape the Scots-Canadian prairie response in Laurence's Manawaka novels: Scots against the English who won at Culloden in 1746, Scots against the Métis under Louis Riel in the 1870 and 1885 rebellions in Manitoba and Saskatchewan, and Scots in their battalions against the Germans in World Wars I (1914-1918) and II (1939-1945). War led to separation of cultural groups and individuals. In World War I, mother-in-law Elsie Fry Laurence was alone at home while her husband was away fighting. World War II had a similar effect of isolating women; Margaret Laurence had no male classmates in her last year of high school in Neepawa because they worked in the war effort or had already enlisted. The references in the Manawaka novels to the cultural wars in Scotland and Canada show her integrated vision and their importance to the protagonists.

Within the multicultural perspective, three essays discuss oral traditions. Perceptively, Fiona Sparrow analyzes examples from *A Tree for Poverty* to demonstrate Laurence's admirable poetic ability in her translations of Somali traditional *gabei* and modern *belwo* oral literary forms. After living in Britain, Somalia, Ghana, Canada, and Croatia, Sparrow's research adds critical comparisons in this essay as she does in her book *Into Africa with Margaret Laurence* (Toronto: ECW, 1992). Further details by Donez Xiques in her Introduction to *A Tree for Poverty* (Toronto: ECW, 1993) expand on Laurence's immersion in Somali desert culture and language based on her correspondence with the retired linguist B. W. Andrzejewski who, and the Somali interpreter Musa Galaal, with other Somalis, worked out literal translations and helped Laurence translate Somali words into English images and verbs. Sparrow notes that Laurence "soon found she had to expand compressed one-word images in order to suggest their complexity of meaning" (*Into Africa* 52); she assesses that "Laurence's aim was to construct independent poems" and that her "translations have an elegant literary style that compensates for any slight loss of accuracy" (53). Sparrow's *Into Africa with Margaret Laurence* also provides much-needed evaluation about each of Laurence's five African books.

Cecil Abrahams provides a perspective new to many North Americans; he shows Laurence's adaptive use of folklore tradition from both Africa and North America, especially to enhance her characters' insights about their ancestors. He compares Laurence and the ancestral tradition in Africa and in Canada with its Scottish and Métis emphasis. Laurence's innovative narrative construction culminates in *The Diviners* where she reworks the history and myths into a new possible Canadian identity previously not portrayed in Canadian literature. Morag of the Scots-Canadian and Jules of the Métis (French and Indian) tradition have a child, Pique, who combines these major Canadian identities into one, an innovative resolution to the "conflict of cultures" novel. Even yet, few novels, certainly in Canada, combine most of the identities of a nation as Laurence does. She goes further than Hugh MacLennan's *Two Solitudes* which brought together English and French traditions in Canada. She, as Chinua Achebe did for Nigeria, instills a true sense of history into her fellow Canadians to redefine the Canadian past and to stir within the Canadian psyche an awareness of and a pride in the ancestral past from which the nation emerged. To evoke creative responses from an audience and to correct an inhumane view of part of Canada's people, Laurence grappled with the best technique, the storyteller's tale. She demonstrates a literary adaptation of oral techniques of a more global mass-media oral "McLuhan age" composite from Britain, Africa, and North America in written literature.

An important essay by the American folklorist Lynn Pifer examines the use of ordinary history in *The Diviners*. Through oral literary techniques Laurence mythologizes the history of the Scots in Scotland and Canada and the Métis.

Part IV focuses on feminist perspectives in Laurence's works. Rosalie Murphy Baum presents the mother-child bond in relation to some of Laurence's older women characters. Her stimulating essay on aging as self-alienation in the Manawaka novels shows that Karen Horney's three basic patterns of neurotic behavior are relevant and evident within parent-child relationships created by Laurence.

An important feminist perspective by Cynthia Taylor presents the subject of aging through the image of the mother in *The Stone Angel*. The focus is on the characterization of an aging Hagar Shipley.

The essay by the late Mitzi Hamovitch is not so much a feminist approach but an historical analysis which incorporates the rise of the women's movement, of how the voices of women characters are presented. Mitzi Hamovitch applies critical theory to her discussion of the style of the technique of the subversive voice in *The Fire-Dwellers*. Stacey does not just learn endurance but learns to protest; she wants her share of the action and considers her options to assert herself in a patriarchal society. Compare the complementary essay by Barbara Powell, "The Inner Conflicting Voices of Rachel Cameron," *Studies in Canadian Literature* 16.1 (1991), which shows how one voice evaluates what another voice says. Laurence portrayed Stacey in the 1950s as she breaks free of male-controlled language, but her voice is double. What women have to say and how they say it are equally important. Laurence, like Tillie Olsen and Adrienne Rich, spoke out in her literary works with women talking to other women, but Laurence's 1960s resolution of the novel reconciles the two voices of a woman talking to both men and women.

The critical perspective on the use of oral tradition is placed in historical perspective. Instead of the America-Europe axis in American fiction, Laurence had her revelations in the Third World which revealed her own self more fully to herself. This included how she was part of the imperialist situation in the eyes of the Somalis. Each new generation can learn this insight from Laurence without having to go through learning the awareness all over again, advises Lidwein Kapteijns, Dutch scholar. As a teacher in the Sudan and Chad (*Margaret Laurence Review* 1.1 1991: 10, 43-44), Kapteijns assessed the contemporary influence of Margaret Laurence in Somalia and for expatriates there and elsewhere.

"Morag Gunn in Context: The Career Woman Theme in *The Diviners*" by Susan Ward presents one answer by Laurence to the contemporary woman who juggles raising children and pursuing her career. Ward shows the role of Morag's mentor-models related to the development of her career. Ward's identification of *The Diviners* as part of the tradition of the *Kunstlerroman* demonstrates both perception and insight. Readers will like the reference to Willa Cather as well as other women writers. The career woman theme found in several American and British nineteenth and twentieth century novels is documented by Susan Ward as the context for protagonists writer Morag in *The Diviners* and teacher Rachel in *A Jest of God*. This excellent essay reinforces literary appraisal that Margaret Laurence shows expertise in rendering the career woman theme in a Canadian and prairie setting. She goes much further than her precedent in Nellie McClung's Manitoba schoolteacher suffragette. The narrative techniques, image patterns, and characterization Margaret Laurence evolved for each of her heroines were innovative and sophisticated. A significant factor is that the subject of old age enables an author to look over more than one generation in the protagonist's whole life.

"Wordsmith and Woman: Morag Gunn's Triumph Through Language," Laurie Lindberg's excellent essay, reveals and documents the growth of Laurence's protagonist of *The Diviners*, Morag Gunn.

Finally, Alexandra Pett critiques Laurence's last book, *Dance on the Earth: A Memoir*. To Pett, Laurence's structure in *Dance* shows the closeness of mother and daughter. Margaret Laurence finally refers to herself as a feminist, some would say an early one because the term was coined in the 1960s. However, she did not exclude men, and even had a male narrator in her first novel *This Side Jordan*; yet as she says in her memoir, *Dance on the Earth*, a male critic panned the birthing scene, the most awesome moment of life for a mother. Yet, this critic and other male novelists portrayed male characters encountering women as nameless objects. This surprising review caused Laurence to rethink her purposes and creativity. Ever after, she had female protagonists and described the life of each from within as that character experienced it: taking care of a parent, husband, children; developing into a woman; remembering the past; facing situations in life at all ages. Grateful readers are abundantly richer for her choice.

Part I

Language, Theme, and Image in Laurence

Chapter 1

Margaret Laurence: Novelist-as-Poet
Walter E. Swayze

To approach the subject of novelist-as-poet[1] we might look at the verse that the young Morag Gunn in *The Diviners* tries to write for a Christmas poem, "The Wise Men" (89-90NCL, 89UC), verse which fills her with shame when Mrs. McKee reads her Hilaire Belloc's "When Jesus Christ was four years old" (91NCL, 66UC). But this venture leads into the question of intention in context. In *The Fire-Dwellers*, Stacey MacAindra's embarrassing telling of the joke about the great god Thor and the lovely country girl, when Stacey is desperately drunk at Mac's boss's Richalife party in the hotel banqueting room (103NCL, 109UC), has significance quite unrelated to the quality of the joke itself. Regardless of how good it or any other joke may be in itself, the joke is superb here in its contribution to our understanding of three characters-- Stacey, Mac, and Thor--and the situation in which their characters are being revealed to us and to them. So, young Morag's Christmas poem could not profitably be considered simply as Laurence's attempt to write a poem, but as an expression of the vulnerability of the beginning writer. Similarly, in creating Christie Logan's tales of Piper Gunn, Laurence has quite remarkably reproduced many of the cadences and rhetorical patterns of James Macpherson's prose "translations" of Romantic pseudo-Ossianic tales in the volume that Christie showed Morag (73-75NCL, 51-53UC), except, of course, that Christie's diction is laced with deliberately unromantic, or at least, "improper," words--*silly bugger, shit-houses of hell, christly* (63NCL, 61UC) and deliberately Canadian terms such as *muskeg* and *half-breeds* (96NCL, 69UC) that one will not find in Macpherson, regardless of edition. The question is not whether Christie's stories are great prose poetry (or whether or not Macpherson was a genuine poet), but whether or not this uneducated old garbage collector, when really drunk, can create effectively for Morag a myth of identity sufficiently exciting and compelling to inspire and nourish her own search for her roots, values, and ultimate sense of significance.[2]

Let us start, however, with a poem that Margaret Laurence wrote and published over or under her own name, in which she may be considered, for the moment, to be

4 Language, Theme, and Image

speaking in her own voice, not that of one of her fictional characters. Signed Peggy Wemyss, it appeared in the United College undergraduate magazine *Vox* in the spring of 1945:

> This is a land of living things,
> Of life within life,
> A land aware, vibrant,
> Strong with the sinew of youth.
> The heart-pulse that beats through earth
> In all its growing things
> Sings of death becoming birth.
> Now I hear the many voices
> Of the wakening prairie
> From greening bluffs
> And from the cool waiting fields,
> A golden weaving of melody.
> Sweet small leaves slowly unfold,
> And new grasses
> Yearn toward the warmth
> Of coming suns.
> Nothing here is of the dead.
> Quietly I walk, wind-cloaked,
> Hearing the rain's promise
> That this land will be my immortality.

As undergraduate verse this is very good poetry, but hardly great poetry. What makes it different for us, forty-three years later, from thousands of other poems written with conviction, care, and sensitivity to rhythm by thousands of other undergraduates of the time, is the effective presentation of the author's own sensibly perceived experience, of--as she put it in 1972, twenty-seven years later--"A world which gave me my own lifework to do, because it was here that I learned the sight of my own particular eyes" (*Heart of a Stranger*, hereafter *Heart* 219). This sight includes more than the "greening bluffs" and the "new grasses"; at its heart is the vision of the relation between present, past, and future, between mortality and immortality, the vision of a place to stand on (*Heart* 155-57, 213-19) and to believe in--in other words, essential themes of the Laurence canon as we know it, but at that time still unwritten.

With this poem I compare the following, published nineteen years later:

> Summer and winter
> she viewed the town
> with sightless eyes.
>
> She was doubly blind,
> not only stone
> but unendowed
> with even a pretense
> of sight.
>
> Whoever carved her
> had left the eyeballs

blank.

It seemed strange to me
that she should stand above the town,
harking us all to heaven
without knowing who we were
at all.

But I was too young then
to know her purpose,
although my father often told me
she had been brought from Italy
at a terrible expense
and was pure white
marble.

I think now
she must have been carved
in that distant sun
by stone masons
who were cynical descendants of Bernini,
gouging out her like by the score,
gauging with admirable accuracy the needs
of fledgling pharaohs
in an uncouth land.

This, of course, is simply a paragraph of continuous prose taken from the opening page of *The Stone Angel* (3), with no changes except in spacing on the page, my arbitrary breaking up of the sentences into separate lines of verse. Yet in many respects this prose is more closely textured poetry than the undergraduate verse. The opening paradox is emphasized by the repeated *bl* and *d* in *doubly blind*, and of its interesting development. Scansion reveals metrical patterns closely related to meaning. Sound patterns also reinforce meaning. The alliterated sibilants of *distant sun, stone masons, cynical descendants* link the romantic softness of the Italian climate and the exotic associations of the Italian Renaissance (in contrast to the harshness of the Manitoba climate and the young Hagar's lack of awareness of artistic history) with ideas of inherited moral corruption. (*Cynical* sounds like *sin*, and linked with *descendants* it may suggest a bond of guilt linking generations of inherited depravity.) The consonance of *gouging* and *gauging* relates commercial exploitation to the actual cutting of the stone, and the unfeeling hardness is emphasized by the implicit pun in *score*. Similarly the alliterated *f*-sounds in *fledgling pharaohs* may suggest an ironical association of the Egyptian rulers with angel feathers and the pervasive association of Hagar, the stone angel, with Egypt throughout the novel (e.g. 40, but every mention of Hagar's name keeps the association alive), and the variations on the biblical allusions that many readers have detected, while the epithet *uncouth* in the following line, by indirection, might bring to mind the pharaoh who "knew not Joseph" (King James Version [KJV] Exodus 1:8) and whose hardness of heart led not only to the persecution of Joseph and his brethren and the enslavement of the Israelites, but also to their exodus, to the generations of wandering in the wilderness, and to the eventual fulfillment of a promise that neither Hagar, Abraham, nor even Moses survived to experience.

Regardless of the author's conscious intention, it is obvious to anyone who has read *The Stone Angel* that a number of its major motifs, themes, and value judgments are present implicitly in this microcosmic passage. Without attempting any formal distinction between the qualities of prose and of poetry,[3] I am merely pointing out that this passage of prose not only sounds like what we normally regard as poetry but also functions like it.

The functioning is so indirect as to be unobtrusive. The voice is Hagar's, but how much is it that of the Hagar of her childhood or youth in Manawaka, or how much that of the nonagenarian in Vancouver looking back over an eighty-five-year span of changing consciousness and perspective? How fully aware is the speaker of the multiple ironies implicit in the associations and reverberations set off by some of the images in this passage? The better we know the novel and Hagar, the more fully, intelligently, and interestingly we can answer such questions. Meanwhile, even on a first reading, we encounter nothing that seems "poetic" in any artificial sense, nothing that is out of character for this woman who has had a Presbyterian upbringing, with some inevitable acquaintance with the most familiar biblical stories and standard hymns, and some training in poetry in the young ladies' academy in Toronto (42).

Little of the novel is ostentatiously "poetic," but frequently passages function very much as this one does. Reference to two others should suffice. Speaking of her father, who has been catechizing his children on the Highland heritage of the Curries,--clan, sept, pipe music, and war cry--Hagar says:

How bitterly I regretted that he'd left and had sired us here, the bald-headed prairie stretching out west of us with nothing to speak of except couchgrass or clans of chittering gophers or the gray-green poplar bluffs, and the town where no more than half a dozen decent brick houses stood, the rest being shacks and shanties, shaky frame and tarpaper, short-lived in the sweltering summers and the winters that froze the wells and the blood. (15)

The patterns of assonance (re*gre*tted . . . l*e*ft . . . h*e*aded . . . str*e*tching . . . w*e*st . . . exc*e*pt), of vowel mutation (gr*ay*-gr*ee*n p*o*plar bl*u*ffs), of alliteration and other consonantal recurrences (stret*ch*ing . . . *c*ouchgrass . . . *c*lans . . . *ch*ittering, do*z*en . . . de*c*ent . . . stoo*d*, *sh*acks . . . *sh*anties . . . *sh*aky . . . *sh*ort . . . *s*weltering *s*ummers), of almost-onomatopoeic rhythms (the *sweltering summers* seem to go on effortlessly in spite of being short-lived, but the winters seem to bring everything to a dead stop with the climactic succession of strong monosyllables--*that froze the wells and the blood*). The casual reader may not be conscious of such patterns, but must at least be aware of the way Hagar's vision of the landscape is so frequently formed by strongly emotional attitudes of class jealousy, pride, and scorn.

My final example is in the fourth chapter. There Hagar is remembering driving herself in the buggy to the hospital to give birth to John:

It was early fall, the oak leaves mottled with brown, the maple leaves dappled green and that queerly translucent yellow, the leaves of berry bushes colored cochineal, and goldenrod dusty with pollen shining like coinage along our road deep-rutted from wheels that had struggled through the mud of past rains. I wished the drive had been longer, so peaceful and light I was, with none to bother me. (122)

Not only are there many long *e*-sounds here (l*ea*ves . . . l*ea*ves . . . gr*ee*n . . . qu*ee*rly . . . l*ea*ves . . . cochin*ea*l . . . d*ee*p-rutted . . . wh*ee*ls . . . p*ea*ceful . . . m*e*), but other vowel sounds approach and recede from those long *e* sounds in varied musical patterns that prolong and sustain, without obvious insistence, the recurrent musical sound that culminates in the satisfying final m*e*. Rarely, if ever, elsewhere in the novel, does Hagar have this feeling of peace with herself and with her world. The special place that John held in her love, the special tragedy that his death was for her, the complicated relationship of both his birth and his death to Hagar's psychological and spiritual condition, are all pointed to by this presentation of her memory of her feelings as she drove to the hospital to give birth to him.

In terms of dynamic imagery in *The Stone Angel*, one need only mention the scene in which Lottie Drieser ("light as an eggshell herself") takes a stick and crushes "the eggshell skulls" of the chicks that had hatched in the sun in the town dump, just after Hagar has refused to play mother to her dying brother Dan (27-28). Elements of this scene are recalled when Hagar frightens the six-year-old boy and girl playing house on the beach at Shadow Point (187-90), and when she, soon after, remembers plotting with Lottie to prevent the marriage of Lottie's daughter Arlene and Hagar's son John by arranging for Arlene to be offered a job in the East. Hagar remembers the chicks, but Lottie does not (213). A month later, both Arlene and John are dead (239-42).

From *This Side Jordan* through *The Diviners* the novels abound with passages in which, without any interference with the functioning of conventional prose, effects are gained that we might loosely call poetic, by devices that we normally associate with poetry.

In *This Side Jordan* the export-import firm of Allkirk, Moore & Bright deals in many commodities, but "the textile trade was the biggest branch of the business. Bolts of tradecloth had been piled on these low wooden platform tables since the year of the last Ashanti War, more than half a century ago" (34). James Thayer tells Johnnie Kestoe that the "prestige and stability of the Firm depend to a very large extent on the right choice of patterns for tradecloth" (35). Patterns and textures of cloth are mentioned in connection with almost every character in the novel, and virtually all these references relate to the characters' attitudes or relations to changing patterns of social, cultural, and psychological aspects of emerging new Africa. Cora Thayer's inability to adapt to inevitable changes is epitomized in her compulsive buying of luxurious brocades that do not suit her, that she cannot afford and that she will never wear (124-25), as a protest against the inevitable wearing of "shapeless cardigans and heavy shoes" (130). Nathaniel Amegbe is haunted by the memory of his father's body "lying on its left side, dressed in the best cloth it had owned in life, a magnificent vari-coloured Kente" (31). But Nathaniel Amegbe himself, with his "khaki slacks and his cheap cotton shirt, threadbare at the collar" (181) and his new glasses with "heavy horn rims," worn of necessity, not to give himself dignity (42), Lamptey, with his "lavender silk shirt and fawn draped trousers" (18), Jacob Abraham Mensah with his "grey pinstripe suit, a yellow shirt of fine poplin, a blue Paisley tie, all shouting guineas, guineas, guineas" (23),[4] Victor Edusei, with his "soiled green shirt . . . glued with sweat to his chest" and "low-slung shapeless corduroy trousers" (114), are wearing European clothes indicative of their relation to Europeanization.

On the second page of the novel the author says, "Into the brash contemporary patterns of this Africa's fabric were woven symbols old as the sun-king, old as the oldest continent." All the fabrics that the characters wear or dream of are part of this "Africa's fabric." So far, these symbolic suggestions are standard qualities of conventional prose fiction. But at times incidental images of clothing operate in ways that suggest both the indirection and, to use Coleridge's term, the "esemplastic power"[5] that we associate with poetry.

Nathaniel Amegbe, with minimal European education, but a determination that his child will be born in a European hospital and that his wife Aya will have the protection of European medicine, is having trouble with Aya, who may be a Christian, but is very much the illiterate girl who feels safe only in her tribal culture and who wants to return to her village to have her child. The day after a heated argument on this subject, Nathaniel returns home from work, knowing as he enters the gate, from the "hoarse throaty laughter" and the "sweet-acrid smell" of palm oil chop, that Adua, Aya's mother, is in the house. Knowing that she is preparing the chop especially for him, he wonders what she wants. He sees her beside the charcoal brazier: "her cloth was black and red, patterned in hands outspread. It billowed hugely around her, and the dozens of scarlet hands clutched at that massive body" (70). After serving him all his favorite foods, before making her demand of him, "Adua wrapped her cloth around her, belched, then sighed" (71).

Isolated for examination, these references to Adua's cloth may seem too obvious. In the context of all the other details in the scene, they may go unnoticed by most readers. But once noticed, the hands on the cloth suggest all the hands, literally and figuratively, outstretched to Nathaniel for sympathy (82), for cooperation with the white man and white woman (97-107). "How many nights I weep and pray and still you never come or send Some Small Thing for help--" (192). "Kwaale wanted money. Aya wanted money. Aya's mother wanted money. The uncles wanted money" (18). In a dream the devil of the night, Sasabonsam, plucks at him with gorilla-like hands (74), and in another dream, King Jesus, arrayed like a King of Ashanti, stretches his hands out to the drowning man (77). The design of Adua's cloth, so apparently incidental, subtly heightens the reader's awareness of both Nathaniel's nervousness and the far-reaching, intricate patterns of "Africa's fabric."

Much of the most illuminating criticism of Laurence's fiction deals with the functioning of metaphor, of clusters or constellations of images. One of the most convincing of these is David Blewett's article "The Unity of the Manawaka Cycle," which examines the symbolic effectiveness of Manawaka itself, the use of contrasted pairs of individuals and images (especially relating to the cemetery and the garbage dump), and "an elaborate imagery of the four elements, one of which predominates in each of the four novels" (36), resembling the image structure of T. S. Eliot's *The Waste Land*. Blewett concludes:

> The symbolism of the four elements and the parallel with *The Wasteland* [sic], the continuity

of major paired images, the interplay of character, and the recurrence of Manawaka, are means to an end. Together they reinforce our growing sense throughout the cycle that the inner lives of individuals, the relationship between human beings, the passing of the generations, the ordering of society are profoundly interconnected. The source of the Manawaka cycle's impressive unity is Margaret Laurence's vision that the fragments of experience are part of a larger, universal design. (39)

This vision, as analyzed by Blewett, is communicated through techniques that we normally regard as poetic.

In *The Diviners*, the most highly patterned, most densely textured novel that Laurence wrote, in addition to scraps of hymns, patriotic songs, nursery rhymes, quotations from poems remembered from school readers, a verse from a song that Louis Riel wrote in prison, and other bits of "poetry" characteristic of the Laurence fiction that the reader is familiar with, one encounters for the first time what one might expect to find in a Sean O'Casey play--four original lyrics printed in verse form in the body of the novel and reprinted with music at the end (481-90NCL, 371-82UC). Unlike an O'Casey play, the novel was issued with a record on which these songs are performed, produced for sale with the novel, with a jacket design matching that of the dust jacket of the novel.[6] (One should note that the performers on the record do not sing exactly the lyrics or the music printed in the novel, but exercise the freedom that most folksingers, amateur and professional, do. The effect of the record is that of an informal amateur performance, appropriate to the context of the novel, but unlikely to make the record climb the charts. At least three of the songs deserve a better recording in terms of sound quality.) As with Stacey's joke about Thor in *The Fire-Dwellers* (103NCL, 109UC), one must deal with these lyrics not only as poems to be read, or as songs to be sung, but as poems that were written and songs that were sung by fictional characters in specific contexts in the novel, and hence as integral components of the novel.

Three of the four songs are composed and sung by Jules "Skinner" Tonnerre, the Métis or half-breed who is Morag Gunn's classmate, then her lover, and then the father of her daughter, Pique. He is alluded to as Pique's father on the third page of the novel (13NCL, 5UC), though not named or characterized in any way, and the reader is not introduced to him until about fifty pages later, in Morag's memories of her experiences in Grade Six:

The other boys in the class . . . never tangle with Skinner. They're scared of him. Also, they think they're better than he is. Skinner is taller than any of the other boys, and has better muscles. He is about three years older than any of the rest of the class, which is why he and his sister Piquette are in the same class. Both have missed a lot of school. Sometimes Skinner goes off with his dad, old Lazarus Tonnerre, and disappears for weeks, setting traplines way up at Galloping Mountain, some say. The Tonnerres (there are an awful lot of them) are called *those breeds*, meaning halfbreeds. They are part Indian, part French, from away back. They are mysterious. People in Manawaka talk about them but don't talk *to* them. Lazarus makes homebrew down there in the shack in the Wachakwa valley, and is often arrested on Saturday nights. Morag knows. She has heard. They are dirty and unmentionable. (76NCL, 54, 88, 95UC)

At home, Christie has been reading Archibald Clark's versified version of James Macpherson's *Ossian* to Morag and showing her the strange, unknown Gaelic works that are supposed to be her incomprehensible heritage (74-75NCL, 52-53UC). At school Miss McMurtrie has been teaching the class "O Canada" in English and French, and "The Maple Leaf Forever."

Morag loves this song and sings with all her guts. She also knows what the emblems mean. Thistle is Scots, like her and Christie. . . . Shamrock is Irish like the Connors and Reillys and them. Rose is English like Prin. . . . Suddenly she looks over to see if Skinner Tonnerre is singing. He has the best voice in the class, and he knows lots of cowboy songs, and dirty songs, and he sometimes sings them after school, walking down the street.
    He is not singing now.
    He comes from nowhere. He isn't anybody. (80, 88, 95NCL, 57UC)

Years later, when Morag is in Grade Eleven, she goes home after school with Skinner, now a private in the Queen's Own Cameron Highlanders on leave, to his shack in the valley. She makes love with him, meets his father Lazarus, hears Skinner sum up his father's life in terms as depressing as Morag's visual and olfactory impressions, and probably about this time, hears Skinner's tales of Rider Tonnerre and his involvement in the Massacre of Seven Oaks, and of Skinner's grandfather, Old Jules, and his part in the Battle of Batoche. These stories are quite different from the ones Morag had heard from Christie or the ones learned at school. While Skinner is overseas and taking part in the Dieppe raid, Morag, as a reporter for the *Manawaka Banner*, is sent to the valley where Piquette and her two children have been burned to death in the Tonnerre shacks.

Morag meets Skinner briefly on his return to Manawaka. She cannot tell him much about his sister's death, and he cannot say much about Dieppe, except that as a lone wolf he saw a fellow soldier die "Like a shot gopher. His guts. Not his eyes, though. . . . Like a horse's eyes in a barn fire" (180NCL, 133UC).

When Morag next meets Skinner she has been to college in Winnipeg, married her English professor, Brooke Skelton, moved to Toronto, had her first novel published, and is obviously at the end of her marriage without fully realizing it. On the street she thinks she sees Lazarus Tonnerre, but it is Skinner. Now he makes his living as a singer in small clubs and coffeehouses--"Oh, country and western, mostly. Lotta them are crap. I sing some I made up, too. Maybe they're crap as well, but at least it's my own crap" (286NCL, 217UC). Morag spends the night with Skinner, decides to leave Brooke, and after three weeks with Skinner moves to Vancouver. She is now bearing Skinner's child, but she hasn't heard him sing his own songs.

When Morag's and Skinner's daughter Pique is five, Skinner appears for a brief visit in Vancouver. He doesn't have much to say, is frequently depressed and drunk. "He will not let Morag take his picture, not even with Pique." "Maybe I don't want to see what I look like" (367NCL, 281UC). (We know about the Indian taboo.) But he will reveal himself in song to Morag and Pique as he sings "The Ballad of Jules Tonnerre" (367-69NCL, 282-83UC), all fifteen stanzas:

They are silent for a while. Morag wonders whether he has not, after all, sung it for her as much as for Pique. Pique likes the tune, and the strong simple rhythm, but otherwise it is lost on her. It is not lost on Morag. The echoes and all the things he could never bring himself to say in ordinary speech, have found their way into the song. (369NCL, 283UC)

Skinner says, "It's too long for a lotta people, and they can't listen right through. . . . Or they don't wanna know about it, and start yellin' why don't I sing 'Yellow Rose of Texas' or like that" (369NCL, 283UC).

"The Ballad of Jules Tonnerre" is not a great poem with universal appeal. In context it is written and sung by a high-school dropout, a social outcast, a despairing alcoholic who is seeing his remaining sister die as surely and as tragically as most of the rest of his family. But Morag is impressed, and we are impressed because so much of the Métis experience which was ignored in the histories learned in school and excluded from the racial symbols embodied in our official anthems and public monuments, and which had reached Morag through some of Skinner's tales and has now reached us through a long pent-up spate of literature on the subject (consider the number and variety of recent distinguished works on Riel and Dumont--biographies, novels, editions of letters and notebooks, plays, radio and TV programs, lawsuits)--so much of this is condensed and given memorable shape in a ballad that employs traditional techniques and conventional mannerisms without artificiality or affectation, that achieves dramatic force with eloquent, spare simplicity, without its being unlikely as the creation of the character in the novel. It is a ballad that gives dignity to the subject without distorting or denying the almost-despairing drabness of the lives of the enduring descendants of Jules Tonnerre.

Pique asks for a song about her. Skinner says maybe she'll make up a song for him. "He says he is working on a song about Lazarus his father, but he does not sing that one" (284). One morning Morag wakens to find him gone.

Ten years later, after Morag and Pique have lived in England and visited Scotland with Dan McRaith, Morag has bought an old log house--"History. Ancestors" (439NCL, 338UC)--at McConnell's Landing in Ontario, and Morag has tried to tell Pique something about her father, Jules, and her grandfather Lazarus (392-93NCL, 301-02UC), Jules (or Skinner), now about forty-seven, but looking "more like Lazarus than he did ten years ago" (449NCL, 345UC), arrives at McConnell's Landing. Jules sings "The Ballad of Jules Tonnerre," which Pique barely remembers from ten years before, and then goes on to "Lazarus," on which he had been working then. The events are closer in time and have been witnessed by Morag herself, and recounted to Pique, and they have been experienced by Skinner himself; Skinner so closely resembles his father when Morag first knew him; Morag, Pique, and Skinner are now ten years older; moreover, this is a better ballad with a better musical setting (assuming that the tune that Skinner sang is similar to Ian Cameron's on the record), and it affects the reader much more powerfully than the former. Again, the power of the few spare words to awaken echoes, not only from *The Diviners*, but from all the Manawaka volumes except *A Jest of God* (e.g., *Diviners* 79-80NCL, 56-57UC; 82NCL, 59UC; 156-57NCL, 114-15UC; 172-76NCL, 127-30UC; 172-76NCL, 132-33UC; *Stone* 127, 177; *Fire* 240-44NCL, 263-68UC; *Bird* 108-20NCL, 114-27UC), and to distill the emotion from all these echoes, is what makes this ballad into poetry that raises the

12 Language, Theme, and Image

emotional pitch of the novel:

> Lazarus, he had a bunch of children;
> He raised them in the Valley down below.
> So that they could eat, he shot rabbits there for meat,
> Where his ancestors had shot the buffalo.
>
> Lazarus, he lost some of those children,
> Some to fire, some to the City's heart of stone.
> Maybe when they went, was the worst time that was sent,
> For then he really knew he was alone. (453NCL, 349UC) [Record, Side Two, Band 1]

Hearing this, Pique says, "I didn't know it was like that."

> "There's a lot you don't know," Jules says harshly. "Your mother probably didn't tell you that when my sister died in that fire, with her kids, she was stoned out of her head with homebrew, on account of she didn't give a fuck whether she lived or died, and she had her reasons." (454NCL, 349UC)

Pique admits that she didn't know and says she doesn't want to hear any more. Jules says he has to tell her, and he sings the song he has written for his sister Piquette.
    These six parallel quatrains, with only one word changing in the first line of each stanza, the second line identical ("Fire and snow--") throughout, and the same o-rhyme of the second and fourth lines throughout, by focusing our attention on the symbols "fire and snow" and the white listeners' incapacity to understand, ironically concentrates everything we have experienced of the Métis in dozens of poignant pages of the Manawaka volumes and universalizes it all with an unforgettable clarity and searing reverberation:

> My sister's eyes
> Fire and snow--
> What they'd be saying
> You couldn't know.
>
> My sister's body
> Fire and snow--
> It wasn't hers
> Since long ago.
>
> My sister's man
> Fire and snow--
> He ate her heart
> Then he made her go.
>
> My sister's children
> Fire and snow--
> She prayed they'd live
> But it wasn't so.
>
> My sister's death
> Fire and snow--
> Burned out her sorrow

> In the valley below.
>
> My sister's eyes
> Fire and snow--
> What they were telling
> You'll never know. (454-55NCL, 350UC) [Record, Side One, Band 2]

This song leads to Jules's summary of what has happened to the rest of his family, to Pique and Jules exchanging the plaid pin that John Shipley had traded to Lazarus in *The Stone Angel* (*Stone* 177) for the knife that John had sold to Christie Logan for the price of a package of cigarettes, and that Morag had kept after Christie's death with the few books dealing with her Scottish heritage. It is inevitable that Pique will accept the invitation to visit Jules' brother Jacques at Galloping Mountain (*Diviners* 5, 351), where he is bringing up not only his own four children, but also the three orphaned children of his sister Valentine, who died in Vancouver, and the son of their brother Paul, who drowned mysteriously while guiding American tourists, and some younger children "whose parents have died or vanished" (463NCL, 359UC).

As Pique prepares to leave Morag for this trip to meet her father's "family" and to do her part in attempting to help in some way with their future, she sings her own song for her mother. The musical setting and Joan Minkoff's performance on the record make Pique's song, perhaps, the most memorable of the four. As a printed lyric isolated from its context, it is not as impressive as Skinner's "Lazarus" and "Piquette's Song." In context, however, this is a song written by a teenager who sings it with diffidence to the mother with whom she has spent most of her life, but is just now getting to know, a mother who has spent much of *her* life with her daughter while searching for her own identity and her heritage in Canada, England, and Scotland. This is a teenager who, in addition to suffering the agonizing amalgam of total iconoclasm and uncompromising idealism of millions growing up in the 1960s, has known only unpredicted and unpredictable visits from a father as inexplicable and unforgettable as Jules Skinner Tonnerre, and who, herself, has had shattering discoveries of her vulnerability as girl, as teenager, and especially as half-breed girl teenager on the highway in Manitoba (117-20NCL, 86-88UC; 252NCL, 191UC) and in high school in Ontario (447NCL, 344UC).

> There's a valley holds my name, now I know
> In the tales they used to tell it seemed so low
> There's a valley way down there
> I used to dream it like a prayer
> And my fathers, they lived there long ago.
>
> There's a mountain holds my name, close to the sky
> And those stories made that mountain seem so high
> There's a mountain way up there
> I used to dream I'd breathe its air
> And hear the voices that in me would never die.
>
> I came to taste the dust out on a prairie road
> My childhood thoughts were heavy on me like a load
> But I left behind my fear

> When I found those ghosts were near
> Leadin' me back to that home I never knowed.
>
> Ah, my valley and my mountain, they're the same
> My living places, and they never will be tame
> When I think how I was born
> I can't help but being torn
> But the valley and the mountain hold my name
> The valley and the mountain hold my name. (464-65NCL, 360UC) [Record, Side Two, Band 2]

The impact of Pique's song is presented economically and convincingly:

> Then silence. Pique could not speak until Morag did, and Morag could not speak for a while. The hurts unwittingly inflicted upon Pique by her mother, by circumstances--Morag had agonized over these often enough, almost as though, if she imagined them sufficiently, they would prove to have been unreal after all. But they were not unreal. Yet Pique was not assigning any blame--that was not what it was all about. And Pique's journey, although at this point it might feel to her unique, was not unique. Morag reached out and took Pique's hand, holding it lightly.
> "Could I have a copy of the words, Pique?"
> This was apparently all she could say. Pique's fingers tightened around Morag's, then let go.
> "Sure, I'll write them out for you now." (465NCL, 360UC)

Here a moment of lyric poetry has illuminated for daughter and mother a realization that neither of them could explain in normal consecutive prose. Blame is not what it was all about. It was the experience itself of finding identity, place, and relationships in the universe. Analysis, evaluation, and perhaps eventual praise or blame are quite different matters.

This leads me to the heart of my subject. Informally in some of the works, I have touched on some matters as patterns of sounds, recurrent images, the structural use of poems, quoted or original, to convey experience and highlight moments of awareness. But what about poetry in a deeper sense? The most central definition of poetry that I know is Frederick A. Pottle's in his book *The Idiom of Poetry*: "[P]oetry is language in which expression of the qualities of experience is felt to predominate greatly over statement concerning its uses" (71-72). In terms of this definition, *all* of Margaret Laurence's fiction is poetry. Critics and scholars have contributed to our awareness of themes and theses that permeate the fiction. If there are issues in life, they should be discernible in artistic presentations of human experience. But to substitute a thesis, a "statement," be it political, economic, biological, or theological, for "expression of the qualities of experience" in Laurence's fiction is, I think, to misread it. Many critical examinations of her fiction are based on such misreading.

The African stories are not theses or statements about imperialism, colonialism, nationalism, or missionary activity. They express with rare immediacy what it is to be a human being, white or black, in the middle of cultural evolution and revolution, having all the human experiences that have hitherto been defined in recognizable, even foreseeable terms, now become absurdly unfamiliar and irrelevant, and challenging or forcing the individual to risk everything for a new life in a new set of terms. *The*

Stone Angel among other things makes us feel what it is like to be inescapably old, to realize that one has not always been what one might have wanted to be and not be able to do much about it, but still not want to give up, and to experience grace that is there for the accepting or the taking. *A Jest of God* makes us feel what it is like to be in a trap, but able to make a gesture towards responsibility and freedom, and to experience the frightening but reassuring infinity of that freedom. *The Fire-Dwellers* makes us share the experience of feeling how little we know ourselves, our mates, our children, our neighbors, and how reassuring it is to get glimpses of our common humanity and of a meaningful coherence beyond our individual and collective horrors. *A Bird in the House* makes us feel what it is like to grow up, to come to terms with our own most stubbornly resisted identity and with our own mortality. *The Diviners*, among many other things, make us feel what it is like to be an outcast, an emigrated Scot, a Métis, a teenager and a teenager's mother, a victim of sexism, and to be a diviner--whether a garbage collector, a water-diviner, or a writer--and to experience the mystery that makes all our identities significant. What emerges from all these books at their most successful, in language that is nearly always memorable in itself, is the expression of the qualities of experience. In terms of Frederick Pottle's definition, Margaret Laurence in her fiction has written little but poetry.

NOTES

Page references to novels refer to the New Canadian Library reprints (noted as "NCL") published by McClelland and Stewart and the University of Chicago Press reprints (noted as "UC"). Paginations for both in-print editions are given.

1. Margaret Laurence and poetry is a much larger and more complex subject. Her first published volume is a collection of translations of poetry and poetic prose. All her books except the collections of short stories and the books for children have epigraphs, most of them poetic, that direct the reader to what the author considered to be important in the volumes that they introduce. The titles of four books come directly from the epigraphs. Snatches of songs and nursery rhymes and stanzas of hymns pervade the novels and short stories. The versions of some of these raise interesting questions, and the quotations themselves are always significant in context. These topics deserve treatment elsewhere.

2. Cf. Clara Thomas, "The Chariot of Ossian: Myth and Manitoba in *The Diviners*," *Journal of Canadian Studies* 13.3 (Fall 1978): 55-63.

3. Cf. William Wordsworth, Preface to the Second Edition of *Lyrical Ballads*, *The English Romantics: Major Poetry and Critical Theory*, ed. John L. Mahoney (Lexington and Toronto: Heath, 1978), 100.

4. The African country of the setting was the Gold Coast before it became Ghana.

5. As Coleridge uses the term in *Biographia Literaria*, Chapter 13, Mahoney, p. 243.

6. McClelland and Stewart Limited in association with Heorte Music. Lyrics Copyright © 1973, Margaret Laurence; Music Copyright © 1973, Ian Cameron. Recording remastered and produced by Quality Records. Vocals by Ian Cameron and Joan Minkoff. Guitars, Ian Cameron, Bob Berry, and Peter MacLachlan.

WORKS CITED

Blewett, David. "The Unity of the Manawaka Cycle." *Journal of Canadian Studies* 13.3

(Fall 1978): 31-39.

Laurence, Margaret. *A Bird in the House*. Toronto: McClelland and Stewart, New Canadian Library, (1970, 1989, 1991) 1994; Chicago: University of Chicago Press, 1993.

___. *The Diviners*. Toronto: McClelland and Stewart, New Canadian Library, (1974, 1988) 1995; Chicago: University of Chicago Press, 1993.

___. *The Fire-Dwellers*. Toronto: McClelland and Stewart, New Canadian Library, (1969, 1988) 1991; Chicago: University of Chicago Press, 1993.

___. *Heart of a Stranger*. Toronto: McClelland and Stewart, 1976.

___. *A Jest of God*. Toronto: McClelland and Stewart, New Canadian Library, (1966, 1974, 1988) 1993; Chicago: University of Chicago Press, 1993.

___. *This Side Jordan*. Toronto: McClelland and Stewart, New Canadian Library, (1960, 1976) 1995.

___. *The Stone Angel*. Toronto: McClelland and Stewart, New Canadian Library, (1964, 1968, 1988) 1995; Chicago: University of Chicago Press, 1993. For details of the recording, see Note 6.

___. "Poems." *Vox* 18.3 (Graduation 1945): 32.

Macpherson, James. *The Poems of Ossian In the Original Gaelic, with a Literal Translation into English and a Dissertation on the Authenticity of the Poems*, by the Rev. Archibald Clark, together with the English translation by Macpherson. 2 vols. Edinburgh and London: Blackwood, 1879; Macpherson, James. *Poems of Ossian in the Original Gaelic*. 3 vols. Ed. John M'Arthur. St. Clair Shores, Michigan: Scholarly Press, n.d.; and MacPherson, James. *The Poems of Ossian*. New York: AMS Press, Inc., 1992.

Pottle, Frederick A. *The Idiom of Poetry. Messenger Lectures on the Evolution of Civilization 1941*. Rev. ed. Ithaca: Cornell University Press, 1946.

Chapter 2

The Angel and the Living Water: Metaphorical Networks and Structural Opposition in *The Stone Angel*
Michel Fabre

The opening of *The Stone Angel*, whose statue in the first paragraph provided Margaret Laurence with the title of her novel, has often been studied for its emblematic and mystical content. It is in fact easy to see in the blind angel that marks the grave of Hagar's mother a prefiguration of the emotional blindness that will afflict Hagar for a long time; to see in the opposition between the beautiful layout of the cemetery and the proliferation of the wild flora, the reflection of a chronic struggle between cultural order and disorder in nature; finally, to underline that the pioneers of Manawaka, those would-be pharaohs in an uncultivated country, have founded their dynasties to the detriment of the aborigines, the white success upsetting once more the Indian harmony.[1] Inscribed in the first paragraph a clue should, however, draw the attention more, for it signals a characteristic displacement in the expected balance, setting off the beginning of a structural opposition (and not only a symbolic one), a lack that will be partially canceled at the end of the novel.

The essential clues in the first three pages first order space in the tale: the verticality of the angel, as the elevated location of the cemetery (and the garbage dump) on the whole, indicates its consecration whereas the little city, a space at first conquered over the uncultivated areas of the geographical "wilderness" then built with brick and stone, is already in a privileged position in relation to the few, scattered outback farms, such as Shipley's, and the even more remote cabins of the half-breeds, then, finally, the prairie. The monumental angel represents also permanence of time inscribed in the eternal in opposition to the changing reoccurrence of the two seasons brought by the wind, which blows alternately snow and dust.

Another pregnant contrast is that of the cultivated flowers and of the wild plants. Within the civilized space can be found pompous peonies whose haughty heads weigh too much for their stems. These bitter-sweet smelling funeral bouquets, pink or a detestable crimson color, are in harmony with the little girls in their Sunday clothes ("prim" calls to mind "proper") who hop about in the straight paths. To the propriety of order is opposed the native flora, "scrub oaks" and "couch grass," and especially the invasion, badly contained in its proliferation, of marsh marigolds with a smell as strong as theirs are deep, "musty, dust-scented smell of things that grew untended" (5).[2] These plants spread the musk of primitive sexuality, anterior to the construction of the town, contemporary to those Indians whose faces are as impenetrable as the beginning of the world.

This symbolic opposition between culture and nature structures the novel just as solidly as does the story of the pioneers of Manitoba who imported their customs, the Presbyterian religion, and the moral values of their ancestral Scotland. With an uncommon strength of character and a desire for success, they imposed this "civilization" upon the hostility of the great spaces and people met in their progression towards the west.

Retrospectively, from the height of her ninety years of inexperience, Hagar can indeed mock this enterprise; she can indeed, instead of using her father as the only target of her bitterness, engulf him within the group of founding fathers, these "fledgling pharaohs in an uncouth land" (3). This expression brings to mind the majestic rhythms of Shelley's "Ozymandias" that also evoked destroyed monuments and extinct dynasties; it sends one back to the rulers of ancient Egypt and begins the characterization, so ambivalent, of Hagar the Egyptian (to whom we will return). An enterprise of colonization, the material and political domination of the country reputed to be "uncultivated" was also an enterprise for the perpetuation of a lineage, the Clanranald of the MacDonalds' ancestors whose warring lifestyle, holidays and castles--the castles especially--seduced Hagar as a girl. It was the illusory enterprise of escaping death and forgetfulness, "forever and a day" (3)-- futile desire, as is emphasized, in her precarious survival, the descendant disinherited by the founding father.

Finally, an obvious emblem is the blindness of the marble angel: "She was doubly blind, not only stone but unendowed with even a pretense of sight" (3). Sanctified by popular speech, the expression "stone blind" is twice as strong because of the absence of any pupil or a visible iris: "Whoever carved her had left her eyeballs blank" (3). The angel thus becomes the symbol of a destiny, assuredly Christian for it calls up Heaven, but derisory because it does not know the inhabitants of the little town any more than God will recognize his own in the cruel games of existence.

Ordinarily, the angel incarnates complementary traits. Intermediary between heaven and earth, human beings, and the divinity, it is also the bird-man; it is also (the medieval controversy on the sex of angels says a lot on this subject) the androgyny which unifies the complementary masculine and feminine principles. Here, the stone angel is feminine immediately on the second line but, at the same time, disposed of this femininity by the masculine will so strongly evoked by the reference to the father. The angel is dedicated to the mother, but she is weak, quasi-nonexistent in life as in death, unlike her daughter--"she relinquished her feeble ghost as I gained my stubborn one" (3)--as of her selfish husband--"bought in pride to mark her bones and proclaim his dynasty" (3). The mother disappears herself completely before the father and the child, so much so that the angel as the incarnation of a mother gone to heaven to intercede is immediately eclipsed by the angel, such an ostentatious work of art, marked with all the signs of cultural consumption approved by the local elite: it comes from Italy (reference to Bernini and the official sculpture of the Renaissance); it is of pure hard white marble (revindication of the authenticity of the material); it was very expensive--facts that the retrospective irony of Hagar exploits magnificently when she evokes the cynical descendants of Bernini, "gouging out her like by the score, gauging with admirable accuracy the needs of fledgling pharaohs in an uncouth land" (3).

This angel, which surpasses the others by its size and cost, if not by its age, is of a particular race. It sets itself apart from the chubby and smiling cherubs, bearers of hearts or players of harps, as if it were some warrior creature of the Ancient Testament who does not suit the deceased mother, or rather, she is hardly suitable to it. Invisible and anonymous mother, her only role will have consisted of giving her life in exchange for that of her daughter, a substitution that the father forgave explicitly to Hagar whom, when she became a woman, he declared himself to be more proud of than of his broodmare. Besides, if Hagar does not remember her mother, or conceals her memory, the text gives us immediately another tomb which characterizes this mother by contagion: that of Regina Weese, a being apparently as pusillanimous as the initial syllable of her patronymic. What is striking in the opinion that Hagar maintains on the deceased is her all-encompassment for a too-devoted woman that she judges without consistence: "I always felt she had only herself to blame, for she was a flimsy, gutless creature, bland as egg custard (we will see the horror of eggs that characterizes Hagar), caring with matured devotion for an ungrateful fox-voiced mother. (The eater of eggs and chicken?)" (4). The evocation causes Regina to die of some secret and virginal illness, almost shameful and, in the same breath, presents Hagar as a child, "neat and orderly, imagining life had been created to celebrate tidiness, like prissy Pippa as she passed" (5). Certainly, the allusion to the character of Browning is ironical, but leaves a double impression: the hostility towards the devoted woman as a model serves as an excuse for the obliteration of the mother; the projection of Hagar as a young girl as the incarnation of the virtues of civilization, of the dynastic plans of her father, even if the discourse of a Hagar-narrator brings them back for cushioning.

The opening does not, therefore, just set in opposition the structural poles around which the conflicts and dramas of Hagar's existence are ordered. It suggests also the process of a critical distance that is enhanced by a retrospective humor which, beginning with the contestation of femininity in the androgenia of the angel, will allow Hagar who begins as a worthy "son" of her father to regain the reputedly stingy side of her nature, or rather that to which a patriarchal culture has reduced feminine nature.

Let us, however, follow our textual tracks. First of all, is the angel an emblematic representation of the protagonist? If yes, on what terms: Hagar being neither a paragon of piety, nor an example of gentleness, any allusion to these would appear suspicious. Only John treats her as an angel, just once, to make fun of his mother when she reproaches him for giving too much to drink to the dying

20 Language, Theme, and Image

Bram: "Why yes," John said, "don't frown like that, angel, he's getting what he needs (172). Also, the opposite association is only encountered once when Hagar, having with great pains climbed back up the slope near Shadow Point, compares herself with humor to the rebellious archangel: "Proud as Napoleon or Lucifer, I stand and survey the wasteland I've conquered" (191).

Not too much should be read in this, in comparison with the blindness, and especially the immobility of the stone angel. It is in fact along the axis of petrifaction by opposition to movement (water that flows or bird that flies) that the imaginary space of the novel is organized. The statue of the angel seems a bit paradoxically like the blocked flight of an imprisoned spirituality. Its two symbolic attributes will be prolonged, on one hand, by the theme of flight and the motif of the wing: sea gulls in the canning factory; Hagar's heart which knocks against her sides like a bird in a cage; and even when she is hospitalized in the new pavilion, her bad pun--"'That's all I need.' I say snappishly, 'a new wing'" (280), which makes of her a reincarnation of the sea gull she has wounded. On the other hand and foremost, the angel is the stone statue, authentic or fake, into which Hagar is transformed by her immobility. She remarks, "I sit rigid and unmovable, like one of those plaster of Paris figures the dime stores sell" (172). She sees herself as some token angel, for these cheap statues which can be found among the knick knacks of Lottie's living room, the little bourgeoisie, contribute sometimes to subtract value by contagion, sometimes to give more value by opposition, to the marble angel of the cemetery and to Hagar herself.

The angel is equally blind, and Hagar claims for herself this spiritual blindness, but at the same time, she makes this the lot of everyone, cursing the supreme sculptor for having chiseled humans without pupils: "I could not speak . . . for anger--not at anyone, at God perhaps, for giving us eyes but almost never sight" (173). The illusory position of superiority that the exalted position of the angel gives, is illustrated elsewhere by the ditty: "If I had the wings of an angel / . . . / I would fly to the top of T. Eaton's / And spit on the people below" (106). Hagar, of course, denies any importance to angels, as opposed to Murray Lees, the believer, who speaks incessantly of them: "I talked like Corinthians says with the tongues of men and angels" (229), and "she could have prayed the angels themselves right down from heaven" (227).

However, in some scenes, the angel keeps its biblical attributes, fighting particularly with Jacob at the foot of the ladder. His flight occurs twice. First, when Hagar asks John to take her to the cemetery to make sure that the Currie tomb is well maintained, she finds the angel fallen over and asks John to straighten it:

He put his shoulders to the angel's head, and heaved. . . . I wish he could have looked like Jacob then, wrestling with the angel and besting it, wringing a blessing from it with his might. But no. He sweated and grunted angrily. His feet slipped and he hit his forehead on a marble ear, and swore. . . . finally the statue moved, teetered, and was upright once more. (179)

Note here that the angel has gone from the feminine to the neuter, which distances it from the mother. It is, however, from the Currie dynasty, not from

Hagar, that John must obtain a blessing, in vain, for the marble ear that the statue lends him wounds him symbolically on the forehead. During this visit to the cemetery by Hagar, already quinquagenarian, nature, normally full of life, is perishing due to the drought while culture, represented by the eternal peonies, is flourishing because it is watered in accordance with the wishes of the rich deceased. In this triumph of culture the fall of the angel clashes; it is felt as an outrage, and the ants which crawl in the stone locks are desecrators. Hagar is not fooled by it, she who suspects her son of as sacrilegious a gesture as his father's once pissing long ago in Jason's shop. And John reconveys that it must be the act of a man who has had too much to drink. The degradation also comes from the marks of red on the lips and cheeks of the statue which make her look vulgar--"Vulgar pink" (179). Here the mouth is "pouting," contrary to the initial scene, which brings the angel closer to the bland little angels of the other tombs and the statuettes belonging to Lottie, and also to her daughter Arlene, described elsewhere as "cooing like a pouting pigeon" (173) and whom Hagar detests because she could marry her son. There is, therefore, a taint to be erased, even if "a faint blush" still remains from this much too indelible a stain.

The second visit to the cemetery takes place with Marvin and Doris. This time again the angel is in peril, not that a human has pushed it, but because the earth, swollen by the frost, has made it lopsided, "askew and tilted" (206), a little like Hagar herself. However, thank heaven, its mouth has become white again. This time, the visitors are concerned to look at the statue, and it is later, not long before she dies, that Hagar evokes her eldest son's struggle with the angel when Marvin clutches her hand:

Now it seems to me that he is truly Jacob, gripping with all his strength, and bargaining. *I will not let thee go, except thou bless me.* And I see I am thus strangely cast, and perhaps have been so from the beginning, and can only release myself by releasing him. (304)

"Cast," which evokes at the same time the role imposed upon Hagar by fate, and the mold in which statues are formed, reestablishes the mother in the role of the all-powerful angel against which the son exhausts himself fighting. This time, Hagar identifies herself under the double aspect of the angel to anguish--"a holy terror" (304)--and the heir to the Shipley-Currie lineage. She admits that her own salvation implies having a more humane attitude towards Marvin whom her blessing will appease; she does not hesitate to lie in proclaiming him the best of her sons to liberate him of his jealousy towards John.

The acceptance of Marvin's devotion (which, like Regina Weese's, has its value), therefore, the repudiation by Hagar of her prejudices towards the oversensitive people that she found too soft, allows the reconciliation of the artificial aspects of the protagonist and the elements of reality which they represent.

Through this bias, the nature-culture opposition reappears. On the social level, the latter was codified in the John Currie-Bram Shipley couple. Jason (the man with the Golden Fleece) possesses it, the merchant whose tenacious labor has no equal other than his sense of thrift, and his appetite for success. This "self-made man" soon occupies an enviable position in the local hierarchy and in the church of which he is the benefactor. As for Bram Shipley, he is Abraham, therefore, the founder (ridiculous?) of a dynasty but even more "Bramble Shipley," as he is nicknamed, that is to say the primitive, who lives off berries like the birds and is not worth more than dung in the eyes of the community. He is the marginal that associates with the half-breeds and defies the established order in the little town with his drunken flings. He is the man of nature, as Jason is the one of culture. Even his brown skin ("brown" contrasted to "white") and the black hairs of his beard and thighs denote a sensuality, a sexuality that the Church condemns. He is also the man of liberty, of joie de vivre, of pleasure in the present moment, who turns up his nose to propriety, pretensions, overly pious behavior what-will-they-says. This savage who does not know how to blow into a handkerchief, who calls a spade a spade, this peasant who likes horses too much to sell them, incarnates a vital spontaneous, warm, and exuberant element which is precisely what the protestant work and family order ethic condemns.

These antitheses of what Jason represents, Hagar in rebellion against her father will hurry to seek precisely because of his interdictions. She flees her home and community in search of a liberty possible with her husband. But she remains conditioned, despite what she has acquired, by the education she has received and will soon no longer tolerate, in the man she loves and whose boorish manners shocked her as much as his sensuality fascinates her, the traits of character that make up his charm. She will, therefore, obstinately apply herself to socialize the savage, to attempt to polish him, to instill in him the respect for institutions. It is only much later, after she has left this husband in order to, as she likes to believe, give to her youngest son the possibility of becoming, by education, a worthy grandson to Jason, that Hagar accepts what Bram represents, by having him buried in the Currie vault. The cemetery angel thus regains its symbolic duality as it recovers the denied side of its androgynous nature when the spontaneity of Shipley joins the petrifaction of Currie, the highness of the one uniting itself to the substance of the other:

I had him buried in the Currie plot, and on the red marble namestone that stood beside the white statue I had this family name carved, so the stone said *Currie* on the one side and *Shipley* on the other. I don't know why I did it. I felt I had to. (184)

At that moment, it is John who expresses the complementarity of what the two men represent: "They're different sides of the same coin, anyway, he and the Curries. They might as well be together there" (184). Hagar does not understand right away what he means, and it is later, during the last visit to the cemetery, that the same expression is used on her own account: "Unusual, eh? This is the *Currie-Shipley* stone. The two families were connected by marriage. Pioneering families, the both of them, two of the earliest in the district" (206). And for Hagar to meditate: "The both of them. Both the same. Nothing to pick and choose between them. That was as it should be" (206). Not only does she explicate here John's sentence about the two sides of the same coin, the face and back, but she states their equivalence and accepts this order of things.

Association of the mobile and the solid, of the aerial and the earthy, the symbolism of the stone angel structures also a whole constellation of motifs and episodes which correspond throughout the novel to the great anthropological categories of the moving and the fixed, of chaos and order, which can be inversely given value according to the time of the narration and the personality of who considers them. For, as Hagar says, things do not have the same aspect when considered from outside or from inside.

Following in fact the metaphors of the stone and of the petrification, we find not only everything that relates to the edifices of man (durable houses as opposed to the shelters, huts, hearths, monuments) but also what signals the blocking of elements or of normally dynamic functions--what one might call the constipation motif. "Rigid and unmovable," Hagar is almost always like this to protect herself from the stare of others. Confronting her father, she resembles a soldier, "standing there rigidly on the bottom step, buttoned and armored in my long dark gown" (44). Her dress has become armor, her epidermis a carapace, hardened envelope to protect her, which she will elsewhere call "my shell." Later, sitting on the bus, her imperturbable appearance only hides her distress: "Rigid as marble I sit, solid and stolid to outward view, inwardly my heart thunders until I fear other passengers may hear" (96). This hardening could be found in the behavior of the young girl who rarely ever let her hair, usually braided or in a bun, loose seeing it as a sign of weakness, of slackness, almost of immorality: "my hair pinned on top of my head would come undone and fall around my shoulders in a black glossiness that the boys would try to touch" (22). Often, one sees her withdraw--"I stiffened and drew back my hands" (25)--to avoid contact, when she cannot, for example, play by the dying Dan the role of her mother, exactly because she had been too soft, too weak in her eyes. The epitome of this hardness is in the constipation of the aged Hagar facing the pastor: "My bowels are locked today. I am Job in reverse. . . . I sit uncomfortably. I am bloated, full, weighted down, and I fear I may pass wind" (40). A physical blockage to be sure, but how could grace enter into such a body? Further, the same remark: "My bowels knot. . . . Now I am locked as a bank vault with no key" (191). Constipation of body and soul evoke so rigid a structure that she becomes a vault holding breath and spirit prisoners.

The solidity, which Hagar likes to find in some old objects and which she contrasts to the fragility of today's junk in furniture, becomes, therefore, a sign of degeneration, of powerlessness instead of proving resistance and strength. Banal, the expression "stone cold," which is applied to the cooling tea is back suddenly, can connote the complete stop of vital heat. The single word "marble" freezes everything. It reminds one in fact of Dan's fall through a hole in the ice of the frozen river. The fact is that even running water becomes petrified: "In winter the Wachakwa River was solid as marble" (23). This ice connotes also funeral parlors where the dead are embalmed, and the congealed water contrasts sharply with the all-important symbolism of the living, free, redemptive water.[3] As with Robert Frost, damnation is a hell of ice and not of flame.

By contrast, after having drunk too much with Murray Lees and also having thought too much about what weighs upon her conscience as much as on her stomach, Hagar cannot keep herself from throwing up. This regurgitation from the innermost of her being becomes a true liberation and, at the same time, an interior debacle. This letting-go, which in her half-sleep she equates to a urination (thinking herself at Doris's, she wants to get a basin), spreads Hagar's secrets at the same time as the debris of her food. Upon exclaiming, "Oh, Lord, you've brought it all up" (247), Lees does not know how true her words are. Consequently, a little later, the memory of Hagar, liberated by the melting of her interior ice, is "unhappily clear now as spring water, [it] bubbles up coldly" (248).

Hagar's itinerary toward contact with others is thus marked with the symbolism of water and tears--water that flows out of her like never before. [As a] child, she resisted the punishments of the father, who "looked at my dry eyes in a kind of fury as though he'd failed unless he drew water from them" (9-10). In the same vein, she never cried for her dear deceased ones--Dan, Bram, John--because her Presbyterian upbringing had taught her never to show her emotion in public. In return, as she gets older, she is angry at herself for her own disbelief, of losing her toughness, not only that of a skin now flabby and wrinkled, but also toughness due to moods once held in and which overflow too easily now, whether it is about her nightly incontinence or the grateful tears that swell stupidly to her eyes when a young girl shows her way. What disgust in the statement: "I'm limp as a dishrag" (152), when Hagar falls back on the soiled mattress in the abandoned cannery! And still, it is there that she will shelter the fantasy which springs from her after she has fled the potential prison of "Silverthreads." She who wanted to close herself up now dreads being confined.

In opposing itself to moral connotation strengthened "with backbone," "limp" evokes the shapeless and chaotic aspect of human beings that strangely sicken Hagar. Where, for instance, does her repulsion for eggs come from?[4] One certainly thinks of the episode of the chicks dying on the heap of refuse, perhaps symbolic of the human condition in an absurd world ruled by a cruel God:

We saw with a kind of horror that could not be avoided. . . . The chicks, feeble, foodless, bloodied and mutilated, prisoned by the weight of broken shells all around them, were trying to crawl like little worms, their halfmouths open uselessly among the garbage. . . . For pity's sake they were put out of their misery, or so I believed then, and still in part believe. But they were an affront to the eyes, as well. (27-28)

Why does Hagar, unlike Lottie, detest this spectacle to the point that she can neither look at it, nor act on it? Does it seem to her to incarnate the metaphysical obscenity of a revolting condition--that of reprieved death that all life is. One can think that is also a repugnance for the egg substance whose running fluids are almost undifferentiated, and of a revolt against the fragility of the shell, a false protection which becomes quickly squashed heads of the chicks or skulls exploding in an accident. It is, at the same time, a jealous attraction and a movement of rejection: "Lottie was light as an eggshell herself, and I felt surely toward her littleness and pale fine hair for I was tall and sturdy and dark and would have liked to be the opposite" (27). In refusing to untangle this psychological viper now, the narrative allows seductive interpretations of the egg symbol. It is a fact that, by an irony of fate, Hagar will become, in order to find the necessary money for John's education, an "egg woman" hawking the eggs of her hens. But what a humiliation to find herself reduced to this role near Lottie, who, when she once gave the coup de grâce to the unfortunate chickens, carries the eggs as if they were a precious load: "the way she took the basket so tenderly as if it mattered to her not to break the frail nestled globes within, as though they were a kind of treasure to her" (132). The egg is, therefore, this thing without a defense, this embryo of being that one must surround with care, like the nonagenarian that she is herself who has to be wedged between pillows and cushions "like an egg in a crate" (93). The egg brings to mind the cozy enclosure of the cocoon which she accepts now to ward off the intolerable physical pain. Cozy is a word which she refused vehemently once, which she even condemned in the brother whose sickly appearance called up her scorn because she saw in it a bad excuse for his laziness. But the egg is also the foetus, the child to be born, whom Hagar is not exactly sure, when she is in labor, she wants: "What could I say, that I'd not wanted children? . . . that the child he wanted could be his and none of mine?" (100)

In a Jungian perspective, the egg is obviously the symbol and the attribute of maternity, of the goddess-mother, by its spherical perfection and its ability to germinate. This something which can blossom and proliferate disconcerts Hagar for whom procreation represents the somewhat obscene outpouring of a life that one cannot stop. This to the extent that, in spite of its irony, she shares the views of a father who has planned in his will a perpetual fund "so that his soul never peer down from the elegant halls of eternity and be offended by cowslips spawning on his grave" (63). If "spawn" did not connote a certain repugnance to procreation, how else can one explain this aversion for eggs and chickens?[5] There is certainly the fear of what-will-they-say and appearing vulgar when Hagar is indignant about Bram's advice to take hard-boiled eggs to eat on the train. But there is more: from the egg that runs to the head that bursts, it is important to Hagar to avoid all that spreads and overflows; thus, she fortifies herself, she shuts herself up much too long in spirit and emotionally, until such a time as the benefits of a liberating flux are recognized by the nonagenarian and that at the eve of her death begins the dissolving of the stone, the bursting of the ice of her heart.

At this stage, one can see with what pertinence the description of the stone statue is assimilated with that of the decrepit monument that the aging body is:

As I brush my fingers over my own wrist, the skin seems too white [the white was valorized in relation to the brown] after the sunburned years, and too dry [before, the humidity of the tears got in the way], powdery as blown dust when the rain failed, flaking with dryness as an old bone will flake and chalk, left out in a sun that grinds bone and flesh and earth to dust as though in a mortar of fire with a pestle of crushing light. (54)

The biblical echoes of this vision of the valley of bones puts on the same plane the flesh and the rock, if not the flesh and the grass that go on drying under the sun of time.

The value of any human monument thus seems to be put again into question.

26 Language, Theme, and Image

One has seen that the monumental angel was no more offensive than any other monument. Indeed who would not think of surviving through their possessions or their descendants? Striking in Jason, this ambition simmers also in Bram whom Hagar sees with surprise is glad to have an offspring to whom to leave his name and his farm: "I saw then with amazement that he wanted his dynasty, no less than my father had" (101). Further on, Hagar remarks ironically regarding the handkerchiefs that she buys him and that pile up, unused, in a drawer: "I used to wonder whether he wanted to be buried with them like an ancient king" (131)-- which echoes back to the grass pharaohs who were the titled founders of Manawaka. Other than the family tomb, Currie's generosity gets him a municipal park in which the petunia flower beds (hereafter also spurned by Hagar as the peonies) "proclaimed my father's immortality in mauve and pink petals" (64). Bram erects a tomb for his favorite horse:

I'm certain he put a boulder on the place, like a gravestone. But later that summer, after the grass and weeds had grown back, when I mentioned the rock curiously and asked how it had got there, Bram only looked at me narrowly and said it had been there always. (88)

The motif of the monument creates an interesting link with reappearance of the Egyptian woman several times in the novel. Thus, in the basement of the hospital where she is having an X-ray, Hagar wonders, "Is it a mausoleum and I, the Egyptian, mummified with pillows and my own flesh, through some oversight embalmed alive?" (96). In this context, "Egyptian" refers first to the corpse of some sister or wife of a pharaoh, an image incidentally taken up again in "perhaps when I'm let out, launched in wind and sun, I may disintegrate entirely like the flowers found on ancient young Tutankhamen's tomb" (111). Through the daughter of the aspiring-pharaoh of Manawaka, the allusion to Egypt refers, therefore, to the concept of an antique dynasty surviving in the secret of the pyramids:

I am Pharaoh's daughter reluctantly returning to his roof, the square brick palace so oddly antimacassared in the wilderness, back to the hill where his monument stood, more dear to him, I believe, than the brood mare who lay beneath because she'd proved no match for his stud. (43)

On the other hand, upon one of her encounters with Mr. Troy, Doris's pastor, Hagar designates herself as "I, the Egyptian not dancing now with rowanberries in her hair but sadly altered" (40), that is to say as an ex-young dancer who owes to her contact with nature (the berries in her hair connect her to her "Bramble" Shipley) a vitality that makes her oppose culture in favor of order. This Egyptian, as we will see, is that of the Bible, but also the "gypsy," the bohemian, represented in the Shadow Point episode, by the evocation of the character of Meg Merrilies, borrowed by Keats from Walter Scott, thus from the best romantic tradition. Hagar identifies right away with Meg, judging that the verses of the poem that celebrate her bring her more comfort than the Twenty-third Psalm: "I'm like Meg Merrilies," she concluded, "old Meg she was a gipsy" (151). Physically, and by her clothing, Meg the gypsy brings to mind the sort of scarecrow that Hagar was as an egg vendor, rigged out in a much too large overcoat and a string scarf (see 133). As a vagabond at Shadow Point, Hagar is the triumph of natural finery (in the canning factory she sprinkled her loose hair with golden green mists to play at being the queen of the ear-wigs and moths) over the hats and outfits "prim and proper" of Lottie and Doris. By this metamorphosis, Hagar defines herself as a nonconformist, a bohemian, as much as a wandering gypsy; she rebels against the order that her pharaoh of a father incarnated. "Egyptian" explodes, therefore, as do other notions or images, into opposite and complementary meaning. Here, it is, according to Genesis, Abraham's wife who gave birth to Ishmael, before that Sarah, according to the divine promise, could be at the origin of the Jewish dynasty of Isaac and Jacob. Because of his pride, Abraham repudiated Hagar, whose name signified "she who flees." It is very obvious that Margaret Laurence in no way models the Shipley family on that of Abraham. However, the Hagar-Bram couple reproduce the natural union of the flesh (as opposed to the marriage according to the Alliance-culture), that is to say, the union which, this time according to the epistle of Saint Paul to the Galatians, begets the heirs fated to slavery in the desert. But the notion of desert and slavery is essential in Hagar's determining confession: "Pride was my wilderness and the demon that led me there was fear, I was . . . never free for I carried my chains with me, and they spread out from me and shackled all I touched" (292). In addition, is Hagar's favorite son, John, not a sort of Ishmael in search of a home and belonging? And the rivalry between Marvin and John, that their mother projects alternately but in vain into the role of Jacob, does not it bring to mind the biblical rivalry between Jacob and Esau. No more than she, John, the son who resembles Hagar, will never be the founder of a dynasty, even if, in an irony of history such as forgetful men make it, the two pioneer families of Manawaka find themselves reunited by new generations in the same cult of origins.

The structural opposition, whose key elements and major orientations could be seen clearly in the initial episode in the cemetery, is present throughout the novel without ever quite resolving itself. Whether it passes through the themes of living water and of free flight, or of ice and of petrifaction, whether it incarnates itself in the androgyny of the angel or in the conflict of Jason and of Bram between whom Hagar finds herself constantly pulled, whether it informs us of the motifs of the Egyptian-gypsy, the egg, the tears, or the flowers, this opposition does not prevent, however, the protagonist from progressing with age towards a reconciliation with herself and a conciliation of the extremes. Having begun from the pole of hardness, order, and culture, Hagar repudiates these values with as much passion as inefficiency in her rebellion as a young woman. Gradually, through the slow but inevitable ripening of her flesh and her heart, she is led to accept things as they are, to appreciate and accept those elements that she had before considered as scornful, even intolerable, in her own personality. To the pride of the stone angel is slowly substituted, by the fire and ice of trials, an opening to pity, a stammering progression towards the joy which will be possible only at the moment of her death. Even though Hagar, who occupies the forefront as both narrator and protagonist, captivates and captures the reader by her discourse on her own story whose structural opposition we have noted and which goes beyond individual destinies, invites one, nevertheless, to see the drama of this woman as a failure of the relation between order and chaos, between the social and the instructive drives, between culture and nature--in brief, of those great categories that allow a humanity subjected to the pains of mortality to project on a larger stage the pleasures and the suffering of its too brief existence. *The Stone Angel* is thus much more than a chronicle, full of sound and fury, of a thirst for survival. By the association and dialectical relationship of motifs and concepts that could be seen only as details or accidental, the novelist in fact creates, in the text, a fabric of symbols and networks whose psychological, poetical, even mythical echoes enrich even more the dimension of a metaphysical parable that this story of an indignant old woman becomes.

NOTES

This essay was first published in *Etudes Anglaises* (Paris) 35.1 (1985): 57-70, translated by Marie Bell-Salter, Middlebury College, and edited by Raymonde Neil, University of Memphis.

1. Numerous analyses on symbolism in *The Stone Angel* are often excellent. I am inspired here by some suggestions and conclusions presented particularly in the introduction by W. H. New in the edition of the novel published by New Canadian Library (1968); from the chapter that Clara Thomas devotes to her in *The Manawaka World of Margaret Laurence* (1975) and of her article "The Wild Garden and the Manawaka World," *Modern Fiction Studies* (Autumn 1976); and finally, by the article by Joan Caldwell, "Hagar as Meg Merrilies, the Homeless Gypsy," *Journal of Canadian Studies* (Summer 1980).

2. All quotations refer to *The Stone Angel* (Toronto: McClelland and Stewart, New Canadian Library, [1964] 1995; Chicago: University of Chicago Press, 1993).

3. The important symbolism of the water deserves a special study (lustrous water, allusions to the curse of the Ancient Mariner of Coleridge and the albatross). By means of the curse which deprives the earth of rain, we rejoin the motif of the sea gull, quasi-divine bird with an immense flight which is here in a closed space where Hagar wounds it without meaning to and is condemned to take its place.

4. At the hospital, shortly before dying, Hagar complains of her diet and of the soft boiled egg, which she associates with "the shrunken world," her universe which shrinks, as if to become a symbol for it (264).

5. The word comes back in Hagar's evocation of the disastrous eventuality and unhappy offspring that John and Arlene might have.

Chapter 3

Stacey Cameron MacAindra: The Fire *This* Time

Lyall H. Powers

"**GOD GAVE NOAH THE RAINBOW SIGN, NO MORE WATER, THE FIRE NEXT TIME!**" (James Baldwin, Epigraph, *The Fire Next Time*)

One of several important similarities between the Yoknapatawpha fiction of William Faulkner and the Manawaka fiction of Margaret Laurence is the central idea that a healthy life depends on the frank recognition of mutability and human mortality--facing the fact of death.[1] That idea enjoys distinct prominence in the middle book of the Manawaka Saga, *The Fire-Dwellers* (1969): it is specifically announced by both the title and the recurring nursery rhyme that opens the novel-- "Ladybird . . . Fly away home, / Your house is on fire, / Your children are gone." The idea is developed dramatically in the career of Stacey Cameron MacAindra, with corollary development in that of her husband, Mac. Stacey's obsessive concern with her own aging and with all the signs--especially the physical--of her lost youth, her association with Buckle Fennick, and her brief affair with Luke Venturi all express her attempt to deny the twin facts of mutability and mortality. The novel equates denial of death with denial of life. Stacey's denial is exhibited also in her excessive concern to protect her children, her attempt to anticipate and thwart the stroke of death. Of principal importance in her maternal anxiety is her relationship with her daughter Katie, a relationship that echoes that between Rachel and Mrs. Cameron in *A Jest of God* and anticipates that between Morag and Pique in *The Diviners*. The constant threat in a world on fire--as Stacey's TV set, the EVER-OPEN EYE, persistently reminds her--is real enough, to be sure; what is at issue here, however, is Stacey's attitude. Technically and thematically *The Fire-Dwellers* is *her* story.

The corollary career of Mac involves his association with Richalife products-- including the necessary "rejuvenating" brush-cut hair style--his little affair with Delores Appleton, his long friendship with Buckle Fennick, and his reticence with Stacey.

From the opening of the novel we are given ample evidence of Stacey's fear of losing her youth, her vowing to diet to achieve a more svelte and youthful figure, her envy of Tess Fogler's appearance. One of Stacey's recurring memories is of her early years as an active and vital young woman swimming and dancing and fantasizing about sex. She worries constantly about the vulnerability of her four children: her house, her world, is indeed on fire, and she dreads that the children will be left alone and vulnerable. The responsibility for them and for her aging self is onerous; she wants out from under, she wants to escape--if only (like Tom Sawyer) temporarily. She is jealous of Tess Fogler's apparent freedom and youthfulness; Tess's husband tells Stacey she has a death wish (14) and comments on her imagination of disaster: *"You're not afraid it'll happen; you're afraid it won't"* (117). One of Stacey's reveries in the opening chapter of *The Fire-Dwellers* illustrates the justice of Jake Fogler's observation, for it is indeed life that frightens her--life at its most vivid and vital is threatening, is on fire:

The hillside is burning. Who dropped a lighted cigarette? Did she? Evergreen catches fire with terrible ease. . . . The children have no business to be there. . . . She is holding the hands of one. Which? . . . Only this one can she take with her, away from the crackling smoke, back to the green world. . . . She must never know who was left behind. (30-31)

As the novel rises to its climactic midpoint, at the end of the fifth of its ten chapters, Stacey is offered a dramatic means of escape. She has been indulging in a couple of her favorite evasive devices: first, reliving the dancing youth of Stacey Cameron--"*The music crests . . . blue-green sound, saltwater with the incoming tide . . . the green beckoning in voices, the men still unheld* " (125)--and second, downing generous glasses of gin and tonic. She burns her hand on the stove in a kind of self-realizing prophecy, and thinks that she just cannot cope, that she does not want to go on living (130). The next day, she goes secretly to a Richalife rally in a pathetic attempt to get closer to Mac and his work; there she gets instead a glimpse of his relationship with the slim, young Delores Appleton: "he has one arm around her, not casually but tightly, like a wall against the world" (137).

At this stage of Stacey's dilemma, Mac's old buddy Buckle Fennick, "prince of the highway," enters with what seems an attractive offer of temporary diversion. She accepts. We know already that in her eyes Buckle is at once attractive and repulsive; he represents raw, blatant masculinity--"His jeans are always too tight and they bulge where his sex is, and it embarrasses me and infuriates me that it does, yet I always look, as he damn well knows and laughs at" (48). We also know that Buckle's customary trucking runs take him north up the Cariboo Highway (50); and he plays "chicken" with his big diesel--evidently to relieve the boredom and also to assert his masculine dominance.

On their brief ride to Coquitlam Stacey fantasizes going up north with Buckle: "*the truck stops. . . . He is poised above her--hard, ready, taut--and she can hardly wait for him to*" (141). She begins to realize that fantasy as she accepts his invitation to his apartment; she is then ready to accept his expected offer of himself to her--"She can almost feel his sex in her" (147). But Buckle does not share his sex; he keeps it to himself, onastically and narcissistically. Stacey flees. Buckle tells Mac that she seduced him; Mac refuses her denial.

"DEATH DESTROYS A MAN: THE IDEA OF DEATH SAVES HIM."
(E. M. Forster, *Howard's End*)

The full significance of Stacey's escapade with Buckle and of Mac's association with him since the Second World War is withheld until the culmination of Stacey's subsequent escapade with Luke Venturi. That delay is an important stroke in Laurence's narrative strategy, as we shall see. Her affair with Luke, which occupies much of Chapters 6 and 7, has obvious parallels to her adventure with Buckle. It begins with another reaction to evidence of Mac's antipathetic response to her and also with her partial understanding of Buckle's motivation in telling Mac of their visit to Buckle's apartment: "Mac wasn't paying enough attention to him" (156).

The reasons for Luke's attractiveness are quite apparent: not only is he the host at the shore of the Sound who welcomes Stacey on her new flight from her house "on fire," he is understanding and sympathetic in his response to her dilemma, and he affords her the symbolic freedom of unfettered sex; beyond that he is young and restores something to her damaged view of her aging self. He is after all just twenty-nine, he tells her, and she "confesses" to thirty-five! After each visit--there are only three in all and they actually make love on only two of them--Stacey returns home ridden with guilt yet clearly revitalized if not exactly rejuvenated. Most important, Luke manages, by coincidence and a kind of magic, to contribute to her *anagnorisis*: he leads her to confront herself and the nature of her fears and thus to her self-acceptance. That process begins early in this affair, on the initial flight to the shore.

Stacey has been dreaming of Diamond Lake and visits she made there at age ten and again at age eighteen; things had changed in the interval: the loons had gone. She therefore fantasizes another lake, *"a deep oil blue . . . somewhere in the Cariboo. The Cariboo country. Up there"* (160); but she returns to the memory of Diamond Lake--swimming, dancing, "the pressure on her lake-covered thighs of the boys" (161). It is the Cariboo, echoing Buckle's customary route up north on the Cariboo Highway, that provokes her first bit of recognition. She addresses God:

--Okay. I see it, Sir. I didn't see it before, but I see it now. . . . That's the place I want to get away to, eh? . . . up there somewhere. When I imagine it, it always looks like Diamond Lake. Like, I guess I mean, everything will be just fine when I'm eighteen again. Come on, Stacey. Home. 161)

But at that moment Luke Venturi enters.

Coincidentally, Luke is soon recounting his experiences up north, "up in the Cariboo, hitching," where he came upon a little farm-house in the middle of nowhere and a twelve-year-old who announces that his Mum *"took off, two-three months ago"* (165). Stacey bursts into tears. Luke, surprised, asks, "Is that where you live?" Dramatic irony: he has innocently put together a great deal for Stacey to ponder. Four days later she returns and in her conversation with Luke is able to admit her fears, to recognize specifically how she has been encouraged since childhood to deny the fact of death. That confrontation has been carefully prepared for at the beginning of the second half of the novel by means of Stacey's memory of telling her mother about a gopher that had been shot; her graphic account is interrupted by Mrs. Cameron--*"Please, dear, don't talk about it--it isn't nice"* (155). Stacey unmistakably reflects the influence as she tells Luke about keeping her father's revolver after his death, in case of emergency:

I thought--*if anything happened*--that's the way I always thought of it . . . that phrase only, just like my mother could never bring herself to say anyone had died--they had always passed on. (179)

Before the third meeting with Luke three noteworthy events occur that directly prepare for that meeting and set up Stacey for the decision she consequently takes. Returning home after her second visit to Luke, she is immediately greeted (at the beginning of Chapter 7) by news of Tess Fogler's obliging Jen to witness her big goldfish's eating a little one. Jen seems fine. Still, the confrontation with Tess's fascination with death draws Stacey and Katie together: "*We*. They have never before encountered one another as persons. At the same time, Katie has been unwittingly calling her *Mum* instead of *Mother*" (192). That evening, Stacey learns from Duncan that Ian has very nearly reenacted the death of his friend Peter Challoner by running in front of a car in pursuit of his football. She thinks:

Ian thinks about death--how much? Some people don't know they're ever going to die until it happens to them, but Ian knows he's going to die . . . and *his* father deals in rejuvenating vitamins. (197)

Third, Julian Garvey comes over later that evening to see Mac about some Richalife pills; that provokes in Stacey the thought that Julian is seeking something to restore his virility or to prolong his life eternally (199). She is ready to visit Luke again--and finally.

They make love for the second time, and then coincidence and magic begin to work on Stacey. Luke resumes his tales of "up north," and they are heavy with echoes and allusions:

There's this place where there's a ferry. . . . [T]his beat-up old raft crawls across the Skeena . . . the old guy who runs it is calm as anything, probably been there forever. Charon. . . . And there's this village . . . Indian village. . . . The attraction is the totem poles . . . the totems of the dead. And of the living dead. (208)

Charon, ferryman to the land of the dead, provides clear enough identification of the true destination of Buckle, prince of the highway--up north. And then, magic or coincidence, Luke responds to Stacey's refusal of his invitation to accompany him up across the Skeena by quoting "Ladybird, ladybird." He then surprisingly confesses to her that his true age is twenty-four; and Stacey is faced with the fact that what Luke has seen in her (whether or not he was conscious of it) is not an eternally youthful partner but very nearly a Jocasta to his Oedipus: "I'm old enough to be his mother. She's the same age as I am [thirty-nine]" (210). When Stacey leaves they both know the affair is over.² And when Stacey reaches homes she is confronted with a most eloquent announcement in Mac's laconic revelation, "Stacey, he's dead" (211). The statement is effectively ambiguous.

"DEATH IS THE MOTHER OF BEAUTY." (Wallace Stevens, "Sunday Morning")

On the death of Buckle Fennick, as a result of his playing "chicken" on the highway, we get a completed account of Buckle's role in the novel. He is a kind of "little brother Death" (an epithet Faulkner's Quentin Compson would readily understand); he offers a meaningful *liebestod* to those who feel his attraction--those who would deny the facts of mutability and mortality. Buckle is the embodiment of the suicidal urge. In Chapter 8 Mac recounts his saving Buckle's life during the Italian campaign of the Second World War. There are two items of particular interest in his story. First, when their truck reached a bridge and Mac wanted to get out to check it for mines and booby traps, Buckle replied, *"Okay, chickadee, you get out and walk because I'm driving across"* (218). The derogatory term "chickadee," suggesting cowardice in this context, is inescapably echoed in "chicken," the name of the game Buckle plays with his diesel on the Cariboo Highway. Second, after the bridge blew up and Mac had rescued him, "Buckle kept coming to . . . and from the way he looked it wasn't only because he was in pain it was something else entirely":

I couldn't figure it out at the time. But later on I thought maybe it was just that I hadn't done him any favor. I hadn't done anything he wanted me to do. (219)

This information completes Stacey's understanding of Buckle and of her own (and Mac's) attraction to him--which is a meaningful synecdoche in the novel. At the outset of the chapter Stacey has pondered Buckle's death as a result of his game of "chicken"; her explanation of his fascination with the game anticipates Mac's war story. She recalls Buckle's bravado:

. . . *I've never yet met a guy who didn't give way.*
--I thought it was pure ego, superconfidence, when he said that. But maybe after all it was only disappointment. (213; cf. 142)

With this, other features of Laurence's portrayal of Buckle crowd in on Stacey; two of them in particular establish the relation between his performance as a trucker and his qualifications as a sexual partner.

The initial sketch of Buckle describes him as a trucker: he drives a huge diesel. "Buckle loves it. It is his portable fortress, his moveable furnace. It is his lover and himself all in one" (50). In addition, he uses his diesel--"his lover and himself"--to challenge other drivers on the highway. The fire in that moveable furnace is certainly destructive, and, as Mac and Stacey both perceive, it is ultimately and intentionally *self*-destructive. Stacey discovers when she has accepted Buckle's invitation to his apartment something of his qualifications as a sexual partner, and they repeat his mastery of the diesel--his lover and himself all in one: "What he is doing now concerns only himself, his sex open and erect in his hands. But although he retreats from her presence, he watches her, needing to see some image in her eyes, some witness to the agony of his pleasure" (147). "Agony" is an eloquent touch! Buckle has been more than half in love with easeful death; he has been an active opponent of the human creative impulse.

The novel strongly implies that Stacey has made the connection between the Narcissus of the highway and the Onan of the bedroom. The dialogue she initiates with Mac as he completes the story of saving Buckle is heavy with such implication. She assures Mac he need feel no responsibility for Buckle--"You're not God. You couldn't save him"--then shifts abruptly (it would seem) to a recapitulation of her moment with Buckle. "I never went to bed with him," she affirms, then continues:

> Look--I might have. I guess I actually might have. But that wasn't what he wanted. I don't guess he was all that interested in women, Mac. That was why Julie [née Kazlik] left him. He liked it with himself but with somebody looking on. (219)

Stacey then gives another turn of the screw with her suggestion, "Maybe he wanted you" (219).

From the beginning of her marriage--"in our years of competition for Mac" (48) --she has seen Buckle as an opponent. She noted carefully the intimacy implied in Buckle's "lighting two cigarettes, holding them both in his mouth at once" (57) for him and Mac in the darkened TV room downstairs. She detected the note of jealousy--a particularly well justified jealousy--over Mac's association with Thor Thorlakson (140-41) at the outset of her crucial encounter with Buckle; in trying to account for his telling Mac about it, Stacey explains to herself, "Mac wasn't paying enough attention to him. Buckle is like a kid. Oh? None of my kids could conceivably be that vicious" (156). The homoerotic and autoerotic features of Buckle coincide with the suicidal: all are reductive and destructive, negations of human creativity[3]--like Brooke Skelton's frustration both of Morag's maternal and of her artistic creative impulses in *The Diviners*. Thus a new significance is added to Stacey's reaffirmation of not going to bed with Buckle: it is an affirmation of a nascent recommitment to life. But the same token, Mac's almost immediately subsequent confession of his taking Delores Appleton to bed--"Only once, though" (220)--is both a rejection of Buckle's sterile and baleful attraction and an affirmation of *his* new-born recommitment to life.

The sturdy comedic conclusion of *The Fire-Dwellers* has begun. Chapter 8 ends with repetition of Stacey's recognition that the Luke affair is distinctly over and with explicit emphasis--"Shameless, shameless attempt at rejuvenation. Pitiful, really" (222); with definite indication that Mac is ridding himself of Thor Thorlakson's influence as rejuvenation peddlar--Mac's brush-cut is growing out (226); and, most important of all, with Stacey's dream that closes the chapter.

"AFTER THE FIRST DEATH THERE IS NO OTHER." (Dylan Thomas, "A Refusal to Mourn the Death by Fire of a Child in London")

The air has been cleared: Stacey and Mac together have confronted and accepted the fact of death and have thus confronted and accepted each other; they are recommitted to life. For all Mac's involvement with Richalife and the youthful appearance (the brush-cut) Thor Thorlakson encourages and with the lissom Delores (a pale parallel to Stacey's involvement with Luke Venturi), his commitment to the means of denying mutability and mortality has been less urgent than Stacey's. To a considerable extent, in fact, Stacey has been herself largely responsible for that commitment of Mac's; certainly that is her guilt-ridden view of the situation--and her view in this is somewhat persuasive. Mac will do what he must to be a reliable bread-winner for the MacAindras; he feels, rightly, that Stacey's support and approval of his Richalife role is less than hearty. His little fling with Delores Appleton is compensatory.

To speak of Stacey's "view" of things, however, is to be guilty of some inaccuracy. From the opening pages of *The Fire-Dwellers* we have been privy to her constant dialogue with herself--a debate between two Staceys with two different views of life. One of those Staceys has always recognized the need to accept the fact of death as an inescapable "given" of the human condition: the view of that Stacey opens the novel with a comment on the "Ladybird" quatrain. "Half those nursery rhymes are gruesome," she observes, and couples with them the line, "Here comes a chopper to chop off your head" and the prayer, "If I should die before I wake," then concludes: "Maybe it's okay, though. Prepares them for what they can expect" (7). This "view" anticipates the dream at the conclusion of Chapter 8. Further preparation for that dream appears in another statement of the same view, the reverie that ends the opening chapter (quoted p. 30); it begins with the burning hillside and the evergreen catching fire and leads to the telling observation, *"Not to be born would be not to have to die. But that would be useless"* (31).[4] Then comes the dream:

The place is a prison but not totally so. It must be an island . . . where people are free to walk around but nobody can get away. . . . Lying together . . . she and Mac listen to the guards' boots . . . and there is nowhere to go but here. (235-36)

Stacey's dream is a dramatic rendering of Martin Heidegger's existentialist idea of the limitations of the human condition. One must accept the limits of the "ground" onto which one is "cast" at birth, that is, all the contingencies of one's self, one's past, one's geographic location--all the features of life that are *given* rather than *chosen*, including the fact of death. Freedom and true being come from recognition of the limiting forces of existence but also from realizing that choices are still available to us to build our world within those inescapable limitations.

The last two chapters of the novel rush ahead to the consequent comedic ending. Not everything in the concluding tumble of events is "happy," but it all sums up and establishes Laurence's claim for the success of the sane view, of accepting the human condition and its limitations--especially mutability and mortality.[5] First, a figure from Stacey's past--and not just hers but the past of all the Manawakans in the saga, whether they have tried to escape it or not--reappears in her life in the person of the Métisse Valentine Tonnerre.[6] She speaks to Stacey the undeniable message of death. Not only is Valentine about to embark, as she says, on a "Long trip. The last one" (242), but she gives news of the death of her sister Piquette and her children back in Manawaka. Death by fire. Stacey immediately makes the personal application: "Piquette and her kids, and the snow and fire. Ian and Duncan in a burning house" (241). That dire application is realized and proven in Duncan's near drowning, an event late in Chapter 10 that gives Ian an opportunity for heroism and draws him and Mac and also Duncan and Mac much closer; also, Duncan will subsequently confront the baleful challenge of the sea again and meet it successfully.

Between those two events we have the attempted suicide of Tess Fogler, the eternally slim and youthful envy of Stacey--and obviously a fictional cousin of Buckle Fennick. Mac's father falls on the stairs; Stacey decides that "Dad" (as she is able at last to call him) will move in with them. Mac brings the news that he is the new local manager of Richalife, as Thorlakson has been called to the head office down east. Jen speaks!

In the midst of this comedic tucking in of loose ends the vexed relationship of Stacey and Katie is brought to a promising stage of development.[7] This concern of the novel has been corollary also to the main theme under discussion. Two features of the relationship demand Stacey's recognition: one, that Katie is inevitably growing into adulthood and (it is to be hoped) maturity, and two, that she herself has left her youth behind and reached adulthood and (it remains to be seen) maturity. At issue here, again, is the necessity of recognizing mutability and its final term, death. (As is the case elsewhere in the novel, so in this we find the two conflicting "views" of Stacey.) Her ability to accept Katie's maturing is evidence of her own true maturity.

Stacey's anxious protection of Katie often expresses itself as fussy moralism of the sort that characterized Mrs. Cameron's treatment of her and her sister Rachel; and her occasional memories of that treatment help to mellow her treatment of Katie. Yet her anxiety over Katie, added to her other worries, drives Stacey to seek escape--with Luke and in her dreams of her youth (which may be seen as two sides of the same coin). Salvation comes with her recognition of the two features I mention above and a consequent third (which helps indicate the thematic consistency and the unity of the Saga). She sees--one side of the Stacey mind has always seen--that her treatment of Katie is unreasonable, for example, that refusal to let her go to an Adult movie is ill-founded--"Do I really believe it's going to alter her out of all recognition? No" (45); also, she sees that her own evasions make her moralism hypocritical--"If it was Katie going to this guy's [Luke's] shack . . . I'd have a fit" (162). So she has ended her affair with Luke, can allow Katie to go to the movies with Don somebody (274-75), and faces the truth:

> that I haven't been Stacey Cameron for one hell of a long time now. Although in some ways I'll always be her, because that's how I started out. But from now on, the dancing goes on only in the head. (276)

At the same time the novel has been developing the theme of the exchange of roles between mother and daughter. It begins early, with Katie maternally comforting Stacey after the automobile accident involving Peter Challoner and Stacey's recognition that "It's supposed to be the other way around" (16); also, it is stated finally on the occasion of Tess Fogler's attempted suicide--Stacey thinks, "One day she will have to take over as the mother, and she's beginning to sense it. . . . I give in like now, and lean on her" (249). *The Fire-Dwellers* thus echoes the changing relationship of Rachel and her mother in *A Jest of God* and anticipates that of Morag and her daughter in *The Diviners*.

The comedic ending of the novel is largely made possible by Stacey's successfully confronting and accepting the twin facts of mutability and mortality. Consequently, the motif introduced by the Ladybird quatrain demands a second look and a new understanding--one that in turn reinforces the comedic ending. Professor Clara Thomas in *Manawaka World* has helpfully observed:

> Stacey has to recognize once and for all that, dangerous and frightening as the fire-element is, neither she nor the ones she loves can move to or live in any other. Her own weeks of intensified flame [with Luke Venturi] have, however, had a clarifying effect on her. (123)

One of the few passages that specifically mention the element of fire in the sense of Professor Thomas's "flame" is Stacey's memory of her mother's caution against her temper--"you must learn to bank your fires"; Stacey's response is noteworthy: "How right she was. . . . she'd never had any fires so couldn't know" (194). Another such passage, however, appears at the very end of the novel and confirms that fire is really the element of life; it is certainly the flame of love (although much of the merwoman's affair with Luke seems to have taken place in "the chambers of the sea"), and it is surely the spark of vitality and perhaps truly the gift that Prometheus brought to mankind. In this Laurence has resumed and fleshed out further an idea already present in one of her early African stories, "The Rain Child" (1962); there she refers to the frank recognition of human love, "shoot an arrow":

> Mother Nyame created the sun with fire, and arrows of the same fire were shot into the veins of mankind and became life-blood. I could have said that the custom was a reminder that women are the source of life. (*Tomorrow-Tamer* 128)

The vital flame is also the force that Dylan Thomas recognizes in his lines:

> The force that through the green fuse drives the flower
> Drives my green age; that blasts the roots of trees
> Is my destroyer.

For in the closing lines of *The Fire-Dwellers*, after the last ray of the EVER-OPEN EYE illuminates the burning streets in cities "Not so far away" and the final reiteration of the Ladybird nursery-rhyme, Stacey raises a question that implicitly supports the understanding of the term just proposed. "Will the fires go on, inside and out? Until the moment when they go out for me" (280).

Stacey's river of life as seen in her dual view of things flows both ways, ahead into the past, and back into the future, until she can lay claim to her title, not merwoman but fire-dweller--until. . . . But, after the first death there is no other.

NOTES

1. For discussion of this idea in Faulkner, see my *Faulkner's Yoknapatawpha Comedy* (Ann Arbor: University of Michigan Press, 1980), 16, 54-56, 64, 70, 116-19, 123-24, 183-89.

2. Luke's final good wishes to Stacey reiterate a subtheme in the novel that has been dominant during their affair: "Ease up on yourself, merwoman" (210). Luke appears to Stacey on the shore of the Sound (Stacey has just been daydreaming about swimming in Diamond Lake); his dwelling is full of marine paraphernalia--fishnets, smoke-green thick glass bubbles, curtains of moss-green sackcloth; on the floor a green and grey rug sustains the sea-green motif; he constantly refers to her as "merwoman" (166-67); his astrological sign is the crab--"I'm Cancer" (175). The water theme might be thought to express fertility, and there is something invigorating in Stacey's association with Luke. But more insistent than that is the theme's function to express escape and, indeed, death. The water element is for Stacey the merwoman similar to what it is for Eliot's Prufrock, who lingered in the chambers of the sea and listened to the mermaids singing until *human* voices awakened him. Stacey does not drown in these fantastic waters, but Duncan very nearly does in the water of English Bay, and even Tess Fogler's fish bowl is an arena of death. This theme in *The Fire-Dwellers* remains something of a puzzle, I think, one of the themes not completely integrated into the novel. Luke Venturi (the Cancer) is associated closely with another such theme; see Note 5, below.

3. Laurence does not see homoeroticism generally as destructive, suicidal; her depiction of Buckle *groups* the homoerotic, autoerotic, and suicidal elements as interrelated and mutually reinforcing features of his character, and together they function as a counter to life-giving, procreative forces.

4. See also the anticipatory passage at the close of Chapter 3: "*The thin panthers are stalking the streets. . . . The Roman legions are marching. . . . Strange things are happening. . . . There is nowhere to go this time*" (85).

5. Laurence gave specific encouragement to this approach to *The Fire-Dwellers* in her comments on the novel in her 1969 essay "Gadgetry or Growing." She there identifies two of its "interlocking themes":

the sense of anguish and fear which Stacey feels in bringing up her kids in a world on fire; and also the question of a middle-aged woman having to accept middle age and learn how to cope with the essential fact of life, which is that the process of life is irreversible. (87)

Yet her achievement in this novel extends well beyond what that comment would seem to cover.

6. In her essay "Gadgetry or Growing" Laurence said about *The Fire-Dwellers*: "I had, or

felt I had, perhaps rather too many interlocking themes to deal with, but these were all inherent in Stacey and her situation" (Gadgetry 87). One of those is surely the Indian theme, which seems puzzling, not fully integrated in the novel, even self-contradictory. The theme is clearly and unambiguously stated with the entrance--or intrusion--of Valentine Tonnerre, "Prairie Indian but not entirely" (239; see the full identification on 240). She awakens another kind of moral guilt in Stacey that we see elsewhere in the novel, and a guilt appropriate to all white Anglo-Saxon Protestant (WASP) Canadians (at least) in fact. The episode is full of pathos--heavier for those who know *The Diviners* (and Laurence, again like Faulkner, seems to have written each of the novels of the saga as though she assumed in the reader full knowledge of the entire saga). Complications arise when we consider the character of Buckle Fennick: "He has a face like an Iroquois, angular and faintly slanted dark eyes, [etc.]" (48); he is blatantly (if deceptively) sexy in an attractive-repulsive way, and he is suicidal. Stacey's lust for him is clearly misguided. Where, then, does the Iroquois appearance fit in? Another complication resides in Stacey's boy lover: Luke's customary garb seems to be his "brown-and-off-white Indian sweater in thick wool with Haida or something motifs of outspread eagle wings and bear mask" (162); (see also 174, 205, 210); he tells the moving story of the Indian village at Kitwanga and invites Stacey to go up there with him (208). The novel strongly implies that his invitation is a virtual equivalent of Buckle's invitation to his apartment. Yet the guilt involved in the story of the Indian village is the same as that involved in the case of Valentine and Piquette Tonnerre. Mixed signals concerning Luke are appropriate enough, perhaps, but the full significance of the Indian theme seems to me unclear: how, exactly, is it "inherent in Stacey and her situation"? Is she a Cancer too?

7. Mother-daughter relationships are a constant and important concern of the Manawaka Saga, as Professor Helen Buss has demonstrated most instructively in *Mother and Daughter Relationships in the Manawaka Works of Margaret Laurence* (Victoria, British Columbia: University of Victoria, 1985).

WORKS CITED

Laurence, Margaret. *The Fire-Dwellers*. Toronto: McClelland and Stewart, New Canadian Library, (1969) 1991; Chicago: University of Chicago Press, 1993.

___. *The Tomorrow-Tamer and Other Stories*. Toronto: McClelland and Stewart, New Canadian Library, (1963, 1970) 1993.

___. "Gadgetry or Growing: Form and Voice in the Novel." *A Place to Stand On: Essays By and About Margaret Laurence*. Ed. George Woodcock. Edmonton: NeWest Press, 1983, 80-89.

Stevens, Wallace. *The Collected Poems of Wallace Stevens*. New York: Knopf, 1968, 68.

Thomas, Clara. *The Manawaka World of Margaret Laurence*. Toronto: McClelland and Stewart, 1975.

Thomas, Dylan. "A Refusal to Mourn the Death of a Child by Fire in London." *The Collected Poems of Dylan Thomas: 1934-1952*. New York: New Directions Books, 1957, 112.

Chapter 4

A World Divided, A World Divined: Two North American Fictions
Neil Besner

Margaret Laurence's *The Diviners* appeared in 1974, John Irving's *The World According to Garp* in 1978. The 1975 and 1979 paperback editions celebrate these novels as the "#1 Canadian bestseller" and "America's most jubilant bestseller."[1] For bestsellers, their major themes might seem esoteric: each novel charts the intertwined course of a writer's life and art. The life of the writer in each novel bears some resemblance or connection--metaphorical, biographical, or autobiographical--to the life of the writer of each novel; both fictional writers and the novels' narrators have much to show and say about the nature of the past, the uses of memory, the workings of language, and the status of fiction. Both novels, like many other North American fictions, present characters who are drawn to a European homeground, variously conceived of as a museum for the young writer's imagination, a repository of wartorn monuments, a deadly playground for sexual initiation, or an ultimately deceptive setting for a return to origins.

Beneath these superficial similarities, however, lie some intriguing differences that are worth attention--chief among them, the differences between the novels' visions of writers' fictions in relation to writers' lives, and the closely related differences between the novels' conceptions and uses of the past. My contention is that the shared North American preoccupation with displacement in time and space that these writers and their protagonists explore is manifest quite different in its Canadian and American versions, and that this difference reflects the divergences that continue to distinguish Canadian and American representations of their respective cultural legacies--even when, if not particularly when, these representations appear to be subsumed in the metafictional and postmodern intentions of two novels that, each in its own way, have bridged the gap between high and mass culture to speak so powerfully to the popular imagination about the position of the writer and the importance of fiction.

The central problem for Morag Gunn, the writer in *The Diviners*, and for Morag's creator, Margaret Laurence, is how to conjure with the past. One of the earliest signs of the abiding presence of the past in this novel emerges from the title of the novel's first section--"The River of Now and Then"--which refers both to the opposed directions of wind and current on and in the river that Morag watches from her window as she writes, and to the insistent pull of the past within the present, a movement that measures the rhythms of Morag's narration. As other readers have noted, shifts in tense and point of view also help to convey the interplay of past and present; and the novel's often-discussed formal devices--memorybank movies, innerfilms, Morag's Tales, and her photographs--provide various means to convey Laurence's protagonist pastwards (Gom 48-58). As she reaches pastward, Morag meditates on the possibilities of language conveying external reality or states of mind and reflects on the status of various versions of the past--the documentary status of her photographs, the fictional status of the stories she has invented to explain the poses of the figures in these photographs, for example.

Another of the novel's powerful pastward impulses, and an important, if long misunderstood one for Morag, is Christie Logan's series of tales about Piper Gunn, Morag's heroic, mythologized ancestor. Christie's tales, like the Métis Lazarus Tonnerre's stories about the legendary Rider Tonnerre, provide contemporary characters like Morag, Jules (Skinner) Tonnerre, and Morag's and Jules's daughter Piquette with necessary routes into their past: mythologized narrations which are eventually seen to merge with Western Canadian history. Finally, divining is the novel's controlling metaphor for all pastward searching, thus connecting all of these kinds of storytelling with Royland's divining of water beneath the surface, guided by a gift of faith inaccessible and unanswerable to reason.

The various forces of "then"--mythology, history, memory, tales, memorybank movies, snapshots, innerfilms--are also the sources for fiction and for the writing of fiction in this novel. But they are opposed to the other impulse which drives Morag's life, and which she reflects on along with her other memories: her powerful urge to escape her biography, her origins, the history of her parents' death when she was a child, of her adoption by Christie and Prin Logan, of her growing up in the small puritanical Western Canadian town of Manawaka. Morag's apparent compulsion to escape her biography, however, is belied by the fiction she begins to write in Toronto, married now to Brooke Skelton, formerly her University literature teacher in Winnipeg. *Spear of Innocence*, Morag's first novel, is about Lilac Stonehouse, a "fluffily pretty girl from a lumber town who lights out for the city," whose "staggering naïveté is never presented as anything but harmful and in fact damages not only herself but others" (244NCL, 184UC). Shortly after completing her novel, Morag breaks out of what has become her prison of a marriage with Brooke and goes to Vancouver, where she writes her second novel, *Prospero's Child*. This novel is at once more allegorical and written about matters closer to Morag's recent experience than was *Spear of Innocence*; as Morag describes the plot in a letter, it reads in part like a version of the evolution of her relationship with Brooke: the child of the novel's title, writes Morag, is

the young woman who marries His Excellency, the Governor of some island in some ocean very far south, and who virtually worships him and then who has to go in the opposite extreme and reject nearly everything about him, at least for a time, in order to become her own person. (353NLC, 270UC)

Of her next book, a collection of short stories which appears after Morag has moved to England, we learn little except its title, *Presences*; but the next novel, *Jonah*, can be seen in part as Morag's attempt to imagine the shape of her troubled relationship with Christie Logan, of whom she has always been ashamed. The narrator explains that *Jonah*

> is the story of an old man, a widower, who is fairly disreputable and who owns a gillnetter in Vancouver. . . . It is also about his daughter Coral, who resents his not being a reputable character. Jonah inhabits Morag's head, and talks in his own voice. In some ways she knows more about Coral, who is so uncertainly freed by Jonah's ultimate death, but it is Jonah himself who seems more likely to take on his own life in the fiction. (390NCL, 299-300UC)

Following directly on this description are Morag's tales, narrated to her daughter Piquette, of Christie Logan and Lazarus Tonnerre--tales which Piquette needs just as Morag needed Christie's tales of Piper Gunn.

Morag's last novel--the last, that is, before the novel that Morag finishes on the last page of *The Diviners*--is *The Shadow of Eden*, written in the log house near McConnell's Landing that Morag has bought after her return with Piquette from England and after her last trip to Manawaka to see Christie before he dies and to bury him. This novel, Morag writes in a letter, deals with the same period as did Christie's tales of Piper Gunn; now Morag's fiction reaches further pastward than the stretch of her own life or experience to encompass her ancestral past; and now, too, Morag writes, "I like the thought of history and fiction interweaving" (444NCL, 341UC). The pastward progress of her fiction and the recollective progress of *The Diviners* are about to reach a temporary balance as we arrive at the present time and place--the house at McConnell's Landing--from which Morag began to recollect her life and her art in the first section, "The River of Now and Then"--and where *The Diviners* ends as well.

The end of *The Diviners*, however--the end of Morag's book-long, life-long process of "look[ing] ahead into the past, and back into the future, until the silence" (477NCL, 370UC)--balances uneasily between the gain and the loss of navigating this kind of "river of now and then." The old man of the river, Royland, has lost his gift of divination, although he tells Morag that his is "not a matter for mourning" (477NCL, 369UC); and perhaps Morag, going inside to write the last words of her novel and give it its title, has lost hers in completing this novel--a novel that might be understood to signify for Morag Gunn what *The Diviners* came to signify for Margaret Laurence when she said in 1974 that it would be her last--as if, like her diviners, Royland and Morag, Laurence herself had sensed an end to her writing of fiction.

The story of Morag's life, the central impulse of her fiction, and the imaginative direction of *The Diviners* form complementary narrations towards the past, always pushing against the current of the present that Morag inhabits. Morag's novels win her imaginative access to the past (as perhaps *The Diviners* did for Laurence) by allowing her to integrate the complementary resources of biography and fiction, memory and imagination, mythology and history. For Morag, memory becomes a conduit that can correct, but not oppose, imagination; history becomes a narrative that can complement, but not invalidate, mythology; photographs become documents that can engender, but not confirm or deny, fictions; and biography and autobiography become narratives that will insistently emerge, whether Morag suppresses them in her life or reshapes them in her fiction.

The concern with reaching pastward sketched out here is typical of what Northrop Frye has suggested is a perennial Canadian preoccupation, the legacy of what he calls Canada's "foreshortened history" and what others see in historical and political as well as in cultural terms as the inevitable legacy of a colony--to be tied to, if not indeed bound by an almost inaccessible past, a past perceived as remote from, removed from the present, and a past, therefore, that ironically and definitively also sets this version of Canadian experience apart from the indigenous one (826). In this regard, Morag's anxiety over the past might be read as a reflection of her culture's, and her fiction as a compelling representation of one of Canadian culture's central fictions--first, that there can be no inhabiting the present without a "divined" past to look ahead to as Morag does at the end of *The Diviners*; but second, that the issue of such divining is in some measure a sense of loss, of incompletion--in this novel, loss of the gift of divination itself, as if to suggest that the rewards of such divination might include the end of fiction.

One does not need to look very far in contemporary Canadian fiction to see the rendering, transformation, excavation, or transcription of the past as a central motif. Think of Atwood's *Surfacing*, Davies' *Fifth Business*, Kroetsch's *Badlands*, MacLennan's *Voices in Time*, Findley's *The Wars*, or Kogawa's *Obasan* for a few cases in point. Yet *The Diviners* seems to be a particularly apposite and cautionary reflection on one of the larger fictions which sustains Canadians: that the past must be divined, recovered, reordered, and narrated, if Canada's culture or our writers' imaginations are going to do more than grimly survive.

The World According to Garp is as North American as *The Diviners* in its preoccupation with origins, and perhaps as American as *The Diviners* is Canadian in its fictional resolution of this preoccupation. From birth to death, Garp's life, like his art, is held hostage between the opposed forces that are imagined as complementary in *The Diviners*; and this violent, apparently irreconcilable split might be understood as an astute representation of the long-standing American preoccupation to preserve its myth of separation from origins.

First, and most obviously, *The World According to Garp* depends upon the radical severance of its protagonist / writer from any kind of past, be it familial, ancestral, or historical. If in *The Diviners* Morag must ceaselessly recover her past, in John Irving's novel the past is banished from the start; in fact, the course of Garp's life runs almost free of time, from his near-immaculate conception to his martyr's death. Rather than merging with Irving's life, as Morag's might in some respects be imagined to merge with Laurence's at the end of *The Diviners*, Garp's life ends well before Irving's novel ends, so that Garp's last words come from an Epilogue.

The point of view and the structure of Irving's novel are also very different from those of *The Diviners*. Unlike the narrator of *The Diviners*, Irving's narrator is lifted free of time to range omnisciently over the present and the future as freely as Morag's memory ranges over her past. One of the recurrent uses this narrator makes of Garp as a writer is to predict and recall what Garp "would" write on various, still future occasions. But for all of Irving's hijinks with fact and fiction, and for all this novel's justly acclaimed energy and exuberance, the *structure* of *The World According to Garp* is actually more conventionally linear than that of *The Diviners*, beginning a little before Garp's birth and closing some years after his death.

It is in the development and the uses of Garp's fiction, however, that we can see the most interesting contrasts between the two novels begin to take shape. If the past in its several narrative forms provides Morag with the source she divines for her fictions, it is the always volatile present which impinges most significantly on Garp's writing. Whereas Morag's fiction grows to its maturity as she learns to incorporate more of the past in more of its forms into her life and her art, Garp's fiction becomes progressively diluted in direct proportion to the incursions of the present. Garp's most brilliant creation is his first short story, "The Pension Grillparzer"; his imagination, free to roam amidst the museums and monuments of postwar Vienna, a city apparently immured in the past, can play rich and freewheeling variations on Irving's recurrent bear-stories.

But Vienna after Freud is also where the first fatal connections between sex and death are established for Garp, and it is the city where Marcus Aurelius died--and where Garp first reads Aurelius's lines on life's phantasmagorical brevity. Garp returns from Vienna as an unknown writer, but his mother Jenny Fields, writer of Sears Roebuck prose (this is Garp's phrase), becomes an instant celebrity with the publication of her autobiography, *A Sexual Suspect*.

For North American readers as Garp (and, perhaps, as Irving) conceives of them in this novel, fiction--conceived of solely as the work of imagination--thus becomes split off from autobiography, conceived of as the more literal work of memory. Severely constrained by this fatally binding opposition, the singular, richly imagined world created by Garp begins its inevitable decline. As Garp's fictions become increasingly thinly disguised versions of his experience, they become increasingly weaker; the violence of contemporary American political and social movements, and the violence wrecked by Garp in the travails of his libido and in his jealousy over Helen's affair, intrude upon both his life and his art, until everything goes smash in the fateful driveway collision. The "X-rated soap opera," *The World According to Bensenhaver* turns the screw yet again; now Garp transforms his nightmarish reality into nightmarish fiction, and his American reading public devours this fiction precisely because it is loosely based on (and baldly promoted as) a distillation of Garp's real and tragic life. If Garp's aesthetics demand allegiance to an autonomous imagination, his readers seem to demand relevant sex and violence; it is not very far from these fatally divided worldviews to Garp's end in the wrestling room, assassinated by a maddened, tongueless Ellen Jamesian who turns out to be Bainbridge "Pooh" Percy.

In Garp's world, it appears that there can be no dialogue between memory and imagination, between autobiography and fiction, or between a writer of fiction and his reading public. Garp's story, unlike Morag's, is one in which the convergence of life and art threatens to destroy both--and eventually does. While Garp insists on the free play of his imagination, Irving shows us how everything beyond an imagination thus conceived must become inimical to the imagination. *The World According to Garp* becomes a critique of Garp's attempts to cleave to the ideal of an autonomous imagination--and a critique of a reading public unwilling or unable to understand imagination as anything other than either history or sheer invention. The admirable energy of Garp's imagination must be expended over and again to conceive an identity free from origins, a "new" Garp. If the world according to Garp must be a new and unique world, quite separate from the world according to everyone else, then the life of the ideal individual in Garp's world would drain social reality of any authenticity, empowering only each separate individual as a creative agent divorced from the world of time. Garp pays the price for his aesthetics: the artist imagined as a Christ might die like a Christ, but not to save all men. On the contrary, in *The World According to Garp*, and perhaps in more ways than he could imagine or than the novel's closing lines suggest, we are all doomed to be terminal cases.

One powerfully recurrent Canadian perception of American culture is evoked in the often quoted closing lines of Earle Birney's "Can. Lit.," first published in 1944: "It's only by our lack of ghosts we're haunted" (138). The poem draws a bitter and angry contrast between a culture that wants no Whitman and has no Dickinson, that builds railways to avoid being alone, that has not purged itself through a real civil war, that cannot break with the past, and a culture that violently and definitively broke with its past, that fought its civil war, that found its first distinctive and essentially "new" voice in Whitman. In Birney's poem, to be haunted by no ghosts seems to arouse more anxiety than to be haunted by a ghostly past, a severed past, a past historically, politically, socially, morally, linguistically, and aesthetically sloughed off. Yet *The Diviners* and *The World According to Garp* seem to suggest, as if from opposed ends of the same continuum, that neither of these North American fictions of the past is adequate. The world that Morag divines brings her to the end of her novel and Laurence to the end of hers, and although readers have justly celebrated the courage and faith that such an act of divination entails, perhaps *The Diviners* can also be understood to record, with grace and humility, a loss of faith, or to document the painful failure of such an obsessively pastward vision to fully inhabit the present. Perhaps *The World According to Garp*, for all its bountiful energy and exuberance, can be read as a virtuoso demonstration of the poverty and ultimately the failure of an imagination severed from its roots in time. Both novels ask what the imagination is and what nourishes it. Also, both novels respond to the question they pose about the imagination with fictions which all too accurately reflect their respective North American cultures' continuing preoccupation with a search for origins. Garp's world divided and Morag's world divined are bestselling North American fictions--bestsellers, perhaps, because for the time being, North American fictions and their North American readers are still jointly troubled above all by the displacement they imagine and remember.

NOTE

1. Margaret Laurence, *The Diviners* (Toronto: McClelland & Stewart, New Canadian Library, [1974] 1995; Chicago: University of Chicago Press, 1993); John Irving, *The World According to Garp*, rev. ed., (New York: Ballantine, [1978] 1990). All references are to these editions.

WORKS CITED

Atwood, Margaret. *Surfacing*. Toronto: McClelland & Stewart, 1972.
Birney, Earle. "Can. Lit." *The Collected Poems of Earle Birney*. 2 Vols. Toronto: McClelland & Stewart, 1975.
Davies, Robertson. *Fifth Business*. Toronto: Macmillan, New York: Viking, 1970.
Findley, Timothy. *The Wars*. Toronto: Clark, Irwin, 1977.
Frye, Northrop. "Conclusion." *Literary History of Canada: Canadian Literature in English*. Toronto: University of Toronto Press, 1965.
Gom, Leona. "Laurence and the Use of Memory." *Canadian Literature* 71 (1976): 48-58.
Irving, John. *The World According to Garp*. New York: E. P. Dutton and Pocket Books (1978) 1979; rev. ed. New York: Ballantine, 1990.
Kogawa, Joy. *Obasan*. Toronto: Lester & Orpen Dennys, 1981.
Kroetsch, Robert. *Badlands*. Toronto: New Press, 1975.
Laurence, Margaret. *The Diviners*. Toronto: McClelland and Stewart, New Canadian Library, (1974) 1995; Chicago: University of Chicago Press, 1993.
MacLennan, Hugh. *Voices in Time*. Toronto: Macmillan, 1980.

Part II

Narrative Structure in Laurence

Chapter 5

Hagar Shipley's Rage for Life: Narrative Technique in *The Stone Angel*
Alice Bell

In *The Stone Angel*[1] Margaret Laurence extends the range of first-person point of view by selecting and arranging elements of the narrative to form an intricate network of associations in which one part is related to another and adds to its meaning. Verbal motifs, images, and symbols gain greater significance each time they appear in a new context. In addition, one part of the network modifies another so that the import of the completed pattern is greater than that of the sum of its parts. With these techniques Laurence is able to communicate more than Hagar Shipley actually tells us about herself and to create a multifaceted portrait of a complex and self-contradictory woman.

Examination of the structure of the first chapter and of how the ideas Laurence introduces there gather meaning as they recur throughout the novel will demonstrate how skillfully she has composed her picture of Hagar and will reveal qualities for the reader to consider in assessing this complicated character.

In the brief reverie which opens the book, Laurence identifies personal values which shaped Hagar's character and communal attitudes which were the foundation of her society and presents images associated with these concepts. For Hagar, the stone angels in the Manawaka cemetery are symbols of passive, weak-spirited women who acquiesced with death because they did not have the strength to cope with life. Her sympathies are with the rugged, strong-willed, albeit irascible, women who survive. She has more respect for the "ungrateful, fox-voiced" Mrs. Weese, a "disreputable lady" who rose from her sick bed and lived for another decade, than for her martyred daughter, Regina, a "flimsy, gutless creature, bland as egg custard." Hagar's own mother "relinquished her feeble ghost" at the same time that Hagar gained her "stubborn one." For ninety years Hagar has lived with vigor and determination and has raged against the limitations of life.

The graveyard area and the flowers that grow there represent two social groups in Manawaka. Within the cemetery bloom the cultivated peonies, with their "funeral-parlor perfume." Hagar associates them with both civilization and death.

Just outside the fence grow the gaudy, tough-rooted, cowslips, which give forth a faint, musky, dust-tinged odor of wild plants that grow untended and that have endured since Indians roamed the land. The young Hagar walks primly along the paths of the cemetery in white kid boots, anxious to be "neat and orderly" and to "celebrate tidiness." The novel shows us why this proud, high-spirited woman chooses to move outside the sheltering and confining boundaries of her father's social position and what happens to her when she attempts to integrate the refinement and propriety of the peony culture with the rough ways of the world of uncultivated cowslips and couchgrass.

Conceptions introduced in these opening pages acquire increased significance with incremental repetition and disclose aspects of Hagar's personality which she does not call to our attention and which readers often overlook. For example, in the first paragraph Hagar tells us that her father bought the stone angel "in pride to mark her [mother's] bones and proclaim her dynasty, as he fancied, forever and a day." A few paragraphs later she mentions that the wild cowslips "were held back at the cemetery's edge, torn out by loving relatives determined to keep the plots clear and clearly civilized" (5). In the second chapter Hagar recalls that at his death her father left a sum of money "to pay for the care of the family plot, in perpetuity, so his soul need never peer down from the elegant halls of eternity and be offended by cowslips spawning on his grave" (63). This statement indicates that Jason Currie wanted to preserve his social position, even after death, and that he had no "loving relatives" to tend his grave. In the third chapter Hagar remembers an event that occurred before her father's death: Bram hoped their first child would be a boy, so that he would have someone to leave his farm to. She was amazed to realize that her husband, like her father, wanted to establish a dynasty. When Bram died several years later, his daughters thought that he should be buried beside his first wife. But Hagar put her foot down and insisted that he be buried with the Curries. She even had Shipley carved on the reverse side of the red marble namestone. Just as Hagar broke with tradition to marry Bram, she defied tradition by honoring him with burial in her family plot. In addition, she gave Bram the opportunity to found a dynasty: at the time of his death he had two sons and a grandson to carry on his name--but because of his negligent ways he had little property to leave to them. An additional reference emphasizes the importance of Hagar's generous act. On her final visit to Manawaka, the cemetery custodian comments on the unusual stone which bears two family names. This network of associations attests to Hagar's loyalty to her husband. But she undercuts this demonstration of her fidelity by musing that she doesn't know why she had Bram buried in her family plot; she just felt she had to. Then she wonders whether either she or John had cared about him, but she concludes: "And yet he mattered to me" (184). For those who are critical of Hagar's marriage relationship, the words of her question seem to drown out the significance of her deed. Thus this pattern of related ideas reveals an important aspect of Hagar's character: she repeatedly notes her weaknesses and failings, but she does not speak about her finer qualities. In like manner, she is extremely articulate in expressing dislike and disapproval but very reticent about voicing gentle emotions and may even pretend she does not have them.

The narrative-present interlude which follows the opening paragraphs shows us that the crusty Hagar is also a sensitive, caring individual, mindful of the feelings of others and aware of the effects of her own sharp tongue. Many readers see the passage at the end of the book in which Hagar tells Marvin that he has been a better son than John as evidence of an inner change in her, of a new concern for relationships. But she is more considerate of Marvin than may appear at first reading. For example, at ninety she finds each new day a precious rarity, but she "dissembles, usually, for the sake of such people as Marvin, who is somehow comforted by the picture of old ladies feeding like docile rabbits on the lettuce leaves of other times, other manners" (5). Hagar reminds herself, however, not to get so caught up in her memories that she speaks aloud because Doris and Marvin will be sure to notice and exchange meaningful glances. Then she asks an important rhetorical question: "What do I care now what people say? I cared too long" (6). This introduces a main theme of the novel--the effect on Hagar of other people's opinions. For example, because of her concern for what people in Manawaka thought about Bram's crudities of speech and behavior, she gave up contact with her former friends and associates and secluded herself on the Shipley farm. She even stopped attending church, preferring "possible damnation in some comfortably distant future, to any ordeal then of peeking or pitying eyes" (90). Ironically, when Murray Lees tells Hagar about his mother, Hagar comments, "Fancy spending your life worrying what other people were thinking. She must have had a rather weak character" (227). This appraisal foreshadows Hagar's new insight into her own behavior a few days later.

The next paragraph demonstrates that at ninety Hagar is still affected by the judgments of others. She vows not to think of her "lost men" because she considers it a disgrace for her daughter-in-law to see her crying. This apparently trivial statement becomes more meaningful a few pages later when we see how Hagar obstinately refused to cry when her father punished her by striking her palms with a ruler. This passage sets the stage for the poignant episode in which Hagar falls in Doris's presence:

Then, terribly, I perceive the tears, my own they must be although they have sprung so unbidden I feel they are like the incontinent wetness of the infirm. Trickling, they taunt down my face. They are no tears of mine, in front of her. I dismiss them, blaspheme against them--let them be gone. But I have not spoken, and they are still there. (31)

"The incontinent wetness of the infirm" becomes painfully significant in Chapter 2 when Hagar learns that she has been wetting her sheets every night without being aware of it. When Marvin and Doris suggest that she needs professional nursing care, her reaction is to "betray" herself "in shameful tears" (76). A few days later Hagar is so touched by the kindness of a young woman who gives her a seat on the bus that she again weeps "unseemly tears" (92). With these deft verbal echoes Laurence depicts the anguish of a strong, stubborn woman who in her old age can no longer control her bodily functions or conceal her emotions as she did when she was young.

Although Hagar grumbles about the minor irritations of life, her tears and her concern for the opinions of others give evidence that she is a person with tender feelings. For example, when she bickers with Doris about having tea, she is immediately sorry, but she is also uneasy about what Doris will think of her if she apologizes. "I repent, curse my churlishness, want to take both her hands in mine and beg forgiveness, but if I did she'd believe me daft entirely instead of only half so" (30). And Hagar acknowledges her own acerbity. Just after she admits that she dissembles for Marvin's sake, she chides herself: "How unfair I am. Well, why not? To carp like this--it's my only enjoyment, that and the cigarettes" (5). Although she is critical of Doris and Marvin, she is objective about her own shortcomings. When she recalls that they have lived with her for seventeen years, she asks, "How have I borne it? How have they?" (37). And she is ashamed of the self-pity and reproach in her voice when she says that she has never wanted to be a burden. These passages indicate that Hagar is impulsive and frequently utters words which she regrets. But she is also sensitive and compassionate.

The second and longer retrospective section in this chapter recounts the youthful experiences and family relationships which molded Hagar's personality. Her very first memory is not of a person or an event but of a dress which she wore when she was about six years old. She recalls it in detail: the pattern of the fabric and the style of the garment ("plaid pinafore"), the precise color ("pale green and pale red-- not pink, a watery red, rather, like the flesh of a ripe watermelon"), the trimming ("grandly piped in black velvet"), where she got it ("made by an aunt in Ontario"), and how she felt about herself when she wore it: "There was I, strutting the board sidewalk like a pint-sized peacock, resplendent, haughty, hoity-toity, Jason Currie's black-haired daughter" (6). By beginning this section with the memory of a garment rather than with the recollection of a relative or a happening, Laurence suggests that Hagar has no strong emotional bond with anyone in her family. She also shows us Hagar's great interest in clothing. Both these concepts are soon reinforced.

After thinking about her plaid pinafore, Hagar recalls members of her family, following the traditional order of mother, father, siblings. This arrangement highlights the most significant fact about Hagar's home--the absence of a mother. To add to Hagar's plight, she feels that everyone holds her responsible for her mother's death. She first remembers her Auntie Doll and how she used to tease the widow who had been the family's housekeeper since Hagar's birth. At no time do we see Auntie Doll fulfilling a nurturing role for Hagar. In fact, she favors Dan. Hagar never has anyone to teach her how to be a woman, a wife, a mother. Hagar's first recollection of her father is as a stern taskmaster who makes her learn weights and measures, scolds her for inattention, but never praises her when she recites correctly. Hagar's first memory of her older brothers is also unpleasant. They used to whip her with maple branches in retaliation for the whippings they received from their father. As she matures and realizes that they will not dare to carry out their threat to slash her throat with the bread knife, Hagar speaks out in her own behalf. After watching her father punish the boys, she tries to apologize to them, but they refuse to listen to her.

Laurence further characterizes Hagar by comparing and contrasting her with her brothers and her father. Dan and Matt are "graceful unspirited boys" who resemble their mother and always try to please their father but rarely can. Hagar fears her father but makes little effort to please him. She has what he terms "backbone," and she is "smart as a whip." He wishes she had been born a boy. Hagar does not want to be like her father, but she acknowledges that she has his hawkish nose and defiant stare. The narrative discloses that she has adopted his practice of emphasizing the negative and ignoring the positive aspects of her own and other people's behavior.

Many of the events which Hagar recalls from her childhood involve death: the death of a baby, the death of Lottie Dreiser's mother, the death of Matt's fighting cock, the death of her brother Dan, and the death of the chicks hatching in the town dump. Analysis of Hagar's attitude toward death is essential for an understanding of her actions and her state of mind throughout the novel. The first of these death-related episodes is the visit to the basement of the funeral parlor to see the body of a playmate's baby sister. Hagar, about six years old at the time, "didn't like the looks of that baby at all." Later Matt and Dan exploit these feelings when they enforce Hagar's silence by threatening to slash her throat and let her bleed to death until she is as empty and white as this stillborn child. In contrast to Hagar, Lottie Dreiser strokes the infant's face and clothes and vows that if she ever has a baby which dies she will have it done up in satin just like this one. This statement proves to be prophetic because Lottie loses two babies before she bears a daughter who survives.

Hagar's refusal to drape herself in her mother's plaid shawl and hold her brother Dan as he is dying of pneumonia is one of the most enigmatic occurrences in the novel. All she can say to Matt is, "I can't. I'm not a bit like her." But as she refuses, she is crying, "shaken by torments he never even suspected, wanting above all else to do the thing he asked, but unable to do it, unable to bend enough" (25). In her own mind she offers this additional explanation: "But all I could think of was that meek woman . . . from whom he's inherited a frailty I could not help but detest, however much a part of me wanted to sympathize" (25). Before we criticize Hagar for inflexibility, we need to identify what she is being inflexible about. In what way is she unable to bend? What is the frailty she detests? The incident which follows tells us more about this one.

When Hagar and her friends see the feeble, bloodied chicks hatching in the town dump, Lottie Dreiser takes a stick and clubs them to death and even steps on some of them. Laurence suggests that the episode of Dan's death and that of the chicks should be examined together because she places them next to each other in the text, brings them together in Hagar's mind, and links them with a verbal repetition. (When Hagar declines to cooperate with Matt and Lottie, each gives the same reply: "All right. . . . Don't then.") At ninety Hagar reassesses Lottie's killing of the chicks:

It was the only thing to do, a thing I couldn't have done. And yet it troubled me so much that I could not. At the time it stung me worse. I think, that I could not bring myself to kill those creatures than that I could not bring myself to comfort Dan. I did not like to think that Lottie might have more gumption than I, when I knew full well she did not. Why could I not have done it? Squeamishness, I suppose. Certainly not pity. For pity's sake they were put out of their misery, or so I believed then, and still in part believe. But they were an affront to the eyes as well. I am less certain than I was that she did it entirely for their sake. I am not sorry now that I did not speed them. (28)

    These two episodes illustrate the most important theme in the novel--Hagar's ideas and feelings about death. Hagar is a survivor, and the epigraph is her motto: "Rage, rage against the dying of the light." Hagar is one who rages against the dying of the light and wants others to do the same. Although this event predates her conscious memory, she first exercised her "stubborn" spirit to survive in a pioneer environment without a mother's care and nurture. As a consequence, she is unable to assist anyone in going gently into the night of death. Although her affection prompts her to comfort Dan, her life-affirming spirit will not permit her to help him die. In Chapter 2 Matt dies of influenza, without struggling to breathe or to hang on to life. Hagar finds his submissiveness harder to bear than his death. She asks herself, "Why hadn't he writhed, cursed, at least grappled with the thing?" (60). Hagar also has great respect for animal life. As she recalls on the drive out to Silverthreads Nursing Home, "I always had some feeling for any creature struggling awkward and unknowing into life" (94). For this reason she cannot kill the baby chicks, even though they have little chance for successful existence. The frailty which Hagar detests is passivity or surrender in the face of either death or the difficulties of life. Her inflexibility is her inability to help anyone die without an all-out struggle to live. Hagar fears the nursing home because it is a prelude to death. She says to herself, "I'd never get out. The only escape from those places is feet first in a wooden box" (185). Running away to Shadow Point is her final rebellious attempt to defy death.

    The incident about the chicks is significant for other reasons. On one level, it is the center of a cluster of egg and chicken images which are associated with passivity, weakness, and death. In the opening section we are told that the martyred Regina Weese was "bland as egg custard." Lottie, who clubs the chicks, is "light as an eggshell" herself. When Marvin and Doris take Hagar out for a drive, she is "bundled around with a packing of puffy pillows . . . held secretly like an egg in a crate" (93). As they approach the Silverthreads Nursing Home, she pushes aside her "shroud of pillows," her heart "beating like a berserk bird" (95). When she is restrained so that she cannot get out of the hospital bed, she is "knotted and tied like a trussed fowl" (285). Also she complains to Marvin about the hospital food, especially "the soft disgusting egg" they served her for supper. She states emphatically, "I hate eggs" (263). On the farm, Hagar learned to raise chickens, but she always disliked them:

Messy things--how I detested their flutter and squawk. At first I could hardly bring myself to touch them, their soiled feathers and the way they flapped in terror to get away. I got so I could even wring their necks when I had to, but they never ceased to sicken me, live or dead, and when I'd plucked and cleaned and cooked one, I never could eat it. I'd as lief have eaten rat flesh. (126-27)

The chicken references are also part of a strategy for portraying Hagar's character and identifying qualities which she values. On various occasions she likens the docile Doris to a hen, a broody hen, and a shot partridge. But she thinks of herself in different terms. When the doctor addresses her as "young lady," she glares at him "like an old malevolent crow, perched silent on a fence, ready to caw and startle the children when they expect it least" (91). As she prepares to run away to Shadow Point, she is "gay . . . and flighty as a sparrow" (144). Then when Marvin and Doris find her in the cannery, she lies still and silent, "huge and immovable, like an old hawk caught, eyes wide open, unblinking." (251). Thus we see that Hagar judges feathered creatures the same way she judges people: she admires the ones with bold, assertive spirits, regardless of their social standing. She especially likes sparrows. She recalls how they congregated in the maple tree outside the bedroom window on the farm "to argue, splattering their insults in voices brassy as Mammon." She would hear them and laugh, "liking their spit and fire" (81). At Shadow Point she sees "a raucous gang of sparrows with voices bigger than themselves flicker their wings, spin and dart in a burst of frenzy of high-heartedness" (186). She follows them "in envy and admiration," and they lead her to the water she desperately needs.

The passage in which Hagar evaluates the killing of the chicks also establishes a contrast between Hagar and Lottie Dreiser. At ninety Hagar questions whether Lottie had unmixed motives, and she is confident that her decision not to help was the correct one. She does not specify what Lottie's motives might have been, but her reservations suggest that we should look more closely at Lottie and at her relationship with Hagar. Throughout the novel Lottie is Hagar's antithesis. On the most obvious level, the two differ in appearance and social position. Lottie is tiny and blond while Hagar is big boned, sturdy, and black haired--and would like to be the opposite. Hagar's father is the leading merchant in town, but Lottie's mother is unmarried and Lottie is never invited to the Currie home. As they mature, Lottie and Hagar reverse social roles. Lottie becomes concerned about proprieties and warns Hagar that Bram Shipley is "common as dirt." While Hagar abandons her social position to marry an improvident widowed farmer, Lottie marries a classmate who later becomes president of the bank and mayor of the town. After their school days, Lottie enters Hagar's life at significant points. Meeting Lottie's fastidiously groomed daughter and surveying Lottie's comfortable and cheerful kitchen--while delivering eggs at the back door--prompt Hagar to reassess her own unkempt appearance. This leads to a reevaluation of her life as Bram Shipley's wife. When Hagar decides to leave Bram, she goes to Lottie to sell the Currie china and silver in order to get the money to begin a new life on her own. Years later Hagar's son and Lottie's daughter develop a relationship which causes tension because of their differing social positions. Despite the disapproval of her parents, Arlene continues her affair with the reckless but charming John, insisting that he is not at all like his father. In this situation Hagar is forced to go to Lottie as an ally, and for the first time she feels kindly disposed toward the woman. At this meeting she asks Lottie whether killing the baby chicks didn't make her feel peculiar, but Lottie has no recollection of this event which is indelibly imprinted on Hagar's memory. After

Arlene's death Lottie takes to her bed--a luxury which Hagar cannot afford. The flimsy bond between them is broken, and they have nothing to say to each other. Lottie has become one of the Manawaka peony women, associated in Hagar's mind with weakness and death. Lottie, not Hagar, is the one who devises the scheme to separate John and Arlene. How much this plan contributes to their death, however, deserves further discussion.

Near the end of her life, Hagar again faces the situation she confronted at the town dump. In her attempt to frighten away the gull trapped inside the old cannery, she wounds it so that it is left bloody and helpless--as unfit for life as the baby chicks. She desperately wants to stop its crying, and she thinks she would gladly kill it. But she can not bring herself to go near enough. Her sadness when she learns that the dogs outside got the bird, however, proves that her attitude has not changed. She is still unable to end a disabled animal's distress by killing it.

Hagar's reverie in Chapter 1 ends when Doris taps on her bedroom door and brings her back to the narrative present. The first thing Hagar notices is that her daughter-in-law is wearing a dark-brown artificial silk dress. Doris believes drab shades are dignified, but Hagar thinks the younger woman has no taste. Hagar has on a lilac dress (which Doris considers unsuitable for a ninety-year-old woman), and she finds satisfaction in believing that it is made of real silk ("spun by worms in China, feeding upon mulberry leaves"), although Doris swears it is acetate. Hagar is always interested in and concerned about clothing. In Chapter 2, she chooses a muted gray silk jersey print as appropriate to wear when the minister calls, and she remembers the bottle green costume with feathered hat which she had on when she returned from finishing school. In the following chapter, she puts on her lilac silk again when she visits the doctor, saying to herself, "I never have believed a woman should look more of a frump than nature decreed for her" (90-91). Hagar also wants other members of her family to be well dressed. She has a picture of Marvin the day he started school clad in a navy blue sailor suit. She recalls that he disliked the suit and that she later had to let him wear hand-me-down overalls. "I soon gave up trying to dress him decently. . . . We hadn't the money for fancy clothes, anyway" (69). This network of associations documents Hagar's wish to be tastefully and appropriately attired. She never loses this desire. When Marvin asks what she needs in the hospital, she directs him to bring her two satin nightgowns, a bun for her hair, the lightweight hair nets, some hairpins, and the bottle of perfume her granddaughter gave her. Being well groomed--with attractive clothing, neat coiffure, and such niceties as perfume--is an important part of Hagar's self-image.

This repeated evidence of Hagar's concern for her appearance adds to the dramatic tension of the scene in which she looks at herself in the mirror in the public rest room and contemplates her son's castoff overcoat, her unfashionable scarf and tam, and her straight gray hair which she has cut herself. At this moment she is no longer interested in being attractively dressed; she merely wants some *decent* clothes. To get them she is willing to do something she has never done before--ask for credit at her father's former store. But her hopes for credit are thwarted when she overhears Bram cadging stale doughnuts and trying to buy lemon extract for resale to the Indians. At this time her need for self-respect and dignity for herself and for John requires her to leave her husband and the community in which he has made himself an object of ridicule and embarrassment.

The network of associations initiated in the first chapter extends throughout the novel, as has been shown. In succeeding chapters Laurence employs additional narrative strategies to supplement Hagar's account of herself. For example, in the second chapter we see Hagar as a young woman who casts aside her social position and her inheritance to marry a ne'er-do-well farmer with two adult daughters. In assessing their marriage decades later, she astutely concludes that they each married for those qualities in the other which they later found they could not bear: Bram for Hagar's manners and speech, she for his flouting of them (79-80). Hagar is aware that she is attracted by Bram's independent and unrestrained spirit, but Laurence reveals that she is also misled by her romantic imagination. Despite her fastidious habits, she is not repulsed by Bram's dirty fingernails; she thinks he looks like a bearded Indian, "so brown and beaked a face." Although she is a practical young woman, she ignores the fact that he has failed as a farmer; she fancies she hears the "bravery of battalions" in his laughter. Then she imagines him "rigged out in a suit of gray soft as a dove's breast-feathers" (45). Concerning her youthful ideas about love, Hagar says, "Love, I fancied, must consist of words and deeds delicate as lavender sachets" (80). The Holman Hunt picture which she brought back with her from finishing school represents this conception of love. After she experiences physical desire and satisfaction with Bram, however, she realizes that the romantic lady swooning in adoration of her knight is only playing at passion. But Hagar has not relinquished all vestiges of her romantic sensibility. She still finds pleasure in the idealized horses of Rosa Bonheur's "The Horse Fair," although she was very much afraid of Bram's real horses.

Through the device of the plaid pin, Laurence lets us know, before Hagar is aware of it, that she is mistaken in her evaluation of John. Although he is an able and resourceful young man, John is a Shipley, not a Currie. When he is six, Hagar gives him the Currie plaid pin, explaining its history and cautioning him that it is not a plaything. But he puts it casually in his pocket. When they leave Manawaka, John tells her that he lost the pin; then later he confesses that he traded it to Lazarus Tonnerre for a knife. Years later, he admits that he sold the knife to buy cigarettes. So the emblem of Currie pride, which has no value for John, goes up in smoke.

Through parallel incidents Laurence also makes plain that neither Lottie nor Hagar is primarily responsible for John's death. His fate is hinted at when Hagar recalls that he was "wild as mustard seed," and two earlier incidents foreshadow his final reckless behavior. Some time before John was twelve, Hagar chanced to see him and the Tonnerre boys crossing the railroad trestle bridge by balancing on the rails. To John's embarrassment, she yelled at him and insisted he go back to firm ground. Years afterward John told her that he and the Tonnerres later devised another game to play on the bridge. They would walk to the middle, wait for a train to come along, and see who could stay in place longest before dropping over the side and climbing the girders to the creek. Driving his truck across the bridge is merely an adult version of this daredevil game.

Laurence portrays Hagar at the most vulnerable time in her life--when she is dying--when she can no longer control her body, or repress her fears and emotions, or maintain a facade of dignity and autonomy. Under these circumstances, we see her weaknesses and her strengths, her self-knowledge and her self-deception, and her regret for might-have-beens. Insights communicated via the network of associations we have just examined offer us greater understanding of Hagar's first-person account. Thus we recognize that she has admirable qualities for which she gives herself little credit. First of all, she is hard working and always fulfills her obligations. The pampered daughter of the leading merchant in town who has never learned how to cook or keep house, she is suddenly placed in charge of a dirty, barren farmhouse. A determined survivor, she gets busy scrubbing and does her best as she can provide. Hagar is unselfish and committed to the welfare of others. She wants her father's money for her sons, not for herself, and she desires material success so that people in town will respect Bram, not so that she can display her possessions, as Lottie does. When she filches from the egg money, she buys a gramophone and records for John, not clothes for herself. Her repeated impulse to talk about her feelings and to explain her actions shows that she is concerned about relationships and longs for greater intimacy with those near to her. She still torments herself with futile what-ifs in the vague belief that something she might have said would have radically altered her relationship with such strong-willed men as Jason Currie and Bram Shipley. With John she pleads openly for communication, "You don't think I'd understand--is that it? How can I, unless you tell me? Don't you think I care how you feel, or what happens to you?" But John's reply is, "You must be tired, after the train . . . I put your suitcase in Marv's old room" (204-05).

Hagar's flaws are obvious. Her preference for plucky, independent-minded people leads her to become emotionally attached to individuals who cannot fulfill her need for middle-class achievement and respectability. At the same time she undervalues her diligent and stable, but dull and unimaginative, son and daughter-in-law. She has never learned how to express affection and approbation, and the tender feelings she has suppressed for decades now return to haunt her.

We also notice that Hagar judges herself as severely as she judges others. She is cross with herself whenever she confuses the past with the present, and she berates herself when she says something which displeases or embarrasses others. During the visit to the nursing home she thinks, "Doris is right. I'm unreasonable. Who could get along with me?" (99). Although she has spent her adult life caring for other people, in the hospital she can't recall anything she has done for someone else--except to help Dan with his spelling.

When the minister sings a hymn for Hagar, she experiences a moment of truth in which she sees her life in a disturbing new light. First, she realizes that she has not been true to herself. She has been much too concerned about "proper appearances" and about what people might say. Then in a brief torrent of emotion she gives vent to a lifetime of passion and loneliness, of grief and guilt:

Pride was my wilderness, and the demon that led me there was fear. I was alone, never anything else, and never free, for I carried my chains within me, and they spread out from me and shackled all I touched. Oh, my two, my dead. Dead by your own hands or by mine? Nothing can take away those years. (292)

Those who have described Hagar as destructive[2] may have been reacting to this flood of intense feeling. Yet an understanding of all that Hagar has told us and of the overtones communicated through the network of associations reveals that Hagar is burdening herself with unwarranted guilt. She recognizes that her pride and her concern for proper appearances have directed her behavior, but there is no evidence that her middle-class standards adversely affected Bram and John. They preferred to be part of the cowslip and couchgrass culture, and they successfully resisted cultivation. Gifts of handkerchiefs never altered the way Bram blew his nose, and possession of the Currie plaid pin did not endow John with the qualities which Hagar associated with it. Neither Hagar's pride nor her peony-class goals caused the death of either Bram or John. Always conscientious, Hagar holds herself responsible for choices and decisions made by other people.

When Hagar identifies fear as the force behind her pride, we recognize that throughout the novel she has been telling us about her fears and her efforts to conceal them. As a child she feared her father and the imaginary monster which lived in the closet. She has always been afraid of animals, both large and small, including Bram's bees and his horses and the gull trapped inside the cannery. During her first pregnancy, she was convinced that she would die in childbirth--as her mother had. Whenever she is alone in a house, or thinks she is alone, the thought of an intruder terrifies her--in the house at Shadow Point, on the farm at the time of John's accident, and when she hears Marvin coming up the stairs of her home in the city. Throughout her life she has been afraid of darkness which teems "with phantoms, soul-parasites with feathery fingers, the voices of trolls, and pale inconstant fires like the flicker of an eye" (205). Hagar first discloses her fear to another person when she tells Murray Lees that she was frightened when she heard the dogs outside the cannery. This prepares the way for her admission to Marvin a few days later, "I'm--frightened, Marvin, I'm so frightened--" (303). This confession leads to her final rapprochement with her older son.

Thus we discover that Hagar's rage for life has a dark dimension: a deep-seated fear of death and of many of the ordinary experiences of living. She becomes a heroic and a tragic figure when we realize that with her outwardly courageous behavior she has concealed a myriad of repressed fears.

This multifaceted portrayal of Hagar is the product of the novel's unique structure. Laurence supplements the retrospective first-person narration with a network of carefully selected and arranged details, images, verbal motifs, and parallels which provides a contrapuntal commentary on Hagar's account and tells the reader more than Hagar can put into words. The result is a fictional character of unusual depth, breadth, and complexity--a character which cannot be fully appreciated without reference to the network of associations which adds significance to all aspects of her story.

NOTES

1. Page references are to Margaret Laurence, *The Stone Angel* (Toronto: McClelland and Stewart, New Canadian Library, [1964] 1995; Chicago: University of Chicago Press, 1993).

2. Reviewers, critics, and those who write blurbs for paperback editions have often labeled Hagar as destructive. For example, the cover of the 1978 edition reads: "She keeps from everyone her bitter secret: that any man she loves, she destroys." On the cover of the New Canadian Library 1968 edition she is accused of destroying her son John. In *The Manawaka World of Margaret Laurence* (Toronto: McClelland and Stewart, [1975] 1976), Clara Thomas writes: "Hagar lived in battle, pitted against everyone who came close to her and, tragically, she betrayed them all--her father, her brothers, her husband, and her sons. Even for John . . . her love was blind and ultimately destructive" (69).

Chapter 6

"Sisters Under Their Skins": *A Jest of God* and *The Fire-Dwellers*

Nora Foster Stovel

A Jest of God (1966) and *The Fire-Dwellers* (1969) are sister novels, both literally and figuratively. Laurence writes, "In *The Fire-Dwellers*, Stacey is Rachel's sister (don't ask me why; I don't know; she just is)" (Ten 21). Opposing personae of the author perhaps, Rachel Cameron, the heroine of *A Jest of God*, and Stacey Cameron MacAindra, the protagonist of *The Fire-Dwellers*, could not appear more different in personality or situation, although they share a common Cameron heritage. Rachel is a gawky, introverted spinster schoolteacher who has returned home to Manawaka from university in Winnipeg upon the death of her alcoholic undertaker father, Niall Cameron, to care for her hypochrondriac mother, May. Stacey is a broad-beamed, hard-drinking, middle-aging extrovert who has escaped the clutches of the Cameron clan in Manawaka to live in the big bad city of Vancouver with her salesman husband, Mac, and their brood of four children.

Nevertheless, the family resemblance is obvious: their shared Scots-Presbyterian ancestry, which Laurence views as distinctively Canadian, provides an armor of pride that imprisons both sisters (like all of Laurence's Manawaka heroines) within their internal worlds, while providing a defence against the external world.[1] To overcome that barrier between personalities, both sisters must learn to understand and accept their heritage in order to liberate their own identities and free themselves for the future. Both women must also learn to love themselves before they can love each other or anyone else. Rachel and Stacey each receive a sentimental education through a brief love affair; as a result of learning to empathize with their lovers, they learn to love themselves and the people they live with. The sisters have not seen each other for seven years, but by the end of each novel they will be *en route* to reunion. Laurence's emphasis is, as always, on the importance of love in the sense of compassion, as each of her solipsistic protagonists develops from claustrophobia to community.

A Jest of God and *The Fire-Dwellers* are sister novels in practical terms also. Published consecutively in 1966 and 1969, the two novels were composed almost simultaneously, since Laurence interrupted work on *The Fire-Dwellers* to write *A Jest of God* (Hind-Smith 37). "Stacey had been in my mind for a long time--longer than Rachel, as a matter of fact" (Ten 22), Laurence explains. Both novels are even set in the same summer, as Rachel and Stacey, aged thirty-four and thirty-nine respectively, endure parallel but opposing turning points in their lives. The letter Stacey writes to her mother in *The Fire-Dwellers* is the very letter that Mrs. Cameron reads aloud to Rachel in *A Jest of God*. Three letters form a framework for the novels, structuring the development of the sisters' relationship, as we will see.

With classic sibling rivalry, each sister envies the other, thinking that the grass is greener on the other side of the Rockies. Rachel reflects:

It's all right for Stacey. She'd laugh, probably. Everything is all right for her, easy and open. She doesn't appreciate what she's got. She doesn't even know she's got it. She thinks she's hard done by, for the work caused by four kids and a man who admits her existence. She doesn't have the faintest notion. She left here young. She gave the last daughter my name. I suppose she thought she was doing me a favor. Jennifer Rachel. But they call her Jen. (105)

The two novels are an exercise in point of view, or the road not taken, as each woman must learn to empathize with her sister, to view her with compassion and charity. "Only connect" (epigraph to E. M. Forster's *Howard's End*) is a tall order, but one that Laurence believes in.

The artistic parallels between the sister novels are as striking as the literal ones. The two primary fictional techniques Laurence employs to delineate the sisters' character development are symbolism and structure. The titles, epigraphs, nursery rhymes, names, and settings are all clues to the symbolism. The name *Rachel* inevitably connects Laurence's heroine with her Biblical namesake and her elder, fertile sister Leah (King James Version [KJV] Genesis 29:16). The titles of both novels, *A Jest of God* and *The Fire-Dwellers*, are significant, generating central themes and motifs. Both sisters open their narratives with nursery rhymes--*"The wind blows low, the wind blows high"* and *"Ladybird, ladybird, / Fly away home"*--containing keys to their characters, as well as to the patterns of imagery. The epigraphs for both novels are drawn from Carl Sandburg's poem "Losers": Rachel's archetype *Jonah* and Stacey's prototype *Nero* also provide crucial clues to their characters. But Laurence's losers win, as we will see.[2]

Laurence interweaves structural with symbolic techniques to dramatize the sisters' identity crises, manipulating narrative method to convey the divisions between the characters' inner and outer lives, subjective and objective realities. This manipulation of narrative method also structures the time sequence in a flashback technique, relating memory and desire, as the protagonists attempt to come to terms with the past in order to free themselves for the future. As Laurence explains in "Sources" and "Time and the Narrative Voice," "both Rachel and Stacey are threatened by the past" (Sources 15), for "the past and the future are both always present" (Time 157). Both sisters are haunted by their living death in the mausoleum of the Cameron Funeral Home, and they must both lay to rest the ghosts of the past in order to survive for the future. While the polyphonic narrative structure dramatizes each protagonist's fractured psyche and the society's fragmented culture, the undercurrent of symbolism interweaves character and theme into an artistic unit.

Although *A Jest of God* and *The Fire-Dwellers* have been recognized as sister novels from the outset, the connections between them, curiously, have not yet been fully explored.[3] Let us consider first the structural and then the symbolic parallels between *A Jest of God* and *The Fire-Dwellers*.

Even though *A Jest of God* won the Governor General's Award in 1966, early critical response to Laurence's first-person, present-tense narrative method was negative. In "Lack of Distance," Robert Harlow "applaud[s] with only one hand," judging, "this book is a failure": Rachel's character is "carpeted wail-to-wail with her failures. . . . The reader, instead of identifying, finds himself (herself, too, I should think) silently shouting at her to get some eye-liner, save for a mink, strong-arm a man, kill her mother and stop bitching."[4] Clara Thomas judges that "artistically, as a novel, it slides out of balance. Because everything comes through Rachel's consciousness and because her mind is so completely, believably, neurotically obsessed, she cannot really see the world around her or the people in it" (51). That, of course, is the point: Laurence shows us a schizophrenic character waking up to reality, as the narrative method recreates this development dramatically. Laurence defends her narrative method: "*A Jest of God*, as some critics have pointed out disapprovingly, is a very inturned novel. I recognize the limitations of a novel told in the first person and the present tense, from one view point only, but it couldn't have been done any other way, for Rachel herself is a very inturned person" (Ten 21).[5]

Laurence's use of narrative method in *A Jest of God* mirrors Rachel's dilemma perfectly. The protagonist is her own narrator: "the thin giant She" (7) is our I / eye in both senses. As she relates her inner and outer experience, the narrative forms an exercise in psychoanalysis, for Rachel is in dire need of therapy. Hanging on to sanity by her fingernails, she is obsessed with fear of madness: "Am I doing it again, this waking nightmare? How weird am I already? Trying to stave off something that has already grown inside me and spread its roots through my blood?" (24). Consciousness for Rachel is "*Hell on wheels*" (24), and she is bound to the clock's nocturnal circling as to a cosmic Catherine wheel. Oblivion is preferable, or at least the little death of sleep, for Rachel inhabits a nightmare world, which she describes in surrealistic pictures: "The darkening sky is hugely blue, gashed with rose, blood, flame pouring from the volcano or wound or flower of the lowering sun. The wavering green, the sea of grass, piercingly bright. Black tree trunks, contorted, arching over the river" (91-92). Laurence says that "we must attempt to communicate however imperfectly, if we are not to succumb to despair or madness."[6] *A Jest of God* records Rachel's struggle to save her sanity and survive in a sometimes insane world.

Nick Kazlik is not the only character with a phantom twin, for Rachel is a *divided self*, in the terms of R. D. Laing. The 1969 film version of *A Jest of God*, directed by Paul Newman and starring Joanne Woodward, was appropriately titled

Rachel, Rachel, for there are indeed two Rachels, and they live in two different worlds, seen through opposite ends of a telescope: "I have no middle view. Either I fix on a detail and see it as though it were magnified--a leaf with all its veins perceived, the fine hairs on the back of a man's hands--or else the world recedes and becomes blurred, artificial, indefinite, an abstract painting of a world" (91). Doubly divided, Rachel addresses herself as a separate person, saying, "We have discussed this a long time ago, you and I, Rachel" (77). Her ultimate humiliation occurs when two adolescent aliens overhear her address her image in a washroom mirror, saying, "*Maybe it wasn't the sun*" (159). She sees herself reflected in a glass window wearing her white hooded raincoat, like the negative of a photograph (35)--her own *döppelganger*. Scarcely a material girl, she is not sure if she is even alive.

Rachel hardly inhabits the real world, so threatening does it appear. In her paranoid state, she interprets a former student's innocent greeting as hostility (62). Her former "children" (8), grown into adolescents, appear to her as "Venusians" (18), with their jeweled eyes and candy-floss hair, invading her planet earth, dispossessing her. Instead, she lives in her own imagination, in the "deep theatre" (97) of the mind, where "I dramatize myself" (10). But this inner theater is dangerous too, for the paranoid Rachel imagines "an unseen audience ready to hoot and caw with a shocking derision" (101). Not even the star of her own drama, the heroine of her own life, Rachel is an uneasy extra, fearing ridicule. Nor is she in control of her private theater, for the willed masturbation fantasy of the "shadow prince" (25) gives way to the involuntary nightmare of the kingdom of death, where corpses powdered like clowns stare at her with glass eyes, their rouged lips twitching to mock her terror (25).

Laurence wants to help women find their own voice, to give her heroines "the gift of tongues" (32). But Rachel's voice is stifled in interior monologues. Her only real outcries are silent screams like Munch paintings, rendered in emphatic italics: "*My God. How can I stand--*" (23). When she does speak, it is in artificial or borrowed voices: the "Peter-Rabbitish voice" of a simpering schoolmarm (11) or the "robot's mechanical voice" (54) of the dummy she feels she is, or, most insidious of all, "Mother's voice, lilting and ladylike" (84)--and false: "Whoever said the truth shall make you free never knew this kind of house" (106). Not until the turning point of the novel will Rachel's inner and outer voices unite, when she enters the real world. Meanwhile, the only person she can talk to is a God she claims not to believe in. Repressed, Rachel is like a volcano ready to explode. Her own voice, long stifled in the crypt on Japonica Street, finally surfaces in cryptic cries in the *Tabernacle of the Risen and Reborn* (35), where the "*gift of tongues*" (33) has been given to the congregation. Rachel's friend Calla Mackie explains, "We hold ourselves too tightly these days, that's the trouble. Afraid to let the Spirit speak through us. Saint Paul. . . . says *I thank my God I speak with tongues more than ye all.* And what about *the tongues of men and of angels?* What else does the tongues of angels mean, if not glossalalia?" (33). Rachel fears that Calla will "suddenly rise and keen like the Grecian women wild on the hills" (37), but it is Rachel who finds her tongue: "Not Calla's voice. Mine. Oh my God. Mine. The voice of Rachel" (43). But the outburst is abortive, for Rachel rejects it as "Hysteria," along with Calla's kiss, proffering love (44).

The voice of Rachel is "mourning for her children" (187). A childless spinster, Rachel calls her pupils "my children" (8), although she knows she must not. She mourns most for James Doherty, the creator of *splendid* spaceships, where astronauts ascend ropes "like angels climbing Jacob's ladder" (12). Since Rachel, unlike his mother Grace, has no right to touch James with tenderness, her repressed affections erupt in an act of violence, as she strikes him across the face with her wooden ruler, causing a river of blood, emblem of vitality, to stream down his face--prefiguring the Wachakwa River Valley where James likes to play hookey and where Rachel will come to life by learning to love (58-59).[7]

In both sister novels, a love affair with a man of different ethnic background provides the catalyst for each heroine's development. Rachel has a summer romance with Nick Kazlik, a high-school teacher from Winnipeg, visiting his parents in Manawaka for the summer. The Scots-Presbyterian spinster from the right side of the tracks envies the indigent Ukrainians for having more fun--"Laying girls and doing gay Slavic dances," mocks Nick (94). Appropriately, "the milkman's son" awakens "the undertaker's daughter" (73), a modern sleeping beauty, on the banks of the Wachakwa River. "As private as the grave" (96), this tomb becomes a womb for Rachel, delivering her from the mausoleum of her Cameron Funeral Home. By making love to her, Nick gives Rachel "the gift of tongues," so that she can finally speak, touch, and love--even herself. Since Nick "inhabits whatever core of me there is" (153), Rachel learns to live in her own body at last, no longer wearing her hands "like empty gloves" (15).

Realizing that she can give houseroom to another creature, she says, "If I had a child, I would like it to be yours," echoing her biblical namesake's cry, "*Give me my children*" (154). Nick's response, "I'm not God. I can't solve anything" (154), is a lesson to Rachel.[8] When Nick mysteriously disappears, after showing her a shadowy boyhood snapshot, Rachel realizes, "He had his own demons and webs" (197). Driven by parental pressure to replace his dead brother by inheriting the dairy farm from his father, "Nestor the Jester," Nick quotes Jeremiah: "*I have forsaken my house--I have left mine heritage--mine heritage is unto me as a lion in the forest--it crieth out against me--therefore have I hated it*" (116). Rachel has a parallel problem: Laurence writes, "She tries to break the handcuffs of her own past, but she is self-perceptive enough to recognize that for her no freedom from the shackledom of the ancestors can be total" (Ten 21). Rachel has learned more than she realizes from Nick Kazlik.

Stacey's sense of identity is not as shadowy as Rachel's, but it has been badly bruised and battered in the marital wars. Somebody's wife, somebody's mother, somebody's daughter, and somebody's sister, Stacey in *The Fire-Dwellers* has forgotten who she is:[9] "I'm not myself" (156NCL and UC). She asks, "Who is this *you*?" and replies, "I don't know" (159). She begins to doubt that she even exists, "now that I'm not seen" (138). An invisible woman, she looks into the mirror "to make sure I'm really there" (132). She dreams that she is carrying her own severed head into the forest (115), suggesting the severing of her essence from her existence. Caught between her past name, "Stacey Cameron," and her present label, "Mrs. C. MacAindra," she addresses herself by various epithets, from "dream girl" (170) to "female Saint" (231), from "clown" (122) to "doll" (189), from "idiot child" (177) to "rotten old bitch" (9). She also addresses herself in various voices, inquiring, "Who're you? One of your other selves" (106). Impatient with her Jiminy Cricket character, she exclaims, "Bugger off, voice" (189). Like Rachel, Stacey has no one but herself to talk to, except "God, Sir," although she is unsure of his existence. Bliss for Stacey means "no voices. Except yours, Stacey. Well, that's my shadow. It won't be switched off until I die. I'm stuck with it, and I get bloody sick of it, I can tell you" (158-159).

In *The Fire-Dwellers*, Laurence elaborates the fictional techniques that she developed in *A Jest of God*, manipulating narrative and structure skillfully to dramatize a crazily complex culture and the efforts of the individual to survive in a society that swamps her: "Narration, dreams, memories, inner running commentary--all had to be brief, even fragmented, to convey the jangled quality of Stacey's life" (Gadgetry 86). Communication is a central theme,[10] emphasized by the fact that Stacey's youngest child Jennifer Rachel, her "flower" (118), does not speak: the breakthrough of the novel occurs when Jen turns to her mother and inquires casually, "Want tea, Mum?" (273). Stacey cannot communicate with any of her children: "I can't get through the sound barrier" (203), she complains, as she contemplates "All your locked rooms" (198). Stacey's relationship with her eldest daughter, Katie, epitomizes the generation gap: a hangover from the jitterbugging generation of boogie-woogie, Stacey is "a stranger in the new world" (274)--the 1960's counterculture of marijuana and flower power.

The major communication gap, however, occurs between Stacey and her husband, Mac, who has escaped from frenetic family life into an underground cave inside his skull, where Stacey cannot follow (24): "whatever the game happens to be, it's a form of solitaire for Mac" (44). The couple's communication gap is sexual as well as verbal: "in bed he makes hate with her, his hands clenched around her collarbones and on her throat until she is able to bring herself to speak the release. *It doesn't hurt. You can't hurt me*" (150). But he can, and it does.

Ostensibly *The Fire-Dwellers* is told in the third person, for Stacey is not the official narrator of her own experience that Rachel is in *A Jest of God*. But Laurence insists in "Time and the Narrative Voice" that *The Fire-Dwellers* "is really a first-person narrative which happens to be written in the third person, for the narrative voice even here is essentially that of the main character" (Time 157).[11] Stacey's salty vernacular, which Laurence calls "my own idiom" (Ten 22), does dominate the narrative, but her vivid undercurrent of imagery is just as poetic as Rachel's. *The Fire-Dwellers* is also as schizoid as *A Jest of God*, since Laurence creates a counterpoint of viewpoints, alternating first- and third-person narrative techniques, as Stacey contradicts each actual utterance with a tacit comment introduced by a subtle dash: "These lies will be the death of me" (34), she fears; "God forgive me a poor spinner" (119), for "My kingdom it extendeth from lie to shining lie" (177). Stacey is split like Rachel in character and experience: she exclaims, "Help, I'm schizophrenic" (106), because "What goes on inside isn't ever the same as what goes on outside" (34), and it is always a shock to be transported "Out of the inner and into the outer" (161). Stacey writes two letters home to her mother, the actual one and the imaginary one, as she wonders "what would happen if just for once I put down what was really happening?" (138).

Laurence symbolizes this schizoid existence by the mirror motif introduced on the opening page of the novel, where "Stacey sees mirrored her own self in the present flesh" (8), next to her slim image in her wedding photograph. The real and unreal war in mirrors as well as on television, where newsreels of the war in Vietnam appear as unreal as Western serial violence: "The full-length mirror is on the bedroom door. Stacey sees images reflected there, distanced by the glass like humans on TV, less real than real and yet more sharply focused because isolated and limited by a frame" (7). But Stacey is in control of her perspectives, whereas Rachel is the victim of psychic forces beyond her control. An escape artist, Stacey left the manacles of Manawaka far behind, emerging from the mausoleum of the Cameron Funeral Chapel. Stacey recalls her farewells: "Good-bye to Stacey's sister, always so clever. (When I think you're still there, I can't bear it.) Goodbye, prairies" (12). Stacey's children force her to keep a hold on reality, unlike Rachel, who realizes, "They think they are making a shelter for their children, but actually it is the children who are making a shelter for them" (*Jest* 56).

Counterpointing inner and outer realities is only the beginning in this novel, however. In *The Fire-Dwellers*, Laurence combines this technique used in *A Jest of God* with another method employed in *The Stone Angel*. The past is ever present for Laurence's characters, and Stacey, whom Laurence calls "Hagar's spiritual grand-daughter" (Ten 22), counterpoints past and present in a series of memories indicated by indentation (*Fire* 8). Reminiscence becomes psychoanalysis, as Stacey lays the ghosts of her past, recognizing that her heritage from her parents' past will be her legacy for her children's future.

Laurence considers the form of *The Fire-Dwellers* wider than *A Jest of God*, including what she calls "third-person narration as well as Stacey's idiomatic inner running commentary and her somewhat less idiomatic fantasies, dreams, memories" (Ten 22). Running parallel, Stacey's memories of the past are her fantasies of the future--daydreams and nightmares which Laurence presents in italicized paragraphs counterpointed with the actual occurrences (22). Many are science fiction fantasies, but none is more fantastic or poignant than this one: "*Out there in unknown houses are people who live without lies, and who touch each other. One day she will discover them, pierce through to them. Then everything will be all right, and she will live in the light of the morning*" (85).

The catalyst for overcoming Stacey's identity crisis and communication gap is the same as Rachel's--a summer romance. In the depths of her despair, upset by Mac's suspicion that she has gone to bed with his best friend, Buckle Fennick, Stacey heads, as always when in need of spiritual sustenance, straight for the sea. Luke Venturi, an Italian dressed in an Indian sweater with Haida totems of eagle wings and bear masks (162), materializes beside her, fearing that she intends to drown herself. A cool counterculture type, a sometime fisherman and science fiction writer, and a healer of sorts, like his New Testament namesake, he invites her into his borrowed A-frame filled with fishnets, where he dispenses, if not tea and sympathy, then "coffee and sex" (206). Every housewife's fantasy figure, he listens and loves--with no strings attached, assuring Stacey that "You're not alone" (165), that real mothers do cry, that everything *really is all right*. Fortified by fantasy come to life, Stacey can go home again to cope with her realities, for Laurence believes that "You have to go home again" (*Diviners* 324NCL, 290UC).

Both sister novels are very rich in symbolism, for Laurence employs titles, epigraphs, songs, names, and settings as clues to her themes. Both novels open with nursery rhymes. Rachel's rhyme reflects her duality:

The wind blows low, the wind blows high
The snow comes falling from the sky,
Rachel Cameron says she'll die
For the want of the golden city.
   She is handsome, she is pretty,
   She is the queen of the golden city-- (*Jest* 7)

Poignant in its multiple implications, the song suggests the discrepancies between Rachel's repressive reality and her liberated ideal. The symbol of a golden city, echoed in the hymn "Jerusalem the Golden" (48), signifies Rachel's goal, but she fears the winds of fate that will waft her thither. Inserting her name *Rachel Cameron* into the song emphasizes her Cameron ancestry, as well as her biblical namesake, mourning her lost children. But Rachel is not ready to be a mother, for she is still an infant, as Calla's continual epithet *child* (52, 15) emphasizes. Hearing her "children" sing the same song that she sang in the same schoolyard twenty-seven years before reinforces our impression that Rachel is entombed in a perpetual childhood in the mausoleum of the Cameron Funeral Home.

Settings are symbolic in Laurence's Manawaka novels, and Rachel's existence above the mortuary where her father reigned as king of the dead emphasizes her living death, even though she denies the facts of death: "No one in Manawaka ever dies, at least not on this side of the tracks. We are a gathering of immortals. We pass on, through Calla's divine gates of topaz and azure, perhaps, but we do not die. Death is rude, unmannerly, not to be spoken to in the street" (19-20). Rachel is a zombie; in her white hooded raincoat she resembles a ghost. No wonder one suitor, a traveling salesman in embalming fluid, like an Egyptian Pharaoh's gravedigger, admired her for her "good bones" (23).

Both sister novels employ identical time settings, beginning with the approach of summer, and concluding with the onset of fall. Laurence makes rich use of seasonal and landscape symbolism, as well as imagery of flora and fauna. Calla, named for the lily, but brash as a sunflower (15-16), initiates the motif of rebirth by proffering Rachel a "hyacinth, bulbously in bud and just about to give birth to the blue-purple blossom" (15). "April is the cruelest month" for Rachel, recalling her humiliation at being ridiculed as a "peeping Thomasina" (85), outcast from life's feast by the young lovers, when she crouched to smell the crocuses on the hill beyond the cemetery: "*I wandered lonely as a cloud*--like some anachronistic survival of Romantic pantheism, collecting wild flowers, probably, to press between the pages of the *Encyclopaedia Britannica*" (86).

Characters are also symbolized by birds and animals, emblems of the threat they represent to the paranoid Rachel. Willard Siddley, the sadistic school principal, appears to Rachel as a reptile (14); her mother, May, named for spring, looks like "a butterfly released from winter" (46); and Nick slithers out of his flannels "like a snake shrugging off its last year's skin" (97)--like the slippery character he turns out to be. Rachel's self-images are the most telling: she views herself as "a lean greyhound" (46), "a giraffe woman" (81), or as "gaunt bird[s]" (121)--an awkward "ostrich" (183), a "crane" (121), or "a tame goose trying to fly" (136), for she has yet to try her wings.

A Jest of God, almost as full of birds as *A Bird in the House*, is also inhabited by angels, birds of a different feather. Calla whistles, *"She's Only a Bird in a Gilded Cage"* (53), suggesting that Rachel's situation is symbolized by her canary's gilt cage. The canary is clearly a symbol for Rachel: Calla calls him Jacob, name of the biblical Rachel's husband: "'So-named because he climbs the ladder all the time. He won't sing. No ear for music. All he does is march up and down that blasted ladder. . . . Maybe the angel at the top can't be seen by me'" (143). Like Jacob, Rachel has not yet found her voice; the question will be, Can she see the angel at the top of her ladder? She does imagine angels, but they are the "Angel[s] of Death" (100) or the "angel-maker[s]" (179) of abortionists, until she eventually progresses to "a joke about an angel who traded his harp for an upright organ" (132).

The most important animal in *A Jest of God* is Jonah's whale, which provides the epithet to the novel in this line from Sandburg's "Losers": *"Because I was swallowed one time deep in the dark"* (Sandburg 189). Resurrection from what Laurence calls "the tomb-like atmosphere of her extended childhood" (New 21) is essential for Rachel. The winds of tempest that God sent to engulf Jonah are also overwhelming Rachel. Stretched out in her bathtub, with its "claw feet taloned and grasping like a griffin's" (143), she considers that her "flesh does have a drowned look" (145), as she recalls *The Tempest* and *Moby Dick*. Jonah cried, "The waters compassed me about, even to the soul" (KJV Jonah 2:5), and Rachel also fears she has "drowned" (145). Like Jonah, Rachel will be rescued from the belly of the whale, but not until she has suffered a sea change. Laurence echoes the biblical Jonah in the name of Hector Jonas, the new proprietor of the mortuary downstairs. Rachel enters the whale's belly when she descends the forbidden steps of her early nightmare down to the land of the dead (25). The courage required to confront her fear of death, "the skull beneath the skin" (128), gives her the nerve to express herself: for the first time in her narrative, her inner and outer voices unite when she says to Hector, "Let me come in" (125). The Japonica Funeral Chapel is a comically grotesque Hades, resembling a cartoon version of "Ye Olde Dungeon" (124), presided over by a "comic prophet, dwarf seer" (131), who leads Rachel, a Persephone figure, "like a bride up the aisle" (132) of his Chapel of Death in a parody ritual resurrection.

Rachel has always been haunted by the ghost of her dead father, and to penetrate

72   Narrative Structure in Laurence

his mystery, she must quest him in his own kingdom. But she searches in vain among the green glass bottles for clues to his secret. Desperate, she turns to Hector Jonas to solve the mystery of her missing father. His reply, "he had the kind of life he wanted most" (131), prompts Rachel's recognition: "*The life he wanted most. If my father had wanted otherwise, it would have been otherwise. Not necessarily better, but at least different. Did he ever try to alter it? Did I, with mine?*" (131). Finally she realizes that she must be the author of her own life. Having accepted the fact of death, she now has the courage to face the facts of life.

But Rachel has another lesson to learn. Softened by Hector's sympathy, Rachel weeps--an outburst as significant as her first orgasm with Nick--when Hector serenades her with this saccharine song echoing her "*golden city*":

There is a happy land
Far far away--
Where saints and angels stand
Bright, bright as day-- (133)

Touched by her newfound vulnerability, Hector--named incongruously for the Trojan warrior prince--shares his own sore point (or Achilles' heel) with Rachel: "At the crucial moment my wife laughs. She says . . . I look funny" (134). Hector's confession prompts Rachel to see another human being from inside for the first time: before, "Hector's eyes are lynx eyes, cat's eyes, the green slanted cat's eyes of glass marbles" (130), echoing her nightmare (25); but now, "I look into his face then, and for an instant see him living there behind his eyes" (134). Encouraged by this communion, Rachel aborts her compulsion to apologize and replaces it with appreciation. Having reached the turning point in her development, Rachel climbs the stairs out of Hades back to life.

But she has not yet emerged from the belly of the whale. A putative pregnancy provides the pestle with which Rachel is ground: "There are three worlds and I'm in the middle one, and this seems now to be a weak area between millstones" (100). Torn between her private desire for birth and the public need for abortion, Rachel agonizes: "*What will become of me?*" (166), and "It can't be borne" (166). Suicidal, she settles down with lethal legacies from both parents--a bottle of her father's whiskey and fourteen of her mother's sleeping pills--one for each of Rachel's years as a spinster schoolteacher in Manawaka and Jacob's years of labor for his Rachel. Realizing, "*They will all go on in some how, all of them, but I will be dead as stone and it will be too late then to change my mind*" (176-177), she tosses the pills onto the mortuary lawn, where they belong.

In the belly of the whale, she falls on her knees and prays to God, the "last resort": "*Help me*" (177)--like Jonah, who "prayed unto the Lord his God out of the fish's belly . . . out of the belly of hell cried I, and thou heardest my voice" (KJV Jonah 2:1:2). But Rachel does not hear any reply: "If You have spoken, I am not aware of having heard. If You have a voice, it is not comprehensible to me. No omens. No burning bush, no pillar of sand by day or pillar of flame by night" (177). She finally realizes, "There isn't anyone. I'm on my own. I never knew before what that would be like. It means no one. Just that. Just--myself" (171). Rachel rejects death for the sake of the embryo she believes is "lodged" within her bonehouse (179). Realizing, "I could bear a living creature" (169), she elects life for herself and her offspring: "Look--it's my child, mine. And so I will have it. I will have it because I want it and because I cannot do anything else" (177). As a result of choosing to bear a child, with all the trials that it must involve for a single woman, Rachel develops into an independent, responsible adult. She even liberates herself from her chains of guilt when her mother plays her trump card, a weak heart: "My mother's tricky heart will just have to take its own chances" (183). Rachel realizes that she is not God.

Here comes the punch line, the jest of God of the title: Rachel is not gestating life but death. She imagines that Doctor Raven's waiting room is "death's immigration office and Doctor Raven some deputy angel allotted to the job of the initial sorting out of sheep and goats, the happy sheep permitted to colonize Heaven, the wayward goats sent to trample their cloven hoofprints all over Hell's acres. What visa and verdict will he give to me? I know the country I'm bound for, but I don't know its name unless it's limbo" (183). Doctor Raven, well named for a harbinger of death, sends her plummeting into purgatory when he discovers that she is incubating not an embryo but a tumor. "How can non-life be a growth?" (187), she questions. Overwhelmed like Jonah by the waters of grief, a new voice wells up from the depths of her spirit: "My speaking voice, and then only that other voice, wordless and terrible, the voice of some woman mourning for her children" (187)--the voice of Rachel. Surgery proves that "Doctor Raven was right, dead right" (189): the growth was a deadly, not a living one. Stretched on a metal table like the one in Hector's mortuary, with her feet strapped in the stirrups to ride birth, Rachel delivers death.

This is the ultimate jest of God, for the decision that cost Rachel so much seems all for nothing. However, the tumor is not *malignant* but *benign*--like God Himself, for Rachel does give birth--not to an infant but to an adult self. She has also gained a child, for she realizes "I am the mother now" (191, 203). God has the last laugh, but Rachel finally gets the joke. She has always been terrified of being foolish: "I'm not a fool" (52), and "I can't bear watching people make fools of themselves" (34). "If I believed, I would have to detest God for the brutal joker He would be if He existed" (48). St. Paul taught, "*If any man among you thinketh himself to be wise, let him become a fool, that he may be wise*" (141). Rachel has taken a long time to develop a spiritual sense of humor: embarrassed by her sexual awkwardness with Nick, she said, "All right, God--go ahead and laugh, and I'll laugh with you, but not quite yet for a while" (121). Finally she gets the joke: "All that. And this at the end of it. I was always afraid that I might become a fool. Yet I could almost smile with some grotesque lightheadedness at that fool of a fear, that poor fear of fools, now that I really am one" (188). Having become a fool, she can now be wise--wise enough to pity the joker: "God's mercy on reluctant jesters. God's grace on fools. God's pity on God" (209).[12]

Like Jonah and Job, Rachel has survived her suffering and learned joy, as she recalls the words of the Psalm: "*Make me to hear joy and gladness, that the bones which Thou hast broken may rejoice*" (208). The novel concludes with embarkation, as Rachel sets out on the road of life with her "elderly child" (208). Finally allowing the winds of fate to waft her, she sets off for her "*golden city,*" *en route* to reunion with her sister Stacey in a new spirit of freedom, combining optimism with realism in an affirmative vision of the future: "Where I'm going, anything may happen. . . . The wind will bear me, and I will drift and settle, and drift and settle. Anything may happen, where I'm going" (208-09).

Stacey's journey parallels Rachel's artistically, for Laurence employs the title, epigraph, and opening nursery rhyme of the novel to symbolize Stacey's development. The title, *The Fire-Dwellers*, introduces the central symbol of the purgatorial flames that Stacey must endure before she can be saved.[13] Stacey's prototype, the Emperor Nero, who fiddled while Rome burned, underlines the main emblem of fire in this epigraph from Sandburg's "Losers": "*I who have fiddled in a world on fire*" (Sandburg 189). The familiar nursery rhyme that opens Stacey's narrative emphasizes the fire motif, applying it to Stacey's situation as wife and mother:

Ladybird, ladybird,
Fly away home;
Your house is on fire,
Your children are gone. (Fire 7)

This insidious little rhyme is repeated at three significant points in the novel: at the beginning (7), at the turning point (209), and at the end (280), structuring the narrative. The significance of the rhyme is double-edged for Stacey, the original ladybird (13), suggesting both her desire to escape from the trap of her four walls and her fear that Providence will punish her for her sins through her most vulnerable point, her children, hostages to fortune.

The theme of Judgment (270) is underlined by the motif of thunder and lightning, echoed comically in the name of Thor Thorlakson, the phoney god of thunder, and Valentine Tonnerre, French for thunder, who will free Stacey from her false god. "I seem to believe in a day of judgment" (241), says Stacey, the original sinner. Recalling the fire that burned Piquette Tonnerre with her children, she fears the same fate for her own offspring: "Piquette and her kids, and the snow and fire. Ian and Duncan in a burning house" (241). Fear of fire fuels her paranoid fantasies: "The house is burning. Everything and everyone in it. Nothing can put out the flames. The house wasn't fire-resistant. One match was all it took" (141). Her first fantasy involves a forest fire, where she must traverse a tree bridge across a bottomless void, but she can rescue only one of her children from the fire, while she hears the voices of the other three calling to her from the flames--*Stacey's choice* (30-31).

Stacey's world is on fire both literally and figuratively, internally and externally. Fiery by nature, Stacey was always warned by her mother, "*you must learn to bank your fires*" (194). Surrounded by flaming red-haired MacAindras indoors and "the eternal flames of the neon forest fires" (154) outdoors, smothering her own flames proves difficult. Sexually and emotionally unsatisfied in her marriage, she recalls, "Better to marry than burn, St. Paul said, but he didn't say what to do if you married *and* burned" (193). Stacey is burned literally when she scorches her hand on the red-hot burner of her stove, branding her palm with two crescent lines--"My brand of stigmata. My western brand. The Double Crescent" (130)--recalling the crucified Christ (Bevan's "fire-hell symbol hunt" xi).

But it is not just Stacey's inner world that is burning; the whole outer world is in flames, as the news constantly reminds us in capital letters:

EVER-OPEN EYE. . . . MAN BURNING. HIS FACE CANNOT BE SEEN. HE LIES STILL, PERHAPS ALREADY DEAD. FLAMES LEAP AND QUIVER FROM HIS BLACKENED ROBE LIKE EXCITED CHILDREN OF HELL. VOICE: TODAY ANOTHER BUDDHIST MONK SET FIRE TO HIMSELF IN PROTEST AGAINST THE WAR IN (116)

"*Doom everywhere*" (58) is Stacey's impression, recalling "the fall of Rome" (117), when Nero fiddled. She watches transfixed as napalm spreads its stain across an infant's face on a newscast (90), and listens appalled as a disembodied voice announces another Vietnamese village burned or American city aflame.

The torch of war is carried back into the past and forward into the future: Stacey recalls her father's Great War, with his tears over the boy caught between the legs by an exploding shell, as well as her husband's Second World War, with the mine blast that left him forever responsible for the life of Buckle Fennick. Forecast of the holocaust triggers her fantasies, as she imagines escaping to the northern wilderness with her family. Her two lethal legacies from her undertaker father are firewater and firearms: she has saved his army revolver as a souvenir so that, in case of a cataclysm, she can dispatch the final thunderbolt that will free her offspring from suffering. Eventually, the purgatorial flames that persecute Stacey will become a refining fire from which she will emerge, if not purified, at least tempered.

The antidote to fire is water: after trying to drown her sorrows in spirits, Stacey awakens with a hangover, thinking, "Help. Water. Water. I'm dying of thirst" (104). But her need for healing water is spiritual as well as physical. If Stacey's nightmares involve fire, her daydreams include water. Stacey lives in the "jewel of the Pacific Northwest" (10), and the first time she escapes from her "Home Sweet Home" (104), she heads straight for the waterfront, where she admires the free-flying gulls. Birds are a symbol of the spirit in all of Laurence's writing, and Stacey, living now on Bluejay Crescent, recalling her past persona whirling in the Flamingo Dance Hall, sees the seagulls as "prophets in bird form" (13), although vultures, the "tomb birds" (270), also threaten.

Fish, inhabitants of water, do not fare so well as waterbirds, if we think of Tess Fogler's goldfish, symbol of "Nature red in tooth and claw": "Dog eat dog and fish eat fish" (92), Stacey thinks, when Tess recounts watching the big fish eat the little fish, suggesting the depths of her sickness (191). Fish symbolism is sinister for Stacey, always a strong swimmer (161), who envisions herself as a mermaid (15).

Luke calls her "merwoman" (166)--appropriately, for Stacey's thoughts are free-floating, like seaweed under water:

Everything drifts. Everything is slowly swirling, philosophies tangled with the grocery lists, unreal-real anxieties like rose thorns waiting to tear the uncertain flesh, nonentities of thoughts floating like plankton, green and orange particles, seaweed--lots of that, dark purple and waving, sharks with fins like cutlasses, herself held underwater by her hair, snared around auburn-rusted anchor chains (34)

Stacey's happiest memories are of lakes, as she recalls her first love-making with the airman from Montreal on the shores of Diamond Lake (71) and her Edenic honeymoon at Timber Lake, where she said to Mac, "I like everything about you," and he replied, "*That's good, honey. I like everything about you too*" (38). Regretting the loss of the loons from Diamond Lake, with their "voices of dead shamans, mourning the departed Indian gods" (159), she fantasizes about escaping with her family from the fiery cataclysm to a cool lake up north in Cariboo country.

Timber Lake features in her "death wish" (14) also, for it is there that she drowns her father's infamous revolver. Like Rachel, Stacey sometimes longs for oblivion. She sings an escapist song that echoes the saccharine hymn with which Hector serenades Rachel in the underworld:

There's a gold mine in the sky
  Faraway--
We will go there, you and I,
  Some sweet day,
And we'll say hello to friends who said goodbye,
When we find that long lost gold mine in the sky.
  Faraway, faraw-a-ay-- (129)

In the depths of her despair, Stacey is blinded by tears of sympathy for her father-in-law Matthew, when he repeats the Psalm, "*Save me, O God, for the waters are come in unto my soul*" (152). But Stacey does not drown; like Rachel, she suffers a significant sea change--a "change of heart" (221).

Stacey's lover Luke, a fisherman named for the Apostle, seems to Stacey "like the rain in a dry year" (187), bringing salvation. Surnamed Venturi, suggesting adventure, Luke offers to fulfill her escape fantasy by taking her north with him to Cariboo country. A fisher of souls, he invites her to blissful oblivion by crossing the Skeena River on a ferry driven by a "Charon" figure (208). Confronted by choice, Stacey knows she can never abandon her children. Mocking her sense of responsibility, Luke repeats the Ladybird rhyme for the second time (209), as Stacey decides, "I have to go home" (209). She returns home to a reprieve: sensing disaster, and fearing that Ian has died for her sins, she is forgiven when Mac explains, "Stacey--it's not Ian. . . . It's Buckle" (211). But Stacey does not escape disaster that lightly, and the motif of drowning is not yet finished, for her favorite, Duncan, is almost drowned at the seashore. Blinded by salt tears, she watches the seawater pump from his mouth until she hears him utter the infant wail of a newborn (267-68).

Finally, Mac confronts his ultimate fear, Stacey's suicide stunt, by asking her what she did with her father's revolver. Rejecting "premourning" in favor of affirmation, she threw the gun into Timber Lake, drowning death, like Ethel Wilson's "Swamp Angel"--a new Excalibur. Ultimately, Stacey and Mac are reconciled and truly make love for the first time in the novel, for Stacey has realized that Mac is not really an Alien Other or "Agamemnon king of men" (8), but a person, like herself, who needs support and sympathy as much as she does.

At the conclusion of *The Fire-Dwellers*, Stacey repeats the Ladybird rhyme for the third and last time, thinking "Will the fires go on, inside and out? Until the moment when they go out for me, the end of the world" (280). Speaking of her sister novels, Laurence writes, "Optimism in this world seems impossible to me. But in each novel there is some hope, and that is a different thing entirely" (Ten 15). So Laurence does not promise the reader perfect happiness, but Stacey has surfaced from her despair and survived: as she falls asleep on the eve of another decade, she prays, "Give me another forty years, Lord, and I may mutate into a matriarch" (381)--"Hagar's spiritual grand-daughter" indeed.

So both sister novels end with acceptance and affirmation, as Rachel and Stacey, having laid to rest the ghosts of the past and survived the present, are ready to embark on the future. Reconciled with the people they live with, but accepting their human limitations, they are ready for a change. At the end of *The Fire-Dwellers*, Stacey, who has recently given houseroom to Mac's aging father, receives a letter from Rachel announcing that she is moving to the coast with their elderly mother (276). Anticipating reunion, Stacey and Rachel realize that they can forgive each other for living. "Sisters under their skins,"[14] they may even learn to feel for each other the compassion that their creator has taught us to feel for both of them.

NOTES

1. G. D. Killam, Introduction to *A Jest of God*, by Margaret Laurence (Toronto: McClelland and Stewart, New Canadian Library, 1966), writes, "The principal characters in the Canadian novels . . . live in almost total isolation from the world around them, unable to give expression to their most profound desires and concerns."

2. The final line from Carl Sandburg's poem "Losers" from *Smoke and Steel* (New York: Harcourt Brace and Company, 1920), p. 87, in which the brave sergeant urges his men to advance into the drumfires at Belleau Woods, suggests the kind of good loser or even tragic hero that he had in mind: "Come on, you. . . . Do you want to live forever?"

3. When this paper was originally composed for the Margaret Laurence Conference at the University of Brandon in 1988, there were few articles on either of the Cameron sister novels and none comparing them. Subsequently, numerous interesting essays have been published about each, including Aritha Van Herk's "The Eulalias of Spinsters and Undertakers" in *Crossing the River: Essays in Honour of Margaret Laurence*, edited by Kristjana Gunnars (Winnipeg: Turnstone, 1988), pp. 133-46, and Christl Verduyn's "Language, Body, and Identity in Margaret Laurence's *The Fire-Dwellers*" in *Margaret Laurence: An Appreciation*, edited by Christl Verduyn, *Journal of Canadian Studies* (1988), pp. 128-40, as well as Coral Ann Howell's "Weaving Fabrications: Women's

Narratives in *A Jest of God* and *The Fire-Dwellers*" in Colin Nicolson's *Critical Approaches to the Fiction of Margaret Laurence* (Vancouver: University of British Columbia Press, 1990), pp. 93-106.

4. Robert Harlow, "Lack of Distance," *Canadian Literature* 31 (1967): 71. Patricia Morley responds in *Margaret Laurence* (Boston: G. K. Hall, 1981): "Harlow misses the multiple voices of Rachel, who thinks and voices a very complex self. . . . The first-person point of view subsumes the many voices of Rachel, while the larger fictional form contains an ironic, implicit commentary through event, image, juxtaposition, and the reactions of the other characters" (90).

5. George Bowering, in "That Fool of a Fear: Notes on *A Jest of God,*" *A Place to Stand On: Essays By and About Margaret Laurence*, ed. George Woodcock (Edmonton: NeWest Press, 1983), writes in 1971: "The form of the novel, first person and present tense, works as Rachel's opening-out does, to get naked" (211). In "Gadgetry and Growing: Form and Voice in the Novel" (subsequently referred to as Gadgetry), p. 84, a 1969 address reprinted in Woodcock, Margaret Laurence says of *A Jest of God*: "I tried again and again to begin the novel in the third person, and it simply would not write itself that way. . . . [T]he character of Rachel would not reveal herself. So finally I gave up and stopped struggling. I began to write the novel as I really must have very intensely wanted to write it--in the first person, through Rachel's eyes. I knew that this meant the focus of the book was narrow--but so was Rachel's life" (84-85).

6. G. D. Killam, Introduction to *A Jest of God*, by Margaret Laurence (Toronto: McClelland and Stewart, New Canadian Library, 1966), quotes Margaret Laurence's comment from her *Long Drums and Cannons* (London: Macmillan, 1968; New York: Praeger, [1969] 1970), pp. 124-25.

7. A nosebleed figures in *The Fire-Dwellers* also, when Thor Thorlakson hits Mac with a ball at a Richalife party, marking a turning point in Mac's attitude toward Thor and Richalife (232).

8. Stacey makes a similar remark to Mac about Buckle Fennick's death: "You're not God. You couldn't save him" (219). Laurence remarks, in "Margaret Laurence: The Black Celt Speaks of Freedom," in Donald Cameron's *Conversations with Canadian Novelists* (Toronto: Macmillan, 1973), that, as a novelist, you must "realize that you are *not* God" (104).

9. Margaret Laurence, *The Fire-Dwellers* (Toronto: McClelland and Stewart, New Canadian Library, [1969] 1991), p. 90, and (Chicago, University of Chicago Press, 1993), p. 90. Subsequent references to both in-print editions will be given in the text. Christl Verduyn observes, in *Margaret Laurence: An Appreciation* (Peterborough, Ontario, Canada: Broadview, 1988), "*The Fire-Dwellers* reflects a number of the predominant themes which have emerged in contemporary feminist writing" (128).

10. Laurence told Cameron, "I feel that human beings ought to be able, *ought* to be able to communicate and touch each other far more than they do, and this human loneliness and isolation, which obviously occurs everywhere, seems to me to be part of man's tragedy" (105). See C. M. McLay, "Every Man Is an Island: Isolation in *A Jest of God*," *Canadian Literature* 50 (1971): 57-68.

11. F. M. Watt's review of *The Fire-Dwellers* in *The Canadian Forum*, July, 1969, judges that "This book contains flaws enough to sink half a dozen books by lesser novelists. . . . *A Jest of God* stuck to the discipline of a single point of view; here the shifts to third-person narration are the technical aspects of the novel's lack of artistic rigor" (87; reprinted in New 198-99). Laurence explains: "I did not want to write a novel entirely in the first person, but I did not want to write one entirely in the third person, either. The inner and outer aspects of Stacey's life were so much at variance that it was essential to have her inner

commentary in order to point up the frequent contrasts between what she was thinking and what she was saying" (Gadgetry 86).

12. Bowering concludes "That Fool of a Fear: Notes on *A Jest of God*" eloquently: "God's jests are not just vocal--the word is made flesh, that is, the eternal present. It is in understanding this that Margaret Laurence chose wisely to write in the present tense, to present the fool made wise by folly" (Woodcock 225).

13. A latter-day Hedda Gabler, Laurence says of her problems with *The Fire-Dwellers*, "I even once burned, dramatically, nearly a hundred pages of a second draft, and then sat down at my typewriter and wrote a deeply gloomy letter to a friend, which began 'I am a firebug'" (Gadgetry 87).

14. In *Collected Verse of Rudyard Kipling* (London: Hodder and Stoughton, 1912), pp. 408-10, Rudyard Kipling's 1896 poem "The Ladies" (408) employs the refrain "For the Colonel's Lady an' Judy O'Grady / Are sisters under their skins!"

WORKS CITED

Bevan, Alan. Introduction to *The Fire-Dwellers*, by Margaret Laurence. Toronto: McClelland and Stewart, New Canadian Library, (1969) 1973.

Hind-Smith, Joan. *Three Voices: The Lives of Margaret Laurence, Gabrielle Roy, Frederick Philip Grove*. Toronto: Clark Irwin, 1975.

Laurence, Margaret. *The Diviners*. Toronto: McClelland and Stewart, New Canadian Library, (1974) 1995; Chicago: University of Chicago Press, 1993.

___. *The Fire-Dwellers*. Afterword by Sylvia Fraser. Toronto: McClelland and Stewart, New Canadian Library, (1969) 1991; Chicago: University of Chicago Press, 1993.

___. *A Jest of God*. Toronto: McClelland and Stewart, New Canadian Library, (1966) 1993; Chicago: University of Chicago Press, 1993.

___. "Gadgetry and Growing: Form and Voice in the Novel." *A Place to Stand On: Essays By and About Margaret Laurence*. Ed. George Woodcock. Edmonton: NeWest, 1983.

___. "Sources." *Margaret Laurence*. Ed. Wm. H. New. Toronto: McGraw-Hill Ryerson, 1977, 15.

___. "Ten Years' Sentences." *Margaret Laurence*. Ed. W. H. New. Toronto: McGraw-Hill Ryerson, 1977, 17-23.

___. "Time and the Narrative Voice." *Margaret Laurence*. Ed. W. H. New. Toronto: McGraw-Hill Ryerson, 1977, 155-59.

New, W. H. *Margaret Laurence*. Toronto: McGraw-Hill Ryerson, 1977.

Sandburg, Carl. *Complete Poems of Carl Sandburg*. New York: Harcourt Brace Jovanovitch, 1969.

Thomas, Clara. *Margaret Laurence*. Toronto: McClelland and Stewart, 1969.

Van Herk, Aritha. "The Eulalias of Spinsters and Undertakers." *Crossing the River: Essays in Honour of Margaret Laurence*. Ed. by Kristjana Gunnars. Winnipeg: Turnstone, 1988, 133-46.

Woodcock, George, ed. *A Place to Stand On: Essays By and About Margaret Laurence*. Edmonton: NeWest, 1983.

Chapter 7

Coherence in *A Bird in the House*
Bruce Stovel

From the start, readers of *A Bird in the House*, Margaret Laurence's book of short stories about growing up in Manawaka, have been particularly struck by two things. One is the author's artistry, and the other is the book's unity and wholeness. As for the first quality, Henry Kreisel says in his review of the book, "The prose is clean and simple and beautifully shaped" (94); Patricia Morley in her book *Margaret Laurence* speaks of her stories as "beautifully crafted" (114); Barbara Hehner, in an article on Laurence's fiction as a whole, refers in passing to "the almost perfect narrative form . . . of *A Bird in the House*" (45); and Sherrill Grace, in "Crossing Jordan: Time and Memory in the Fiction of Margaret Laurence," an essay that contains a very penetrating discussion of the book, considers it "a small masterpiece . . . perhaps her finest work" (329). The second quality has been just as evident: the anonymous reviewer in *Choice* observed that the stories "are best understood and appreciated when read all together rather than as separate short stories" (Review 1374), and William French noted in his review that "the cumulative impact is greater than the sum of the parts" (15). Laurence herself says in "Time and the Narrative Voice," a commentary upon two of her short stories, that although seven of the eight stories in the book appeared separately before it was published as a single volume in 1970, the stories "were . . . conceived from the beginning as a related group. Each story is self-contained in the sense that it is definitely a short story and not a chapter from a novel, but the net effect is not unlike that of a novel" (Time 157). It was to describe this mingling of genres that Kent Thompson, in his review of *A Bird in the House*, framed a new and influential critical term: the whole-book: "a book which is more than a collection of short stories and yet, though like a novel in some ways, not a novel" (*Place* 232).

Readers, then, have found these stories both highly crafted and unusually integrated. There is, I believe, a direct connection between these two facts; much of the artistry in each story lies in the interconnected, cumulative resonances that bind the stories together into a single, coherent whole. In this essay I will explore the nature of this larger coherence. My argument will fall into two stages: first I will show that the stories in this volume, considered simply as separate short stories, are essentially alike and are thus knit together by many resonances connecting them; then I will outline some ways in which the stories form a single, cumulative progression which has a "net effect . . . not unlike that of a novel."

The eight stories in Laurence's Manawaka collection are essentially the same in setting, character, point of view and voice, style, subject, structure, symbol, image, and theme. This fact creates much of the concentrated intensity of effect that impresses the reader of the book: the stories recapitulate each other and resonate among themselves, telling in the end a single, developing tale. Furthermore, throughout the book the elements of fiction--point of view, symbol, theme, and so on--depend upon and support each other in an unusually integral way. The book is thus much more coherent in impact than most short-story collections (and than Laurence's other collection of stories, *The Tomorrow-Tamer* (Toronto: McClelland and Stewart, New Canadian Library [1963, 1970] 1993). A brief account of the nature of each of these elements of fiction in *A Bird in the House* will give some substance to these claims.

All of the stories have the same setting. Uniquely among Laurence's works of fiction, this book is set wholly in Manawaka when Laurence herself was growing up, between the mid-thirties, when Laurence and her heroine, Vanessa MacLeod, were ten, until the early forties, when both Laurence and Vanessa left Manawaka and went to university in Winnipeg. Furthermore, the stories are not primarily set in Manawaka as a whole, but in the two homes in which Vanessa lives: the MacLeod house, presided over by her Grandmother MacLeod, and the Brick House, the home of her Grandfather and Grandmother Connor. For most of the book, as Vanessa remarks in "Horses of the Night," "What I really saw was only what went on in our family" (*Bird* 128). Both houses are imposing brick structures, built to their specifications by the two sets of grandparents as embodiments of their status as pillars of the community.

The stories also have the same set of characters. The central character is Vanessa MacLeod, present in two roles: as a young girl and then as a young woman, she is the protagonist in each story, while the narrator in each is a much older and wiser Vanessa, implied throughout the narration, glimpsed at the end of the third story, "The Mask of the Bear," and presented as a forty year old woman with children of her own in a two-page epilogue to the final story. Around Vanessa we see her family and, later, a few characters who enter into or impinge upon the family circle. The characters of the family members do not change, although their situations do, and this serves to dramatize and gauge the changes within Vanessa herself, who matures within the narrative from a child's awareness--certain, comforting, self-centered, but also ignorant of other people's states of mind and so powerless in action--to an adult understanding of the confusing, complex, unfair realities that have produced her. This understanding is not easily or immediately achieved, but the stories show that Vanessa is sufficiently curious, perceptive, sympathetic, humble, and tough-minded to learn the truth of things--and so to attain some degree of freedom over her circumstances. If Vanessa the child believes, even in the concluding pages of the final story, that she can rebel against the Brick House and all that it represents, destroying its brick battlements with the war-cry of her trumpets, Vanessa the adult writes the book's first sentence: "That house in Manawaka is the one which, more than any other, I carry with me" (11).

The stories thus all have the same point of view and narrative voice: a wonderfully evocative double perspective that presents simultaneously the world as it registers upon the child and the world as the narrating adult understands it. In "Time and the Narrative Voice," Laurence says of *A Bird in the House*: "The narrative voice had to speak as though from two points of view, simultaneously" (158). For instance, the opening pages present the ten-year-old Vanessa's impression of Grandfather Connor, prevented by his principles from working on the Sabbath, "lumber[ing] around the house like some great wakeful bear waiting for the enforced hibernation of Sunday to be over"; this picture is immediately followed by the explanation, "I did not know then the real torment that the day of rest was for him, so I had no patience with his impatience" (16). This implicit split between the Vanessa who acts and the narrating Vanessa who understands becomes explicit twice, as mentioned above, once in the final two pages of the book, and once in the last paragraph of the third story, "The Mask of the Bear"; the paragraph begins, "Many years later, when Manawaka was far away from me, in miles and in time, I saw one day in a museum the Bear Mask of the Haida Indians" (86).

This double perspective is reflected in Vanessa's own prose style. Each of the characters has a distinctive way of speaking: Grandfather Connor grumps and trumpets, Grandmother MacLeod pronounces, Aunt Edna talks tough, Piquette Tonnerre squawks, Vanessa's parents explain, console, and waver. Vanessa's idiom as a narrator is always simple, direct, and unaffected, a style which at times conveys the simplicity of naivete, as when Vanessa describes her Grandmother Connor as a Mitigated Baptist, since she has heard her grandfather say of her that at least she is not an unmitigated Baptist who believes in total immersion (24); at other times, we find the unstripped simplicity of bitter irony, as when at the end of "The Loons," Vanessa relates without comment that "Galloping Mountain was now a national park, and Diamond Lake had been renamed Lake Wapakata, for it was felt that an Indian name would have a greater appeal to tourists" (119). Most often, however, the two simplicities coexist: when Vanessa describes her hopes of learning about nature from Piquette, a real-life Indian, the child's simplicity and the adult's ironic awareness are blended:

It seemed to me that Piquette must be in some way a daughter of the forest, a kind of junior prophetess of the wilds, who might impart to me, if I took the right approach, some of the secrets which she undoubtedly knew--where the whippoorwill made her nest, how the coyote reared her young, or whatever it was that it said in Hiawatha. (112)

One of the many sources of irony here is that Piquette *does* turn out to have some secret knowledge of the wilds and *does* impart it in the end to Vanessa. This two-toned simplicity, then, extending back to childhood from the narrator's present and forward into adulthood from the dramatic present, is the prose medium by which Laurence creates her double-narrative perspective and her distinctive narrating voice.

Each story, as well, has the same subject. In each, Vanessa comes up against one character in her world, "Central Figure," note the chart. This term is a little misleading, however, for the subject of each story is not so much the character Vanessa confronts in it, her father or Piquette or Chris, as Vanessa's relationship with that character.

A BIRD IN THE HOUSE: A BIRD'S-EYE VIEW

The Sequence of Stories	*Central Figure*	*Vanessa's Age*	*Time Encompassed*	*Number of Dramatized Days*
"The Sound of the Singing"	Grandfather Connor	just turned 10	two hours	one
"To Set Our House in Order"	Grandmother MacLeod	10 1/4	two or three weeks	three
"The Mask of the Bear"	Grandfather Connor	10 1/2, 10 3/4	two months (and a glimpse from "many years later")	three (plus the final glimpse)
"A Bird in the House"	Vanessa's father	12, 17	five years	nine
"The Loons"	Piquette Tonnerre	11, 15, 19	eight years	five
"Horses of the Night"	Chris (a distant cousin)	6, 9, 11, 13, c. 15, c. 20	about fourteen years	twelve
"The Half-Husky"	Harvey Shinwell (the paper boy)	15, 17	two years	nine
"Jericho's Brick Battlements"	Grandfather Connor	4, 12, 14, 17, 18, 20, 40	thirty-six years	fourteen

For instance, the three stories just alluded to all end with a paragraph in which Vanessa comes to understand the central figure, her own relationship with and to that figure, and how and why she came to this knowledge. "A Bird in the House," the story devoted to her relationship with her father, ends with the seventeen-year-old Vanessa, as she burns the photograph of the French girl from her father's past, grieving for her father "as though he had just died now" (107). She realizes the truth about her father's life, about all that they would have in common and could discuss together if he were still alive, about how much she failed to comprehend when she was a child; herself "desperately anxious to get away from Manawaka and from my grandfather's house," she has no trouble now understanding his need for "some momentary and unexpected freedom" (107).

A consequence of this sameness of subject is that the stories also have the same structure. In each story, Vanessa takes us through a series of puzzling events and troubling awarenesses to a final moment of recognition in which she comprehends everything in the story. As Robert Gibbs points out, these final moments of recognition are not Joycean epiphanies, but rather "one understanding, a culminating one, of many in the story" (i). Vanessa does not move from childhood to adulthood in one leap, but through a series of small jolts and dislocations which occur within each story and from story to story. These concluding moments of recognition are stated in each case as a riddle: Vanessa grieves for her father as if he has just died (107), she realizes that Piquette might well be the only one who actually heard the crying of the loons (120), she puts away the miniature saddle branded with the name of Chris's imaginary ranch "gently and ruthlessly" (144). A riddle, by definition a puzzle which has an answer, is a fitting vehicle for Vanessa's realizations: a riddle represents both the opacity of the world as the child experiences it and the adult's ability to pierce that opacity. Furthermore, each story is organized around a central symbol alluded to in its title, and Vanessa's concluding recognition in each case is conveyed through that symbol: through the opposition between the Brick House and Uncle Dan's joyful singing in the opening story (42), through the disarray created by Grandmother MacLeod's ferocious determination to clean her house and keep it neat in the second story (61), through the sad fact, in the third story, that Grandfather Connor's bear mask conceals a bewildered man (86), and so on. The truths that Vanessa discovers come to her in riddles and symbols: she learns, not directly and by exercise of reason, but obliquely and by an effort of imagination; Gibbs remarks, "Truth . . . is imaginative insight, which sets her free" (v). Vanessa's childish imagination is ambiguous. It leads her far away from the life around her, as her romantic expectations of Piquette indicate; during the book we see her abandon the three glamorous stories she is composing in notebooks because she finds them to be untrue to her own experience. On the other hand, though, it is Vanessa's capacity to live imaginatively in other worlds than her own that in the end enables her to understand other people by empathizing with them. Imagination provides us with human truths that we can get in no other way. The adult Vanessa has not simply abandoned the epic tale "The Pillars of the Nation" or "The Silver Sphinx," the Egyptian story of love and death, or the romantic tale of the Quebec girl Marie imprisoned in the grey stone inn: *A*

Bird in the House tells each of these stories, but in a form that is truer than, not false to, actual experience.

Furthermore, the stories develop the same set of symbols and images. One quick way to see this is to note that in three of the eight stories the central symbol is a Brick House--Grandfather Connor's sturdy brick house in the first and last stories, Grandmother MacLeod's more embellished house in "To Set Our House in Order"--and that in four stories the central symbol is an animal, unfree and vulnerable because a creature of instinct--"The Mask of the Bear," "The Loons," "Horses of the Night," "The Half-Husky." The one remaining story, which gives the volume its title, combines these two central symbols: "A Bird in the House." As Margaret Laurence presents it, Vanessa's predicament is also that of all the people around her: the human being is trapped within the rigid walls, protective yet isolating, of family pride and social convention.

Just as the same symbols recur throughout the stories, so a single set of images supports and elaborates these symbols. For instance, the spontaneous singing of Uncle Dan, Grandfather Connor's shiftless brother, in the opening story can be related to Grandmother Connor's caged canary, which hardly ever sings, to Vanessa's boisterous singing of a cowboy song in the title story and to her subsequent inability in the same story to sing more than the first stanza of the hymn celebrating "*Rest beyond the river*" (104), to the wild song of the loons (and, by suggestion, of Piquette Tonnerre, whose hoarse voice seems so unmusical), to the jukebox in the Regal Cafe "booming like tuneful thunder" as Piquette, "leaning lightly on its chrome and its rainbow glass," tells Vanessa of her dreams of married love in Winnipeg (117), and to Aunt Edna's ragtime piano in the final story--which, like Uncle Dan's singing, is silenced by Grandfather Connor (167). Similarly, given Vanessa's ever-greater need to escape from the Brick House, the notion of travel becomes a charged one from the first story onward: in fact, in every one of the stories except the sixth, "Horses of the Night," Vanessa leaves the family house at the end of the story and has her moment of recognition after she has moved outside the brick walls.[1]

Another image running through the stories is that of battle. Vanessa, like her grandfather, is a warrior: if, in the opening lines of the book, his house is "sparsely windowed as some crusader's embattled fortress in a heathen wilderness" (11), Vanessa thinks with Old Testament ferocity "*How are the mighty fallen in the midst of the battle,*" when he is humiliated in front of the family at the end of the story (39); similarly, when she and her grandfather attack each other in the final story, she imagines, again in Old Testament terms, that "if I sounded all my trumpets loudly enough, his walls would quake and crumble" (184). In "A Bird in the House" Vanessa refuses to go to the Remembrance Day parade because she considers her father and the other veterans in their World War I uniforms to be "impostors, plump or spindly caricatures of past warriors" (88). Meanwhile, real battle is revealed as a much more harrowing thing: in the second and fourth stories, we hear that Vanessa's father has had, at the age of nineteen, to watch his eighteen-year-old brother die in the muddy trenches of World War I; the first paragraph of "The Loons" informs us that after the Battle at Batoche the voices of the Métis entered their long silence--just as at the end of the story the loons and Piquette will have become silent; in the last story young men from half the families in Manawaka have died in the Dieppe raid of 1942 (181). In "Horses of the Night," Chris's imaginary horses, Duchess and Firefly, are set against not only his family's actual plow horses, Floss and Trooper, but also against the army horses Vanessa's father has described dying berserk with fear as they sank in the mud. Chris says to Vanessa, "Ewen said a guy tended to concentrate on the horses because he didn't dare think what was happening to the men. Including himself" (141). When Chris himself goes off to battle, Vanessa realizes that his retreat into madness is simply "the final heartbreaking extension of that way he'd always had of distancing himself from the absolute unbearability of battle" (143). It is because Chris is a Connor who refuses to fight that Vanessa puts away his saddle "ruthlessly": people who are Connors and live with Connors have to become tough. As Uncle Terence observes in "The Mask of the Bear," "everybody to his own shield in this family" (86).

Finally, these stories all have the same principal theme. *A Bird in the House*, of course, develops many themes, and especially those found throughout Laurence's fiction, the themes represented by the words ancestors, freedom, self-knowledge, communication, love. But one theme is central here in a way that it is not in the rest of Laurence's fiction: the difference between child-awareness and adult-awareness. Each of the stories hinges upon Vanessa making the transition from the first to the second, and as a result the book as a whole explores the nature of that transition. On the one hand, Vanessa clings to the comforting and self-absorbed world of childhood, where her parents are all-knowing, all-powerful, perfect ("perfect" meaning complete as well as without fault). Vanessa's childhood certainty is both present and threatened throughout the book--as when, for instance, in the first story she suddenly notices "intricate lines of tiredness" in her mother's face: "The sight frightened me, for I still needed the conviction that no one except myself ever suffered anything" (19). Later in the same story Vanessa runs downstairs to answer the phone, fleeing the sight of her aunt and her mother comforting each other: "Their sadness was such a new thing, not to my actual sight but to my attention, that I felt it as bodily hurt, like skinning a knee, a sharp stinging pain. But I felt as well an obscure sense of loss. Some comfort had been taken from me, but I did not know what it was" (28). This same sense of loss haunts Vanessa's dreams and imaginings in "To Set Our House in Order," in which her mother is rushed to hospital before her time and gives birth to her brother Roderick; it enters her life and changes it completely when her father dies in the story "A Bird in the House." On the other hand, if Vanessa does not know exactly what comfort has been taken from her, she is determined to find out: until she knows, she is cut off from the real world, powerless: unable to understand, to sympathize, to help, to act. Vanessa the narrator stresses the child's powerlessness to us again and again. When her father describes his own father's loneliness in "To Set Our House in Order," she comments, "It seemed to me that my father was talking oddly. There was a sadness in his voice that I had never heard before, and I longed to say something that would make him feel better, but I could not, because I did not know what was the matter" (54). In "The Mask of the Bear," she realizes that her Aunt Edna's confession of helplessness is not directed at her: "what she had to say could not be spoken to me. I felt chilled by my childhood, unable to touch her because of the freezing burden of my inexperience" (71). The poignancy of "A Bird in the House" is summed up in Vanessa's thought while talking to her father about his war experiences, "I wanted to speak in some way that would be more poignant and comprehending than anything of which my mother could possibly be capable. But I did not know how" (91); Vanessa's account of her last real conversation with her father ends with the words, "But I did not know and so could not tell him" (101). The word *know* becomes the most important one in Vanessa's vocabulary. The child's predicament is summed up in "The Half-Husky"; her dog Nanuk is being tormented by Harvey Shinwell, and the fifteen-year-old Vanessa is capable only of fantasies of revenge: "I still did not know what to do in reality" (152).

Vanessa does, however, come to know herself and her world, as the last line of "The Half-Husky" suggests: Vanessa does not reply when Harvey Shinwell's aunt, who raised him, greets her on the street, "although I knew that this was probably not fair, either" (160). Vanessa comes to her knowledge by an effort of attention: where the child looks at an undifferentiated world surrounding him or her, the adult notices. In "To Set Our House in Order" Vanessa notices her father's collection of travel books, "which I had looked at often enough, but never before with the puzzling compulsion which I felt now, as though I were on the verge of some discovery, something which I had to find out and yet did not want to know" (56). Vanessa says that Piquette Tonnerre "dwelt and moved somewhere within the scope of my vision" (109), but only on one occasion, in the Regal Cafe, does Vanessa actually see her: "I saw her. I really did see her, for the first and only time in all the years we had both lived in the same town" (117). Similarly, Vanessa at the age of fifteen realizes that, when Chris had spilled out his ambitions and fears on their camping expedition, back when she was thirteen, "I had listened to his words, but I had not really heard them, not until now" (142). When Vanessa realizes that Piquette might be "the only one, after all, who had heard the crying of the loons" (120), in that very awareness Vanessa herself hears the loons cry for the first time--now that they are silent. To attend to someone else requires an effort because of what Laurence calls in "Time and the Narrative Voice" "the pain and bewilderment of one's knowledge of other people" (158), but Vanessa consistently demonstrates that she is willing to pay the price exacted for adult knowledge.

Because all of the stories in *A Bird in the House* have essentially the same concerns and techniques, resonances that unite them occur at every point. Much of the book's coherence comes from this sort of resonance. Vanessa confronting the Indian bear mask, Vanessa mourning her father's loss as she watches the photograph of the French girl burn, Vanessa realizing that only Piquette heard the loons cry, Vanessa putting away Chris's saddle: all four moments are parallel in meaning, in function, and in tone. Each recalls and enriches the others. In "Time and the Narrative Voice," Laurence provides an interesting description of this sort of connection among the stories in *A Bird in the House*: "In a novel, one might perhaps imagine the various themes and experiences and the interaction of characters with one another and with themselves as a series of wavy lines, converging, separating, touching, drawing apart, but moving in a *horizontal* direction. The short stories have flow lines which are very different. They move very close together but parallel and in a *vertical* direction" (157).

If we look closely at one moment in the book, we can get a clearer idea of how these resonating parallels tie the stories together. Towards the end of "The Sound of the Singing," Vanessa presents Grandfather Connor acquiescing, astonishingly, to his wife's request that he call back Uncle Dan:

How are the mighty fallen in the midst of the battle. The line slid stealthily into my mind, and I felt a surge of spiteful joy at it. Then I looked again at my grandfather's face, and saw there such a bleak bewilderment that I could feel only shame and sadness. His eyes chanced upon me, and when he spoke it was to me, as though he could not speak directly to any of the adults in that room.

"When he gets too old to look after himself, it'll be me that pays to have him kept in a home. It's not fair, Vanessa. It's not fair."

He was right. It was not fair. Even I could see that. Yet I veered sharply away from his touch, and that was probably not fair, either. I wanted only to be by myself, with no one else around. (*Bird* 39)

This moment extends outward to many others in the book. Perhaps most important is the irony in Grandfather Connor's immediate appeal to Vanessa for understanding and sympathy; right through the collection of stories, as the title "Jericho's Brick Battlements" underlines, Vanessa thinks of her grandfather as her great antagonist, the enemy who prevents her from entering into her own promised land. In the final pages of the book, however, Vanessa finally does extend that understanding and sympathy: she realizes, not only how much she resembles him, but also that she has hardly repudiated him: when she visits the Brick House one last time at the age of forty, her instinctive indignation at its disrepair is the final proof that he is "immortal" (189), that "he proclaimed himself in my veins" (191). The fact that Grandfather Connor resembles the ten-year-old Vanessa is equally ironic: his repeated complaint that "it's not fair" suggests that, morally speaking, he is imprisoned within a perpetual childhood. The adult Vanessa looking back can see that her refusal to respond is "probably not fair, either": the action, the awareness, and the exact words recur, as we have seen, at the end of "The Half-Husky." The book's final verdict on the grandfather comes after his funeral when Vanessa's mother asks, "Edna--were we always unfair to him?" and her aunt replies, "Yes, we were, . . . And he was to us, as well" (189). Furthermore, her grandfather's "bleak bewilderment" at this moment in "The Sound of the Singing" is echoed at the end of "The Mask of the Bear" when Vanessa says, "I imagined that I could see somewhere within that darkness a look which I knew, a lurking bewilderment" (86). Vanessa penetrates many times the mask that conceals the suffering person, perhaps most notably when Piquette's "defiant face, momentarily, became unguarded and unmasked" (117) as she spoke of her intended marriage. Again, Grandfather Connor's collapse in "The Sound of the Singing" anticipates his grief-stricken collapse in "The Mask of the Bear" and his rout at the hand of Aunt Edna's suitor Wes Grigg in "Jericho's Brick Battlements." Vanessa's collapse in this passage from triumphant joy to "shame and sadness"--an instinctive and involuntary sympathy--echoes her grandfather's, once again underlining the likeness between the two, and anticipates several collapses from ferocious combat to puzzled submission on Vanessa's part. In fact, Vanessa's movement from joy to shame and sadness epitomizes the whole movement of the book from single-minded certainty to complex, troubling, sympathetic awareness. Simple oppositions between people collapse into a common identity. All of Vanessa's discoveries will amount to one, that she can never "be by myself, with no one else around." There is a fine symbolism in the fact that Vanessa's move into independence, her departure for university, is paid for by money collected by her mother from the members of her family, with the largest amount coming from her grandfather--even though Vanessa's first reaction to this scheme is one worthy of the old man himself, "Him? . . . I'm not taking a nickel of his money" (187).

As we have seen, Laurence speaks in "Time and the Narrative Voice" not only of parallel lines, but of parallel lines which move together in a single (vertical) direction; it is for this reason that, as she says in "Time and the Narrative Voice," "the net effect [of *A Bird in the House*] is not unlike that of a novel" (155). In short, the stories are not only connected with each other, but connected into a single, progressive, cumulative story. Vanessa changes year by year: when, at the age of eleven in "Horses of the Night," she tells her cousin Chris, now a vacuum-cleaner salesman, "I bet you'll sell a thousand," she realizes, "Two years ago, this statement would have seemed self-evident, unquestionable. Yet now, when I had spoken, I knew that I did not believe it" (133). Vanessa gets older as we advance from one story to the next, and the changes in her in one story carry over into the subsequent stories. For instance, Vanessa responds so intensely to Piquette Tonnerre's death and the disappearance of the loons from Diamond Lake in "The Loons" because both events are associated in her mind with her loss of her father, an event whose full impact upon her we have come to understand in the previous story, "A Bird in the House." Sherrill Grace observes, "Laurence has the best of both worlds--the formal purity of the story plus the scope and sense of movement and growth that are possible in the novel" (332).

Much of our sense of the book's coherence derives from this ongoing, deepening, novel-like progression. Without it, the resonating parallels within the stories would be repetitive: Laurence would have told the same story eight times. In fact, one reviewer in 1970, "J. P." in *The Malahat Review* said, without particularizing: "her stories . . . are organized according to precisely the same principle, not to say formula, so that to have read one of them is virtually . . . to have read them all" (114). For most readers, however, the novel-like qualities of *A Bird in the House* have been apparent: it is quite common to come across references to it as a novel or to the *five* Manawaka novels (for example, Wiebe 17), and the annual *MLA Bibliography* lists entries on the book under the heading, "*Novel / A Bird in the House* (1970)."

A Bird in the House is not actually a novel. In *Dance on the Earth*, her posthumous memoir, she says that her one major disagreement with her editor of many years at Knopf, Judith Jones, occurred when the latter tried to persuade her to make the collection of stories into a novel, since novels sell much better than story collections; Laurence felt, "I would rather not have the book published at all than make the stories into a novel" (198). Yet the notion that the book is a novel is understandable. The first and last stories especially straddle the border separating the short story and novel forms. These two stories are both centered upon the book's dominant figure, Grandfather Connor, and upon the Brick House, his dwelling-place-cum-monument; each is longer by several pages than the other stories in the volume; the one serves as a rich exposition, and the other as a ringing conclusion, to the book as a whole. In fact, we are twenty-seven pages into the thirty-two page "The Sound of the Singing" before the events that make this Sunday dinner distinctive occur, and conversely, "Jericho's Brick Battlements" has, as I read it, four different paragraphs that might well serve as the book's finale. The first story contains a page of dialogue (29-30) between Vanessa and her Aunt Edna which suggests the latter's fear of independence--a fear that is of no importance in this story, but which will become central in "The Mask of the Bear" and "Jericho's Brick Battlements." Similarly, the final story, like the last chapter of a traditional novel, reintroduces all the major characters and sketches their fates: Uncle Dan reappears in the paragraph devoted to the impoverished funeral he received and the flamboyant funeral he deserved (188); Grandmother MacLeod is present in the Limoges china that Grandfather Connor dismisses to the basement, but which Vanessa's mother sells to help pay the cost of sending Vanessa to university. Both stories, in short, exist more to serve the volume as a whole than as separate and separable stories. It is a striking fact that although four of the stories in *A Bird in the House* have frequently been anthologized--"To Set Our House in Order," "A Bird in the House," "The Loons," and "Horses of the Night"--these two framing stories have never been reprinted; "Jericho's Brick Battlements," in fact, is the one story of the eight that only appeared in print as part of *A Bird in the House*.

One way of demonstrating this novel-like progression within the stories--and the coherence that results from it--is to note the pivotal force of the fourth and title story, "A Bird in the House." At the simplest level, Vanessa's life is completely different once her father dies. She is now alone and attuned to suffering as she had not been before. Her relationship to Manawaka becomes simplified and polarized when she moves into the Brick House, since the MacLeod family no longer exists in Manawaka. The starkness of her predicament is symbolized in the central scene in which she flails out after her father's death at Noreen, the hired girl. Vanessa hits Noreen "as though she were a prison all around me and I was battling to get out" (105). The symbolism is rich and suggestive. The prison is at least three things: the religious faith that Noreen represents for Vanessa, the fact of death (her father's and her own) that Vanessa is confronting, and her own ignorance and powerlessness. Arnold Davidson argues that Vanessa rebels here against being caged with "her own childhood . . . her innocence and experience" (95). Whatever exactly the prison is, however, one thing is clear: Vanessa will not be like her pious Grandmother Connor, who, emblematized by her pet canary, accepted her cage, nor like her father, the impostor-warrior, who capitulated out of guilt and duty. From this point on, Vanessa is determined to struggle against her captivity with all her might. Whatever faith she has from here on will be of her own creation. At this stage, however, Vanessa is "fighting blindly, my eyes tightly closed" (105); like the sparrow, she does not understand what she is fighting against and why, and so she collapses once again in unwilling submission.

Everything is different after the fourth story in several other ways. Whereas each of the first three stories builds to moments of recognition in which Vanessa realizes her essential difference from those around her and commits herself to being unlike them, the fourth story is the first one which ends with Vanessa realizing that she and the central figure are alike. Once Vanessa can see that she and her father shared the same predicament, she can go from disavowing Grandfather Connor or Grandmother MacLeod to acknowledging, as she does at the end of the book, that her grandfather lives on in her, that in an important sense she *is* her grandfather. In the end, Vanessa will understand that all the members of her family, including her grandfather, are equally trapped within its protective structure, and the realization that her father was, as she is, a bird in the house is an important step towards this awareness of a common identity. One of the book's climactic moments epitomizes Vanessa's volume-long change of attitude. In the final story, Vanessa, aged twenty, remembers on the day of her grandfather's funeral how when she was twelve, after her father's death, she sat in her grandfather's car remembering how she had sat beside him while he drove through town in the car when she was four. The twelve-year-old Vanessa had been unsettled to recall how happy she had been as a small child--in the memory, "I was gazing with love and glory at my giant grandfather as he drove his valiant chariot through all the streets of this world" (166)--and had simply removed herself from her grandfather's car, deciding that the loft was a better place for writing her stories. But the twenty-year-old Vanessa can see "what the car might have meant to him, to the boy who walked the hundred miles from Winnipeg to Manawaka with hardly a cent in his pockets" (190). From being a giant that the child can love and worship, the grandfather has become a boy that Vanessa, now adult, can understand by an effort of sympathetic imagination. This "memory of a memory" (190) epitomizes not only, as Sherrill Grace has shown (331), the book's narrative technique of creative remembrance, but also its theme.

The story "A Bird in the House" marks a turning point in many ways, then. Vanessa's new and adult capacities are reflected in the subject matter of the fifth, sixth, and seventh stories, in which Vanessa's attention turns outward from her immediate family to Piquette, who lives outside Manawaka in several senses, to the loner Chris, and to Harvey Shinwell, the dead-end drop-out. Furthermore, each of these three central figures is radically alone and comes from a house that is not a home; through Vanessa's eyes, we see each of these nonhomes in sordid detail, sharing her unstated shock at the implicit contrast between them and the two complacent and prosperous homes that are all she has known (and we have seen) up to this point. Each of these solitaries escapes from Manawaka, but only into an even greater state of unfreedom: into death, into madness, into prison. Not only, then, is the setting greatly expanded in these stories, as Vanessa turns her eyes on the world beyond the family circle, but, by implication, she discovers that to have a stifling home and a threatened future is better than being without either. Vanessa begins to grasp that her family has granted her some everyday decencies--privacy, dignity, respect and self-respect, conversation, comfort--and that she has taken them for granted. Vanessa finds that her family has given her "a place to stand on"-- a phrase that Margaret Laurence applied in an interview to Grandfather Connor (Thomas 102), citing the two lines from the poem "Roblin Mills" (2) by Al Purdy that provided her with the epigraph to her last novel, *The Diviners* of which the last line is "and left a place to stand on" (57). Vanessa's new capacities and her new relationship with her family are reflected in a simple plot device: in each of the first three stories Vanessa receives some information necessary to her final realization by *overhearing* adults talk, whereas the facts Vanessa needs to know about Piquette, Chris, and Harvey Shinwell are told to her directly and in answer to her own questions by her mother.

Perhaps the primary source of this cumulative coherence in the progression of stories is Laurence's handling of time, and here again the fourth story serves as the hinge on which the book as a whole turns. It is the first story to show us Vanessa, the protagonist, as more than a child: the glimpse of the adult Vanessa at the end of the previous story, "The Mask of the Bear," can be seen, to use an analogy from music, as a brief anticipation of this central theme. Beginning with the fourth story, however, as a glance at my chart will show, the stories end with Vanessa at or about the age of eighteen: the age at which she reaches her majority and leaves Manawaka for university (see Baum 202). Even more importantly, however, the fourth story is the first story that treats a relatively long expanse of time. The first story takes place within two hours or so at dinnertime one Sunday; the second story spans two or three weeks during August of the year Vanessa's brother is born; the third story, apart from its anticipatory final paragraph, covers two months. The fourth story, however, spans five years, and from this point on the stories range backward and forward through increasingly large sweeps of time, as the chart indicates. In fact, time becomes increasingly prominent after the fourth story: Vanessa simply gets older in each story up to that point, but, beginning with "The Loons," the stories go back to events *before* those in the fourth story. Laurence says that Vanessa's growth can be conceived of as a single vertical line--and during the last half of the book we go down as well as up that line. "The Half-Husky," which is arguably the slightest story in the book, breaks this regular progression to a degree, as the chart indicates, but the concluding story is the culminating one in its treatment of time, as in so many other ways, since it contains virtually the whole of Vanessa's life: the thirty-six years that connect the small child who rode in her grandfather's car and the forty-year-old woman who revisits his house at the story's end. Furthermore, there is a similar increase in the number of days dramatized in each story: whereas the first story covers only one day, the last story contains fourteen different days on which significant events happen. And, again, the fourth story is notable as the first one to contain a relatively large number of specific days: nine.

These time-patterns in *A Bird in the House* illustrate the perfect matching of form and theme that I alluded to at the start of this essay. The changes in structure as we move from one story to the next *enact* the changes in Vanessa's awareness that Laurence has made her central theme. The stories cover more and more separate episodes because for Vanessa to understand her experience she must learn to abstract herself from absorption in the immediate moment, to stand outside herself and see her situation from the outside, to compare and connect an increasing number of increasingly various separate moments. She must learn to *comprehend* her life, both in the root sense of "hold together" and in the figurative sense of "understand." To be an adult is to comprehend. "To Set Our House in Order" ends with Vanessa thinking, "I could not really comprehend these things, but I sensed their strangeness, their disarray" (61). I have already cited Vanessa's frustration in the story "A Bird in the House" at her inability to speak to her father in a "poignant and comprehending" way (91); similarly, the thirteen-year-old Vanessa in "Horses of the Night" feels humiliated by her inability to "reply as I would have wanted, comprehendingly" (141), to Chris's outpouring. The adult Vanessa at the book's end can, however, set her house in order: she reflects of her grandfather, "Perhaps he even was immortal, in ways which it would take me half a lifetime to comprehend" (189).

Much of the book's coherence, then, comes from this progression: as Vanessa grows up, she increasingly distances herself from the immediate moment and learns to comprehend the patterns of cause and effect that underlie and explain each single moment. Paradoxically, Vanessa has both lost her family and gained it during this process. On the one hand, as we have seen, she has lost a comforting certainty: the twenty-year-old Vanessa reflects that "in the ancient days" her grandfather "seemed as large and admirable as God" (190); on the other hand, as the end of the story "A Bird in the House" suggests, Vanessa's discovery that she and her closest kin are genuinely akin brings them back to life, makes them immortal for her. Vanessa the character reaches this state of awareness by exercising her sympathetic imagination; Vanessa the narrator--and behind her, Margaret Laurence--has given Vanessa's world lasting life by an exercise of creative imagination. And here, again, form and theme interpenetrate: a work of fiction, just because it presents the coherent patterns found within the confusing facts of a great many separate lives, allows the author and her readers to understand one another, to become one another, in the same way that Vanessa comes to comprehend the people around her. As Jon Kertzer points out, this coherence in *A Bird in the House* is in the end a fictional convention, an ideal of full and complete comprehension--and yet one that is necessary: "We cannot abide the chaos of an incomprehensible life, which is maddening. Therefore we try to understand and to improve our understanding. Vanessa's stories formalize this essential human need, and bring its inner workings to our attention" (34).

No work of non-fiction autobiography, no matter how factually accurate, could convey this kind of truth. Laurence admitted frequently in interviews, in essays, and in her memoir that *A Bird in the House* is "loosely based on my family and childhood" (*Dance* 209), "the only semi-autobiographical fiction I have ever written" (Place 5). For instance, as *Dance on the Earth* explains, her own father died when she was nine (56), and as a result she and her much younger brother moved into the big brick house of her domineering maternal grandfather, John Simpson (63-70). Again, in the memoir a real life cousin who was a dreamer and misfit did go mad in the army like Chris of "Horses of the Night" (71-72, 257-62); the seventeen-year-old Margaret did have as her first love an Air Force man who was ten years older than her, literary in his tastes, and, unknown to Margaret, married (85-88), just as Vanessa does in "Jericho's Brick Battlements." Hundreds of incidents and details from *A Bird in the House* have a real life source: for example, the kitchens of both Grandfather Simpson's actual house and Grandfather Connor's fictitious one are dominated by a big wood-stove, with "McClary's Range" in silver handwriting across the warming oven on top (*Dance* 23; *Bird* 20). And anyone who visits the Simpson house, now preserved in Laurence's native Neepawa, Manitoba, as the Margaret Laurence House, will find upstairs the very same air vent that served Vanessa as a "listening post" (77), allowing someone upstairs to overhear what is said in the kitchen below. Yet Margaret Laurence's own experience is opaque, fragmented, incoherent compared to that of Vanessa: Grandfather Simpson in the memoir, for instance, is a shadowy and inexplicable figure, unlike Grandfather Connor; the real-life model for Chris whom Laurence describes in the memoir (71-72) and makes the subject of an appended poem, "For Lorne (1976)," remains enigmatic, as Chris does not. Laurence says in "Time and the Narrative Voice":

the character is one of the writer's voices and selves, and fiction writers tend to have a mental trunk full of these--in writers, this quality is known as richness of imagination; in certain inmates of mental hospitals it has other names, the only significant difference being that writers are creating their private worlds with the ultimate hope of throwing open the doors to other humans. (156)

Unlike the private world of Vanessa's cousin Chris, the imaginary world in Laurence's book is one that many people can walk into and inhabit. My point has been that it is largely its coherence that makes *A Bird in the House* such a welcoming edifice.

NOTE

1. Patricia Morley discusses the motif of travel in *A Bird in the House* and relates it to "the dominant metaphor of Laurence's work, of journeying in search of freedom and joy" (*Margaret Laurence* 113). See *Margaret Laurence* (Boston: G. K. Hall, 1981); reprint, with an Afterword, *Margaret Laurence: The Long Journey Home* (Montreal: McGill-Queen's University Press, 1991), and her earlier essay, "The Long Trek Home: Margaret Laurence's Stories," *Journal of Canadian Studies* 11.4 (Fall 1976): 19-26.

WORKS CITED

Baum, Rosalie Murphy. "Artist and Woman: Young Lives in Laurence and Munro." *North*

Dakota Quarterly 52.3 (Summer 1984): 196-211; 202.

J. P. Rev. of *A Bird in the House*, by Margaret Laurence. *The Malahat Review* 15.2 (July 1970): 113-14.

Rev. of *A Bird in the House*. *Choice* 7 (December 1970): 1374.

Davidson, Arnold. "Cages and Escapes in Margaret Laurence's *A Bird In the House.*" *University of Windsor Review* 16.1 (Fall-Winter 1981): 92-101; 95.

French, William. "Coming of Age in Manawaka," review of *A Bird in the House*, by Margaret Laurence. *Toronto Globe and Mail* 14 March 1970: *Magazine* 15.

Gibbs, Robert. Introduction to *A Bird in the House*, by Margaret Laurence. Toronto: McClelland and Stewart, New Canadian Library, (1970) 1974, i-vi.

Grace, Sherrill. "Crossing Jordan: Time and Memory in the Fiction of Margaret Laurence." *World Literature Written in English* 16 (1977): 328-39.

Hehner, Barbara. "River of Now and Then: Margaret Laurence's Narratives," *Canadian Literature* 74 (Autumn 1977): 40-47.

Kreisel, Henry. "A Familiar Landscape," review of *A Bird in the House*, by Margaret Laurence. *The Tamarack Review* 55 (1970): 91-92, 94.

Kertzer, Jon. *"That House in Manawaka": Margaret Laurence's "A Bird in the House."* Canadian Fiction Studies. Toronto: Educational Canadian Works (ECW) Press, 1992.

Laurence, Margaret. *A Bird in the House*. Afterword by Isabel Huggan. Toronto: McClelland and Stewart, New Canadian Library, (1970, 1989, 1991) 1994; Chicago: University of Chicago Press, 1993.

___. *Dance on the Earth: A Memoir*. Toronto: McClelland and Stewart, 1989.

___. *The Diviners*. Toronto: McClelland and Stewart, (1974, 1988) 1993.

___. "A Place to Stand On." *Mosaic* (April 1970); reprint, *A Place to Stand On: Essays By and About Margaret Laurence*. Ed. George Woodcock. Edmonton: NeWest Press, 1983, 15-19; reprint, *Heart of a Stranger*. Toronto: McClelland and Stewart, (1976) 1988.

___. "Time and the Narrative Voice." *The Narrative Voice*. Ed. John Metcalf. Toronto: McGraw-Hill Ryerson, 1972, 126-30; reprint, *A Place to Stand On: Essays By and About Margaret Laurence*. Ed. George Woodcock. Edmonton: NeWest Press, 1983, 155-59.

Morley, Patricia. *Margaret Laurence*. Boston: G. K. Hall, 1981; reprint, with an Afterword, *Margaret Laurence: The Long Journey Home*. Montreal: McGill-Queen's University Press, 1991.

Purdy, Al. "Roblin Mills" (2). *Al Purdy. Being Alive: Poems 1958-78*. Toronto: McClelland and Stewart, 1978, 57.

Thomas, Clara. *The Manawaka World of Margaret Laurence*. Toronto: McClelland and Stewart, 1976, 102.

___. "A Conversation About Literature: An Interview with Margaret Laurence and Irving Layton." *Journal of Canadian Fiction* 1.1 (Winter 1972): 65-69.

Thompson, Kent. Rev. of *A Bird in the House*, by Margaret Laurence. *The Fiddlehead* 84 (March-April 1970): 108-11; reprint, *A Place to Stand On*. Ed. George Woodcock. Edmonton: NeWest Press, 1983, 232-35.

Wiebe, Rudy. "Jean Margaret Wemyss Laurence, 1926-1987." *Canadian Women's Studies* 8.3 (Fall 1987): 17; his memorial tribute: "Margaret Laurence did more than publish the five Manawaka novels in ten years."

Woodcock, George, ed. *A Place to Stand On: Essays By and About Margaret Laurence*. Western Canadian Literary Documents 4. Edmonton: NeWest, 1983.

Chapter 8

Dividing *The Diviners*
Ken McLean

The general critical consensus is that in her last novel, *The Diviners*, Margaret Laurence portrays the traditional development of a protagonist from early uncertainty and insecurity to mature certainty and acceptance.[1] Helen Buss's recent summary is representative: "Laurence has structured her novel to show a movement toward personal, artistic, and spiritual wholeness that has involved a journey from loss, through shame, acceptance and growth, to transcendence" (*Mother* 75). While it cannot be denied that there are numerous centripetal impulses in the novel that propel it to such a totalized reading, I contend that there are also generally unacknowledged centrifugal tendencies which work against such a harmonizing, that dialogize any such certainty, and make of *The Diviners* a genuinely writerly text. An examination of Morag's voice and memories, and of the mythic tales embedded in the text, illustrates these decentering forces at work.

Laurence encodes the dialogizing impulses metaphorically in the first sentence of the novel: "The river flowed both ways" (11NCL, 3UC). This image introduces a protagonist whose salient characteristic is her uncertainty; she repeatedly, in the opening section of the novel, states, then qualifies, and retracts, in a rhythm of subversion, of indeterminacy. So Pique is "Not dry behind the ears. Yes, she was, though" (11NCL, 4UC); Pique would not leave again, "Morag was pretty sure [she] wouldn't. Not sure enough, probably" (12NCL, 4UC). Such examples could be multiplied. By the end of the first section, we've come to know a protagonist who is uncertain on all levels, emotional, perceptual, factual, even textual. For, as many commentators have noted, the voice of the third-person narrator is so closely interwoven with that of Morag that we experience the narration as if it were in the first person, or as if Morag were recounting her story in the third person, as she does in her "Memorybank Movies." Hence to destabilize Morag's certainty is to effectively destabilize that of the third-person narrator as well. Laurence further problematizes the status of her narrative by asserting that "of course the novel she [Morag] is writing is *The Diviners*" (Fabre, Interview 205).[2] If this is so, what is the status of the passages dealing with the present? If they are, indeed, part of Morag's own novel, is she then both Morag the character and Morag as author of Morag? Such concerns establish the question of *The Diviners*' difference from itself.

The first page of the novel also introduces the recurrent motif of a scene of reading, a device used throughout the novel to destabilize the status of both memory and myth. Laurence (Morag?) embeds the text of Pique's letter in her narrative and explicitly reads it as the language of another: "Well, you had to give the girl some marks for style of writing" (11NCL, 3UC). Such dialogized reading is then applied to the first of Morag's memories, the six "snapshots" which she explicitly reads, or better, misreads. For she comments of her reading of the second photograph: "All this is crazy, of course, and quite untrue . . . or maybe true and maybe not. I am remembering myself composing this interpretation" (16NCL, 7UC). Similarly, of the last of these readings she remarks, "I can't trust it completely, either, partly because I recognize anomalies in it, ways of expressing the remembering, ways which aren't those of a five-year-old" (21NCL, 11UC), again explicitly dialogizing her own reading. Such reflections replicate thematically the problematized status of the narrative as a whole.

Laurence often renders similarly problematic the authority of the "Memorybank Movies," the memory-texts that make up the main body of the novel. The often cartoon-like captions that serve as the titles of these embedded texts tend to undermine their seriousness by defamiliarization, by drawing attention to them as fictional artifice. The "lateral dance" the reader executes as he moves between title and text intensifies the centrifugal forces.

The accepted view of the mythic tales that Laurence embeds in *The Diviners* is that they contribute significantly to Morag's maturation; they provide her with a past she can take pride in, enabling her to withstand the oppression of Manawaka society; and they inspire her to write her own fiction. Clearly the tales do perform these functions. But it also needs to be noted that they are radically textualized by their conflicting versions of the past and by the highly subjective, and variable, nature of their validity.

Two major sets of mythic tales are in the novel, Christie's tales of Morag's supposed ancestor Piper Gunn and Jules's tales of his own ancestor Rider Tonnerre, both of which draw on historical materials. Laurence chooses to utilize histories that she believed to have been marginalized, those of the Scots crofters and the Métis, in order to undermine the dominant WASP (white Anglo-Saxon Protestant) discourse of Canadian history. Such privileging of the primitive over Western imperialist cultures is, of course, reflected in Laurence's African fiction as well. The conflict between the dominant imperialist discourse and that of the marginalized Scots-Métis is also encoded in the text in Laurence's treatment of Morag's husband, Brooke Skelton, who is established as an imperialist by his Indian childhood, by this notion of Canada as a "colony" (de Papp Carrington 157), and by his attempt to suppress Morag's past.[3] Significantly, that when Morag finally rejects Brooke, she does so by denouncing him in Christie's language ("by judas priest and all the sodden saints in fucking Beulah land" 277NCL, 210UC), and by making love to Jules. But Laurence's attitude to the "official" imperialist discourse is more indeterminate than this might suggest. For she also uses this discourse to problematize Christie's tales; "Oh Christie! They didn't. We took it in History" (145NCL, 106UC) Morag interjects; and Christie confesses, "Maybe the story didn't go quite like I said" (146NCL, 107UC). Similarly, in his "Tale of the Battle of Bourlon Wood" Christie remarks: "[I]t was like the book [*The 60th Canadian Field Artillery Battery Book*] says, but it wasn't like that also. That is the strangeness" (101NCL, 73UC).

"Christie's First Tale of Piper Gunn" (58-60NCL, 40-42UC), which tells of the Highland Clearances and of how Piper Gunn inspired his fellow Sutherland crofters to emigrate to Manitoba's Red River, is essentially historical, though his portrait of the Countess of Sutherland is somewhat distorted (see Linklater 334-36 and Mitchison 377-78). Morag does validate this tale by creating, in response to it, "Morag's Tale of Piper Gunn's Woman" (60NCL, 42UC), the language of which is a hybrid of her own and Christie's. The shift to "Piper Gunn's Woman" might appear to be a feminist critique of the male heroism of Christie's tale; but, on the other hand, the heroine is designated "Piper Gunn's Woman," or "Of piper," to employ the rhetoric of Margaret Atwood's *The Handmaid's Tale* (published later in 1985).

"Christie's Tale of Piper Gunn and the Long March" (94-97NCL, 68-71UC), the second story he recounts, tells of the voyage of the Sutherlanders to "the wrong place" on Hudson's Bay, and of how Piper Gunn led them on a "long march" of "maybe a thousand or so miles . . . to the place where all the supplies was," whence they could take the flatbottomed boats to Red River (96NCL, 69UC). Once again Christie's account is historically accurate in its essentials (see W. L. Morton 49-50 and MacEwan 74-79). After hearing this tale, Morag again writes her own, a story of one "Clowny Macpherson," "a guy who was one of Piper Gunn's men" (98NCL, 70UC). The "Macpherson" she picks up from Christie's reading of James Macpherson's *Ossian* (72-75NCL, 51-53UC); but the name "Clowny" tends to undermine the authenticity of the tale. Much later in the novel, Morag comments on this second tale in a letter she writes to her friend Ella:

Odd--the tales Christie used to tell of Piper Gunn and the Sutherlanders. . . . Christie always said they walked about a thousand miles--it was about a hundred and fifty, in fact, but you know, he was right; it must've felt like a thousand. The man who led them on that march, and on the trip by water to Red River, was young Archie Macdonald, but in my mind the piper who played them on will always be that giant of a man, Piper Gunn, who probably never lived in so-called real life but who lives forever. Christie knew things about inner truths that I am only just beginning to understand. (443NCL, 342UC)

In affirming the "inner" truths of Christie's tale, Morag's remarks here tend to problematize the historical validity of the tale. But this textualizing itself, however, is rendered uncannily indeterminate, not only in that a piper *did* lead the march (MacEwan 78), but in that this piper was in fact named Robert Gunn (Bryce 323).[4] Since Laurence herself apparently did not know this when she wrote the novel, it seems that in this case Christie knew more about "outer" as well as "inner" truths than even she suspected.⁵ In fact, she later referred to this as "an element of magic about the novel" (*Dance on the Earth* 200).

The third and final tale that Christie tells of Piper Gunn is "Piper Gunn and the Rebels" (143-46NCL, 105-107UC), which concerns the role of Piper Gunn and the Sutherland settlers in the Red River Rebellion of 1869-1870; according to Christie, the Sutherlanders recaptured Fort Garry from Riel and the Métis "before even a smell of an army" from "Down East" got there (145NCL, 106UC). Here he is clearly falsifying history (see W. L. Morton 144), as Morag immediately objects: "They didn't. We took it in History" (145NCL, 106UC). A comment by Laurence in "Road From the Isles," an essay written years earlier, also suggests that she sees Christie's portrayal of Piper Gunn as a fabrication: those who experienced the Highland Clearances were "never able to produce strong leaders from among their ranks" (*Heart* 148). The occasion of the telling of Christie's third tale further undermines its validity. Morag has just discovered her sexuality for the first time, and, unable to confront the responsibility and danger this means, she asks Christie to tell her one of his tales, for "the times when she was a kid and Christie would tell those stories, everything used to seem all right then" (143NCL, 105UC). Here she is hoping to use myth to escape adult reality.

Moreover, this third tale is contextualized by Jules's second tale, "Skinner's Tale of Rider Tonnerre and the Prophet" (161-62NCL, 118-19UC), which presents quite a different version of the same events. In Jules's version, Louis Riel, the "Prophet," a leader with "the power" and "the vision," is the hero, not Piper Gunn. Christie and Jules differ even as to the physical appearance of Riel; to Christie, he was a "short little man" (144NCL, 106UC), to Jules, "a very tall guy" (162NCL, 119UC). On the whole, Jules's version is more historically accurate than Christie's (see Jackson 109). Despite Laurence's devaluing of historical accuracy in the case of Christie's second tale, here, then, she uses precisely such historical accuracy as a measurement of validity.

Jules's first tale, "Skinner's Tale of Lazarus's Tale of Rider Tonnerre" (159-61NCL, 117-18UC) concerns an earlier clash between the Métis and the English, the Seven Oaks Massacre of 1817. In the same letter in which she tells Ella of her realization about Christie's tales, Morag identifies Rider's titles and gun in this tale as being "borrowed" from Gabriel Dumont (and see Woodcock, *Dumont* 52) and his horse as deriving "from a Cree legend" (444NCL, 341UC), thereby acknowledging that Jules's tales, too, are not entirely historically accurate. She adds though, that "she likes the thought of history and fiction interweaving" thus (444NCL, 341UC), a sentiment Laurence would clearly echo. Jules's third tale, "Skinner's Tale of Old Jules and the War Out West" (162NCL, 119-20UC), which records the climactic Métis defeat at the Battle of Batoche in the Northwest Rebellion of 1885, is, however, historically accurate in all its details (Desmond Morton 89-92 and Woodcock, *Dumont* 220-21).

Laurence's attitude to the historicity of Christie's and Jules's tales is basically in line with her problematizing of what she saw as the dominant historical discourse. For Laurence and her protagonist the past is not a scientifically verifiable fixed entity. Morag recognizes that "memories" may be "invented" (18NCL, 89UC), the past "embroidered later on" (26NCL, 15UC), and that "everyone is constantly changing their own past, recalling it, revising it" (70NCL, 49UC), with the result that "there's no one version [of the past]. There just isn't" (373NCL, 287UC). These mythic tales may articulate the essential "truth" which the "facts" of history may distort. On the other hand, even here there is some uncertainty. For Christie's third tale actually falsifies history, whereas the first two simply "embroider" it, and it is this third tale which meets with the most skeptical response from Morag, and which is dialogized by one of Jules's tales. So historical accuracy both does and does not matter. Jules's tales are more historically accurate than Christie's, yet the myths they purvey are not those Morag can adopt. Given this element of undecidability in her valorization of myth and history, Morag's "crucial" revelation in Scotland (crucial, that is, from a centralizing reading of the novel) that "the myths are my reality" (415NCL, 319UC) is now seen to have been radically problematized. Which myths? What reality?

Christie does offer Morag another potential mythic hero, one much closer to home, her father, Colin Gunn, in his "Tale of the Battle of Bourlon Wood" (101-103NCL, 73-75UC). Christie prefaces this tale by telling Morag that "your dad saved my life that one time, then" (101NCL, 72UC), and the tale fills in the dramatic details. So perhaps this is a mythic "reality" Morag can depend on. But no: much later, Prin tells Morag, "That Colin. . . . He never done that for my Christie. Saved him, like. Or maybe he done it, I dunno. . . . He would cry, and Christie would hold him" (223-24NCL, 167UC). Morag reflects: "Christie's tale of Gunner Gunn and the Great War. How Colin saved Christie. . . . It hadn't happened that way, then, or probably not" (224NCL, 167UC). So this myth, too, is rendered undecidable; appropriately, as Morag learns, "the chieftainship of Clan Gunn is undetermined at the present time" (58NCL, 40UC).

Christie, in fact, cannot determine the truth about even himself. On one occasion, when Prin is bemoaning her fate, he rebukes her in his characteristic voice: "Goddammit, you make your own choices in this world!" (99NCL, 71UC); but then "his voice drops," and he admits "Although that's not the truth of it, neither. It's all true and not true. Isn't that a bugger now?" (99NCL, 71UC). Then, in an exchange that neatly encapsulates the indeterminacy of the novel, Prin remarks, "I don't understand you Christie Logan," and he replies, "You're not the only one. I don't understand myself" (99NCL, 71UC).[6]

Another mythic set enters the novel in the form of Laurence's intertextualizing of the books of Catharine Parr Traill, who embodies the tradition of the successful upper middle-class British settlers, and is, for Morag, "the epitome of the benign pioneer matriarch" (Thomas, Myth 109). Not only does Morag engage in a dialectic with Traill, but Laurence also dialogizes Traill's voice by juxtaposing to it a rival myth of failure, arising out of Morag's inner mythmaking about the earliest inhabitants of her cabin at McConnell's Landing, the Coopers. Just before the first "C.P.T." (Catharine Parr Traill) dialogue (108NCL, 79UC), Morag reflects that the grandsons of the original settler had "finally giv[en] up, selling out and moving to some town or other" (105NCL, 76UC); she then thinks of the hard life these settlers must have led and fantasizes about the first Mrs. Cooper:

It's the full of the moon, George--Mrs. Cooper always howls like this at such a time--nothing to worry about--she'll be right as rain come the morning--c'mon there, Sarah, quit crouching in the corner and stop baring your fangs like that--George and me's hungry and would appreciate a spot of grub. (107NCL, 77UC)

In the next reference to Sarah Cooper, which immediately precedes the second C.P.T. dialogue, Morag ponders the fact that weeds now flourish where Sarah once started a vegetable garden (186NCL, 138UC). In the binary opposition set up by this rival myth, then, Laurence exposes the dark underside of the C.P.T. pioneering myth, suggesting the horror of those who cracked under the strain.

Another somewhat oblique but nevertheless fascinating form of intertextualizing in the novel may be that between Morag's novels and Laurence's own earlier Manawaka novels. Morag's third novel, *Jonah*, is described as "the story of an old man . . . who is fairly disreputable" and his relationship to his daughter, "who resents his not being a reputable character" (390NCL, 299-300UC). Jonah, we learn, "owns a gilnetter" and fishes for salmon. Laurence's first Manawaka novel, *The Stone Angel*, bears a resemblance to *Jonah* in that it too treats a "disreputable" older person and her relationship to her children. The name "Jonah" and Jonah's fishing echo the sea imagery prevalent in *The Stone Angel*, particularly in Hagar's visit to the old fish cannery. Morag's first novel, *Spear of Innocence*, tells of a young woman who leaves her small town for the city. Rachel, the protagonist of Laurence's second Manawaka novel, *A Jest of God*, does this too; in fact the phrase "Spear of Innocence" describes Rachel's condition quite well. Moreover, a film option is taken out on *Spear* (437NCL, 336UC), as one was on *Jest*. Morag's third book is a collection of short stories entitled *Presences* (384NCL, 295UC). This is all we are told about this book, but it may well be based on Morag's recollections of Christie, for one of the memorybank movies about him is entitled "Christie's Presence and Presents" (98NCL, 71UC). If so, there could be a parallel between this volume and Laurence's volume of Manawaka stories, *A Bird in the House*, for it too is about the author's own immediate family. This possible intertextualizing does not work to subvert the text; here, rather, the indeterminacy lies in the speculative nature of these parallels.[7]

The accepted centripetal reading of *The Diviners* might appear, at first, to get some support from the title concept of "divining" in its many manifestations throughout the novel. Divining, the seeking for "hidden" water, is presented as a metaphor for the logocentric quest for hidden "truths." Just as Royland divines for water, Christie and Jules "divine" in their tales, Christie in his garbage "telling," and Morag in her writing. Christie's garbage telling is, of course, another inscription of a scene of reading; and here, too, an inconsistency can be discovered. Christie tells the garbage to expose the hidden facts of the lives of the bourgeois townsfolk, and this revelation is privileged over their myths of respectability and piety. Yet for the Scots crofters and the Métis, myths rather than facts, are privileged.

Moreover, the diviner holds a forked wand. For even as Morag establishes the parallel between herself and Royland, she problematizes it: "He was divining for water. What in hell was she divining for?" (115NCL, 83UC). At the end of the novel, Morag reiterates the divining-writing parallel, but this time in the context of Royland's losing, or giving up, the gift of divining. There is here the implication that Morag too will do so, though this is not spelled out. Can this really be seen as a fitting resolution in a centripetal reading?

Rather, the reader is invited to be a "diviner" too, as, in the final words of the novel, Morag "set[s] down her title" (477NCL, 370UC). The title is *a posteriori* to the text, as it also precedes it. But then this final title is not actually "set down"--there is instead the absence, the gap, that invites interpretation, divining. Yet again, perhaps *this* is not the end of the novel; the text continues with a section entitled "Album," which contains the songs referred to earlier in the novel. Even the location of the ending is indeterminate.

An appropriate ending is, however, inscribed in the second to last paragraph of the novel proper, in a recurrence of the opening river metaphor; here the description of the river implicitly encodes the illusoriness of resolution: whereas "near shore, in the shallows, the water was clear, . . . only slightly further out, the water deepened and kept its life from sight" (477NCL, 370UC).

SUPPLEMENT, 1993

Since 1987, when this article was first written, the centripetal reading can be said to have remained dominant: of twenty-five studies of the novel that have appeared in the interim, only eight raise some doubts about a centered interpretation. The centripetal approaches can be divided into overviews, political studies, and specialized studies of the use of photography and of the novel's feminism.

In his overview of Laurence's work for the ECW Press "Canadian Writers and Their Works" series, Kertzer seems at first to recognize the centrifugal elements, but he immediately defuses these, noting that "Laurence regarded the novel as an artefact that holds, balances, and resolves opposing impulses" (16). His commentary on *The Diviners* is solidly centripetal, as he describes the novel as a "summation" which "unites the concerns of previous works" (41), draws on "universal" myths (44), and illustrates the need of "grace" and "salvation" (46). Gunnars' Preface to her 1988 commemorative collection is similarly centered and humanist, as she praises Laurence for the "honesty" and "truth" (viii) manifested on her "journey of discovery" (ix). Swayze's essay in this collection is, if anything, more centripetal than any previous discussion: mystifying Laurence as an antiintellectual but intuitive thinker, he finds the conclusion of *The Diviners* to be "triumphantly Christian" (13), as "the miracle of saving grace is mirrored in the miracle of writing" (13). Although Hauge's contribution to the same volume argues that the antimimetic metafictionality of *The Diviners* (as opposed to *The Stone Angel*) undermines the religious function, he confuses the issue by speaking of the former's "idealism" (131). Fulton's article in the Gunnars' volume objects to reading Laurence's "feminism" in the male-centered terms of "humanism," but what she offers instead is equally unitary, simply replacing Swayze's Christianity with her feminism, without providing any supporting evidence from the novel. Buss's study of Laurence's "autobiographical impulse" is not much less centripetal than her earlier discussion, tracing as it does the way in which Laurence's protagonists bring strength and creativity into balance. New's 1989 *A History of Canadian Literature* contains none of the centrifugal suggestions about *The Diviners* found in his 1977 Introduction; rather here he speaks of the novel as "reconciling" Morag to her past and present, just as the Manawaka works as a whole "reconcile" the various ethnicities of Western Canada (247). Finally, Keith's pedantic attack on *The Diviners* in the name of "Close Reading" points to what he considers as flaws in "the verbal and structural elements of the novel" (103) from a solidly centripetal perspective, as he objects to Laurence's grammatical errors, Morag's use of slang, "flat, conventional language" (106) and exaggeration, the implausibility of Morag's "transformation" into an artist given her culturally deprived upbringing (109) and the "lack of cohesiveness" (111) in the later sections of the novel. In his subsequent book on English-Canadian fiction, Keith adds to the list of faults in *The Diviners* that of "contrivance" (130), which he sees as arising from what I would term a centripetal intention, Laurence's desire to "provide some unifying effect" (131).

Four of the recent studies pursue political concerns. Bader presents a fairly straightforward thematic account of the changing "heterostereotype" of Britain in *The Diviners* as compared to Australian fiction. Thieme describes the contestation of the "mainstream Canadian values" by those of the Scots and Métis (156), but he sees the novel as "privileging legend over official history" (159) without noting the problematizing of legend. While Nicholson's more nuanced examination of "Aspects of Scotland" in *The Diviners* is fairly centered, he does take cognizance of the "heterogeneity" of the novel, and of its "contextualizing" of the Scottish references" by a concomitant development within and away from hegemonic English discourse" (167). Finally, in completely centripetal terms, Fraser traces the parallels between Canada's experience as a colony and the "interior colonization" (xi) of Morag within the patriarchy, discovering, for example, that "Morag manages to establish her own form of sovereignty-association with society" (147).

Two recent studies examine the role of photography in the novel. Bowen stresses the subjectivity, the ambiguity (in my terms, the centrifugal aspects) of the photographs in the first part of the novel, but then centripetalizes the later sections, asserting that here Morag overcomes her doubts and arranges the photographs to discover "the true value of the past" (32). York puts more emphasis on Morag's ordering of even the early photographs, seeing this as analogous to fiction's ordering of the chaos of life.

The most recent article on *The Diviners*, by Bök, manifests both centrifugal and centripetal tendencies: his discussion of Laurence's feminist revision of the male *Kunstlerroman* brings out various centrifugal aspects, but his emphasis on the "oracular," "sibylline" protagonist and, especially, on the novel's failure to exhibit its feminism in form as well as content makes his reading primarily centripetal.

The continuing currency of the centripetal view of *The Diviners* is illustrated by the passing comments the novel receives in two general discussions of the

Canadian novel. Hutcheon excludes *The Diviners* from her investigation of the "Canadian Postmodern" because it "reveals more a *modernist* search for order in the face of moral and social chaos than a *postmodernist* urge to trouble, to question, to make both problematic and provisional any such desire for order or truth" (2). Similarly, in Mathews's commentary on the implications of the choice of the ten "most important" Canadian novels (of which *The Diviners* was one) at the 1977 Calgary conference on the Canadian novel, he speaks of *The Diviners'* orthodoxy and conservatism, of its being "respectable and inoffensive," able to be "read with profit by an intelligent fourteen year old" (165), presumably because Morag "achieves self-knowledge based on her acceptance of her personal and cultural past" (101).

The commentaries of six recent critics do, however, run counter to this majority assessment of the novel. In her valuable book on contemporary Canadian women novelists, Howells emphasizes the "registration of contradictions" (44) in *The Diviners*, and the unreliability of both perception and language, with even Morag's final "statements of achievement" being "destabilized" (56). However, although Howells's later article records similar instabilities, its emphasis is more centripetal, as it speaks of Morag's "impulse toward completion" being "aesthetically necessary" (59) and of the novel ending "not in wilderness but with a homecoming" (68). In the only centrifugal discussion in the Gunnars' collection, Hjartarson argues that whereas almost all previous analyses of *The Diviners* have stressed the inevitability of the past in shaping Morag's "subjectivity," the novel actually presents "the dynamic and apparently contradictory process by which she . . . appears, on the one hand to shape and give meaning to the life story she tells, and, on the other, to be entirely shaped, to be herself composed by the stories told" (43), in a dialogic contestation between the "Then" and the "Now." Hunter's interesting study sets up another opposition, that between the illusory "consolation" of an ordering society and the "articulation" by which the individual exposes the contradictions that undermine such consolation; the structure of the novel also enacts this opposition, as the "consoling" content of the memorybank series is undermined by the fragmentation of the narrative.

The remaining three centrifugal studies are feminist. Greene's essay in the Nicholson volume (and her slightly revised version of it in her subsequent book) presents *The Diviners* as a feminist revisioning of Joyce's male *Kunstlerroman*, Shakespeare's patriarchal magician in *The Tempest*, and Milton's conception of paradise, which Laurence redefines as process rather than attainment. For Greene, paradox is central to the novel, resolutions are "provisional" only, and "endings are problematised" (199). Verduyn's investigation of Laurence's treatment of language in *The Diviners* emphasizes the contradictions pervading the novel, both in Morag's "profound ambivalence about conceptualizations of truth, knowledge, and faith" (53), and inherent in language itself (in the process, she implicitly provides an effective counter to Keith's strictures on Laurence's careless use of language, which, ironically, appeared in the same journal). Finally, Godard's lengthy article in *Open Letter* is the most extensive examination of *The Diviners* to date, and it is aggressively centrifugal. In this wide-ranging study, Godard demonstrates, for example, how *The Diviners* enacts a "carnivalesque subversion" of the "dominant" through its "polyglossia" (43), problematizes the "monologic" "discourse of History" (44), "participates in the general post-structuralist critique of representation" (48), and "rewrites the Great Tradition [as represented by Shakespeare and Milton] to displace fathering by (m)othering the text" (68). To read Godard is to wonder how so many critics of the novel can overlook its centrifugal elements.

NOTES

1. Of the thirty-three commentaries on *The Diviners* published prior to 1987, when the first version of this paper was written for delivery at the Margaret Laurence session of the Modern Language Association convention, twenty-seven present such a positivist reading. These twenty-seven can be grouped into general overviews, studies of characterization, studies of Morag as a writer, and investigations of narrative technique and plot structure.

The most significant overview is provided by Thomas: her consistently centripetal reading points the direction for most of the studies which followed. In her 1975 book on Laurence she describes *The Diviners* as "the story of a profoundly religious pilgrimage, the affirmation of faith and the finding of grace" (131), and positions the novel as "a final statement [which] encircles, encloses, and completes" the Manawaka cycle (132). Similarly, in her brief examination of the "religion of heritage" in Laurence's fiction, Mortlock finds the protagonists moving towards "a truly gratifying form of religious assent" (132). Thomas's 1978 study of mythology is as centripetal as her earlier book; she affirms, for example, that, for Morag "the functions of myth have been to give her strength to develop into her own person, to find her own place, and, finally, to rest easy in it" (114).

Like Thomas and many other commentators, Staines, in his Introduction to the 1978 New Canadian Library edition, stresses how the novel is "the culmination and completion of the Manawaka novels" (v) with a "central lesson" (viii) of the need to accept the past and attain "personal peace and contentment" (xiii). In his overview of the novel, Blewett sets up an opposition resembling mine between centripetal and centrifugal tendencies, but he finds Laurence's "habitual cast of mind" (178) drawn to "reconciliation" and "defeat" of divisive forces (185). Similarly, Woodcock sees the Manawaka world as presenting a "paradigm of the Canadian condition, with the relations of its characters exemplifying the divisions and distrusts . . . that make up the collective psyche of Canada," (154) and *The Diviners* providing a salutary "balancing of elements" (159) as the "summation of Margaret Laurence's vision" (160). Although Stratford finds *The Diviners* to "celebrate heterogeneity" (53) by comparison to the "claustrophobic" *Kamouraska*, he erases any centrifugal implication by his centered account of the novel as a "story of a woman's successive liberations" from repressive stereotypes into an "achieved independence" (53). Powe's curiously muddled assessment of Laurence is perhaps the strangest overview of her work. On the one hand he complains that other critics "inevitably burble on about her gutsiness and decency and understanding" (130); but instead of calling attention to the openness and subtlety of her texts, he points out the artistic shortcomings others have overlooked, such as her "dull" writing, predictable plots, lack of ideas, and limited range. Then, conversely, he points to precisely those qualities in her work which he has just said it lacks, such as her "willingness to try almost anything" (139) in *The Diviners*, and concludes by praising her for her "feeling, hard-won and real" (142).

A number of studies of the novel focus on the characterization, particularly of Morag.

Some of the phrasing in Moss's account suggests an awareness of centrifugal aspects--the novel manifests a "brawling vision" (69); Morag "struggles to resolve the several roles and several selves that she finds within her" (75)--but his emphasis is centripetal: *The Diviners* is the story of how Morag's "interior factions" have been "assimilated into the simple complex personality who at the novel's close endures without rancour" (76). Bailey's (1977) Jungian analysis presents Laurence's novels as "progress[ing] almost systematically" to the attaining of "completed individuation" in Morag (306), Buss's study of the mother-daughter relationship draws on Jung to read the novel as presenting Morag's "ritualistic move to wholeness" (67), and Goldie examines the contribution of folklore and culture to Morag's "quest for identity, for individuation" (95). In a 1978 feminist analysis Bailey discovers "Morag's internal development to a creative wholeness which I take to be equivalent to androgyny, [with its] . . . harmonious balance" of masculine and feminine (12). Ross's totalizing reading is similar: in the "central scene" of the novel (93) Morag's "ritual encounter" with the "initiating shaman" Jules "completes" her as a woman (87).

Other studies focus on Morag specifically as a writer. In her important early study Carrington implicitly recognizes some centrifugal features in Laurence's problematizing of "truth" and her "emphasis . . . on tales in the telling (168); however, her approach leans more to the centripetal when she emphasizes Jules's "shamanistic" role and the "magic" of divining. Grace takes a very conservative view of Morag as artist, seeing her as a "full-fledged hero" (64) who goes through three stages to a "final victory [which] is a function of her ability to embrace the totality of her experience" (70). Johnston presents a totalized reading of the novel as Morag's "quest for [the] mysterious core of life" (108), to "divine" which is "to isolate the essential truth" (113). Similarly, examining the relationship between Morag's novels and her life, Wainwright sees *The Diviners* as presenting "Morag's painful but triumphant journey to the summit of a particularly Canadian Kilimanjaro" (293).

One might expect that examinations of the novel's narrative technique and structure would be less centered, more dialogic, but this is not the case. Gom's study of the narrative technique stresses Morag's "acceptance" of herself as she is, noting that she "has already 'arrived' when the novel opens" (247); similarly in her Twayne overview Morley speaks of "Morag's move towards the hard-won maturity that is in the narrative voice from the beginning" (125). Gom's subsequent study of "memory" again finds Morag more aware and "more secure" than the earlier Laurence protagonists and adds that "she not only understands herself, but she understands the memory process" (56). Hehner's investigation of the narrative technique finds "an achieved equilibrium" in the adult Morag (48). Significantly, when Hehner does note the presence of centrifugal features she considers them to be flaws; for example, she claims that "in her presentation of the internal doubts which beset Morag as a writer . . . Laurence comes perilously close to sinking the novel under the weight of its self-consciousness" (52). Finally, Cooper finds no centrifugal tendencies in *The Diviners* at all: oblivious of any destabilizing elements, she asserts that "Morag's art of recollecting and ordering [her] personal history as a final testament is an art of closure" (93).

Of the six studies that could be considered centrifugal, three provide only suggestions of such a reading. These hints first appear in New's Introduction to his 1977 collection, in which he speaks of the novel's "reconciliation" of its "tensions" as "often hesitant, tentative, a matter of making do" (2). Harrison's brief commentary on the novel refers to Laurence's "skepticism about the given past" (183). McCallum's useful contextualizing of *The Diviners* brings out in passing two of the novel's most important centrifugal features: "the radical innovation of the novel lies in its recognition that all forms of communication are limited and distorted by the pressuring social structures they necessarily inhabit" (13), and the novel dramatizes the "resistance" to "the dominating forces in Canada's past" (15).

Two French critics were the first to draw sustained attention to the novel's centrifugal elements. Vauthier's study (unfortunately available only in French) foregrounds the self-reflexivity of the novel, examining the "circulation" of its narratives, their transformations, contestations, and subjectivities, thereby destabilizing a centered reading. Fabre's two 1982 articles take up similar narratological concerns. In "Text, Mini-Text and Micro-Text" he examines the metafictional "narrative units," which he sees as undermining the novel's mimesis (though he does perceive "an attempt to build a pattern" [161] of these fragments). "Words and the World" views the novel as presenting "writing as a creative and communicative process indissociable from the problematic relation between fiction and reality" (247).

A comment Laurence makes in her essay "Ivory Tower or Grassroots?" shows both her awareness of, and ambivalence concerning such centrifugal elements: "My fiction . . . must always feel easy with paradox and accommodate contradiction" (23). Centrifugal "paradox" and "contradiction" are centripetally accepted and "accommodated."

2. For discussions of the internal evidence that the novel Morag is writing is *The Diviners* see Grace 68 and McLean 392-93. Clara Thomas also points out that in the manuscript of the novel the final sentence is followed by the words "The Diviners" (Garden 401).

3. His status as an imperialist is reinforced in that Laurence gave the same name to a British imperialist in her African story "A Fetish For Love."

4. Robert Gunn is the only settler of 266 Bryce names whom he designates "piper." Bryce makes no mention of Piper Gunn's having a wife named Morag but notes that he was accompanied on the march by his "sister" Mary (323).

5. She tells in her memoir *Dance on the Earth* of how she only learned of the Piper being named Gunn from her friend Jean Cole after the novel was published (200-01).

6. Christie's surname may well have been suggested to Laurence by Hugh MacLennan's essay "A Disquisition on Elmer," in which he remarks that his own family name began as "Logan" and that the Logan clan was "one of the weakest clans in Scotland" (122), with the war-cry "The Ridge of Tears"; he adds that the only member of the Logan clan mentioned in the encyclopedia is "an Edinburgh Victorian who wrote a book on the sexual habits of savages," though he doesn't know "whether he left Scotland in order to do it" (123).

7. Godard also suggests an alignment of Morag's fiction and Laurence's, but it is entirely different from mine: *Spear of Innocence* "re / presents" *The Stone Angel* by substituting an "outsider" for an "establishment" figure, *Prospero's Child* inverts the imperialist-colonialist struggle in *This Side Jordan*, "*Jonah* foregrounds the watery descent and rebirth images found in *A Jest of God*," the here and now of *Presences* is contrasted to the "future orientation" of *The Tomorrow-Tamer*, and the intermingling of history and fiction in *Shadows of Eden* repeats the concerns of *The Diviners* (41).

WORKS CITED

Atwood, Margaret. *The Handmaid's Tale*. Toronto: McClelland and Stewart, 1985.

Bader, Rudolf. "The Mirage of the Sceptr'd Isle: An Imagological Appraisal." *Ariel* 19.1 (January 1988): 35-44.

Bailey, Nancy. "Fiction and the New Androgyne: Problems and Possibilities in *The Diviners*." *Atlantis* 4.1 (Fall 1978): 10-17.

___. "Margaret Laurence, Carl Jung and The Manawaka Women." *Studies in Canadian Literature* 2.2 (Summer 1977): 306-21.

Blewett, David. "The Unity of The Manawaka Cycle." *Margaret Laurence: An Appreciation*. Ed. Christl Verduyn. Peterborough, Ontario: Broadview Press, 1988, 176-92.

Bök, Christian. "Sibyls: Echoes of French Feminism in *The Diviners* and *Lady Oracle*." *Canadian Literature* 135 (Winter 1992): 80-93.

Bowen, Deborah. "In Camera: The Developed Photographs of Margaret Laurence and Alice Munro." *Studies in Canadian Literature* 13.1 (1988): 20-33.

Bryce, George. *The Romantic Settlement of Lord Selkirk's Colonists*. Winnipeg: Clark, 1909.

Buss, Helen. *Mother and Daughter Relationships in The Manawaka Works of Margaret Laurence*. Victoria: University of Victoria Press, 1985.

___. "Margaret Laurence and the Autobiographical Impulse." *Crossing the River: Essays in Honour of Margaret Laurence*. Ed. Kristjana Gunnars. Winnipeg: Turnstone, 1988, 147-68.

Carrington, Ildako de Papp. "Tales in the Telling: *The Diviners* as Fiction About Fiction." *Essays on Canadian Writing* 9 (1977/78): 154-68.

Cooper, Cheryl. "Images of Closure in *The Diviners*." *The Canadian Novel Here and Now*. Ed. John Moss. Toronto: New Canadian Press, 1978, 93-102.

Fabre, Michel. "From *The Stone Angel* to *The Diviners*: An Interview with Margaret Laurence." *A Place to Stand On: Essays By and About Margaret Laurence*. Ed. George Woodcock. Edmonton: NeWest, 1983, 193-209.

___. "Text, Mini-Text and Micro-Text: The Forms and Functions of Narrative Units in Margaret Laurence's *The Diviners*." *Commonwealth Novel in English* 1.2 (July 1982): 166-90.

___. "Words and the World: *The Diviners* as an Exploration of the Book of Life." *A Place to Stand On: Essays by and about Margaret Laurence*. Ed. George Woodcock. Edmonton: NeWest, 1983, 247-96.

Fraser, Wayne. *The Dominion of Women: The Personal and the Political in Canadian Women's Literature*. Westport, Conn.: Greenwood, 1991.

Fulton, Keith Louise. "Feminism and Humanism: Margaret Laurence and the 'Crisis of the Imagination.'" *Crossing the River: Essays in Honour of Margaret Laurence*. Ed. Kristjana Gunnars. Winnipeg: Turnstone, 1988, 99-120.

Godard, Barbara. "*The Diviners* as Supplement: (M)othering the Text." *Open Letter* 7th ser. 7 (Spring 1990): 26-73.

Goldie, Terry. "Folklore, Popular Culture and Individuation in *Surfacing* and *The Diviners*." *Canadian Literature* 104 (Spring 1985): 95-108.

Gom, Leona. "Laurence and the Use of Memory." *Canadian Literature* 71 (Winter 1976): 48-58.

___. "Margaret Laurence and the First Person." *Dalhousie Review* 55.2 (Summer 1975): 236-51.

Grace, Sherrill. "A Portrait of the Artist as Laurence Hero." *Journal of Canadian Studies* 13.3 (Fall 1978): 64-71.

Greene, Gayle. *Changing the Story: Feminist Fiction and the Tradition*. Bloomington: Indiana University Press, 1991.

___. "Margaret Laurence's *The Diviners*: The Uses of the Past." *Critical Approaches to the Fiction of Margaret Laurence*. Ed. Colin Nicholson. Vancouver: University of British Columbia Press, 1990, 177-207.

Harrison, Dick. *Unnamed Country: The Struggle for a Canadian Prairie Fiction*. Edmonton: University of Alberta, 1977.

Hauge, Hans. "The Novel Religion of Margaret Laurence." *Crossing the River*. Ed. Kristjana Gunnars. Winnipeg: Turnstone, 1988, 122-32.

Hehner, Barbara. "River of Now and Then: Margaret Laurence's Narratives." *Canadian

Literature 74 (Autumn 1977): 40-57.

Hjartarson, Paul. "'Christie's Real Country Where I was Born': Story-telling, Loss and Subjectivity in *The Diviners.*" *Crossing the River.* Ed. Kristjana Gunnars. Winnipeg: Turnstone, 1988, 43-64.

Howells, Coral Ann. *Private and Fictional Words: Canadian Women Novelists of the 1970s and 1980s.* London: Methuen, 1987.

___. "In Search of Lost Mothers: Margaret Laurence's *The Diviners* and Elizabeth Jolley's *Miss Peabody's Inheritance.*" *Ariel* 19.1 (January 1988): 57-70.

Hunter, Lynette. "Consolation and Articulation in Margaret Laurence's *The Diviners.*" *Critical Approaches to the Fiction of Margaret Laurence.* Ed. Colin Nicholson. Vancouver: University of British Columbia, 1990, 133-51.

Hutcheon, Linda. *The Canadian Postmodern: A Study of Contemporary English-Canadian Fiction.* Toronto: Oxford, 1988.

Jackson, James A. *The Centennial History of Manitoba.* Toronto: McClelland and Stewart, 1970.

Johnston, Eleanor. "The Quest of the Diviners." *Mosaic* 11 (Spring 1978): 107-17.

Keith, W. J. *A Sense of Style: Studies in the Art of Fiction in English-Speaking Canada.* Toronto: ECW, 1989.

___. "Margaret Laurence's *The Diviners*: The Problems of Close Reading." *Journal of Canadian Studies* 23.3 (Autumn 1988): 102-16.

Kertzer, J. M. *Margaret Laurence and Her Works.* Toronto: ECW, 1987.

Laurence, Margaret. *Dance on the Earth: A Memoir.* Toronto: McClelland and Stewart, 1989.

___. *The Diviners.* Toronto: McClelland and Stewart, New Canadian Library, (1974) 1995; Chicago: University of Chicago Press, 1993.

___. "A Fetish For Love." *The Tomorrow-Tamer and Other Stories.* Toronto: McClelland and Stewart, New Canadian Library, (1963, 1970) 1993, 161-81.

___. "Ivory Tower or Grassroots?: The Novelist as Socio-Political Being." *A Political Art: Essays and Images in Honour of George Woodcock.* Ed. William H. New. Vancouver: University of British Columbia, 1978, 15-25.

___. "Road From the Isles." *Heart of a Stranger.* Toronto: McClelland and Stewart, 1976, 145-57.

Linklater, Eric. *The Survival of Scotland.* New York: Doubleday, 1968.

MacEwan, Grant. *Cornerstone Colony: Selkirk's Contribution to the Canadian West.* Saskatoon: Western Prairie Producer, 1977.

MacLennan, Hugh. "A Disquisition on Elmer." *The Other Side of Hugh MacLennan: Selected Essays Old and New.* Ed. Elspeth Cameron. Toronto: Macmillan, 1978, 122-27.

Mathews, Lawrence. "Calgary, Canonization, and Class: Deciphering List B." *Canadian Canons: Essays in Literary Value.* Ed. Robert Lecker. Toronto: University of Toronto, 1991.

McCallum, Pamela. "Communication and History: Themes in Innis and Laurence." *Studies in Canadian Literature* 3.1 (Winter 1978): 5-16.

McLean, Kenneth Hugh. "The Treatment of History in Canadian Fiction." Ph.D. diss. York University, 1980.

Mitchison, Rosalind. *A History of Scotland.* London: Methuen, 1970.

Morley, Patricia. *Margaret Laurence.* Boston: Twayne, 1981. Reprint, with an Afterword. *Margaret Laurence: The Long Journey Home.* Montreal: McGill-Queen's University Press, 1991.

Mortlock, Melanie. "The Religion of Heritage: *The Diviners* as a Thematic Conclusion to the Manawaka Series." *Journal of Canadian Fiction* 27 (1980): 132-41.
Morton, Desmond. *The Last War Drum: The North West Campaign of 1885.* Toronto: Hakkert, 1972.
Morton, W. L. *Manitoba: A History.* Toronto: University of Toronto Press, 1957.
Moss, John. *Sex and Violence in the Canadian Novel.* Toronto: McClelland and Stewart, 1977.
New, W. H. *A History of Canadian Literature.* Houndmills: Macmillan, 1989.
___. Introduction to *Margaret Laurence.* Ed. W. H. New. Toronto: McGraw-Hill Ryerson, 1977.
Nicholson, Colin. "'There and Not There': Aspects of Scotland in Laurence's Writing." *Critical Approaches to the Fiction of Margaret Laurence.* Ed. Colin Nicholson. Vancouver: University of British Columbia, 1990, 162-76.
Powe, B. W. *A Climate Charged.* Oakville, Ontario: Mosaic, 1984.
Ross, Catherine Sheldrick. "'A Singing Spirit': Female Rites of Passage in *Klee Wyck*, *Surfacing* and *The Diviners.*" *Atlantis* 4.1 (Fall 1978): 87-94.
Staines, David. Introduction to *The Diviners*, by Margaret Laurence. Toronto: McClelland and Stewart, New Canadian Library, 1978.
Stratford, Philip. *All the Polarities: Comparative Studies in Contemporary Canadian Novels in French and English.* Toronto: ECW, 1986.
Swayze, Walter. "Introduction: Know Through Writing: The Pilgrimage of Margaret Laurence." *Crossing the River: Essays in Honour of Margaret Laurence.* Ed. Kristjana Gunnars. Winnipeg: Turnstone, 1988, 3-22.
Thieme, John. "Acknowledging Myths: The Images of Europe in Margaret Laurence's *The Diviners* and Jack Hodgin's *The Invention of the World.*" *Critical Approaches to the Fiction of Margaret Laurence.* Ed. Colin Nicholson. Vancouver: University of British Columbia, 1990, 152-61.
Thomas, Clara. *The Manawaka World of Margaret Laurence.* Toronto: McClelland and Stewart, New Canadian Library, (1975) 1976.
___. "Myth and Manitoba in *The Diviners.*" *The Canadian Novel: Here and Now.* Ed. John Moss. Toronto: NC, 1978, 103-18.
___. "The Wild Garden and the Manawaka World." *Modern Fiction Studies* 22.3 (1976): 401-11.
Vauthier, Simone. "La Circulation des récits dans *The Diviners.*" *Echos du Commonwealth* 7 (1981-1982): 59-77.
Wagner, Linda. "Margaret Laurence's *The Diviners.*" *University of Windsor Review* 16.2 (Spring-Summer 1982): 5-17.
Wainwright, J. A. "You Have to Go Home Again: Art and Life in *The Diviners.*" *World Literature Written in English* 20.2 (Autumn 1981): 292-311.
Woodcock, George. *Gabriel Dumont: The Métis Chief and his Lost World.* Edmonton: Hurtig, 1975.
___. "The Human Elements: Margaret Laurence's Fiction." *The Human Elements.* Ed. David Helwig. Ottawa: Oberon, 1978, 134-61.
York, Lorraine. *The Other Side of Dailiness: Photographs in the Works of Alice Munro, Timothy Findley, Michael Ondaatje and Margaret Laurence.* Toronto: ECW, 1988.

Part III

Multiculturalism in Laurence

Chapter 9

War in the Manawaka Novels as Macrocosm, Fictionalized Biography, and Imaginative History
Greta M. K. McCormick Coger

The Manawaka novels fictionalize Scottish and Canadian history in an imaginative way. A major part is the fictionalizing of the history of Laurence's own Scottish ancestry and its context in the Scottish heritage. Particularly, the major theme of surviving wars gives meaning to time and place, provides a macrocosm of background and context to enrich characterization, and suffuses the microcosm of characters' experiences.

The meaning of war to Margaret Laurence involves her Scottish ancestry in the context of the Scottish heritage. The origins of Scottish identity and Laurence's ancestry can be seen from a summary of Scottish history (Muirhead xxviii-xxxiv). Before the Roman invasions of Scotland in A.D. 83, prehistoric Picts (Celts with pre-Celtic stock) occupied the territory north of the Firths of Forth and Clyde. Laurence's roots go back this far for her maiden name "Wemyss" means "cave-dweller" (Thomas 6-7 and Milne 25). Picts were united with Scots (Christian Goidelic Celts from Ireland) from 843 to 1371 when Stewarts of Scotland came to "the throne and remained until 1714. From 1214 until the early eighteenth century was the 'golden age' of Scottish distinctness of clans. Her teacher Wes McAmmond pointed out, "[Laurence] knew her Scottish heritage" (McAmmond 11). Her cousin Catherine Simpson Milne noted: The Wemyss, a sept of the Clan MacDuff (Thomas 6; cf. Muirhead 265, 297), "were a very superior clan . . . [with] titled people in them. . . . Two or three counts and things like that. Mrs. Wemyss was very conscious of it. More so than Mr. Wemyss because it was on Mr. Wemyss' side" (Milne 25-26). Similarly, like Laurence and other Neepawa residents, schoolmate and neighbor Gerald Murray knew his family's long Scottish history; in Scotland he visited Earl Murray County near Blair Castle (Murray 38). Laurence imaginatively worked her Scottish ancestry into her fiction. A major factor in the history of Scottish clans was survival of warring factions.

The theme of surviving wars--Culloden in 1746, Batoche in 1885, and Germany from 1914-1918 and 1939-1945--gives meaning to time and place in the

Manawaka novels. Scottish identity was retained by surviving wars with the English, Métis, and Germans whether Scots suffered defeats or celebrated victories in these battles. These three wars in particular affected Scots in the last two centuries. They lost to the English in 1746 at the Battle of Culloden in Scotland. The crofters survived mainly by emigration to Canada. In 1885 Scots won when the Métis Rebellion was put down. These two groups remained separate, even after some of both fought together in World War II. The third seminal war for Scots' identity was the win against the Germans in the modern First and Second World Wars. The Scots in Canada fought with the English against the Métis in the nineteenth century and then with some Métis against the Germans in the twentieth century, but still retained their heritage. Laurence uses these wars in the time span of the Manawaka novels as she portrays characters with Scottish ancestry. Some key historical aspects have their fictional presentation in the characters' specific activities and attitudes. Historical references of the twentieth century have correspondences with Laurence's Neepawa days. These insights come from her own comments as well as several interviews with Laurence's classmates, teachers, relatives, and neighbors in Neepawa. The characters at the end of each novel assess these wars from Laurence's viewpoint of the 1960s.

The theme of surviving wars as macrocosm of background and context enriches Laurence's characterization. The wider historical view indicates that the Highlanders remained independent despite several wars of the English to pacify the Highlands. Only in the mid-eighteenth century when the Highlanders nearly succeeded in resisting did the English crush them at Culloden in 1746. Laurence makes considerable use of this specific war for it led to Scots coming to Canada. When the Highlanders at last were crushed by the English in the Culloden bloodbath (Muirhead 367-68 and Bell 337-39), British soldiers were ordered to seek out and kill the wounded who had crawled into bushes and the old men, women, and children in nearby villages. So awful was this historic Scottish battle in the clans' memories that 135 years later in 1881 they erected a cairn at Culloden. Only in 1930 was the hate between Scots and English subdued enough that the colors of both sides, "once carried in enmity" were ceremoniously laid side by side in the Scottish National Naval and Military Museum (Bell 339). Time can bring about some unity of divisions.

This macrocosm of Scottish history Laurence presents imaginatively in greatest detail in *The Diviners* (New Canadian Library edition [NCL] and University of Chicago edition [UC]), as it is set forth by Christie Logan. Logan gives Morag a poetical account of this seminal war of Culloden with facts taken from *The Clans and Tartans of Scotland* which he retrieved from the Nuisance Grounds; it augmented any information he had of his Scottish heritage:

A sad cry, it is, for the sadness of my people. A cry heard at Culloden, in the black days of the battle, when the clans stood together for the last time, and the clans were broken by the Sassenach [English] cannons and the damned bloody rifles of the redcoat swine. They mowed the clans down in cold blood, my dear, and it must have been enough to tear the heart and unhinge the mind of the strongest coldest man alive, for our folk were poor bloody crofters, and were not wanting to fight the wars of the chieftains, at all. . . . They believed their chiefs were kings from God. And them who didn't believe was raised anyway, with fire and the sword, until they went off to fight Charlie's battle for him, and him a green boy from France who neither knew nor cared for his people but only for the crown gleaming there in the eye of his own mind. (*Diviners* 57NCL, 39UC)

Tale telling through the voice of a fictional ancestral narrator gives history a storyteller's aura:

It was in the old days, a long time ago, after the clans was broken and scattered at the battle on the moors, and the dead men thrown into the long graves there, and no heather ever grew on those places, never again, for it was dark places they had become and places of mourning. Then, in those days, a darkness fell over the lands and the crofts of Sutherland. (*Diviners* 58NCL, 40UC)

This reference is to another cataclysmic event in Scottish history-the Highland Enclosures. Laurence's teacher, Wes McAmmond, says: "The lairds went into sheep farming. They didn't need farmers anymore. So they just tore down their cottages and said 'good-bye'" (19). In *The Diviners*, Laurence uses this history to vividly paint the great hardships and starvation. Dan McRaith paints a Highland woman in agony. Behind her is a burning croft (*Diviners* 309NCL, 402UC). These Highland clearances are the basis for Laurence to use history imaginatively in a poetic tale; Christie tells Morag of those poor and starving crofters driven off the good land; history tells that they had to resort to eating lichens off the rocks especially in East Ross and Sutherland at the coast:

The Bitch-Duchess . . . sowed the darkness and reaped gold, for her heart was dark as the feathers of a raven and her. . . . tacksmen rode through the countryside, setting fire to the crofts and turning out the people from their homes which they had lived in since the beginning of all time. And it was old men and old women with thin shanks and men in their prime and women with the child inside them and a great scattering of small children, like, and all of them was driven away from the lands of their fathers and onto the wild rocks of the shore, then, to fish if they could and pry the shellfish off of the rocks there, for food. (*Diviners* 58NCL, 40UC)

Some stayed in Scotland for as Christie says in his tale:

But the people were afraid, see? They did not dare. Better to die on the known rocks in the land of their ancestors, so some said. Others said the lands across the seas were bad. (*Diviners* 59-60NCL, 41UC)

Many did leave, for emigration seemed a better choice. Thus the Battle of Culloden led to the diaspora of Scots throughout the world ever since. In her novels, Laurence particularizes this emigration in her clan histories of the Curries, MacLeods, Logans, and Gunns who found their way to Manawaka. Laurence has the imaginative figure of Piper Gunn stand for all emigrants courageously setting forth. As Christie tells Morag: Piper Gunn said, "My woman and I will go and rear our daughters and our sons in the far land and make it ours" (*Diviners* 59-60NCL,

141UC). That land was Canada. So many Scots came by 1812 while few settlers were English (Lemon 272). In 1814 free passage was offered. In 1825 thousands of emigrants were assisted materially; in 1828 land could be purchased for as little as four shillings an acre on credit. By 1842 many more Scots had come because of the Highland Clearances (Lemon 276, 286) "to make way for sheep farms, which were later succeeded by deer forests" (Muirhead xxxiii).

Of the Scots emigrating, a number came to Hudson's Bay and south to Fort Garry (now Winnipeg) at the confluence of the Red and Assiniboine Rivers. Scottish distinctness continued in Manitoba despite attacks by the Métis throughout most of the nineteenth century and despite working alongside the English. Christie represents this attitude for in his tales he refers to the English as Sassenachs not only at Culloden but also at Red River and Batoche where "Sutherlanders didn't trust the goddamn English, them bloody Sassenachs from Down East, no more than what they trusted halfbreeds" (*Diviners* 144NCL, 106UC). Even as late as the 1930s, advertisements for help in Winnipeg papers sometimes said at the bottom "No Englishman need apply." Scottish identity continued in the twentieth century during World Wars I and II; four divisions-the 9th (World War I only), 15th, 51st, and 52d were entirely Scottish (Muirhead xxxiii).

The macrocosm of Scottish ancestry in Laurence's and other Neepawa families is fundamental to all the Manawaka novels though most overt in the last two. In each novel, war which kept the Scottish identity separate in the Highlands is evaluated from about the 1960s viewpoint. These deep Scottish roots in the first Manaswaka novel, *The Stone Angel*, are briefly explicit where the fictional Hagar makes a wish on her death-bed. Because of Culloden and after, she had "never even set foot in the Highlands. . . . And yet--I'd wish it [to be in the Highlands], as I'm gathered to my fathers" (*Angel* 306). Similarly, Morag, "when I am gathered to my ancestors," will give Pique the Currie plaid-pin (*Diviners* 474NCL, 367UC). Of sterling silver, the pin was passed on to each younger generation; Hagar passed it on to her son John at age six (*Angel* 140). Hagar's "genetic memory" is a close combination of heredity and environment; lifelong training by her father had instilled in Hagar that the Curries were "a sept of the Clanranald MacDonalds" and had as their war-cry "Gainsay Who Dare" (*Angel* 15NCL 15UC). She schooled John in the knowledge of his Scottish ancestors, as her father had taught her. She wanted him to be proud that he had a distinguished ancestor, Sir Daniel Currie, though his baronetcy died with him (*Angel* 124NCL, 124UC). This mirrors Laurence's own ancestor Sir John Wemyss who was a baronet (Thomas 6). To her son, Hagar also added the most recent generation's history--that her father, his grandfather, came from the Highlands where, "as a boy before they moved to Glasgow," he would "waken early in midsummer and hear the pipes bring in the dawn" (*Angel* 124NCL, 124UC). Hagar sums up this tenuous connection to Scottish heritage despite being in a new place and contemporary time: "How could anyone explain such an absurdity" (*Angel* 306NCL, 306UC)? The thought of having a piper play a pibroch at her funeral prompted her inner reaching back in her Scottish ancestry. Hagar recognizes the oddity of this combination of physical and psychological connection to the past and demonstrates that Scottish heritage survived the trauma of wars.

Because the Highland clans had warred successfully and their Scottish ancestry persisted, Laurence has more specific Highland history to use in *The Stone Angel* and *A Bird in the House*. MacLeods early in the thirteenth century inhabited Dunvegan Castle, the oldest inhabited house in Scotland (Bell 363). The clan of MacLeod had an established seat at the Castle of Kinlochaline on the Morven coast across from the Isle of Mull (Muirhead 343). Laurence has her fictionalized Grandmother MacLeod tell of her MacInnes ancestors as "lairds of Morven and the constables of the Castle of Kinlochaline" (*Bird* 49, 52, 55). Laurence even integrates the name of a distinguished historic ancestor, Sir Roderick MacLeod, the twelfth chief of the clan MacLeod, knighted by James VI (Muirhead 383). The tradition of Scottish clans passing names down several generations was perpetuated in Grandmother MacLeod naming her second son Roderick. When he was killed in the First World War, she kept the memory of him alive with several pictures in her bedroom but only had one up of her other son (*Bird* 47). Then she works her will on her son Ewen; he gives in and persuades his wife Beth to name their newborn son "Roderick." In resignation Ewen sees that in taking on his family's house he has taken on the family's ancestry (*Bird* 93). To him, Grandmother MacLeod sees young Roderick as "Roderick Dhu" as Sir Walter Scott would romanticize the name (*Bird* 58). Another Black Celt is "Morag Dhu" (*Diviners* 400, 401, 403, 404, 407NCL; 308, 309, 310, 311, 312UC), the name Dan McRaith bestows on his painting of Morag.

Grandmother MacLeod, like Hagar, concerns herself with more than names and mottoes in passing on family Scottish history. When old, just as she leaves for Winnipeg, she gives instructions that when she dies, the MacLeod seal-ring is to belong to Roderick, the youngest male heir of the MacLeods and that the MacInnes seal-ring goes to "Roddie too" (*Bird* 106). Yet, Hagar gives her mother's sapphire ring to her granddaughter Tina (279-80), but she does not give the Currie plaid-pin to the eldest son (*Angel* 140).

Distinctions in Scottish clan heritage come from clan lineage, mottoes, crests, plaid-pins, war-cries, and the knowledge of the great deeds done in the past to strengthen present-day, commitment to their clan. Passing on Scottish heritage is more sophisticated in Laurence's last Manawaka novel. Laurence travels north of Inverness to the Black-Sceptr'd Isles of Sutherland and Ross which have "an old Pictish background of the sixth to eleventh centuries. Here are found early symbols known and unknown and the earliest Celtic Church relics" (Muirhead 68). These are the ancestral homes of the historical Logans (Ross), the Curries (Sutherland), and Gunns (Caithness to the north and also Sutherland). Like those of Laurence's own early Pict ancestry, these crofters in her fiction have the same historical names; Laurence imaginatively creates Christie Logan with ancestors who fought at the Ridge of Tears--Culloden (*Diviners* 57NCL, 39UC) as the MacLeods did (Bell 381).

The triumph of Laurence's Scottish heritage on her mother's side is overt in *A Bird in the House*. Laurence suggests that Scottish heritage is both heredity and environment closely intertwined in Vanessa, who, twenty years later in the 1960s, revisited Grandfather Connors house; she realized that in spite of her turning away, he "proclaimed himself in my veins" (*Bird* 191). Likewise, at the end of *The Diviners*, Morag reminds Dan of Calgary that his father is in his veins which she touches on his hand. He can never leave his father entirely (*Diviners* 378NCL, 291UC).

Two of the Manawaka novels have emphasis almost entirely on the twentieth-century wars. Rachel Cameron in *A Jest of God* and her sister Stacey in *The Fire-Dwellers* know Niall Cameron, their father, repudiated any glory attached to the First and Second World Wars. The sisters affirm their self-determination for peace of mind and love of self and family. For Stacey, the Second World War was upsetting because she could not draw her husband out of his silence before his war buddy Buckle Fennick died. By the 1960s Stacey marches against war of any kind (*Fire-Dwellers* 250).

All three significant wars of the Scots are fictionalized in *The Diviners*: history in Scotland pivoting on proud independence before the defeat at Culloden in 1746 and the subsequent emigration to Canada, the history of Scots wars with the Métis, and the modern wars. In this novel especially, Laurence is most innovative because all three wars are assessed from the 1960s viewpoint not only by Morag Gunn with Scottish ancestry but also the Métis Jules and their daughter Pique. Through her parents' intermarriage, Pique is a blend of Scottish and Métis heritages, seemingly incompatible but she creates her own harmony out of both.

In Manitoba and Saskatchewan, a kind of Canadian "Culloden" occurred for the Métis in 1885 after several battles with the Scottish settlers over land. As Wes McAmmond emphasized, Manitoba history documents "the conflict between the Métis and the Orangemen" (McAmmond 20). In his tale, Christie says: when Piper Gunn and his people arrived at the Red River they fought the Indians and half-breeds. "They weren't bad. They were--just there" (*Diviners* 97NCL, 70UC). Vanessa has a similar insight about the Battle of Britain: the soldiers "were just there, too, and before they knew it, there wasn't any way to get out. Like the clansmen at Culloden" (*Bird* 182). The Scots' land settlement was opposed by Métis and fur traders. Métis harassed Scottish settlers by stealing horses, burning barns, crops, and houses. In 1816, they massacred Governor Semple and his men at Seven Oaks. However, new Scottish immigrants built up the small settlement and moved westward. By 1870, when Manitoba became a province, more Scottish settlers came west from Nova Scotia, New Brunswick, and Ontario. Not only histories of Margaret Laurence's characters but also interviews with Neepawa residents support this history. Gerald Murray said his grandfather came in the early 1870s from New Brunswick and built a homestead six miles west of Neepawa (Murray 8). Another Neepawa resident, Dorothy Campbell Henderson, told of her husband's grandfather being a founder of Neepawa. He "bought the property of which a subdivision was surveyed, streets laid out and cement sidewalks put down" for the town of Neepawa in 1878 (Campbell Henderson 13 and McKenzie 48). Margaret Laurence's grandfather, John Wemyss, a lawyer, incorporated Neepawa in 1883. He had left his law practice in Winnipeg, after emigration in 1881 from Glasgow where he had completed his apprenticeship in law. In Winnipeg, he married Margaret Harrison, daughter of Dr. D. H. Harrison, briefly premier of Manitoba in 1887. Laurence's maternal grandfather, John Simpson, was born in 1856 in Milton, Ontario, of Scots-Irish immigrants from County Tyrone. He came to Portage La Prairie in 1878, and married Jane Bailey of Loyalists near Amherstburg, Ontario, before he moved to Neepawa (Thomas 7).

These historical facts of Neepawa families resemble the novels' family histories of emigration from the east. In close resemblance to Laurence's maternal grandfather, fictional grandfather Timothy Connor came from Ontario to Manitoba by river steamer and walked from Winnipeg to Manawaka, earning his way by shoeing horses (*Bird* 188). In a similar biographical reference, Hagar opens her heart to son John to speak of her father, Jason Currie, his grandfather: "When he came over from Scotland as a boy, he didn't have a bean. . . . He came out West by sternwheeler [from Ontario], and packed his goods from Winnipeg to Manawaka by bull-train" (*Angel* 123). That was after 1870 (*Angel* 306). Laurence creates Christie Logan with origins in East Ross (*Diviners* 56-57, 74NCL; 39, 53UC). He came with his widowed mother from the Highlands to Glasgow to Nova Scotia where she worked in people's houses. He was orphaned--she "kicked the bucket when I was around fifteen or so and I came west" to Manawaka (*Diviners* 74NCL, 53UC). Also, Morag imagines that her grandfather, Alisdair Gunn, came from the Highlands and started "a farm where there was only buffalo grass and Indians" (*Diviners* 16-17NCL, 7UC).

Further west, Scottish settlement led to land deals in which Métis usually sold their land. As Scottish settlers advanced further west, Métis had less land to move to. The tensions between Scots and Métis resulted in a confrontation at Batoche, Saskatchewan, in 1885 led by Louis Riel and Gabriel Dumont. Militia was sent quickly by railroad from Ottawa authorized by John A. Macdonald. They arrived with superior cannon power which routed the ambush, the technique of the Métis. This was the culmination of decades of confrontations. The Métis had killed Governor Semple and his men in 1816: then in 1849 Louis Riel, father of the leader of the 1885 Rebellion, broke the control of the Hudson's Bay Company trying to stop the fur trade going South. Then came the threat of American annexation in the Manifest Destiny of 1866, the fear of Fenian penetration after 1866 into Red River, and a man's proclamation of "the Republic of Manitoba" in 1869 at Portage La Prairie. The critical confrontation came when Governor William McDougall in 1870 asserted his authority before he actually received word of Great Britain transferring the West to Canada. The impetuous younger Riel took over Fort Garry and declared themselves the government (*Diviners* 144NCL, 106UC). This leader of the Métis, unfortunately, executed Thomas Scott. The Canadian historian Lower points out the significance of this act: "In retrospect, the death of Scott looms as the most determinative specific political incident between Confederation in 1867 and the Great War of 1914, for by leading to the execution of Riel in 1885 . . . it dug up the hatchet that was supposed to have been buried in 1867 by the Confederation of Canada and opened once more a gulf between the two races" (Lower 352). The Métis were put out of Fort Garry. By 1885 when the Métis took a stand at Batoche, Saskatchewan, their fighting method of ambush used in hunting buffalo as well as Riel's delayed signal to start, led to the final military defeat of the Métis. To this day, this group remains apart even though they fought together with Scots in the Second World War. Campbell Henderson confirmed this for she told of an Indian, Mr. Prince, (if he left the reservation he would fall in the category of citizen as a soldier) who though he had received many honors in World War II was not welcomed back into his native group. They felt he'd done the wrong thing (Letter 13 August 1988). Apparently, he drank himself to death. This sad division reminds the reader that MacLachlan, editor of the *Manawaka Banner*, deleted a comment from Morag's story of the fire which caused Piquette's death. It would have stated that Lazarus had fought at Batoche; MacLachlan said that some readers would think he fought on the wrong side (*Diviners* 176NCL, 130UC). The *Neepawa Heritage* lists a few of these veterans of the Riel Rebellions among the founding members of the veterans organization formed in Neepawa in 1910 (294).

In her fiction, Laurence creates an innovative portrayal of Manitoba history because she shows the Scots and the Métis coming together. As Wes McAmmond says: "Laurence invents these creations. She created what she writes about. She invented multi-culturalism" (3). She fictionalizes events through the tales Christie invents for Morag of the Scottish side and the heroic tales Jules tells to Morag of the Métis side. Interviews show that Laurence knew few Métis in her Neepawa of the 1930s and 1940s. Several views were expressed of her portrayal of Scots-Métis harmony but interviewees recall few if any Métis in the villages. McAmmond said there were no Métis except for Pat the Breed in the valley. He recalls an occasional name like Les Carrieres and Degas on the school rolls (11). Musgrove said an occasional Métis was treated at Neepawa hospital. One was a Métis girl with tuberculosis of the bone similar to the fictional Piquette's disease. The Wemyss family took this girl to Clear Lake (Musgrove 10). When Laurence left Neepawa she learned of difference which wars made, as well as the ethnic differences and how these might or might not be harmonized. By her last novel Laurence created a possible answer to the most prevalent division between two groups in Manitoba and indeed of all Canada--the Scots and Métis. As noted above, Laurence portrays the very slow coming together of a few Métis with Scots. Jules fought in the Second World War albeit to provide dentures for his father. When he returned he adopted the "grey flannels, grey sports blazer, and grey fedora" at a rakish angle on his head (*Diviners* 179NCL, 132UC). He takes up a singing career traveling across Canada with his guitar. He intersperses modern songs with his Métis-heritage songs, though the latter are rarely popular. Nevertheless, he passes on this musical heritage of songs to his daughter Pique. She also composes her own history in song with the poignant line that she is nearly torn in two: "When I think how I was born / I can't help but feeling torn" (*Diviners* 490NCL, 382UC). These songs and the tales of Rider Tonnerre, the Prophet, Lazarus, and Dumont present the Métis fighters as heroes just as the Scots told of their distinguished leaders, real like Sir Roderick MacLeod and Sir Daniel Currie, or imaginary like Piper Gunn and Piper Gunn's wife.

When examining the twentieth-century wars, Laurence concentrates largely on the more positive aspects. This reflects how she had experienced life in Neepawa and other Westerners experienced it. Scots having fought alongside the English in the nineteenth century did so again in the twentieth century against the Germans. They formed their Queen's Own Cameron Highlanders and had a distinguished history of fierce fighting in both the First and Second World Wars. The experience overseas enhanced their Scottish heritage for some like Gerald Murray. What becomes evident from the fiction and interviews of this period of the First and Second World Wars is that the horrors of war are not talked about realistically, if at all, unless to a person in special circumstances--raising money, entertaining, and dancing. What is affirmed are the social activities in Canada in Neepawa (or Manawaka) or in Vancouver.

Far from the battlefield in Europe, youthful Neepawa residents joined up while those at home entertained soldiers at nearby camps and bases. In both World Wars, enlisted men were very young, in both fact and fiction. Until nearly eighteen when he joined up, Gerald Murray in the Second War at seventeen pumped gas at Clear Lake and turned propellers at the airbase. He has a shortened finger as a result of it (Murray 6). Catherine Simpson Milne tells of Laurence's father and Uncle Roderick joining up (Milne 17). The fictional counterpart, Ewen MacLeod, was nineteen while his brother Roderick was eighteen (*Bird* 59). So was the soldier whom Niall Cameron saw blasted by a grenade (*Fire-Dwellers* 10NCL, 10UC) and Colin Gunn crying amidst the barbaric shellfire (*Diviners* 224NCL, 167UC).

Because the Great Depression preceded the Second World War, Neepawa men enlisted because it was a job with pay. Gerald Murray noted he "got $21 a month. That was a lot of money" (Murray 14). Compare this to the fiction where Jules joined up to earn money to buy dentures for his father, Lazarus (*Diviners* 157NCL, 115UC).

Interviewees did not mention the horrible parts of war. Like the women in much of the Manawaka novels, they told of what they did at home. An important local war effort was growing food, which Dorothy Campbell said she and her husband did as their war effort while others helped on the farm. Too young to join up, these "Sons of the Soil" helped the farmers get the crops up. As Margaret Murray said:

My husband wasn't old enough to go [in the First War], but they let them go from school. They called them "Sons of the Soil." They let them go and help the farmers because they had no help whatever to get the crops up [cut, stook, and thresh or combine fields of ripe grain]. Both Earl and his brother went out then when they were just sixteen. (Margaret Murray 24)

The First War in Neepawa also meant raising money, however small. Margaret Murray tells of raising funds by holding a tea:

Norma and Victory and I, at the time of the First World War, Mrs. Wemyss helped us and we had a tea for the Belgium Relief Fund. The country was needing so much stuff. The Germans had taken over. So, we put this tea on--the three of us. I can remember it so well-- five cents a tea. (Margaret Murray 22)

Victory Bonds in the First World War were purchased. Those her father bought sent Catherine Simpson Milne, Laurence's cousin, to college to be a home economist (Milne 28; cf. Ewen became a doctor). Also, in the novels, small amounts of money were raised for good causes: when Vanessa was to go to university, three hundred dollars came from the sale of the MacLeod silver and Limoges china (*Bird* 187). To get travel funds, Hagar also sells Currie family dishes to the bank manager's wife (*Angel* 136).

Happier events of entertaining and dancing in Neepawa contrasted with the fighting thousands of miles away. During the First War at nearby camps, octogenarian Margaret Murray said:

My mother then used to entertain the boys--have them up and entertain them. . . . Then, the boys were all down at Camp Sewell. That's Shilo now [east of Brandon]. They were down there for their training. Mother and Dad used to make a big picnic lunch and take us down. We'd meet the boys we knew . . . [a] cousin and other boys there. (Margaret Murray 23)

In the Second World War, many entertained pilots training near Neepawa at the "very significant" (Campbell Henderson 26) Air Force base. According to Gerald Murray:

It was run by the Miramichee Flying Club from New Brunswick. Civilians were running it and RAF instructors. They were all English people from England or South Africa. My mother and dad were very, very hospitable to them. (Murray 7)

As Margaret Murray said herself:

We had Indian boys here, even one who wore a turban--a Sikh. We used to entertain the boys a lot in our home. We all did--anyone who could take them in and give them a meal and make them feel at home--because a lot of them were just young boys like our own sons. Then we lived in a great red brick house on Mountain Avenue. (Margaret Murray 3-4)

Some were their house guests: One pilot instructor and his wife lived in the upstairs of his parents' home all the time they were in Neepawa. Gerald still keeps in touch with them. He had visited the instructor's mother in England when he was in an air force command in Yorkshire (Murray 7).

The two to three hundred men at the airbase meant that "the local girls met a lot of the English Air Force boys." Laurence did too for only one boy--most had enlisted--remained in her senior high-school year (cf. *Diviners* 146NCL, 107UC). The senior class discussed the subject of whether the airmen were to be invited to the high-school graduation dance. As editor of the school yearbook, *Black and Gold,* at Neepawa Collegiate, Laurence wrote of it and got others involved in the subject (Musgrove 2, 9) though some local boys objected.

Frequently, Laurence and the girls danced at the airbase, Clear Lake, and at the dancehall [the Old Arcade]. It was the place for dances:

It was run by an old-time resident of Neepawa, C. T. Peddler, a car-dealer, who built the original Danceland at Clear Lake with chandeliers. His brother Bruce who still lives here in Neepawa was the one who really ran it. (Murray 9-10)

"It is now a furniture store on Hamilton Street--Matheson's Furniture Store" (Murray 9). "Many times, Peggy referred to it in one of her books" (Murray 9). For instance, Rachel Cameron sees Val in the cafe ready to go to the dancehall (*Jest* 61). Stacey recalls pleasant dancing experiences, especially with the Montreal airman, Al Duschesne (*Fire-Dwellers* 44-45, 74-75). Morag goes to The Flamingo to dance where in spite of her embarrassment she attempts small talk (*Diviners* 164-65NCL, 121UC).

One of the most poignant fictionalized biographical moments--Vanessa entertaining an airman--resembles Laurence and an airman she met at the local dance. Catherine Simpson Milne said:

I know one instance that she [Peggy] had quite a crush on this boy . . . [one of the] air force British boys around here . . . [from the] air force training school. . . . I think he used to be up at the house a bit, when she was living with grandfather. Grandfather was horrified. He said, "Mark my words; he's a married man. Just mark my words." Sure enough he was. It turned out he was. Grandfather was always right. He was really. . . . He was a very good judge of people. . . . I know that he would be around the house a bit. (Milne 30-31).

Neighbor Phyllis Ralph also noted "Peggy had a RAF boy friend. It went on for quite awhile. They broke up. I guess they were young" (Ralph 8). This close correspondence to Laurence in *A Bird in the House* describes Vanessa inviting an airman home several times to visit. Grandfather Connor comes up from the basement, where he was rocking in his chair, to burst out, "I'll bet a nickel to a doughnut hole he's married." It turned out he was (*Bird* 184). Some romances, however, did develop as a result of the dances. Viola Radford's daughter Sheila (now Morris) was in the same grade as Margaret. "The war years came on. I think they had quite a nice time. . . . There were a lot of outside men in. . . . [My] daughter married [one of the airmen from Oakville, Ontario]. Of course, Laurence did too. He was an air force man" (Radford 9). Thus war--the men at the airbase--brought happiness and more cosmopolitanism to Neepawa. It was part of Laurence's maturing. Margaret Murray pointed out: Laurence "got out and had a good time too and met a lot [of men] her age then. And she was quite popular, I think, in school" (Margaret Murray 16). "She had a good bringing up because her stepmother was a lovely person. Her mother was too" (Margaret Murray 22). Wes McAmmond expanded on this:

Laurence got out and got going to places and going with others. She was a very lively young girl. . . . She couldn't take liberties. She couldn't have fun. I think she was quite glad when she got going to Winnipeg. . . . When she went away, she tried new things. (McAmmond 3-4)

These happier moments of entertaining and dancing were thousands of miles from the horrors of war in Europe of which little is said in the interviews. Even in the fiction, only vignettes about startling details give specifics of war horrors. For both the First and Second World Wars, accounts are low key but stoically awful, such as lists of casualties Morag and Vanessa read (*Diviners* 158-59NCL, 116-

17UC and *Bird* 181). Newspapers tell lies. According to Jules, the Battle of Dieppe, "wasn't quite the way the paper told it, I guess. All any guy thinks of is staying alive. Some guys were scared" (*Diviners* 180NCL, 133UC). When they wrote letters to family members, they lied; they said everything was "going well." This reflects real life for Neepawa; resident Gerald Murray says he wrote this way to his mother (Murray 5-6). Yet he flew twenty-nine missions and saw a buddy bail out from the plane in front of him (Murray 5-6). In *A Bird in the House*, a soldier character, Ewen MacLeod, wrote Grandmother MacLeod about his brother Roderick as dying gallantly (*Bird* 59). The irony of this is compounded when she proudly says, "The MacLeods never tell lies" (*Bird* 48). Yet Ewen was candid with his wife. He had said to her, "Men don't really die like that, Beth. It wasn't that way at all" (*Bird* 59, 141). His wife, Beth, learned from Ewen that he had stumbled upon Roderick by chance; he told her of the muck, the wild-eyed horses, and mud with floating appendages (*Bird* 141). To Christie the worst lies are in official history books like *The 60th Canadian Field Artillery Battery Book*. He cries to Morag that it makes "the war sound like a Sunday School picnic" (*Diviners* 101NCL, 73UC). Relentlessly, the case is built up about the appearance and reality of war in Laurence's novels. In another instance, the blunt word "lies" is used. When Rachel praises the pipe band playing "March of the Cameron Highland Men," Niall Cameron comments, "It's a nice sound, the lies the pipes tell" (*Jest* 63, 207). A comment about war may be perceived as very minimal unless one knows the realities of the First and Second World Wars. For example, Hagar downplays its tragic events: of Marvin in the awful Vimy Ridge battle, she thinks only that "He lived through it" (*Angel* 130).

Details of what actually happened in the wars are very few because often they returned back home, men in Manawaka, as in Neepawa, kept silent. Examples of silence are found in every Manawaka novel. Marvin would never say what he had been forced to look upon (*Angel* 182) nor would Brooke Skelton who did Second World War service in Quebec, a safe place (*Diviners* 233NCL, 176UC). Another kind of silence is the retreat into insanity. After a year in Britain, Chris was brought home to a mental institution (*Bird* 142). For Chris, Vanessa articulates the solutions as "unreal . . . because there were no others, the brave and useless strokes of fantasy against a depression that was both the world's and his own" (*Bird* 143). His mental illness was the "final heartbreaking extension of the way he's always had of distancing himself from the absolute unbearability of battle" (*Bird* 143). They "could force his body to march and even to kill, but what they didn't know was that he's fooled them. He didn't live inside it anymore" (*Bird* 143).

Of those back in Manawaka, the muck and mire of war was far away. Christie would only say that collecting people's garbage was not as bad as the muck and filth overseas of trenches muddied with urine, blood, floating limbs, and floundering flare-nostrilled horses. To Christie, the only thing worse in Manawaka was the dead baby wrapped in newspaper (*Diviners* 86NCL, 62UC; 425NCL, 326UC). A few other characters would break their silence to a special person. "A Private in the Artillery in 1915" (*Jest* 105), Niall Cameron kept silent while drinking his alcohol among the dead in his funeral business until one day he told

Stacey he saw an eighteen-year-old boy get a grenade between his legs. Stacey remembers: "My dad cried when he told it because the kid didn't die" (*Fire-Dwellers* 10). No wonder Niall speaks in a terrifying voice (*Fire-Dwellers* 44). Stacey remembered this when contemplating the silence of Mac about the Second War until he had to identity his former war buddy at the morgue. The moment's stress contributed to Mac telling Stacey why Buckle maintained a twenty-year symbiotic relationship with him: in Italy, Buckle's truck was blown off a bridge the reckless Buckle refused to scout for explosives; Mac tells her how he carried Buckle to a farmer's cart which they rode; fortunately, they rejoined their unit (*Fire-Dwellers* 219). A different reason prompts Brooke Skelton to break his silence but only to talk of auxiliary activities--the women in Montreal (*Diviners* 233NCL, 176UC). For Vanessa's airman Michael, a sensitive poet and story writer, he would confide only to her that he was sweating every time he is up in a Tiger Moth plane (*Bird* 182). Even training for combat was stressful enough to be done dutifully silently bearing the emotional trauma. Vanessa could only hug him tightly. Some silences were broken when a character directly requested details: only then did Skinner Tonnerre give details to Morag of how John Lobodiak died: "They [his guts] were spilling out.... Like a shot gopher.... His eyes.... Like a horse's eyes in a barn fire" (*Diviners* 180NCL, 133UC). Laurence's childhood neighbor, Gerald Murray, four decades after the Second World War, could begin to talk more about his twenty-nine missions (5-6). He had been young enough to shrug off the war. He did see those with psychological exhaustion (5-6).

In fictional Manawaka, the returned men talked of other things like Mac MacAindra did of his jobs. In Laurence's fiction plenty of evidence exists about the ambivalence of silence and talking about war, but words flowed freely about pleasant social activities.

War then, to Laurence, may cause a division between ethnic groups, but time and circumstances may bring some of them together. Where there is intermarriage, the painful process of reconciling two identities can be learned. The will to include all of one's past from all identities will bring the past into the present to make it more meaningful. The particular innovation of Laurence bringing together the prairie groups of the Scots and Métis is notable. Neither has a place to go back to but live in a present time and in several places across Canada. Readers in the American South might find a more positive answer here to their situation. South Africa, where Afrikaners, Africans, and Coloreds have nowhere to turn back to, might learn to live with multifaceted identities. Laurence's answer in *The Diviners* is to have Pique voluntarily find out who she is amidst the Canadian expanses from Ontario to the west coast. Another answer is to put two groups together imaginatively. Stacey had imagined herself as Anastasia of Russia and then had thought, in a melding of her Scottish ancestry with her knowledge of another group, that she is Anastasia of the Hebrides. Trying to unite disparate elements in a character's or a person's life is a microcosm of the larger picture of history, that record of wars where distinct groups, such as the Scots, Métis, French, English, Ukrainian, and any others, did not get together. War and its trauma during and after sometimes has to stimulate the will to survive and to know oneself which is to learn again one's heritage in each generation. Laurence has drawn upon the wars she learned about in Neepawa but explored and fictionalized much from those seminal ones of Scottish heritage, Métis history, and modern times. Against the 1960s background of the Vietnam war--Pique sings the songs of Joan Baez, Bob Dylan, Joni Mitchell, and others (*Diviners* 451NCL, 347UC)--Laurence depicts part of the Canadian dilemma, a kind of dormant civil war stasis, among the Métis and Scots with characters like Morag, Jules, and Pique. Laurence also portrays the answer to war one person can make: women raising families, like Stacey, can arrange time to march against all war; like Rachel, women can be assertive. Hagar and Vanessa both learn they can acknowledge their Scottish ancestry with its wars while aware of the futility of war. War in the final analysis influences what a person can affirm in the present. That affirmation can include some or considerable knowledge of the past--about the war dead and what the living did afterwards.

WORKS CITED

Bell, J. J. *The Glory of Scotland*. London: George G. Harrap, 1932.
Henderson, Dorothy Campbell. Interview. 20 July 1984, Neepawa, Manitoba.
___. Letter from Mr. Prince, August 13, 1988.
Laurence, Margaret. *A Bird in the House*. Toronto: McClelland and Stewart, New Canadian Library (1970) 1994; Chicago: University of Chicago Press, 1993.
___. *The Diviners*. Toronto: McClelland and Stewart, New Canadian Library (1974, 1988) 1995; Chicago: University of Chicago Press, 1993.
___. *The Fire-Dwellers*. Toronto: McClelland and Stewart, New Canadian Library (1969, 1988) 1991; Chicago: University of Chicago Press, 1993.
___. *A Jest of God*. Toronto: McClelland and Stewart, New Canadian Library (1966, 1974, 1988) 1993; Chicago: University of Chicago Press, 1993.
___. *Heart of a Stranger*. Toronto: McClelland and Stewart, 1976.
___. *The Stone Angel*. Toronto: McClelland and Stewart, New Canadian Library (1964, 1968, 1988) 1995; Chicago: University of Chicago Press, 1993.
Lemon, Anthony, and N. C. Pollock, eds. *Studies in Overseas Settlement and Population*. London: Longman Group, 1980.
Lower, A. M. *From Colony to Nation*. London: Longman, Green (1946) 1957.
McAmmond, Wes. Interview. 24 July 1984, Winnipeg, Manitoba.
McKenzie, A. F. (Dick). *75 Years Keystone of the Keystone Province. Neepawa. Land of Plenty*. Brandon, Manitoba: Leech Printing, 1984.
Milne, Catherine Simpson. Interview. 24 July 1984, Neepawa, Manitoba.
Muirhead, L. Russell, ed. *The Blue Guides. Scotland*. London: Benn, 1959.
Murray, Gerald. Interview. 23 July 1984, Neepawa, Manitoba.
Murray, Margaret. Interview. 20 July 1984, Neepawa, Manitoba.
Musgrove, Mildred. Interview. 21 July 1984, Boissevain, Manitoba.
Neepawa Heritage. *A History of the Town of Neepawa and District as Told and Recorded by its People. 1883-1983*. Neepawa, Manitoba: n.p., 1983.
Radford, Viola. Interview. 23 July 1984, Neepawa, Manitoba.
Ralph, Phyllis. Interview. 25 July 1984, Winnipeg, Manitoba.
Thomas, Clara. *The Manawaka World of Margaret Laurence*. Toronto, Canada: McClelland and Stewart (1975) 1976.

Chapter 10

Margaret Laurence of Hargeisa: A Discussion of *A Tree for Poverty*

Fiona Sparrow

When Mary Renault reviewed *This Side Jordan* (Toronto, McClelland and Stewart, New Canadian Library [1960] 1989), published by Macmillan of London in 1960, she thought of its author as Miss Laurence, "A scholar and translator of African folklore and poetry" ("On Understanding Africa," *Saturday Review* 10 December 1960: 24). At this point the compilers of *The British Library General Catalogue of Printed Books to 1975*, Volume 185, knew little more. They had described the author of *A Tree for Poverty*, published in 1954, as "Margaret Laurence, of Hargeisa" (*British* 303). In 1954 Hargeisa was the capital of the British Protectorate of Somaliland, and it was there that the decision was taken to publish Margaret Laurence's first book. Now, of course, Margaret Laurence is known as the first lady of Manawaka, but as Margaret Laurence of Hargeisa she produced a work of scholarship that is still valued by those who study Somali literature in the context of African oral traditions.

In *The Prophet's Camel Bell* (Toronto: McClelland and Stewart, New Canadian Library [1963, 1988] 1991), Margaret Laurence describes how she began to collect Somali poetry and prose and how *A Tree for Poverty* (Nairobi: Eagle, 1954; Dublin: Irish University Press and Hamilton, Ontario: McMaster University Press, 1970; rpt. Toronto: ECW, 1993, designated hereafter as *Tree)* came to be published. Soon after arrival in the British Protectorate in 1950, she had the good fortune to meet a young Polish poet and his Somali assistant. They had a British research grant to study the Somali language and literature. Much of Margaret Laurence's work was done with their encouragement and help. The poet, B. W. Andrzejewski, Emeritus Professor of the University of London, and the Somali, the late Musa Galaal, became the leading scholars in their field and produced, as Margaret Laurence acknowledges, work "of a much more scholarly and accurate nature" than her own (*Tree* 19). Hers, however, was the first published collection of Somali literature in English, and the introduction she wrote for it is a fine piece of literary criticism. A passage in this introduction caught the attention of a member of the British Administration and it was from Colonial Office funds, allocated to the Protectorate, that money was found to publish at Eagle Press, in Nairobi, *A Tree for Poverty* (1954).

This edition is now difficult to find. *The National Union Catalog* knows of two copies in the United States, but there is no record of a Canadian library holding. The book was much in demand, and "The last copies . . .were bought by the Peace Corps for distribution among young volunteers going to the Somali Republic" (*Tree* 19). In 1970 the Irish University Press and McMaster University Press made a photographic facsimile of the first edition and published it with a new Preface by Margaret Laurence. This edition, though out of print, is available from McMaster University Archives, Hamilton, Ontario, Canada.

Not long after its first publication, *A Tree for Poverty* began appearing in bibliographies relating to Somali literature. It was also used as a source in the compilation of anthologies of African oral poetry and prose. Margaret Laurence's work was, and still is, esteemed for two reasons. First, it contains a substantial body of Somali poetry and prose, providing sufficient material for scholars to demonstrate a critical view and for anthologizers to exercise a choice. Secondly, the translations are finely done and they testify to the beauty of the original as well as to the excellence of Margaret Laurence's craft.

A hundred years before the publication of *A Tree for Poverty*, Richard Burton commented on the importance of poetry in Somaliland in *First Footsteps in East Africa* (London: J. M. Dent, 1910), a work well known to Margaret Laurence. He says, "It is strange that a dialect which has no written character should so abound in poetry and eloquence" (*First* 90). In 1954 Somali still had no official written character (it was not until 1972 that an orthography was chosen), and Margaret Laurence was in her turn struck by the vitality of the oral culture: "Although they have no written language, the Somalis are a nation of poets. There is no sign of this art dying" (*Tree* 23).

Margaret Laurence speaks of "ten different types of Somali poetry" (*Tree* 26), but she concentrates on only two, the oldest and the youngest, the classical *gabei* and the modern *belwo* (the spelling used by Margaret Laurence of the variants before 1972). This is her definition of the gabei:

The Somali gabei is considered to be the highest literary form in the culture. Gabei may be on any topic, but the rules of gabei-making are strict and difficult. A gabei poet must not only have an extensive vocabulary and an ability to express himself fluently and in terms of figures of speech. He must also possess considerable knowledge of the country, its geography and plant-life, Somali medicine, and animal husbandry. (*Tree* 32)

The gabei has much in common with Old English poetry. They spring from similar oral traditions and the use of alliteration, a memory aid, is common to both. The demands made on the Somali poet, however, are greater because he does not confine his alliteration to the line but carries it through the whole poem, often of some length. B. V. Andrzejewski and I. M. Lewis believe

[T]he exacting demands of alliteration, maintained throughout the whole poem have had a profound influence on Somali poetic diction. The poet, to supplement his store of words, has to resurrect archaic words, enliven obsolescent ones, and even create new ones, and many arguments arise among Somali audiences as to the precise meanings of such archaisms. (B. V. Andrzejewski and I. M. Lewis, *Somali Poetry: An Introduction* [Oxford: Clarendon Press, 1964], p. 43, hereafter designated *Somali Poetry*)

It follows that the gabei is difficult to translate. Margaret Laurence only attempts short extracts, but on one occasion she tries to convey the effect of Somali alliteration. The poem, "Battle Pledge," opens with praise of the composer's "fleet and fiery horse," with "shining flank and finely arching neck" (*Tree* 56). The English alliteration with "f" is only lightly done but Margaret Laurence's version is not without the sophistication and dramatic effect that she was aware of in the original.

"Battle Pledge" is one piece chosen from *A Tree for Poverty* by Ruth Finnegan for her excellent and well-informed anthology *The Penguin Book of Oral Poetry* (Harmondsworth: Penguin Books, 1982). However, the gabei translation that has attracted the most attention is called "To a Friend Going on a Journey." Anthologizers cannot resist it; it is included in Ruth Finnegan's selection, and it has also been used as an epigraph by Dr. Kevin M. Cahill for his book *Somalia: A Perspective* (Albany, NY: State University of New York Press, 1980), which is a collection of compassionate essays on the suffering caused by disease. This gabei extract is from a long poem by Mohamed Abdullah Hassan, the great Somali national hero, who defied the British for twenty years with his poetry and his sword. Margaret Laurence chose to remember him in his role of friend, not enemy, and her translation is worth quoting in full:

Now you depart, and though your way may lead
Through airless forests thick with "hhagar" trees,
Places steeped in heat, stifling and dry,
Where breath comes hard, and no fresh breeze can reach--
Yet may God place a shield of coolest air
Between your body and the assailant sun.

And in a random scorching flame of wind
That parches the painful throat, and sears the flesh,
May God, in His compassion, let you find
The great-boughed tree that will protect and shade.

On every side of you, I now would place
Prayers from the Holy Qoran, to bless your path,
That ills may not descend, nor evils harm,
And you may travel in the peace of faith.

To all the blessings I bestow on you,
Friend, yourself now say a last Amen. (*Tree* 53)

In their collection, *Somali Poetry*, Andrzejewski and Lewis have a number of

Mohamed Abdullah Hassan's long poems. The Sayyid, as his people called him, spoke to the Ogaden tribesmen through his poems. One, translated by Andrzejewski, is a dramatic description of conditions in the Haud. The passage calls to mind many of the themes central to *The Prophet's Camel Bell*: the hardship of the nomad's life, the need to have faith in God, and the importance of the few desert trees that provide shade for the traveler. Andrzejewski's translation of this passage is impersonal, a virtue because little stands between the reader and the original as regards meaning, but it is also spare so that the Sayyid's rhythmic and alliterative effects must be imagined. This is Andrzejewski's translation:

Nevertheless, what the Haud is known for is hardship and lack of water. / The present season is the time of the light Kahil rains. / God who fills our water-ponds will not make you thirst. / Bush thick and impenetrable, scorched *hagar* trees, the hot air rising from them, / Hot wind and heat, which will lick you like a flame, / A mantle of air and a shade-giving tree will shelter you. (*Somali Poetry* 94)

Margaret Laurence's translations are considered accurate by scholars; indeed, it was Andrzejewski and Musa Galaal who gave her the literal translations in the first place. There is a flexibility in her handling of the material, and the elegant English of her translations is as true in its way to the Sayyid's art as Andrzejewski's faithful rendering.

The *belwo*, the modern lyric love poem, is very different from the *gabei*, and, indeed, as Andrzejewski in "The Art of the Miniature in Somali Poetry," *African Language Review* 6 (1967) has pointed out that the *belwo*, "loved by the new urban generation . . . met with fierce censure from the older people in the interior and the more pious men in towns" (12). The *belwo* was invented in 1944 by a lorry driver, Abdi Deeqsi. "It was, at least at first, a very short poem of two lines, or even one . . . . Initially the subject matter was always love" (5). Like the *gabei* the *belwo* is difficult to translate, and Andrzejewski and Margaret Laurence untie the condensed imagery in different ways. This can be seen in *The Penguin Book of Oral Poetry* because Ruth Finnegan selects examples of both translators' work and has this to say about them:

In the first group given here the translator, Margaret Laurence, has felt forced to lengthen the translations slightly in her attempt to convey the images involved, while the later translations, mainly by B. W. Andrzejewski, approximate more nearly to the length of the originals. (*Penguin* 110)

Sometimes Finnegan seems unaware that they are working from the same original:

All your young beauty is to me
Like a place where the new grass sways,
After the blessing of the rain,
When the sun unveils its light. (*Tree* 50)

Andrzejewski's version is, in contrast, a two-line mirror image of the original:

You are like a place with fresh grass after a downpour of rain
On which the sun now shines. (*Penguin* 112)

He does not attempt anything but a literal translation. When he appears in *The Prophet's Camel Bell*, he seems unprepared to think of his own poetry in any language other than Polish:

"Of course, it is useless," he said with deep Slavonic melancholy. "My poetry can't be published in Poland, and in England who is interested in publishing poems written in Polish?" (*Prophet* 44)

Margaret Laurence's attitude is different, and she will redefine an image or smooth over a grammatical transition, though she always respects the original and her responsibility to convey it truthfully. In Ruth Finnegan's selection there are two similar poems on death. This is a favorite theme with the belwo poets, and the differences in the two following translations may be the result of more than one Somali version. Nevertheless, both translators again demonstrate their particular working attitudes. This is Margaret Laurence:

The merciful will not ignore
A man whose death draws near:
Before the earth receives my bones,
Show mercy unto me. (*Tree* 51)

This is Andrzejewski:

One does not hurry past a dying man,
Before I enter the grave, spare a word for me. (*Penguin* 112)

A Tree for Poverty shows Margaret Laurence working with poetry. Her translations are poems in their own right. Her interest, however, has always been primarily in fiction, and the main part of the book attempts to capture something of the storyteller's art as she encountered it in the Haud. She records most of the stories as paraphrases rather than translations, and she works from versions given her by Hersi, the teller of tales in *The Prophet's Camel Bell*.

Andrzejewski divides oral literature into two streams: time-bound and time-free (*Literatures in African Languages* [Cambridge: University Press, 1985], p. 338). The former is generally poetry that alters remarkably little during transmission. The latter is mostly prose, stories that have been told many times. Their storyline may remain basically stable, but it is expected that individual storytellers will add to their own color and detail. Hersi told Margaret Laurence the Somali stories in his colorful English, acting them out as he did so:

[H]is acting had tremendous value. It compensated to some extent for the fact that I was not hearing the stories in Somali, in which he would have been able to express them with better style. Hersi belonged to the ancient brotherhood of born storytellers. (*Prophet* 177)

Margaret Laurence was then free, according to the oral traditions themselves, to tell the stories in her own way.

Among the best of Hersi's stories are the ones that tell of Wiil Waal, the powerful and wise Sultan who ruled the country around Jijigga. Nuruddin Farah in the novel, *Close Sesame* (London: Allison & Busby, 1983; reprinted St. Paul, Minnesota, Graywolf Publishers, 1992), of his Somali trilogy uses three of the stories Margaret Laurence has preserved, including two about Wiil Waal. The central figure in *Close Sesame*, published in 1983, is a marvelous old Ogaden tribesman, now living in Mogadiscio, who can recall the stories he heard as a child and tell them again for his young grandson. Nuruddin Farah at the end of his novel acknowledges the debt owed to Margaret Laurence who made sure these stories would not be lost. He adds that "being a Somali myself, I've had to depend more on the resources of my own memory than on Laurence's" (208). Yet, the two versions of the Wiil Waal stories are close. Details of plot, dialogue, and the moral of the story are the same, but a difference lies in the mood and language of the storytelling voice.

Margaret Laurence keeps any individual characterization out of the storytelling voice without weakening the dramatic narrative. The denouement is always carefully planned and the dialogue, a large part of the stories, is rhetorical and exuberant. There is an extensive use of the "once upon a time" storytelling tags: "It happened," "It is said that once, long ago," "Once there lived," "Now it is well known that," and "It came to pass."

Nuruddin Farah's storyteller is a known individual, and his character influences the narrative voice. The reader is made aware of who is telling the tale. Deeiye, a devout Muslim, is honored by his family, for the natural authority he possesses and for the price he has paid in the fight for Somali independence. Though Deeriye's attachment to the past is strong, he accepts change and is proud of his two modern children, especially his daughter, a doctor, who takes professional care of her ailing father. The reader is aware of all this as the story is told. Deeriye's language is more archaic and formal than Margaret Laurence's, and the Somali tribesman makes use of this opportunity to remind his grandson of the importance of the faith and traditions of his ancestors.

To demonstrate the comparison from extracts is difficult, but the following two passages, one from each version, give an idea of the differences of mood and style. In the story Wiil Waal is trying to prove once more that there is no man as wise as he is, and he has asked all his people to kill one of their sheep and bring him the piece of meat that "makes men either brothers or enemies" (*Tree* 112)

In *A Tree for Poverty* the story continues:

All day long, the Bartire elders puzzled over the words, and discussed together. But, finding no answer to the strange demand of Sultan Wiil Waal, each decided to take a chance. The sheep were slaughtered in each home that night, and the special piece of mutton was selected. One man decided to take a leg of meat to stir the "shiir." Another thought that a good saddle of mutton might please the sultan. Another, the shoulders of the sheep. And so it went.

One man of the Bartire was very poor. In his flock, he had no more than half a dozen sheep. But, obeying his Sultan's command, he killed a fine sheep that night, and gave it to his daughter to cut up the meat.

Now the girl was about fifteen years old, and very beautiful. But as well as beauty, she had a brain. (*Tree* 113)

Deeriye tells the tale to Samawade thus:

That evening, there was consultations among the men. Many did not know what to do. Word went round that it was one of their King's mad whims and they suspected there was a trick behind this. . . . The rich among the populace had little to worry about. . . . But the poor encountered a difficulty: not only could they not afford an expensive joke of a King's whim, but they did not know whether if they failed they would be fined or, worse still, made to slaughter more.

There was one such worried poor man. This man owned no more than the hut in which he and his only daughter lived and five sheep. But he was a saintly man and a man with a great deal of foresight, for he had believed in the Prophet's tradition that "he who educates a young boy for the future and for Islam educates a man-in-the-future; and he who educates a girl for the future and for Islam educates--symbolically speaking--a larger community": and had cared for his daughter in the way other men pampered their boys; and he educated her by paying from his meager wealth the little that would make a Koranic teacher pass on to her all the essentials. That evening when he went back to his hamlet, he wouldn't eat nor would he say what ailed him or worried him. After a lot of questioning, he told her what the King had said. She said she did not know why her father should be worried; he should let her deal with it. (Farah, *Close Sesame* 124)

In the Haud Margaret Laurence had watched Hersi dramatizing the Somali stories; years later she created a fictional storyteller of her own who, like Deeriye, could enchant a child with tales of the past. Christie Logan in *The Diviners* (Toronto: McClelland and Stewart, New Canadian Library, 1995; and Chicago: University of Chicago Press, 1993), while he speaks with a distinctly individual voice, uses the patterns of oral tradition that Margaret Laurence studied in Africa:

It was in the old days, a long time ago, after the clans was broken and scattered at the battle on the moors. . . . Then Piper Gunn spoke to the people. "Dolts and draggard and daft loons and gutless as gutted herring you are," he calls out in his voice like the voice of the wind from the north isles. (*Diviners* 58-59NCL, 40-41UC)

In her Preface to the 1970 edition of *A Tree for Poverty*, Margaret Laurence admits that she is neither "a literary critic nor an anthropologist," and that her book, therefore, has "shortcomings" (*Tree* 19). If so, they have not been noticed by the linguists and critics who have used her work. *A Tree for Poverty* is not without relevance to Margaret Laurence's fiction, but it is far more important as a work in its own right and in its own field. It contains examples of Somali poetry and prose in translations that achieve a compromise between two languages and two cultures. A work both of scholarship and love, it is a text book and much more. Her first book, the literature it celebrates, is "a tree for poverty to shelter under," a tree that gives shade to the traveler.

Chapter 11

Margaret Laurence and the Ancestral Tradition
Cecil Abrahams

The years Margaret Laurence spent in Somaliland and Ghana had a tremendous impact on her creative and critical work (unpublished interview, 1974). In her impressions of Somali society in *The Prophet's Camel Bell*, and again in her critical reading of West African writing in *Long Drums and Cannons*, she continually asks questions about the African oral traditions, and she demonstrates an authentic concern for African culture which, hitherto, had not been a mark of most Western writers. *This Side Jordan*, which deals to a large extent with the European experience in the days preceding Ghana's independence, has been enthusiastically commended by G. D. Killam and Clara Thomas. Killam regards Laurence as "the best expatriate writing about Africa," and, in particular, he contrasts her "objectivity" with the many other renditions of the expatriate experience in Africa. Although Clara Thomas expresses some reservation about the authenticity of the African characters in *This Side Jordan*, she recognizes the value of this book in the subsequent development of Laurence's fiction, and she goes on to note the "sureness of tone and the success of technique" which Laurence achieves in her first novel" (52). This writer argues that Laurence's authenticity stems from her innate sense of awareness of the ethos of traditional society and that this perception also underlies her vision of Canadian society.

The ethos of traditional society was enshrined in an oral, religious, and literary tradition through which the community transmitted from generation to generation its customs, values, and norms. The poet and the storyteller stood at the center of this tradition, as the community's chroniclers, entertainers, and collective conscience. Their contribution was considered to be of the greatest significance. The oral creative act was a communal one rather than the product of a particular genius. The story was acted out by the villagers in the marketplace or the village square, and this instant feedback from the audience encouraged the artists to give of their best. Because the artistic act was communal, the storyteller emphasized the communal value of art: he was always guided by a broad theme that centered on the need for an ordered society, a stable and harmonious community. For the oral storyteller "art is, and was always, in the service of man" (Achebe 19).

As a writer living in a relatively new nation-state, Laurence admitted in the interview that in her need to establish a viable vision through which the people in her country could envisage themselves, she devoted most of her creative talents to being the oral tale teller for the cultural heritage which her people so often found difficult to relate to a central national pattern. Therefore, she deliberately fashioned out of her material loose historical myths through which she could trace the history of her country's culture, comment on its present development, and chart possible new directions for the future. Hence, she transforms relatively small villages into macrocosms of vast and intricate nations and peoples, and in so doing, she takes the reader back to the true sources of history for the Canadian people.

Laurence's writings cover four generations from her grandparents to her child's generations. Since there is the overwhelming need in Laurence to journey back to the sources from which the current confusion emanates, she demonstrates a tremendous belief in the ancestral past. She says "the past is extremely real," and she emphasizes her belief that a great deal of what we know and are today has been "passed on" by earlier generations. She sees this preoccupation as being aware of her tribal past, and Laurence insists that her sojourn in Africa reawakened her own sense of tribalism. The tribal nature of the chief characters in Laurence's books is further enforced by the type of society which she examines. The Scots-Presbyterians of Laurence's works are tightly structured, highly individualistic, hardworking, and moralistic.

Looking at the work of Chinua Achebe, Laurence sees her task as not being unlike his. But whereas Achebe's definition of the Nigerian people can in a large part be carved out of the colonial invasion and conflict, Laurence is faced with the more challenging and subtle task of demonstrating to her people that not only has colonialism attempted to render the entire nation inferior, but also its divide-and-rule policy has led to civil conflict between the various tribes within the nation. Laurence claims that what she is doing in her fiction as well as what writers, such as Robert Kroetsch, Al Purdy, and Irving Layton, have done "is to try in some way to come to terms with our ancestral past, to deal in this way with these themes of survival and growth, and to record our mythology" (Thomas 67). It is this attempt to charter the Canadian psyche in *The Diviners* which establishes her real value to Canada.

Jules Tonnerre's defense of his father's life is similar to Obierika's defense of Okonkwo in *Things Fall Apart*. He observes that in the final days of his father's life Lazarus did not care "whether he died or didn't die. He had a lotta troubles in his life" (*Diviners* 288NCL, 219UC). Jules portrays Lazarus as a father who cared for his brood and who would "never turn anybody of his out, whatever they had done" (288NCL, 219UC). Yet because of the prejudice of the Anglo-Saxon community of Manawaka, Lazarus was considered to be a "low-bred, halfbreed" with whom the respectable ought not to communicate. Similar to Okonkwo, there is no place in the town's cemetery to rest Lazarus's dead bones. But while Okonkwo is refused permission to the cemetery because he had offended the gods, Lazarus is kept out because "His halfbreed bones [would spoil] their cemetery" (289NCL, 219UC). Like Obierika, Morag Gunn recalls bitterly and sadly that "The Métis, once lords of the prairies," are now "refused burial space in their own land" (289NCL, 219UC). In this tragic instance and in the class prejudice which is shown towards Christie Logan, it is left to Laurence to correct the inhumane view of her people. Like Achebe, Laurence uses *The Diviners* to redefine the Canadian past, to instill a true sense of history into her fellow Canadians, and to stir within the Canadian psyche an awareness of and a pride in an ancestral past from which a part of the nation emerged. In this purpose, both Laurence and Achebe follow the great tradition of the oral storyteller, and as literary chroniclers they desire to achieve the same glorious aims as their predecessors. But the task of recording history and interpreting it for one's fellow participants is not an easy one. Hence both *The Diviners* and *Things Fall Apart* grow slowly and painstakingly as the artists grapple with the best technique to evoke creative responses from an audience whose passivity and obtuseness are unlike the traditional audience who anticipated and eagerly expanded the storyteller's tale.

Laurence and Achebe adhere further to the constraints of the oral tale-teller by giving the distinct impression in their novels that the stories they are recording have been brought down to them by other storytellers of the collective soul of their people. Both writers constantly recall stories that reinforce the moral teachings of their societies and instill a strong element of pride. In *Things Fall Apart*, author Achebe frequently calls upon the wisdom of the past generations to make a telling point or to clarify certain forms of behavior. Margaret Laurence refers often to the creative environment of her stepmother's home where she was permitted and encouraged to form her own tales and where she was constantly fascinated by many tales of her tradition's past. It is, therefore, not by chance that the form of *The Diviners* is framed in the traditional story and that the results achieved by both form and tale-teller are identical with those of the oral performance.

Since Chinua Achebe inherited a rich and recognized oral tradition, he is not faced with the additional task of trying to explain or to establish such a tradition before writing his work. Margaret Laurence recognizes that her task of being her nation's oral tale-teller is significantly more difficult because her nation blends a mixture of literate and oral cultures. In *The Diviners* she uses Lazarus, Jules, and Christie as the visible and viable storytellers. Perhaps more significantly, she uses the "snap-shot" and "Memorybank Movie" techniques as modern extensions of the tale-teller.

The oral teller presented the community with tales that had been carried over from other generations. Since the tale-telling occurred as a dramatic performance, both teller and listener contributed to its form and content. In this regard, Christie Logan's stories of heroism on the part of Piper Gunn are rendered in a dramatic form and his audience, consisting of the young Morag and the obedient Prin, often provides impetus for and augmentation to the tale. This tale-telling further inspires Morag to begin a tale of "Piper Gunn's Woman" (61NCL, 42UC), thus fulfilling the task of the oral storyteller to further the myths of the nation by inspiring the birth of another teller in the form of Morag. This need for continuity pervades Laurence's overall objectives, and it is found in Lazarus Tonnerre's inspiring Jules and his other children to remember the Métis past and to carry their tradition forward; it is found in Jules whose legacy to Pique is not to forget her past and whose gift to her is his songs and the knife; additionally, it is found in Royland who recognizes that the gift of passing on mystery and myth is eternal and inevitable for the forward moving process of the culture and humanity. This need to relate present perspectives to a much wider development which contains the ancestral past preoccupies Laurence's attention. The snapshots are used deliberately to trace both the past history of Morag and the Scots-Presbyterians and to reflect on the present condition of both. Since Laurence is writing for a modern Canadian audience, she transforms the oral technique of the tale-teller (which worked so well in Morag's youth) into visual forms that are more in harmony and effective today.

Essentially, however, the storytellers' objectives are realized in the tales of inhumanity and despair which we find in the treatment of Indians and poorer-class Canadians. Like Achebe, Laurence's task here is to show the irrational causes for these dreadful situations and through illustration to seek active redress. Coming from a prairie world where the Indian has always been a part of the landscape, Laurence in her previous works had made references to the Indians' condition. Invariably, she notes, the Indian was regarded and treated as a heathenish outcast by the God-fearing puritans of the white community. In *The Diviners*, Laurence makes a close study of the root cause of such a belief. She demonstrates a Manawaka white community that had for decades referred to the Indians as "those breeds" (79NCL, 56UC), a subhuman specie that had to be removed to an isolated place in the Wachakwa valley. Regardless of the aspirations and inner workings of the Indian community, the prairie white society expresses their prejudice in their belief that the Indian is generally lazy, always drunk, lives in filth and squalor, is not interested in education, and that their women are prostitutes and their men heartless and poor providers. It is in her close examination of the Tonnerre family that Laurence shows the incorrect view that is held by the white community.

Through Lazarus and Jules Tonnerre, Morag is provided with the Indian's view of the Riel rebellion. Since the disintegration of the Métis community stems from this traumatic event, Laurence shows the two views held in regard to the rebellion. The official or school teacher's view is that Louis Riel was a rebel and that he and the Métis deserved their destructive fate. Lazarus tells Jules of how heroically Riel and the Métis defended their land and their independence and how cruelly they were treated by the whites. Furthermore, the result of the Riel fight is perpetual prejudice and enslavement at the hands of the white community. Lazarus is considered to be a drunken sloth who "makes homebrew down there in the shack in the Wachakwa valley" (79NCL, 56UC); Jules is bluntly informed not to consider the profession of law, but as an Indian he "might do well to set [his] sights a bit lower" like working as an apprentice mechanic at the BA Garage (149NCL, 109UC); also, Piquette and her family are destroyed in a fire, but the blame is not placed on the inhumane living conditions which had been imposed on them, but it is simply assumed that drunkenness had caused the tragedy (173-76NCL, 127-30UC). To show that the prejudice against the Métis is widespread among

Canadians rather than a peculiar Manawaka disease, Laurence shows the seemingly educated Brooke Skelton reacting in a racist manner towards Jules when he refers to the illegality of serving liquor to Indians. Later in Vancouver when Maggie Tefler views the product of Jules and Morag's lovemaking, she states bluntly:

Did you get yerself mixed up with a Chinese or a Jap, dear? No? Well, I wasn't going to say halfbreed--I didn't think it possible. What's that? Maytee? I never heard that word. They're all halfbreeds to me, and I could tell you a thing or two, you betcha. (329NCL, 252UC)

Laurence emphasises the prejudice here and indicates the struggle that Pique and other Métis will have to engage in to lift the prejudice and to restore the respect for the Métis which existed before the Riel rebellion. Hence, the hope of a better integrated nation is expressed in Pique's intimacy with Jules and the lessons through his songs which in its oral form sing the praises and joy of the Métis. Armed in this manner, she sets off to aid her uncle in restoring dignity to the poor and orphaned Indian children and thus prepares the road for the Indian to once more assume his rightful place in the Canadian society. By searching out the source of white prejudice, Laurence, the traditional storyteller, urges the nation to look closely at its irrational past and to redefine its future freed of prejudice towards the Indians in particular but other disenfranchised groups as well.

Since it is Morag who does so much to bridge the gap between the various groups and cultures in Canada, it is not surprising, therefore, that it should be she who recognizes that Jules and Christie Logan are alike and that much of their attitude to life stems from the cruel and inequitable treatment which they have had to endure at the hands of the more secure members of the Canadian nation. In the Christie story Laurence reveals the hollowness of the Canadian belief that the country is classless and egalitarian; furthermore, she demonstrates the destructive consequences that result in such prejudiced behavior.

Christie Logan, as town scavenger, occupies a poorer house and enjoys a poorer living standard than his better-placed neighbors. Only because of his race is he permitted to live among the other Manawakans and not with the Tonnerres in the Wachakwa valley. Yet, for this dubious privilege Christie, and by association Morag, are reduced by their neighbors to a subhuman level. To counteract the shame and pain which both Christie and Morag must experience, Christie reminds Morag that regardless of man's behavior, "by their garbage shall ye know them" (39). His vehement outburst corresponds in bitterness and frustration with that of Jules because both of them are the recipients of the irrational behavior of the same narrow community. In Morag's development the reader is able to view the perniciousness of the community's attitude towards the less fortunate. Morag is ostracized at school and scorned at for the clothes she wears; finally, she is forced to thrust herself more into Jules's company. The result of the community's behavior is to transform Morag into a snob towards Christie and Prin and to hasten the day when she could leave Manawaka.

This unstable and uncertain background Morag has to do battle with amidst the snobbishness and savagery of Brooke Skelton to the extent that she is ashamed of having Christie and Prin at her wedding and that she forsakes them. Morag's reeducation occurs after Prin's death and her renewed friendship with Jules in Toronto. In fact at this stage Morag becomes aware of her past and slowly begins to understand the injustice that had been imposed on Christie and herself by the community of Manawaka. Her education is complete when she finally recognizes Christie as her real ancestor and when she is able to appreciate the value of his teaching and example. This, of course, is the legacy which Morag must now pass on to Pique.

WORKS CITED

Abrahams, Cecil. Interview with Margaret Laurence, May 1974.
Achebe, Chinua. *Morning Yet on Creation Day*. London: Heinemann, 1975.
___. *Things Fall Apart*. New York: Knopf, (1958, 1962) 1992.
Killam, G. D. Introduction to *This Side Jordan*, by Margaret Laurence. Toronto: McClelland and Stewart, New Canadian Library, (1960) 1976.
Laurence, Margaret. *The Diviners*. Toronto: McClelland and Stewart, New Canadian Library, (1974, 1988) 1995; Chicago: University of Chicago Press, 1993.
___. *Long Drums and Cannons: Nigerian Novelists and Dramatists 1952-1966*. London: Macmillan, 1968; New York: Praeger (1969) 1970.
___. *The Prophet's Camel Bell*. Toronto: McClelland and Stewart, New Canadian Library, (1963, 1988) 1991.
___. *This Side Jordan*. Toronto: McClelland and Stewart, New Canadian Library, (1960, 1976) 1989.
Thomas, Clara. *The Manawaka World of Margaret Laurence*. Toronto: McClelland and Stewart, New Canadian Library, (1975) 1976.
___. "A Conversation About Literature: An Interview with Margaret Laurence and Irving Layton." *Journal of Canadian Fiction* 1.1 (Winter 1972): 65-69.

Chapter 12

"It Was Like the Book Says, But It Wasn't": Oral Folk History in Laurence's *The Diviners*

Lynn Pifer

Margaret Laurence's novel, *The Diviners*, effectively re-creates the uses of oral folk history in familial and personal contexts and demonstrates the value of oral traditions in individual characters' lives. Through short snatches of folklore from schoolyard rhymes and songs to family stories, Laurence represents the ethnic coming-of-age of her main characters. Laurence herself notes that her family brought her up with a great knowledge of her Scots background, and her protagonist, Morag Gunn, is raised in much the same way, listening to Christie Logan's tales of her Scottish ancestors. Morag's classmate, Jules "Skinner" Tonnerre, a Métis, or French-Indian half-breed, listens to his father's stories of his ancestor, Rider Tonnerre. Both Morag and Jules depend on family stories for positive identification, but as they grow older, they realize their oral narratives differ from the official versions of history accepted by the larger society. Throughout the course of the novel, Jules and Morag, as well as their daughter, Pique, must come to terms with their ethnic heritage and cultural identity, and their families' quirky tales and stories become more important than they had realized. Laurence's novel is significant because it advocates the importance of oral folk history in individual lives.

Laurence creates a dichotomy between printed text histories, which are alienating and ultimately uninformative, and family stories, which give children the identity they seek. She reinforces this theme by juxtaposing school versions of history with family versions. Although Morag at first clings to her school versions as truth, through her friendship with Jules, she begins to understand that public education presents slanted versions of conquest and domination from the dominators' points of view.

Richard Dorson notes that the community identity of immigrants and minority groups depends upon the development of their own oral folk histories: "Dependent on the spoken, rather than the written word, and strongly bound by ethnic solidarity, these groups perpetuate oral traditions of sufferings and triumphs" (142). Still, official historians have often scorned oral folk history as unprofessional and inaccurate. Larry Danielson explains that this attitude towards oral history is held by many people besides the professional historians:

History for many continues to be spelled in capital letters and describes "important events" in the national past. The life history and community history, which most of us [as folklorists] accept as legitimate historical topics, still bear explanations to many as important subject matter. (63)

Oral folk history can be faulty and confusing, due to memory lapses or other human errors, but it can also provide valuable insight to people's feelings during an event and their perceptions afterwards, whereas official printed sources focus on and honor only the perceived "facts" of the event. The characters in *The Diviners* learn that oral folk history helps children understand their ethnic heritage. After learning their family's or ethnic group's stories, they can better comprehend why other children treat them differently and are better equipped psychologically to defend themselves against ethnic and racial prejudice.

As Morag Gunn and Jules Tonnerre mature in the novel, they become aware of the differences between the family history they know through tales heard at home and the official version of history learned in school. Just as professional historians have equated folklore with hearsay, untruth, and distortion, Morag and Skinner learn to view their family stories as "crap" (*Diviners* 84NCL. 60UC). Yet they both maintain a sense of ethnicity and heritage through the stories, and both rework the stories in their adult lives, Morag through her novels and Jules through his ballads.

Early in the novel, Christie Logan tells his foster daughter, Morag Gunn, stories of her 'fictional' ancestor, Piper Gunn. Morag had been disappointed because *The Clans and Tartans of Scotland* book had nothing to say about her clan: "The chieftainship of Clan Gunn is undetermined at the present time, and no arms have been matriculated" (58NCL, 40UC). In depicting a girl's extreme disappointment in the hollow jargon of a reference book, Laurence emphasizes that one's heritage cannot be found in the pages of a text. When the historical source fails to provide the information Morag seeks, Christie tells her about Piper Gunn, and these tales help satisfy her need for a known ancestor. As folklorist Richard Bauman has noted, oral performance can be seen as "a mode of communication" (3), and Christie's oral performances allow him to communicate with his foster daughter. Simply telling Morag not to mind the gabby little turds at school is not as effective as creating a family ancestor that Morag can be proud of. The heroic Piper Gunn served as the hero of his evicted clan, leading them with the blaring sound of his bagpipes: "he was a great tall man . . . with the voice of drums and the heart of a child and the gall of a thousand and the strength of conviction" (59NCL, 41UC).

Christie's storytelling sessions resemble transcribed oral narratives performed in everyday situations. He speaks in an informal manner, using rambling sentences, idioms, and vernacular expressions. The first sentence of his story about Piper Gunn and the Long March illustrates just how rambling Christie's narrative style can be:

Now that bloody ship, there, who would know what its name was, but with all of them from Sutherland on board, and struck with the sickness and the fever and the devil's plague, well, then, that ship with the children dying of the fever, it crossed the ocean, do you see, and it come to the new land, which was HERE, only very far north. (94NCL, 68UC)

This long and drawn out sentence indicates the rhythm and pitch of Christie's speech: he speaks in a series of short phrases, separated by commas, that build up to the word "HERE," and then taper off with the qualifying phrase, "only very far north." He also uses oral phrases such as "well, then," and "do you see," as transitional devices, which demonstrate Laurence's familiarity with oral storytelling styles and characteristics, as well as contrasting clearly with the wordy style ("undetermined," "matriculated") of the reference book.

In the first tale of Piper Gunn, the Bitch-Duchess evicts Clan Gunn from their farms in Scotland. Christie describes the Duchess as he would a fairy tale wicked witch: "The Bitch-Duchess was living there then, and it was she who cast the darkness over the land, and sowed the darkness and reaped gold, for her heart was dark . . . and she loved no creature alive but only the gold" (58NCL, 40UC). Christie, in fact, refers to Lady Strafford, the owner of the Sutherland estate, and his tale is an oral folk history account of the Sutherland Clearances of 1806 to 1820. Beginning in the early 1800s, Lady Strafford, the Duchess of Sutherland, cleared her land of its tenants in order to make way for extensive sheep farming (Fairhurst 1). As Christie Logan explains, the Sutherland estate will switch from tenant farming to the raising of sheep, *"for they'll pay better than folk"* (59NCL, 40UC).

Lady Strafford acted as many of the Highland landlords did at the time by trying to make her overpopulated estate more profitable. This does not, of course, excuse her capitalistic greed or her methods for satisfying it. Several historians have noted that she carried out extremely severe clearances. In fact, Karl Marx uses the Sutherland Clearances as a classic example of the expropriation of an agricultural population in *Capital* volume one:

From 1814 to 1820 . . . about 3000 families were systematically hunted and rooted out. All their villages were destroyed and burnt, all their fields turned into pasturage. . . . The whole of the stolen clanland she divided into 29 great sheep farms. . . . In the year 1835 the 15,000 Gaels were already replaced by 131,000 sheep. (682-683)

In Laurence's novel, although generations have passed since the evictions, Christie does not forget to include the cruelty of the Duchess's agents who set fire to the tenants' crofts, or the sense of outrage held by the clanspeople who thought the land belonged to them because their families had always lived there "from the beginning of all time" (58NCL, 40UC).

Lady Strafford hired Patrick Sellar, a Morayshire capitalist, to plan the renovation of her estate. Sellar proposed to move the tenants from the interior to the coast. There they would form fishing villages, leaving the land open for sheepwalks (Hunter 14). Christie also describes how the people were driven from their homes and forced to find a living on the coast (*Diviners* 58NCL, 40UC). Neither Sellar nor the Duchess bothered to consult the people living on the estate before they decided to clear the land. In a letter to Sellar, Lady Strafford refers to her tenants as "these barbarous hordes" (Hunter 15).

"How Tame Were the Highlanders During the Clearances?" is his article in which Eric Richards writes that "the people believed that they had traditional rights to their land and the landlords were usurping those rights, and acting against real justice" (41). It is not surprising, then, that many tenants left their small assigned lots on the coast for the factories in Glasgow or, as Piper Gunn and his woman did, sailed to Canada.

The second tale of Piper Gunn tells of the voyages to Canada and the hardships that faced the new settlers, including the hard winter, long march, plagues, and Indians (whom Christie never portrays positively in his tales). Historically, it refers to Lord Selkirk's Red River settlers who established a colony in 1812 in the area which is now Winnipeg, Manitoba (Gressley 287). The settlers, sailing from the Scottish Highlands and Orkney Islands, had a difficult time reaching their destination. W. J. Healey, author of *Women of the Red River*, a book of written accounts of oral recollections of women who lived through the Red River era, notes that the first wave of settlers came on three separate ships. The account of the third shipload's experience sounds very close to Christie's second tale of Piper Gunn. Healey writes:

[There was] a third party, after a voyage on which there had been death from ship fever. Most of the survivors were so weak that the journey of seven hundred miles to the Red River could not be undertaken that fall. Rough log cabins had to be made with axe and spade for a winter camp near the mouth of the Churchill River. Early in April, 1813, twenty-one men and twenty women started from the winter camp for York Factory. . . . There was a Highland piper in the middle of the line. (3)

Piper Gunn becomes the heroic leader in Christie's version of the story, as he plays the pipes while striking a path through the snow, leading his people to a new home: "It could've been maybe a thousand or so miles then. . . . And through the snow and muck and that. And who led them? . . . Piper Gunn. Himself" (96NCL, 69UC).

Christie cannot quote the exact number of miles that the settlers marched, and his guess overestimates the distance. But the people who lived through the experience certainly felt that they had marched a thousand miles, no matter what the actual distance was, and they would have told their children of the long long march in the same inexact style that Christie uses.

While Laurence's novel highlights the differences between printed versions of history and oral folk history, when Morag meets Jules Tonnerre, she learns that there are also discrepancies between different families' versions of an event. Christie's story about Piper Gunn and the Rebels (143NCL, 105UC) is an oral folk history account of the Red River Rebellion of 1870 told from the white settlers' point of view. Jules Tonnerre presents the Métis version of the story in his Tale of Rider Tonnerre and the Prophet (161-62NCL, 118-19UC). In 1870 Louis Riel led the Métis when they took over Fort Garry in order to express their displeasure for the new Governor. Governor MacDougall advocated white Canadian expansion, threatening the Métis and plains Indians who survived by hunting buffalo on the open prairie (Stanley 62). Desmond Morton writes, "Very low on the agenda of Canadiens [sic] who pondered the problems of the North West . . . was any consideration of the feelings of the people who lived there" (24). Such a state of affairs would justify the fears of the Métis and Indians living on the prairie. Here the acts and attitudes of the Canadian officials sound very much like those of the Duchess of Sutherland. Laurence thus parallels the situations of these two ethnic groups, suggesting that those who were themselves dispossessed can, in turn, become the usurpers. Although Christie knows his own history as one of displacement, he cannot see that his ethnic group has displaced the Indians and Métis.

Christie Logan does not consider the Métis' grievances when he summarizes the events leading up to the Red River Rebellion. He notes that the half-breeds living outside of the Scottish settlement "got very worked up" and decided to overthrow the government, "So they got themselves a rebel chief. Short little man he was, with burning eyes. His name was Reel" (144NCL, 106UC). Christie's general account is more or less correct according to his Scottish point of view; he depicts Riel negatively because he has always seen Indians and Métis as a threat to the Scots-Canadians. In earlier stories, Christie enumerates the many hardships that the brave Scottish settlers faced in the new world: "Locusts. Hailstorms. Floods. Blizzards. Indians. Halfbreeds." (96NCL, 69UC), and to Christie, the Métis are just another in a long line of plagues. Morag, however, notices his negative description of Louis Riel as both "short" and "little," and his mispronunciation of Riel's name. According to Christie's view of the event, the half-breeds had no real motive for their actions; they merely "got themselves worked up." Later in the novel, Jules tells Morag his family's account of the rebellion and gives his own description of Riel.

The Tonnerre family tales feature Rider Tonnerre, a brave and skillful ancestor who leads the other Métis in battle much the same way Piper Gunn led his people out of Scotland. Rider also possesses legendary qualities as he can outride any man on horseback and is such a good marksman he never misses a buffalo (160NCL, 118UC). Tonnerre family stories also recreate historical events--battles between the Indians and European settlers from the Seven Oaks Massacre of 1816 (159-61NCL, 117-18UC) to a battle during the Rebellion of 1885 (162-64NCL, 119-20UC). Morag finds herself correcting details in Jules's tales, such as identifying the song his father could not remember as Falcon's Song (161NCL, 118UC), as she tries to piece together the history she learned at school or from Christie with the stories Jules tells her.

In the Tonnerre account of the Red River Rebellion of 1870, Rider is too old to lead the Métis, so he gets "The Prophet," Louis Riel, to take charge of the rebellion. According to Jules, Riel is taller than Rider, who stood an amazing seven feet:

I don't say Lazarus told the way it happened, but neither did the books and they're one hell of a sight worse because they made out that the guy was nuts. . . . the Prophet, then, he's a very tall guy, taller than Rider Tonnerre.

(I thought he was supposed to be a very short guy.) No. Very tall. (161-62NCL, 119UC)

Jules has a definite idea of who Louis Riel was, and the fact that printed sources present a different picture does not shake his opinion. The Métis of Riel's time looked to him as a leader, while the government considered him an outlaw. The Métis of later generations look to him as a hero, although the Anglo-Canadian school books portray him as a lunatic. The need to preserve Riel's story in the oral tradition becomes urgent in this case, as the people who tell the stories realize that their vision of this man and his deeds may not be preserved otherwise.

Morag not only understands Jules's stories but also his need to tell them. The preservation of oral folk history becomes the preservation of a group's culture and cultural identity, and such an identity can be crucial to a group member's personal survival. Both Morag and Jules need to belong to a group from which they will not be rejected. Morag is orphaned at age five, and she must move into town to live with the Logans, who are not related to her, not well-to-do, and not respected by the other citizens of Manawaka. By identifying herself with her own ethnic group, the Scots, and her particular clan, the Gunns, Morag establishes her sense of belonging. Through the deeds of Piper Gunn, Morag develops pride in her family history and in herself, even though the richer and more popular children at school mock her for being poor. Morag's experiences with her family history also help her understand Jules Tonnerre's family stories and his pride in his Métis heritage. The boy she had considered to be without a heritage when the class sings "the THISTLE SHAMROCK ROSE entwine / The MAPLE LEAF FOREVER!" (80NCL, 57UC), a song that celebrates the Scots Irish English domination of Canadian society, does indeed have a rich past and a strong sense of ethnicity. As a member of a shunned ethnic group ("People in Manawaka talk about them but don't talk *to* them" [79NCL, 56UC]) Jules needs to vindicate his family by telling their stories. His songs about his father and sister Piquette show the side of his family that the townspeople would never allow themselves to see. Although Lazarus Tonnerre manages to raise his children by himself, the town only sees an unemployed half-breed who gets drunk and lives in a dirty shack. The children he claims as his own and struggles to feed and protect are only seen as too many unwanted half-breeds.

Morag gains a greater understanding of the Tonnerre family during her brief sexual encounter with Jules before he is shipped off to fight in World War II, and she is distressed by the family's poverty. Later, when she is sent by the newspaper to report on the fire that killed his sister, Piquette, and her children, she is sickened by the scene at the burnt shack. Morag nonetheless finds that she must tell the story of Piquette's death to Jules when he returns from the war. She is not, however, allowed to tell the whole story in her newspaper report. Her editor asks her to delete those details that would displease the citizens of Manawaka (176NCL, 130UC).

The discrepancies between official printed history and oral tradition clash again when Christie Logan tries to tell Morag about his experiences in World War I in the Battle of Bourlon Wood. He first consults a printed account of the battle in *The 60th Canadian Artillery Battery Book*, but he finds the printed version of the event to be painfully inadequate. None of his experiences are recorded in this account of zero hours, gun positions, and enemy attacks. He cannot even identify himself among the rows of men in the battery photo (100NCL, 72UC). He experiences the odd feeling of knowing that he had fought in the battle, even though he cannot find himself in the official record of the event. He can only explain to Morag, "[I]t was like the book says and it wasn't like that also" (101NCL, 73UC). The book records the factual events of the Battle of Bourlon Wood; however, Christie must tell his own version of the battle if Morag wants to learn what it was like. But Christie's narrow and confused version fixes on minute details, such as the abundance of mud and the screams of a dying horse, and he cannot finish his narrative because he becomes emotionally overwhelmed. But even with an unfinished oral narrative, Morag has a greater understanding of the event than what she learned from the text.

Morag never, however, abandons books. After Christie's death, the only belongings of his that she wants to keep are four books, including *The Poems of Ossian--In the original Gaelic with a Literal Translation into English*, and *The Clans and Tartans of Scotland*. She also relies on reference books for cultural information such as the motto of a clan or the meaning of the Gaelic word *dhu*. She realizes, however, the importance of hearing a people's stories and understanding their own accounts of what happened or who they are. Despite the confusion of Christie's personal narrative and the fictions he develops in the tales of Piper Gunn, Morag gleans elements of truth from the oral accounts that she cannot find in the printed authorities. In fact, printed sources, such as *The Clans and Tartans of Scotland* or *The 60th Canadian Field Artillery Battery Book*, repeatedly fail her when she turns to them for information about her family, and she cannot find the word *dhu* in the *Clans and Tartans* glossary. Official historical accounts cannot put one in the boots of the man in the trenches at Bourlon Wood or in the place of an Indian lying in a ditch in the Battle of Batoche, yet an oral narrative by that man or his descendants may succeed in doing so despite its historical inaccuracies. Or as Morag explains, the uneducated trash collector, Christie Logan, "knew things about inner truths that I am only just beginning to understand" (443NCL, 341UC).

By selecting historical events and depicting her fictional characters exchanging different versions of the events, Laurence shows us history as process; people try to find the truth or come to terms with their own interpretation of history. Laurence's characters continue to work through and retell their families' stories throughout their adult lives. Jules's songs and Morag's novels demonstrate the importance of their ethnic consciousness and its expression in their creative lives. Bitter life experiences have taught them what they cannot be: Jules learns he cannot go to law school, and Morag visits Scotland to learn she cannot live there, but their childhood stories will always reinforce who they are. Morag tells Christie's stories to her daughter, Pique, and writes novels that incorporate the old tales. Jules writes ballads about his grandfather, father, and sister, and he sings them to Pique. Pique herself is left with the task of uniting the two sides of her ethnicity, trying to balance her mother's Scottish stories and her father's Métis songs. Her struggle is symbolized in the two family heirlooms--the Scottish pin and the Métis knife. Significantly, her period of apparently aimless hitchhiking and suicidal behavior ends when she begins to write and sing her own songs which assert her heritage and identity: "the valley and the mountain hold my name" (465NCL, 360UC).

WORKS CITED

Bauman, Richard. *Story, Performance, and Event: Contextual Studies of Oral Narrative.* Cambridge: Cambridge University Press, 1986.
Danielson, Larry. "The Folklorist, the Oral Historian, and Local History." *The Oral History Review* (1980): 62-72.
Dorson, Richard M. *American Folklore and the Historian.* Chicago: The University of Chicago Press, 1971.
Fairhurst, Horace. "The Surveys for the Sutherland Clearances 1813-1820." *Scottish Studies* 8 (1964): 1-18.
Gressley, Gene M. "Lord Selkirk and the Canadian Courts." *Canadian History Before the Confederation.* Ed. J. M. Bumsted. Georgetown, Ontario: Irwin-Dorsey, 1972.
Healey, W. J. *Women of the Red River.* Winnipeg, Manitoba: The Women's Canadian Club of Winnipeg, 1923.
Hunter, James. *The Making of the Crofting Community.* Edinburgh: Donald, 1976.
Laurence, Margaret. *The Diviners.* Toronto: McClelland and Stewart, New Canadian Library, (1974, 1988) 1995; Chicago: University of Chicago Press, 1993.
Marx, Karl. *Capital.* Vol. 1. Trans. Samuel Moore and Edward Aveling. Ed. Frederick Engels. New York: International Publishers, 1967.
Morton, Desmond. *The Last War Drum: The North West Campaign of 1885.* Toronto: A. M. Hakkert, 1972.
Richards, Eric. "How Tame Were the Highlanders During the Clearances?" *Scottish Studies* 17 (1973): 35-50.
Stanley, George F. G. *The Birth of Western Canada: A History of the Riel Rebellions.* Toronto: University of Toronto Press, 1978.

Part IV

Feminist Perspectives in Laurence

Chapter 13

Self-alienation of the Elderly in Margaret Laurence's Fiction

Rosalie Murphy Baum

Many modern writers portray elderly characters as self-alienated; that is, in Abraham Maslow's words, they are incapable of self-actualization or of the "ongoing actualization of potentials, capacities and talents" (45). An examination of Margaret Laurence's fictional portrayal of three elderly women, however, suggests that the women's patterns of behavior in old age are simply variations of a neurotic pattern of self-alienation, what Marcia Westkott identifies as a "core dependent character" (87), which is gender-neutral in our culture, begins in childhood, and can continue indefinitely in a parent-child-parent cycle.

Karen Horney's work focuses largely upon three basic patterns of neurotic behavior which the "core dependent character" can take--the compliant or dependent, the aggressive or domineering, and the detached. All three forms are found in Laurence's fiction. For example, Mrs. Cameron, Rachel's mother in *A Jest of God*, is a good example of an elderly woman in whom compliant ("moving toward") tendencies dominate. Such a person frequently controls others through his or her need of them; he may take the stance that "You must love me, protect me, forgive me, not desert me, *because* I am so weak and helpless" (*Our Inner Conflicts*, hereafter *OIC* 53). Hagar Shipley, Marvin's mother in *The Stone Angel*, offers a good example of the aggressive type ("moving against"), who denies his or her softer feelings, abhors helplessness, and seeks independence or mastery. Hagar is a superb example of two varieties of this type which Horney identifies--the perfectionist and the arrogant-vindictive--and is Laurence's supreme achievement in characterization. Mrs. MacLeod, Ewen's mother and Vanessa's grandmother in *A Bird in the House*, offers an excellent example of the detached person ("moving away from"). Such a person feels a strong need for superiority and usually looks at those around him with condescension. He or she frequently suppresses emotion and realizes his need for superiority in a world essentially of isolation.

Laurence's portrayal of these three elderly women and their families offers a bleak view of human potential and, more especially, of the mother-child relationship. Although Horney indicates quite clearly that an individual can become neurotic because of the neurotic elements of his or her society and culture--for example, the contradictions between competition and brotherly love or between "conspicuous consumption" and "the reality of limited economic resources" (Westkott 66)--she also feels that appropriate parenting (that is parenting which successfully struggles with the neurotic culture) could make a difference. In Laurence's novels, it is obvious that the neurotic character of Mrs. Cameron, Grandmother Connor, and Hagar Shipley--which was clear in their early adulthoods--has made it impossible for them to offer such parenting.

According to Horney, the greatest problem in character development occurs when a child has a "neurotic parent," one, for example, whose insecurity and vulnerability to the ideals and stresses of a competitive society create within the family itself the very conditions of the society and culture. Most destructive of all is the "pattern of treating a child as a narcissistic extension of the parent's idealized self," a situation in which the child is made to feel--usually covertly--that "his right to existence lies solely in. . . living up to the parents' expectations--measuring up to their standards or ambitions for him, enhancing their prestige, [or] giving them blind devotion" (*Self Analysis* 44). In all three novels, the offspring of the elderly women have clearly experienced such conditions. Horney suggests that under such conditions the children can only lose what self-confidence they have and begin to think of themselves as "weak, helpless, and worthless" (Westkott 74). The obvious (healthy) reaction would be hostility toward the parent. However, because of a fear of reprisal and loss of love, the child tends to repress the hostility toward the parent and even direct it toward himself or herself instead. In so doing the child gradually loses touch with his or her real self and may no longer know "what she herself liked or wished or feared or resented" (*Self Analysis* 51). In many cases, the child will even admire those who deserve hostility and then turn the repressed hostility on others. Much of this pattern can be found in Rachel, Ewen, and Marvin. Thus, our examination of the three elderly women does not suggest simply a condition of self-alienation in the elderly; it suggests a neurotic cycle in these families which cannot be easily broken. Whether this neurotic cycle is created or perpetuated by Mrs. Cameron and Mrs. MacLeod in Laurence's novels--something we do not know since we know little about the parents of these two women--the cycle certainly continues through them to their children. In Hagar, of course, we see the perpetuation of the pattern created by her mother and father and continued through her son Marvin. The pattern--as presented in the novels--may or may not continue in the grandchildren. At the end of *A Jest of God*, Rachel, of course, has not married or had a child; and we see too little of Marvin's son and daughter to know how their personalities have developed. However, Vanessa, the grandchild in *A Bird in the House*, has so clearly understood and broken the pattern that it is her voice which tells us the story of her family.

In examining these three elderly women in Margaret Laurence's fiction in the light of Karen Horney's work on neurosis, we shall be focusing on the neurotic manner in which each woman interacts--actually conflicts, overtly or covertly--only with the daughter or son with whom she is living. (That is, we shall not consider other family members.) It is important, however, to make clear from the beginning that in no way does Horney suggest that conflict in and of itself--whether it is clashes between ourselves and others or within ourselves--is neurotic. Rather, conflict occurs within and between all of us, the nonneurotic and the neurotic; within the neurotic personality, however, the conflict is distinctive and self-destructive. In addition, we must keep in mind that neurosis is "always a matter of degree" (*OIC* 27) and that there is often much overlap in the behavior of the individuals falling within Horney's three categories; classification depends upon the *most basic* pattern of behavior being exhibited.

The conflicts of the neurotic individual, according to Horney, differ from the nonneurotic in that the neurotic individual has limited "awareness of [his or her] feelings and desires" (*OIC 27*); the neurotic individual has "compulsive standards," which make choice between conflicting drives almost impossible. And as a result of these two conditions, the neurotic individual has a limited "capacity to assume responsibility" (*OIC* 28) for himself because of a "*devastating waste of human energies*" (*OIC* 155). This waste is contributed to by two primary characteristics: first, by "a curious single-mindedness of purpose" (*OIC* 156) or the pursuit of an excessive number of goals or the pursuit of two or more incompatible goals and, second, by "the eclipse of whole areas of the personality due to the suppression of parts of the basic conflict" (*OIC* 156). Symptoms of such an impoverished personality include indecisiveness or procrastination; ineffectualness, which manifests itself by the need for inordinate amounts of effort and forgetfulness; and inertia, which is a "paralysis of initiative and action" (*OIC* 160). The symptoms of an impoverished personality appear with great clarity in the children of Laurence's elderly heroines. However, the pretenses which Horney emphasizes are necessary for the neurotic personality--the pretense of love, the pretense of goodness, the pretense of interest and knowledge, the pretense of honesty and fairness, and the pretense of suffering--are most vivid in Laurence's elderly women.

Type I, the compliant neurotic type, is found in Margaret Laurence's novel *A Jest of God*, in which Mrs. Cameron, Rachel's mother, controls her daughter through her need of her. Horney describes such a type as showing "marked need for affection and approval and an especial need for a 'partner' . . . who is to fulfill all expectations of life and take responsibility for good and evil" (*OIC* 50). He or she may make "demands 'because he is so miserable' or will secretly dominate under the guise of loving" (*OIC* 57). This individual's needs, she explains, "have the characteristic common to all neurotic trends, that is, they are compulsive, indiscriminate, and generate anxiety or despondence when frustrated" (*OIC* 50). They make the individual exceptionally vulnerable and create a sense of "being neglected, rejected and humiliated whenever the excessive amount of affection or approval demanded is not forthcoming" (*OIC* 56).

The compliant type also demonstrates a variety of strongly repressed aggressive tendencies: "a callous lack of interest in others, attitudes of defiance, unconscious parasitic or exploiting tendencies, propensities to control and manipulate others, relentless needs to excel or to enjoy vindictive triumphs" (*OIC* 55).

At the opening of *A Jest of God*, Mrs. Cameron is probably somewhere in her seventies (21) and all that a proper lady should be: slender and cute (21), "bright and flighty" (68); delicate, with a "tricky" (21,183) heart. Her face characterizes her, with its "querulous fragility" and "the over-brightness of her eyes rimmed with the shadows or sickness or disappointment" (100). Her thirty-four-year-old daughter, Rachel, left the university when her father died fourteen years before the novel opens and has taught grammar school and taken care of her mother ever since. Rachel's life is inscribed by her mother in a suffocating manner. When she returns from school at the end of the day, her mother greets her with "Hello, dear. Aren't you rather late tonight?" (20), or "You're late this evening, dear" (63). She fusses about Rachel's being "too conscientious" (20) about her teaching and about Rachel's health. If Rachel plans to go out during the evening, Mrs. Cameron reminds her to bring her her pills from the medicine cabinet--"in case anything happens." Then she assures Rachel that she's sure she'll be just fine, that Rachel should just "go ahead and enjoy" (72) herself. Mrs. Cameron also suggests that since Rachel will be gone and she will have absolutely nothing to do all evening, perhaps she should wash the blankets. She suggests this knowing full well that the doctor has warned her and Rachel that she should not lift things. When Rachel tells her mother she is going out with Nick Kazlik, Mrs. Cameron inquires, "You mean the milkman's son?" (73).

Rachel, in describing Mrs. Cameron's tactics, realizes that her mother's "weapons are invisible, and she would never admit even to carrying them, much less putting them to use" (46). But gently, gently, Mrs. Cameron is parasitic and exploitative, manipulating Rachel with success for at least the fourteen years Rachel has been caring for her. Mrs. Cameron's emphasis is on her love for Rachel--that's why she shows concern when Rachel is late or works hard--and upon her own ill health--that's why she must depend upon Rachel. But, in reality, Mrs. Cameron controls Rachel's life and, rather than showing gratitude for her daughter's sacrifices, constantly reminds her daughter of her shortcomings and failures. Her protestations are deadly: when she is invading Rachel's privacy, she says, "It isn't as though I expect you to tell me everything you do." When Rachel does not do exactly what her mother requests, she says, "I couldn't be annoyed over a thing like that. A little hurt, perhaps," or "Never mind, dear. Everyone's thoughtless at times, I guess. I can't expect--" (84-85). Ignoring the many sacrifices Rachel has made for her, Mrs. Cameron even praises her daughter Stacey, who has visited once during the fourteen years but writes weekly, and who, she implies, shares a special understanding with her mother because the two of them, unlike Rachel, have had families and borne children. Mrs. Cameron relies heavily upon all of the pretenses discussed by Horney--that of interest and knowledge, love, goodness, honesty and fairness, and suffering. Her life is focused upon Rachel--who must make her feel liked, appreciated, and loved; who must need her; and who must help, protect, and take care of her.

At one point in the novel Rachel feels that "a leather thong had lassoed my temples" (87). But she herself--at this point in her life--is as neurotic as her elderly mother. She is clearly a narcisissitic extension of her mother--trying unsuccessfully to be what her mother wishes her to be. She vacillates between a sense of weakness and worthlessness and a deep sense of hostility. With her life for so long focused on another (her mother), she hardly knows who she is--what her own likes or values are. She is indecisive and increasingly tempted by a world of the imagination. An excellent example of an impoverished personality, Rachel is clearly exhibiting characteristics of Horney's third personality type, that of the detached individual. Her friend Calla, "pillar of tabernacles, speaker in tongues, mother of canaries and budgerigars" (205) has already moved in that direction. At the end of the novel, however, Rachel takes a step which may lead to a healthier psychic life: she asserts herself with her mother and makes plans to leave Manawaka and pursue a life with more opportunities for fulfillment. She muses, "Anything may happen, where I'm going. I will be different. I will remain the same. . . . I will be afraid" (209).

Type II, the aggressive or domineering neurotic type, is found in Laurence's novel *The Stone Angel*, in which Hagar Shipley dominates her son Marvin's life by her pride and fear, the "chains" within her which "spread out . . . and shackled" (292) all she touches. Horney describes such a type as seeing life as "a struggle of all against all," even though this attitude is sometimes "covered over with a veneer of suave politeness, fairmindedness and good fellowship" (*OIC* 63). The control over others which the aggressive type needs "may be an outright exercise of power . . . [or] indirect manipulation through oversolicitousness or putting people under obligation" (*OIC* 64). In exploiting others, he or she becomes "hard and tough," regarding feelings as "'sloppy sentimentality'" (*OIC* 65); in fact, the emergence of any "softer tendencies" (*OIC* 71) will create a conflict necessitating the repression of the "softer tendencies" and thereby reinforcing the aggressive tendencies.

At the opening of *The Stone Angel*, Hagar Shipley is about ninety, an outrageous, difficult woman being cared for by her son Marvin and daughter-in-law, Doris. She has difficulty remembering what happens from one minute to the next and sometimes confuses events of the past with those of the present; she cries easily, screeches at her daughter-in-law with little or no cause, and is churlish or combative much of the time. In addition, she wets the bed and insists upon smoking in bed even though she frequently falls asleep with a burning cigarette; her arthritis makes her clumsy; and she suffers pain under her ribs, which is later diagnosed as cancer. At the same time that she is experiencing these humiliations of old age--and inflicting them, without gratitude, upon her son and daughter-in-law--she is "rampant with memory" (5); that is, she relives, through memory, her entire life. In so doing, she recalls her great pride and her fear of emotion. She reviews the many times she has shown strength and control over others, the times she has refused to allow her emotions to show, and the times she has allowed "proper appearances" (292) rather than genuineness or caring to rule her life. In her last days she realizes how pride has been her "wilderness" and fear her "demon" (292). She has lost the two men she loved most in life through her pride: never did she allow her husband, Bram, to see the love and sexual attraction she felt for him, thereby contributing to his alcoholism and death; never did she allow her son John to live his own life until her interference actually led to his death. Hagar realizes in her last hours that she has never really lived, never simply rejoiced. Her life has been all pride and pretense, including many of the pretenses discussed by Horney.

Her son Marvin, with his wife, has devoted the last seventeen years of his life caring for his elderly mother. He has served her in every way he could, cringing from the bickering and recriminations between her and his wife, feeling guilty about the great burden that his wife has to bear from both the physical needs and attitude of his mother. At one point, as he realizes that his wife simply cannot continue to lift his mother when she falls, he is able--for a short time--to consider placing his mother in a home for the aged; but his "hopeful desperation" (96) that she will like the place succumbs quickly to his mother's refusal. As a child, Marvin had also tried to serve his mother well, doing his chores ably and hanging around her, fruitlessly hoping for words of praise or affection. But he has never been important to his mother. Only in her last hours, when Hagar comes to realize something of the emotional desert her life has been, does she see Marvin for who he is--a loving, caring, responsible child begging for a blessing from a parent who has always ignored him. With this insight, Hagar blesses him, saying, "You've been good to me, always" (304); and she deliberately and caringly lies to him by adding that he has been "a better son than John" (304), her favorite son. Thus, Hagar lifts from Marvin his sense of weakness and worthlessness, and he believes her. Who would tell a lie on her deathbed? A son whose impoverished personality--with its neurotic dependency--has struggled responsibly throughout a lifetime of hard work and little joy, Marvin is one of the luckier children in Laurence: he has had limited joy with his wife, Doris, and their children, Tina and Steven, and he receives his mother's blessing and release when she is ninety and he is in his sixties.

Type III, the detached neurotic type, is found in Laurence's collection of short stories *A Bird in the House*, in which Grandmother MacLeod largely directs the lives of her son and daughter-in-law through her pretensions of being a lady. Horney describes such an individual as one who tends to suppress feeling toward others and seeks "utter independence" (*OIC* 77). He or she will forego anything--even basic needs--to avoid "coercion, influence, obligation" (*OIC* 77); "external advantages and inner values will be equally renounced--consciously, by setting aside any desire that might interfere with independence, or unconsciously, by automatic prohibition" (*OIC* 89). This need for independence is closely tied to the individual's sense of superiority. Such a person "does not want to excel realistically through consistent effort. He feels rather that the treasures within him should be recognized without any effort on his part; his hidden greatness should be felt without his having to make a move" (*OIC* 80). The primary aim of such neurotic detachment--or evasion--appears to be, on the one hand, avoiding all conflict by keeping away from any significant relationship with others while, at the same time, enjoying a sense of uniqueness, in fantasy or dream. If at any time the "detached person's feeling of superiority is temporarily shattered, whether by a concrete failure or an increase of inner conflicts, he will be unable to stand solitude and may reach out frantically for affection and protection" (*OIC* 79). This can pose additional problems since his "aloofness is not a matter of his own free choice" (*OIC* 103) but very likely stems from his inability to cope with others.

Grandmother MacLeod appears infrequently in *A Bird in the House* but is a dominant force in her son Ewen's and his family's lives, both because of her personality and because the family had moved in with her during the Great Depression when Mrs. MacLeod could no longer afford a housekeeper. Vanessa, her grandchild, describes the house as "like a museum, full of dead and meaningless objects, vases and gilt-framed pictures and looming furniture" (78). Grandmother MacLeod basically detaches herself from the life of her son and family, spending most of her time in the tower room among her "potted plants drooped in a lethargic and lime-green confusion" (106) or in her room, "with its stale and old-smelling air, the dim reek of medicines and lavender sachets" (47). Grandmother MacLeod has created a romantic, fictitious past for herself: she describes her family as the MacInnes, an ancient clan, "the lairds of Morven and the constables of the Castle of Kinlochaline" (49), even though she was born in Ontario and her father was a horse doctor; and she has idealized her son Roderick, who died in World War I. At a time when the family barely has enough to eat, she hires a girl for the housework; reads the catalogue from Robinson & Cleaver and orders "linen tea-cloths and . . . serviettes" (51-52); and reminisces about the days when she had resident help, dinner parties, and high teas. Grandmother MacLeod reveals no real feeling for her son or any member of his family, and she does nothing to help around the house. The family seal with the MacLeod crest and motto and the seal ring with the MacLeod crest--these are her world. They form the chivalric world of Horney's pretenses--of interest and knowledge, goodness, honesty and fairness, and suffering.

Mrs. MacLeod's son Ewen is a beaten and defeated man in his mother's house and, in his compliance, becomes her accomplice in her fictitious memories. When his brother, always his mother's favorite son, had died, he had written his mother a letter from the battlefield about how "gallantly" (59) Roderick had died, creating an imaginative account that would fulfill her dreams. His guilt that his brother had died, not he, had no doubt been compounded by the fact that he had accidentally blinded his brother in one eye with his air-rifle when they had been children. When Ewen had returned home after the war, he had become a doctor and gone into practice with his father, apparently from a sense of duty to his parents rather than his own wishes. As the novel opens, with his daughter growing up in the house with his mother, Ewen explains away Vanessa's anger that Grandmother MacLeod cannot be "nice" to others for a change instead of their always having to be "nice" (55) to her. He tells her what a disappointment his mother's life has been because she has not been able to live the life of a lady that she had aspired to. It is such "troubles" (55), he says, that account for Grandmother MacLeod's migraines and crossness. Ewen yells at his wife when she tries to get Vanessa out of the living room with its antiques and blue Chinese carpet, even though he knows quite well that his mother has criticized his wife for letting Vanessa endanger her valuable possessions. He remains silent when his mother quietly says, "I see no need to blaspheme, Ewen" (47). And he drives himself at his work, "forever reproaching" (93) himself as a failure because he is not able to earn enough for his family and to maintain his mother in the style she wants. In an argument with his wife, he says, "I haven't only taken on my father's house, I've taken on everything that goes with it, apparently" (93). When he dies midway through the collection of short stories, he dies a man who has never lived, who has never really known who he is. Feeling weak and worthless, like Rachel and Marvin, he has been a narcisissitic extension of his mother, exhibiting both compliance and detachment.

Examining Karen Horney's three basic patterns of neurotic behavior within the parent-child relationships created by Laurence in three of her works of fiction is especially appropriate because of the very nature of neurotic trends. As Horney points out, the neurotic is highly dependent upon other people, whatever form his neurosis may have assumed. He depends upon people for moving toward, moving against, or moving away from. One could almost say that the parent-child relationship offers a particularly revealing (if unfortunate) laboratory for examining the variations of neurotic behavior since the parent-child relationship, by definition, involves two people bound together by the physical and emotional needs of the younger. Laurence's fiction is also especially appropriate for examining such neurotic patterns because Laurence, in the words of John Moss, "celebrates life while lamenting the limitations placed upon it by personality" (157). Laurence's fiction indicates quite clearly that the neurotic bonds established in childhood remain throughout life, even in a case like Marvin, who left home at seventeen, when Hagar was in her early forties, and lived away from her for thirty years. However, the three novels we have examined by Laurence also suggest that when the mother-figure has as strong a personality as those of Mrs. Cameron, Grandmother MacLeod, and Hagar Shipley, the child's personality appears even more impoverished than that of the parent; and the child is certainly a less interesting fictional character than the parent, even in a case like *A Jest of God* where the child, Rachel, is the central figure. Hagar's discovery at the end of her life--that life's purpose is to rejoice--is ultimately Horney's definition of the goal of therapy--to create "*wholeheartedness*: to be without pretense, to be emotionally sincere, to be able to put the whole of oneself into one's feelings, one's work, one's beliefs" (*OIC* 242). But since it is the neurotic character--especially the grand dame of them all, Hagar--who holds the attention of readers, we cannot help being grateful for such neuroses, at least in fiction if not in life.

WORKS CITED

Horney, Karen. *Our Inner Conflicts*. New York: W. W. Norton, 1945.
___. *Self Analysis*. New York: W. W. Norton, 1942.
Laurence, Margaret. *A Bird in the House*. Toronto: McClelland and Stewart, New Canadian Library, (1970, 1989) 1994; Chicago: University of Chicago Press, 1993.
___. *A Jest of God (Rachel, Rachel)*. Toronto: McClelland and Stewart, New Canadian Library, (1966. 1974, 1988) 1993; Chicago: University of Chicago Press, 1993.
___. *The Stone Angel*. Toronto: McClelland and Stewart, New Canadian Library, (1964, 1968, 1988) 1995; Chicago: University of Chicago Press, 1993.
Maslow, Abraham H. *Toward a Psychology of Being*. Princeton: Van Nostrand, 1968.
Moss, John. *A Reader's Guide to the Canadian Novel*. Toronto: McClelland and Stewart, 1981.
Westkott, Marcia. *The Feminist Legacy of Karen Horney*. New Haven: Yale University Press, 1986.

Chapter 14

Coming to Terms with the Image of the Mother in *The Stone Angel*
Cynthia Taylor

In *Diving Deep and Surfacing: Women Writers on Spiritual Quest*, Carol Christ describes a common pattern in women's spiritual quests, which takes a distinctive form in the work of women writers. The first stage in the spiritual quest process is what Christ calls an "experience of nothingness," which precedes the second stage, awakening. Awakening often occurs through the third stage, "mystical identification," and frequently takes place in a natural setting. Awakening is followed by the last stage in the process, which Christ terms "new naming of self and reality" (13). Tracing this pattern in Margaret Laurence's *The Stone Angel* places Hagar Shipley's story in a strong tradition of writing by women: the novel of awakening. In these novels, as in Laurence's, readers attempt to understand the female heroes as they attempt to understand themselves. Laurence's use of this pattern in *The Stone Angel* allows her to explore several ideas common to the novel of awakening: the survival of personality, the function of memory, the importance of coming to terms with female sexuality, and the necessity of accepting the past in order to understand the present. Laurence's achievement is that she makes her protagonist's awakening contingent upon her ability to come to terms with her image of the mother and of herself as mother, and that the awakening in *The Stone Angel* evolves in the consciousness of a ninety-year-old woman.

The awakening process that Christ describes begins in an experience of nothingness. According to Christ, women experience nothingness in their own lives, especially in their relationships with men. That is certainly true of Laurence's protagonist, Hagar Currie Shipley. Early in *The Stone Angel*, Hagar cries, "Oh, my lost men. No, I will not think of that" (6). But Hagar does not have as much control over her thoughts as she would like. In two parallel plots, one devoted to the events of the last two weeks of her life and the other devoted to her memories of that life, Hagar tries to come to terms with her failed relationships with the men in her life: her father, her two brothers, her husband, and her two sons.

Christ says that women also experience nothingness in the values that have shaped their lives. Again that is true in Hagar's case. Because her mother dies when Hagar is born, Hagar's life is shaped and dominated by the patriarchal and materialistic values that she inherits from her stern Scottish father, Jason Currie. Laurence has said that *The Stone Angel* was an attempt to understand her grandparent's generation. Hagar's father represents the best and worst of that generation: an unbending authoritarian, he is afraid to show love, easily angered, bigoted, ambitious, hard-working, dutiful, proud, and strong. From him, Hagar inherits all those attributes, along with the Scottish clan motto that she lives by all her life: "Gainsay Who Dare." From him she also inherits her hatred of even the appearance of weakness. One of her earliest memories is of being beaten by her father and her reaction to the punishment: "I wouldn't let him see me cry, I was so enraged." She also recalls her father's response: "You take after me. . . . You've got backbone" (10). Hagar also inherits her father's brains. Once she overhears her father talking about her: "Smart as a whip, she is, that one. If only she'd been--" (14). Hagar does not need to hear the end of the sentence, and neither do her brothers.

In her first mention of her brothers, Hagar says, "My brothers took after our mother." She describes them as "graceful unspirited boys" (7). Implicit here is the damaging association between women and weakness that Hagar makes throughout most of her life. The same association is implicit in her opening description of the stone angel which guards her mother's grave: "in memory of her who relinquished her feeble ghost as I gained my stubborn one" (3). It is this association that damages her relationship with her brothers. When her brother Dan is dying of pneumonia, Matt, her other brother, tries to talk the teenaged Hagar into wearing their mother's shawl to comfort Dan. Hagar refuses:

But all I could think of was that meek woman I'd never seen, the woman Dan was said to resemble so much and from whom he'd inherited a frailty I could not help but detest, however much a part of me wanted to sympathize. To play at being her--it was beyond me. (25)

Hagar wants to do what Matt asks but, as she puts it, she is "unable to bend enough." When she rejects her mother's weakness, she becomes like her stone image. Hagar loses the fullness of her potential self when she cuts herself off from others.

It is this inability to bend that destroys her relationship with her husband, Bram Shipley. Hagar is first attracted to Bram because of what he represents to her: rebellion against her father's authority and middle-class values, and a response to the natural world. It is significant that the first time Hagar sees Bram at a dance, she "thought he looked like a bearded Indian, so brown and beaked a face." She also "reveled in his fingernails with crescents of ingrown earth that never met a file" (45). She is shocked when during their first dance, he presses his groin against her, but she accepts when he asks her for another dance. It is clear that Hagar is attracted to Bram's earthy sexuality, but it is also clear that the values she inherits from her father and her training in the cult of true womanhood will not allow her to

Coming to Terms with the Image of the Mother 163

acknowledge that attraction. Her Currie inheritance and finishing-school training cause her to denigrate the very qualities in Bram that she is drawn to. When her father refuses to have anything to do with her marriage to Bram, or with her, Hagar is at first certain that he "would soften and yield, when he saw how Brampton Shipley prospered, gentled, learned cravats and grammar" (50). Her ideas about love, like her ideas about everything else, are shaped by her alienating background. If she imagined Bram as a rugged Indian when they first met, in the next instant she "imagined him rigged out in a suit of gray soft as a dove's breast-feathers" (45). Her romantic conceptions about love prevent her from recognizing her true feelings for her husband: "He had a banner over me for many years. I never thought it love, though, after we wed. Love, I fancied, must consist of words and deeds delicate as lavender sachets, not like the things he did sprawled on the high white bedstead that rattled like a train" (80).

Hagar's attempts to tame Bram are futile and destructive. Their battle of wills hurts him, her, and their relationship. She is more successful at taming her own response to her husband:

It was not so very long after we wed, when first I felt my blood and vitals rise to meet his. He never knew. I never let him know. I never spoke aloud, and I made certain that the trembling was all inner. . . . I prided myself upon keeping my pride intact, like some maidenhead. (81)

To show response would be to accept being a woman. Denying her womanliness also means denying her sexuality. Her success at controlling herself is just as destructive as her attempts to control Bram. When she feels tenderness for her husband, as she does when he loses a prized horse, she refuses to express it, seeing such feelings as weak and womanly. The same intolerance of weakness prevents her from telling Bram of her fears when she finds that she is pregnant. At several points in their relationship, Hagar pulls away when they have chances to pull together. When Bram takes her to the hospital to deliver their son, for example, instead of sharing Bram's excitement, Hagar feels ashamed to be seen with him.

It is a concern about what others think of her, her pride, that causes her to leave Bram, just as defiance of what others think, her pride, caused her to leave her father and marry Bram. When she leaves him to support herself and her youngest son, John, by becoming a housekeeper for a rich man on the coast, she proves her strength, her independence, and her ability to survive, but leaving Bram levies a heavy emotional toll. Her memories of him suggest that not only did she miss him in her bed, but she also missed his recognition and respect of *her*. Looking back, she thinks "he was the only person close to me who ever thought of me by my name, not daughter, nor sister, nor mother, nor even wife, but Hagar, always" (80). That Bram is the only one who calls her by her name is important. He recognizes a sense of self which her lack of a relationship with her mother has denied.

Hagar's unexpressed, unacknowledged love for Bram affects her relationship with her youngest son, John. Despite hints in her narrative that John is very much like his father, Hagar insists on seeing him as a Currie through and through. She even gives him one of her prized possessions, her Currie clan pin. He asserts his allegiance to Bram by trading it for a knife. John's similarity to Bram is clearest in his relationship with Arlene Simmons. He assumes that Arlene is attracted to him for the same reason that Hagar is initially attracted to Bram--because she is not supposed to be. They first get together at a dance, like Bram and Hagar did. John gets drunk, like his father, who drank himself to death, and Arlene brings him home. When John learns that Arlene took care of him, he grins, and Hagar describes it as "the same distorted mouth as I'd seen before on someone else" (199). When Arlene defends John by denying that he is like Bram, Hagar gets angry at the implied criticism of her dead husband. It is clear, except to Hagar, that her preference for her youngest son is based on his resemblance to his father.

Just as John resembles the young Bram, Arlene is like the young Hagar. Remembering Arlene taking care of the drunken John, Hagar observes, "She was a very practical girl in some ways" (198). When Arlene's parents lose their money during the Depression, she is proud of her own self-sufficiency when she gets a job. But unlike Hagar, Arlene is able to express her feelings for the man she loves. When Hagar overhears them making love, it is clear to her that Arlene is enjoying herself, and that is when Hagar takes steps to stop them from marrying. Hagar's reaction to John's marriage repeats her father's reaction to hers. She arranges with Arlene's parents to send Arlene away. When John learns of Arlene's departure he gets drunk, drives with Arlene on the railway bridge, and kills them both in a self-destructive game of chicken with a freight train. It is not until Hagar goes through her process of awakening that she is able to come to terms with her guilt over her part in John and Arlene's death.

Whereas Hagar was too protective of John, she almost ignores her older son, Marvin. While she insists that the wild John is a Currie through and through, it is the hard-working Marvin who seems most like Hagar's father. As John tells her, "You always bet on the wrong horse. . . . Marv was your boy, but you never saw that" (237). It is clear from Hagar's memories that Marvin would have done anything to win her approval: "He was a serious and plodding little boy, and seemed to take to chores naturally. But when he'd finished them, he'd hang around the kitchen" (99). He's waiting for approval, or at least acknowledgment, but he never wins them from Hagar. The same pattern emerges when he leaves to join the war. Hagar feels a pang of tenderness: "I wanted all at once to hold him tightly, plead with him, against all reason and reality, not to go. But I did not want to embarrass both of us, nor have him think I'd taken leave of my senses" (129). Once again, Hagar's pride comes between her and those she loves. As she says, "the moment eluded us both." The relationship between Hagar and Marvin doesn't improve when he and his wife, Doris, move in with Hagar to take care of her. Living with an aging and irascible Hagar makes life difficult for all of them, as Hagar herself realizes: "I have lived with Marvin and Doris--or they have lived in my house, whichever way one cares to phrase it--for seventeen years. Seventeen--it weighs like centuries. How have I borne it? How have they?" (37). When Hagar's falls and memory lapses convince them that they can no longer care for her, they investigate the possibility of putting her in Silverthreads, a nursing home. Hagar's pride and self-reliance will not permit; attempting to stop it leads to her awakening.

Coming to Terms with the Image of the Mother 165

As Hagar thinks about her "lost men," it becomes clear that her relationships with them are marked by failure: by her failure to understand those she loves, and by her failure to express her feelings so that they could understand her. Clearly, Hagar experienced the nothingness in her relationships with the men in her life that Christ sees in women's novels of awakening, but even more damaging is the nothingness she experienced in her relationships with women, symbolized by the stone angel. *The Stone Angel* opens with a scene that connects imagery associated with the mother figure and imagery associated with the natural world. The novel begins with a description of the stone angel which dominates the small prairie town of Manawaka, and the whole novel:

Above the town, on the hill brow, the stone angel used to stand. I wonder if she stands there yet, in memory of her who relinquished her feeble ghost as I gained my stubborn one, my mother's angel that my father bought in pride to mark her bones and proclaim his dynasty, as he fancied, forever and a day. (3)

The stone angel is an emblem for the guilt which Hagar feels for the fact that her birth caused her mother's death, for the weakness that she associates with her mother, and for the power that she associates with her father. The mother herself is an emblem and a victim of the colonial system. Yet this image is all Hagar has and her desire for her mother, her need to be protected, and her pain at her mother's suffering characterize her childhood. Hagar stares at the stone angel's blind eyes, but never sees herself reflected there. Traditional accounts of psychological development argue that the child acquires a sense of self from the nurturing gaze of its mother-figure, grows away from her into an independent being, and goes on to master the world outside, symbolized by the father. The mother figure represents the first external mirror, eventually internalized, into which the girl-child looks to discover her identity. *The Stone Angel* provides a striking version of the absence of a mirroring bond and its painful effects on the heroine. Hagar's life story is the narrative of a subject's painful inability to belong to a place in any secure way, to belong to a larger community, until she can come to terms with her image of the mother and with her own role as a mother.

Hagar seems to suffer from what Adrienne Rich calls matrophobia:

the fear not of one's mother or of motherhood but of *becoming one's mother* . . . the one through whom the restrictions and degradations of a female existence were perforce transmitted. Easier by far to hate and reject a mother outright than to see beyond her to the forces acting upon her. But where a mother is hated to the point of matrophobia there may also be a deep underlying pull toward her, a dread that if one relaxes one's guard one will identify with her completely. (235)

Hagar exhibits the dread that Rich mentions when she refuses to wear her mother's shawl to comfort her dying brother. She also exhibits the debilitating effects of matrophobia which Rich describes:

Matrophobia can be seen as a womanly splitting of the self, in the desire to become purged once and for all of our mother's bondage, to become individuated and free. The mother stands for the victim in ourselves, the unfree woman, the martyr. Our personalities seem dangerously to blur and overlap with our mothers'; and, in a desperate attempt to know where mother ends and daughter begins, we perform radical surgery. (236)

Clearly, the stone angel represents the mother as martyr, and Hagar performs the kind of radical surgery which Rich fears. She fits Rich's description of the motherless woman: "the 'motherless' woman may also react by denying her own vulnerability, denying she has felt any loss or absence of mothering. . . . She may feel uneasy with equals--particularly women" (243). This is certainly true of Hagar, whose fear of the female and inability to accept her own womanhood lead to decidedly unflattering images of women in the first half of the novel: Doris is an "unwilling hen" (36); Bram's daughters are like "lumps of unrendered fat" (56); the old women at Silverthreads are "ewes" (98); Arlene is a "pouter pigeon" (173). Although Hagar needs the sense of safety which an acknowledged identification with her mother and other women might confer, the death of her mother and her fear of becoming her bars her from this feeling of unity and dooms her to a sense of fragmentation, which is reflected in her opening description of the angel and its surroundings.

In her opening description of the Manawaka cemetery, Laurence sets up several oppositions that will divide Hagar from herself and from those she loves, especially Bram. The clearest opposition is between the foreign peony and the native cowslip. Hagar remembers "the funeral-parlor perfume of the planted peonies, dark crimson and wallpaper pink, the pompous blossoms hanging leadenly, too heavy for their light stems, bowed down with the weight of themselves" (4). This recollection contrasts sharply with her memories of the cowslips:

They were tough-rooted, these wild and gaudy flowers, and although they were held back at the cemetery's edge, torn out by loving relatives determined to keep the plots clear and clearly civilized, for a second or two a person walking there could catch the faint, musky, dust-tinged smell of things that grew untended and had grown always, before the portly peonies and the angels with rigid wings, when the prairie bluffs were walked through only by Cree. (5)

Hagar's disdain for the imported peonies and her respect for the native cowslips suggest her ambivalence about the domestication of the prairie which Kolodny discusses in *The Land Before Her*. This passage could be read as a critique of the pioneer experience, as emblem of one woman's struggle with the conflicting values of domesticity and respect for the natural environment. Several contrasts are suggested in the opening scenes of the novel: death-life, artificial-natural, conscious-unconscious, civilization-nature, repression-passion, present-past, order-disorder, Currie-Shipley. Since all Hagar ever knew was the separation and fragmentation suggested by these binary oppositions, she is condemned to repeat them in all of her relationships. The lack of a bond between mother and daughter results in a painful psychological bondage from which Hagar cannot free herself until her awakening in the western Canadian landscape.

According to Christ, as a result of experiencing nothingness, the women in the novels she studies "question the meaning of their lives, thus opening themselves to the revelation of deeper sources of power and value" (13). Hagar's memories can be seen as an attempt to understand her life, and they help prepare her for the transformation she undergoes at Shadow Point. Like her marriage to Bram, Hagar's trip to the abandoned cannery on the edge of the ocean represents her rebellion against authority, against Doris and Marvin and their decision to place her in the Silverthreads nursing home. As Hagar plots her escape to Shadow Point, her defiance is clear: "They're greatly mistaken if they think I'll bend meekly and never raise a finger. I've taken matters into my own hands before, and can again, if need be" (139).

Hagar's trip to Shadow Point is also like her marriage to Bram in that it represents her repressed response to the natural world. At Shadow Point, Hagar gets in touch with external nature and with her own. She goes there because she is drawn to its quiet beauty: "I like this green blue-ceilinged place, warm and cool with sun and shade, where I'm not fussed at. Perhaps I've come here not to hide but to seek" (191-192). What Hagar finds at Shadow Point is her own repressed response to the natural world as opposed to the domestic values that she has used to keep herself in check for so many years. This change is signaled when she replaces her old-lady hat with the dead June bugs she finds in the abandoned cannery: "I take off my hat--it's hardly suitable for here, anyway, a prim domestic hat sprouting cultivated flowers. Then with considerable care I arrange the jade and copper pieces in my hair." Pleased with the effect, Hagar imagines herself "queen of moth-millers, empress of earwigs" (216). Hagar's coronation is in keeping with her comparison of herself to Keats' Meg Merrilies:

Old Meg she was a gypsy,
And lived upon the moors;
Her bed it was the brown heath turf,
And her house was out of doors. (151)

Hagar's house at the cannery, like Meg's, is essentially "out of doors" in Laurence's description of the human elements' surrender to the natural. In these conditions, Hagar's usual concern with protective boundaries is suspended. Like her house, Hagar is open to the natural world, and her openness is signaled by her identification with Meg. According to Helen Buss, Meg also represents Hagar's openness to a new view of womanhood: "Coming to terms with feminine values is largely accomplished for her through her identification of her womanhood with the figure of Meg Merrilies." Buss points out that Meg represents the "woman outside the civilized order . . . that Hagar needs to touch in herself. Meg is also 'brave as Margaret Queen' and 'tall as Amazon' thus representing a womanly strength based on a female tradition rather than a denial of femininity" (17). According to Buss, Hagar's "chant of brave old Meg . . . gives her a vision of female strength that she has previously lacked" (25).

As in the novels that Christ examines, Hagar's awakening takes place in a natural setting, and it is presaged by a storm. Like Edna Pontellier in Chopin's *The*

Awakening, she is both beckoned and menaced by the sea. Since the ocean is the "matrix of creation," in literature it often represents a desire to return to that "pool of darkness" that is associated with women. The ocean represents surrender, release, but also rebirth, a cleansing baptismal plunge. Water imagery represents a condition absolutely opposed to the stony paralysis of the angel. While listening to the soothing sounds of the sea, Hagar does plunge into the depths of her memories with the help of Murray Ferney Lees, agent for Dependable Life Assurance. Christ notes that in women's spiritual quest literature, the awakening often resembles a conversion experience. There are certainly religious overtones to the scene between Hagar and Mr. Lees. They share a jug of wine and tell each other their confessions. Religion figures prominently in Mr. Lees's story, and he tells it in language reminiscent of an itinerant preacher, which is appropriate since he comes from a long line of circuit riders. The confession / sermon he tells Hagar seems tailor-made for her. As Constance Rooke points out, Lee's story is essentially Hagar's, "where the chief villains are a concern for appearances and denial of sexuality, and where the catastrophe involves the loss of a son" (31).

Laurence emphasizes the importance of the night that Hagar and Lees spend together in the abandoned cannery by making it the nexus of her dual plots. As she listens to Mr. Lees's tragedy in the present, her memories take her to John's death in the past. Since Hagar was so traumatized by seeing all that she loved destroyed, it is no wonder that she is compelled to repeat it. Mr. Lees's confession moves her to make her own, but it is not until he responds to it that she realizes that for the first time in her life, she has spoken her feelings out loud. Her reaction is uncharacteristic: "I'm not sorry I've talked to him, not sorry at all, and that's remarkable" (245). They discuss their anger about their senseless losses and then Hagar describes the effect of their revelations: "We sit close together for warmth, both of us, leaning against the boxes. And then we slip into sleep" (245). When Hagar awakes, she feels the affects of spending two nights in the open and Mr. Lees's cheap wine. She is sick and confused. In her confusion she mistakes Mr. Lees for her lost son, and tells him that she won't come between John and Arlene. In one of the most generous acts in the novel, Mr. Lees pretends to be John and forgives her. This allows Hagar to forgive herself. At Shadow Point, Hagar comes to terms with the image of the mother on two levels: the image of Meg Merrilies supplants the image of woman as victim which Hagar has carried with her since the death of her mother, and her confession to Mr. Lees allows her to confront her own failure as a mother. Her journey to Shadow Point is also a journey into that part of her past, her failure as a mother, that she has been trying to avoid remembering, and finally, a journey into acceptance. Her experiences at Shadow Point force Hagar to begin revising her notion of what being a woman means.

It is through Mr. Lees that Hagar achieves the "mystical identification" that Christ cites as a characteristic of women's novels of awakening. The night she spends with him prepares her for what Christ terms "a new naming of self and reality that articulates the new orientation to self and world achieved through" the awakening. While Hagar does not become a sweet old lady over night, the effects of her experience with Mr. Lees are almost immediately apparent. Although her first reaction is anger when she finds that Mr. Lees has betrayed her hiding place to Marvin and Doris, when Doris tells her that Mr. Lees has saved her life, Hagar is brought up short:

> This ridiculous statement almost makes me laugh, but then, looking into this strange man's eyes, an additional memory returns, something more of what he spoke to me last evening, and I to him, and the statement no longer seems so ridiculous. Impulsively, hardly knowing what I'm doing, I reach out and touch his wrist. (253)

Hagar, who always flinches from human contact, touches him because he has touched her. He *has* saved her life.

Signs of Hagar's awakening are numerous in the last weeks of her life. While symbols of frozen womanhood, especially the stone angel, dominate the early chapters of the novel, the last two chapters feature images of women, both patients and nurses, as nurturers. As Buss points out, "We may measure Hagar's growth in her last days by her changing attitudes towards women, her increasing ability to receive mothering love and to offer love in return. . . . Hagar begins a process whereby she allows other women to touch her life" (12). One of the most significant signs of her awakening is that Hagar, who has never been able to form attachments with women, becomes part of the women's community in the hospital where she spends her last days. Initially, she complains to Marvin about the noise and lack of privacy on the women's ward, but when he arranges for her to be moved to a semiprivate room, she realizes that she will miss the other women, and the dialogues that they carry on in their dreams. The night cries in the women's hospital ward express their shared psychic field. Their mental barriers are permeable and their sleeping conversation incorporates all of the women's psychic lives:

> *Tom, don't you worry none--*
> *Mother of God, pray for us now and at the hour of--*
> *Mein Gott, erlöse mich--*
> *You mind that time, Tom? I mind it so well--*
> *I am sorry for having offended Thee, because I love--*
> *Erlöse mich von meinen Schmerzen--*
> *Bram!* (275)

The community of women described here is distinctive for its many lives and many-sided perspectives on womanhood from many cultures. In the hospital, Hagar finally achieves the imaginative identification with other women which allows her to grow. For Hagar, expanded awareness, impetus for change, and renewal result from her merging with different women's lives.

Another sign of her awakening is Hagar's relationship with two young women, Sandra Wong, the teenager who shares her new room, and Doris's daughter, Tina. Hagar, who cannot think of anything that she has done to help someone else, gets out of her own bed, though she is in a lot of pain, to get a bedpan for her young roommate, and then she and Sandra laugh themselves to sleep over the look on the nurse's face when she finds Hagar out of bed. This scene is small, but important, for

Hagar is able to define herself in a new way so that being a woman does not mean becoming her mother, retaining all the old connections with weakness, assuming automatically the outmoded passive roles. Hagar's changing view of womanhood is reflected in her identification with her granddaughter. In Buss's view, Hagar's "gentle feelings toward Tina signal a new stage in her life, one that is to bring her closer to the mother and the values represented by that figure" (12). Hagar's reconciliation with the image of the mother is signaled when she gives Tina the ring which once belonged to her mother. As Constance Rooke points out, the gesture signifies connection between four generations of women (41). According to Adrienne Rich, "Until a strong line of love, confirmation, and example stretches from mother to daughter, from woman to woman across the generations, women will still be wandering in the wilderness" (246). Hagar comes to realize that she has been wandering in the wilderness, and her gift of the ring is her attempt to pass on the love, confirmation, and example which she lacked. The gesture involves not destruction of the "mother" but rather a confrontation with and an incorporation of the matriarchal power to nurture.

The most significant sign of Hagar's growth in the novel comes in its most famous passage, when she faces some difficult truths about herself:

Every good joy I might have held, in my man or any child of mine or even the plain light of morning, of walking the earth, all were forced to a standstill by some brake of proper appearances--oh, proper to whom? When did I ever speak the heart's truth? Pride was my wilderness, and the demon that led me there was fear. (292)

Throughout the novel Hagar is, in effect, reading her own life; in this passage she realizes that she is the author. Although this passage has received a lot of discussion from Laurence scholars, no one has noticed Hagar's emphasis on her sense of loss as a woman and a mother and her recognition that this loss is tied to her ability to respond to her natural surroundings, and caused by the pride and fear of feminine weakness which she inherited from her father. In "speaking the heart's truth," Hagar achieves both a reconciliation with the feminine and a new sense of her own strength as a woman. By facing the stone angel which she has become, Hagar gets in touch with her life-giving forces. Hagar looks Medusa--Stone Angel--in the eye. Instead of being turned to stone, she is released into the world of feeling from the frozen rage which Medusa represents. Facing the truth about herself allows her to speak it. When Marvin asks her how she is, she is set to lie, but instead she tells him "I'm--frightened. Marvin, I'm so frightened--" (303). Even more difficult is the lie she tells him out of love--that he has been a better son to her than John. Hagar considers her final mothering of Marvin a victory and Buss explains why she is right:

When we consider the distance she has had to reach out to find the mother and the scant hand-holds her society offered her in her search . . . we may be inclined to agree with her assessment of victory, and conclude that Laurence's achievement has not been in her portrayal of isolation but in her portrayal of the feminine search for relatedness despite all the forces of isolation. (30)

When he leaves her room, Hagar overhears Marvin and the nurse discussing her in one of the most moving passages in the novel: "'She's a holy terror,' he says. Listening, I feel like it is more than I could now reasonably have expected out of life, for he has spoken with such anger and such tenderness" (304-305). Hagar is a holy terror to the end. In the last scene in the novel, she characteristically refuses to let the nurse help her drink a glass of water and insists on holding it in her own hands, just as she had held her life in her own hands. *The Stone Angel* ends with Hagar triumphantly drinking the water and then the words "And then--" As W. H. New points out, there are several ways to read this ending (191). In a novel shaped by Hagar's memory, "And then--" could mean "at that time in the past," a final expression of the past imposing itself on the present. Or "And then--" could mean "on the other hand," an expression of an alternative possibility. But I prefer to read "And then--" as "next," an expression of continuity. It seems fitting that a novel that begins with death, that has at its center an awakening that places it in a long tradition of writing by women, and that attempts to explore the complex relationship between mothers and daughters, should end countering finality with regeneration. That Hagar's recognition of herself as a woman coincides with her own death is not only the tragedy of restricted choices. It is also her triumphant assumption of the female and of the painful but liberating comprehension of it.

WORKS CITED

Buss, Helen M. *Mother and Daughter Relationships in the Manawaka Works of Margaret Laurence*. Victoria: University of Victoria Press, 1985.

Christ, Carol. *Diving Deep and Surfacing: Women Writers on Spiritual Quest*. Boston: Beacon, 1980.

Kolodny, Annette. *The Land Before Her*. Chapel Hill: University of North Carolina Press, 1984.

Laurence, Margaret. *The Stone Angel*. Toronto: McClelland and Stewart, New Canadian Library, (1964, 1968, 1988) 1995; Chicago: University of Chicago Press, 1993.

New, W. H. "Every Now and Then: Voice and Language in Laurence's *The Stone Angel*." *A Place to Stand On: Essays By and About Margaret Laurence*. Ed. George Woodcock. Edmonton: NeWest, 1983, 171-92.

Rich, Adrienne. *Of Woman Born: Motherhood as Experience and Institution*. New York: W. W. Norton, 1976.

Rooke, Constance. "A Feminist Reading of *The Stone Angel*." *Canadian Literature* 93 (1982): 26-41.

Chapter 15

The Subversive Voice in *The Fire-Dwellers*
Mitzi Hamovitch

The double voice of Stacey MacAindra, central protagonist of Margaret Laurence's *The Fire-Dwellers*, is plainly heard by the reader throughout the novel. In the driven internal monologue that dominates the novel, the voice is muffled and covert, hidden from other characters in the novel because it is subversive of patriarchal society. It is, however, of major importance to the feminist reader. The second voice, overt, but muted in importance, is often wistful, tentative, conformist, occasionally mildly rebellious, easily rebuffed, and sometimes fragmented. Laurence's intention is to reconcile the two voices by the end of the novel, but with the advantage of years of feminist theory, the subversive voice is louder.

Background about the existence of an important subversive voice in Laurence's novels comes from feminist theory as it related to language. In *Language and Woman's Place*, Lakoff describes women's language as lacking authority and seriousness, conviction and confidence. In her view, in comparison with the (ostensibly) forceful and effective language of men, women are hesitant, tentative, even trivial, and are therefore "deficient," as she puts it. Spender disagrees with Lakoff stating in *Man Made Language* that her research and that of others who find women's language, the language of more than half the members of society, "inferior," is based on the fallacious belief that language belongs to men in our patriarchal society, and that women somehow don't use language as effectively or persuasively as men. Spender's thesis is that the English language has been "literally man made and that it is still under male control." Women have to break that control to ensure that what women say and how they say it will be regarded as equally significant. Public discourse has been dominated by men for their own ends, and women have been either excluded or made to feel "uncomfortable," or to serve those ends, if and when, they do participate. In the words of Tillie Olsen, "Not to be able to come to one's own truth . . . even when telling the truth, having to 'tell it slant,' robs one of drive, of conviction, and limits potential stature" (339). Voice and utterance are central in the novel.

Laurence uses a framework of multiple devices to give the reader a sense of the immediacy and urgency of Stacey's life. Thought, directed both toward the past and the present, fantasy, the voice of the media, action, and dialogue impinge on each other in a variety of typography and spacing on the page to give the reader the total effect of Stacey's life as it is being lived at the time of reading. The action of the book is set in the 1950s--an infamous time for women--in which women were isolated in suburbia and totally family-centered. The events occur over a period of a few weeks before Stacey's fortieth birthday. Stacey is the wife of Clifford MacAindra, a salesman, first of encyclopedias, then of essences as they are called, peppermint, and so forth, and now finally of Richalife, an all-purpose vitamin. The fire of the title is the dangerous and frightening element in which they all live--it is also the purifying element out of which the surviving substances are true and essential. The epigraph with which the book begins is "Ladybird, Ladybird, / Fly away home. / Your house is on fire / And your children are gone." Stacey is filled with anxiety, inadequacy, and anger--anxiety about her four children--Katie, fourteen, beautiful and rebellious; Ian, eleven, silent and moody; Duncan, eight, gentle but somewhat of a momma's boy, and creative; and Jen, two, who does not yet speak. The anger is directed at her husband because he is silent, absent. He comes home from work too tired to talk, and resents her questions. Stacey's muffled voice speaks, "Nothing ever can come out. I sometimes see us like moles, living in our underground burrows, with eyes that can't stand any light" (151). At night, too tired for sex, Mac's usual routine is to ask Stacey in bed, "Is everything all right?" Stacey's routine answer is, "Yes. Everything's all right." Mac grunts, turns over, and falls immediately asleep. On another occasion, Stacey reflects to herself:

Does he hate me? If so, how long? Where did it start? . . . Adam. . . . And maybe Eve. . . . What's the matter with us that we can't talk? . . . How come we feel it's indecent? . . . Okay, I get the message. If that's the way you want it, that's the way it'll be. From now on, I live alone in a house where everything is always always all right. (155-156)

Male inarticulateness and the battle of the sexes are familiar themes in novels, but not often are the heroines so self-aware and honest as is Stacey. Metaphors of blindness, silence in an underground mole-like existence, underscore Stacey's duplicitous existence. Everything is always all right means nothing is all right.

Stacey's need to break out of the suburban trap and the continuing spaces of the house is evident in the opening pages of *The Fire-Dwellers*. Vancouver, labeled by advertising experts "the jewel of the Pacific Northwest," conceals from the ordinary city-dweller, a part not usually visited by the casual walker in the city, its seedy waterfront. Stacey has lived in the city for twenty years and feels she does not know a thing about it. Social conscience surfacing, Stacey feels it is time she learned about the "other":

In the lobby of the Princess Regal Hotel, some yawning yellow-toothed fishwife, fleshwife, sagging guttily in a print dress sad with poppies, is sweeping up last night--heel-squashed cigarette butts, Kleenex blown into or bawled into, and ashes. Old men are sitting there too, sitting in the red-plastic-covered chairs, waiting for the beer parlor to open, so somebody can

stand them a drink and they can accept haughtily, their scorn some kind of sop to their pride.
What is it like really? How would I know? People live in those rooms above the stores, people who go to the cafes and bars at night, who prowl these streets that are their territory. (10-11)

In T. S. Eliot's words, "She has such a vision of the streets" (*Selected Poems* 23). "The buildings at the heart of the city are brash, flashing with colors, solid and self-confident" (*Fire* 14). Stacey is reassured by them until she looks again and sees them "charred, open to the impersonal winds, glass and steel broken like vulnerable live bones, shadows of people frog-splayed on the stone like in that other city" (*Fire* 14-15). Stacey has the imagination of disaster. Hiroshima in its atom-bombed anguish is always in Stacey's consciousness . . . but, of course, there is no one to talk to about that.

Newspaper headlines and television voices batter her spirit as well. "'Seventeen-Year-Old on Drug Charge.' 'Girl Kills Self, Lover.' . . . 'Car Smash Decapitates Indian Bride, Groom.' 'Man Sets Room Ablaze, Perishes.' . . . What do I know of it?" "--What is it like really? How would I know?" "Nearly twenty years here, and I don't know the place at all or feel at home" (11). Isolated in suburbia and before that nurtured in small-town Manawaka's parochial environment, Stacey craves communion, to experience the world in all its variety.

As she returns to her home on Bluejay Crescent, Stacey imagines herself as her seat-mate, a young girl with flawless skin, must see her:

--What's she seeing? Housewife, mother of four, this slightly too short and too amply rumped woman with coat of yesteryear, hemlines all the wrong length as Katie is always telling me, lipstick wrong color, and crowning comic touch, the hat. . . . I want to explain. *Under the chapeau lurks a mermaid, a whore, a tigress.* (15)

The self-parodistic viewpoint antedates Adrienne Rich's odd apt insight in "When We Dead Awaken: Writing as Re-Vision": "We have been expected to lie with our bodies, to bleach, redden, unkink or curl our hair, pluck eyebrows, shave armpits. . . . take little steps, glaze finger and toe nails, wear clothes that emphasized our helplessness" (188). At this date, before the feminist movement, Stacey feels herself a misfit. Under the impact of the advertising of the patriarchal world, a reality has been constructed that diminishes the real woman who does not fit the media package--which is to be sleek, coiffed, and stylish at all times.

Stacey's husband has started a new job as salesman of Richalife vitamins which promote health for the entire family. Stacey is enraged by the hypocrisy and pseudogospel quality of the program as well as by the strangely menacing silver-maned director, Thor Thorlaksen. In a crucial and comic scene, Stacey, who has, against Mac's injunctions, drunk too much at a Richalife social gathering of salesmen and wives--to which she has been dragged and then abandoned--dares to tell Thor what she thinks of the quiz he has foisted on the family, calling it an "infrusion," her drunken amalgam of "intrusion" and "infringement." Mac shepherds her away, and is, of course, judgmentally silent, speaking only to give her a figurative slap on the wrist--"no use talking to you in your condition." If Stacey had known the work of feminist writers like Mary Daly and Adrienne Rich--who had not yet written--she would not have felt so isolated in her attempt to make her muffled voice heard in the phony world of salesmen, peddlers of quackery. To Daly, Rich, and others, it is important that women cease to be muted and find their voice, that women's language be liberated. To quote Daly, "The development of this hearing faculty and power of speech involves the dislodging of images that reflect and reinforce prevailing social arrangements" (62). Of the 1950s, Adrienne Rich writes that "middle-class women were making careers of domestic perfection --people were living in the suburbs, technology was going to be the answer to everything--even sex; the family was in its glory. Life was extremely private; women were isolated from each other by the loyalties of marriage; women didn't talk to each other much in the fifties--not about their secret emptinesses, their frustrations" (42). Women have been forced to lie, for survival, to men. How to unlearn this among other women? In fact, when Stacey's friend, Tess, some-time babysitter for Jen, attempts suicide, Stacey is stunned. What really lay behind the facade of meticulously groomed perfection that Tess unfailingly presented?

An ardent, short-lived love affair brings brief fulfillment to Stacey, who realizes then that, although she could gain the freedom she craves and go away with her lover, Luke Venturi, she will never leave her family. The love she feels for her children is what holds her to her unsatisfying marriage, she realizes. A number of events and a contrived ending bring *The Fire-Dwellers* to a close; close friends die or attempt suicide, Duncan is saved by a hair's breadth from drowning, a near-catastrophe which draws Stacey and Mac closer together, Jen finally utters a few words, "Want tea, Mum?"--and Mac's promotion to director of the Vancouver branch of Richalife with concomitant raise in pay and departure of the ominous Thorlaksen, bring a temporarily affirmative ending to the novel. "Give me another forty years Lord, and I may mutate into a matriarch. . . . The house is quiet. The kids are asleep. . . . Mac is asleep. . . . Temporarily, they are all more or less okay" (281). They are all stronger than they thought they were, Stacey reflects.

To the contemporary reader, *The Fire-Dwellers* is particularly interesting because it acknowledges the subversive feminine voice of the 1950s that murmured beneath the surface of events. The typical feminine metaphors of traps and confinement are evoked in Stacey's life. On one hand, she hungers to be free, to go to the Northwest Territories, perhaps, and teach the Indians. "I'm bloody sick of trying to cope. I don't want to be a good wife and mother" (161). On the other hand, the overt message in *The Fire-Dwellers* is that, like it or not, a woman's place is in the home. What Margaret Laurence does, in a 1960s resolution of the novel, is to reconcile the two voices. By her fortieth birthday, Stacey learns to accept what she cannot change. She has learned the importance of endurance, the panacea recommended to women throughout time, the answer to life's demands. Today's woman, however, wants more than that--she wants her share of the action and considers her options. At the very least, she hears more clearly the voice of protest, the voice of resistance. Laurence's protagonist in *The Fire-Dwellers* is an early instance of a feminine subversive voice asserting itself in a patriarchal society.

WORKS CITED

Daly, Mary. *Beyond God the Father*. Boston: Beacon Press, 1973.
Eliot, T. S. *Selected Poems*. New York: Harcourt, Brace, & World, 1936.
Lakoff, Robin. *Language and Woman's Place*. New York: Octagon Books, 1975.
Laurence, Margaret. *The Fire-Dwellers*. Toronto: McClelland and Stewart, New Canadian Library, (1969, 1981) 1991; Chicago: University of Chicago Press, 1993.
Olsen, Tillie. "One Out of Twelve: Women Who Are Writers in Our Century." *Working It Out*. Ed. Pamela Daniels and Sara Ruddick. New York: Pantheon Books, 1977.
Rich, Adrienne. "When We Dead Awaken: Writing as Re-Vision." *On Lies, Secrets, and Silence*. New York: W. W. Norton, 1979.
Spender, Dale. *Man Made Language*. Boston: Routledge and Kegan Paul, 1980.

Chapter 16

Morag Gunn in Fictional Context: The Career Woman Theme in *The Diviners*

Susan Ward

The Diviners is, as much as anything else, the story of a woman and her career. As such, it takes its place in a long line of American and British novels about career women, a line which continues into the present day. With the middle of the nineteenth century marking the point at which it began to be acceptable for middle-class women to work outside the home and with the professions beginning to open for women about the same date, novelists, many of them women, began to experiment with the new career woman as a fictional heroine. Although, for reasons having to do with conservative audience values and the difficulties that the choice of a working heroine posed, the career woman heroine was not a constant subject for any one writer, a number of nineteenth-century novelists wrote about her. Sara Parton (or "Fanny Fern") in *Ruth Hall* (1855); Charlotte Bronte in *Jane Eyre* (1847) and *Vilette* (1853); Louisa May Alcott in *Work* (1873); Elizabeth Stuart Phelps in *A Silent Partner* (1871), *The Story of Avis* (1877), *Doctor Zay* (1882), and a number of short stories; Sara Orne Jewett in *A Country Doctor* (1884); George Gissing in *The Odd Woman* (1893); and Kate Chopin in *The Awakening* (1899) all experimented with this figure. In the first decades of the twentieth century, Mary Hunter Austin in *A Woman of Genius* (1912); Willa Cather in *O Pioneers!* (1913, *The Song of the Lark* (1914), and a number of short stories; Dorothy Canfield in *The Home-Maker* (1924); Ellen Glasgow in *Barren Ground* (1925); Sheila Kaye-Smith in *Joanna Godden* (1921) and *Susan Spray* (1931) continued the experimentation. Virginia Woolf wrote about the career woman in essays and made her a subject in her fiction throughout the twenties, thirties, and forties. Recently, career women have appeared regularly as heroines in the works of Lisa Alther, Margaret Atwood, Margaret Drabble, Marilyn French, Gail Godwin, Mary Gordon, Erica Jong, Doris Lessing, Alison Lurie, Joyce Carol Oates, Marge Piercy, Sylvia Plath, Judith Rossner, and countless others. Morag Gunn, then, has plenty of fictional company.

Although a few studies have been written on the female *Kunstlerroman*, the career woman novel, featuring heroines with careers outside as well as in the arts, broadens the genre and allows discussion of several themes pertinent to others besides the practitioner of the arts.[1] In the nineteenth century, the genre took its form partly from the female *Bildungsroman* and partly from the genre Susan Roskowski has termed "the novel of awakening." In the twentieth century, writers are engaged in the process Rachel Blau du Plessis has termed "writing beyond the ending," inventing new narrative strategies for a still developing form. It is possible, nevertheless, to identify certain formal and thematic concerns in the genre and to view Laurence's *The Diviners* against a common backdrop. In the reminder of this essay, I will sketch out some of these concerns as they are portrayed in the work of some of Laurence's predecessors and contemporaries and discuss some of the ways in which Laurence, in writing *The Diviners*, chooses to meet them. It will become apparent that *The Diviners* is part of a developing genre and that Laurence, in choosing to work within it, does so with both artistic integrity and imagination.

A primary thematic concern in career woman novels is the heroine's motivation. Why does the heroine turn to a career in the first place? The answers are varied. Some do it for the money; Ruth Hall in Sarah Parton's novel, for example, begins to write to support herself and her children after her husband dies. Others--Christie Devon in Alcott's *Work*--embark on a career to establish independence from traditional feminine roles. Still others--Glasgow's Dorinda Oakley in *Barren Ground* and Phelps' Perley Kelso in *The Silent Partner*--choose careers to fill voids in their lives. In *The Diviners*, Laurence combines many of these motives in providing Morag Gunn with the rationale to become a writer. An orphan raised by the town refuse collector, she early learns the value of money; after she leaves Brooke, the only person she leans on for support in her adult life, she depends on her career for income. "Look at it this way," she tells A-Okay Smith, who teases her about the overgrown state of her garden, "If I spent all my time gardening, how in hell could I get any writing done? . . . I need a minimal income" (66NCL, 46UC). Even as an established writer, she muses: "Finances are getting low. Pray God they hurry with the advance on royalties" (443NCL, 341UC). Yet money is not the only reason for her decision to earn her living as a writer. Writing furnishes her with a route to independence after she leaves Brooke. Divorced and alone with Pique, she grasps at her publisher's suggestion to write light articles for money. Also writing provides her with a means for making sense of the fragments of her past. All of Morag's novels, from *Spear of Innocence*, which uses the story of Eva Winkler, to the novel she is writing as the novel we are reading progresses, interweave pieces of Morag's past into the fictions she creates.

Talent and the notion that one's career can be and often is a part of one's identity unite to form a second thematic concern in many novels featuring career women as heroines. Some heroines--Cather's Thea Kronberg in *The Song of the Lark*, for example--are simply driven by their talent. Others--Atwood's Joan in *Lady Oracle*, Godwin's Violet Clay in her novel by that name, and Lurie's Janet Belle Smith in *Real People*--run from their talent by producing bad forms of art only to realize that they must produce better. Still others--Godwin's Jane Clifford in *The Odd Woman* and Rossner's Anna Burke in *August*--choose careers which fit particularly well with their own personalities.

Talent and the harmonious fit of Morag's career to her personality and her abilities are major themes in *The Diviners*. It is evident from the first pages of the novel that its protagonist is a writer. On page three, as she reads Pique's farewell note, she muses: "Well, you had to give the girl some marks for style of writing," revealing her ever-present interest in writing as craft (11NCL, 4UC). Throughout the novel, she records mental descriptions and then revises wordings: "[the river's] surface was wrinkled by the breeze," but "the river wasn't wrinkled or creased at all--wrong words, implying something unfluid like skin, something unenduring, prey to age" (12NCL, 40UC). The snapshots, beginning in the first chapter, the memorybank movies, the inner films, the dialogues with Catherine Parr Traill, all attest to her imagination and her ability to weave the fact and fiction of the past into a new whole. Moreover, the early parts of the novel are filled with images of the young Morag writing: the child writing in her notebook after listening to Christie's tales of Piper Gunn; the student submitting her first story to the university paper; the young wife writing stories and a first novel during the hours her professor husband works at his own career; the professional struggling to finish her latest novels even as she worries over the whereabouts of her nineteen-year-old daughter. Writing is central to Morag, and her growth as a writer provides the novel with much of its plot, placing it squarely in the tradition of the *Kunstlerroman*.[2]

Training and the role of mentors and teachers poses a third thematic concern in many novels tracing the development of career women. According to Linda Nochlin, in an early feminist essay entitled "Why Are There No Great Women Artists?" women historically often lacked the teachers and mentors so necessary to men as they began to develop in artistic careers. Mentors often aid in the career development of women with nonartistic interests as well. The spirits of ancient Indian artisans of the Southwest perform this function for Cather's Thea Kronberg in *The Song of the Lark*, and Ursula DeVane in Godwin's *The Finishing School* fulfills this role for Justin Stokes.

In *The Diviners*, Laurence provides Morag with two mentor-models: Christie, who weaves his tales of Piper Gunn out of small bits of fact and large lengths of fiction, and Skinner Tonnerre, who employs the same method to fashion the legends of the Tonnerre family. The relationship between Christie's tale-telling and her own fiction writing is evident; directly after Laurence records the telling of Christie's first Piper Gunn, she shows us the young Morag composing the Tale of Piper Gunn's Woman and recording it in her notebook. Similarly, Morag reuses Skinner's tales when she retells them to the child Pique. As well, the relationship between facts from her own life and Morag's fiction becomes evident when we review the content of her novels: the heroine in *Spear of Innocence* aborting herself as Eva Winkler had done; the heroine of *Prospero's Child* struggling to overcome the dominance of the man she has married as Morag has struggled with Brooke; the old man in *Jonah*, who is disreputable and whose daughter resents it, as she resented Christie; the content of *Shadow of Eden*, based on the Canadian settlement of the Scots Christie immortalized for her in his tales of Piper Gunn. "I like the thought of history and fiction interweaving," Morag writes to her friend

Ella. It is clear that she learns this technique from Christie and from Skinner as she first listens to and then analyzes the tales they tell.

A fourth thematic concern in novels featuring career women as heroines stems from the tension between the heroine's career and expectations placed on her, either by herself or by others, to fulfill traditional feminine roles. According to Grace Stewart in *A New Mythos: The Novel of the Artist as Heroine, 1877-1977*, such a conflict forms a vital part of the novel of the artist as heroine (15); this statement may be broadened to apply to most novels featuring career women as heroines. Two plot patterns emerge from the aforementioned conflict: the plot of the successful career woman who sacrifices her ambitions to the demands of husband and family--as in Phelps' *The Story of Avis* or, more recently, in Miriam's history in Piercy's *Small Changes*--and the plot of the ambitious career woman who abandons traditional female role expectations to devote herself to her career--as in Lydia's story in Godwin's *A Mother and Two Daughters* and in Mira's story in French's *The Women's Room*. Both of these plots surface in *The Diviners*: the first in the section in which Morag sacrifices her university ambitions to marry Brooke and then finds she can write only when he is out of the house, and the second in the immediately succeeding section in which Morag leaves Brooke because he is stifling her creative self. The section preceding the marriage breakup is filled with scenes emphasizing Morag's unhappiness with the traditional role of faculty wife Brooke tries to foist on her: Morag turning to writing a novel because she finds her life empty; Morag unable to finish her daily stint of writing before Brooke returns home (248NCL, 187UC); Morag disregarding Brooke's advice and sending *Spear of Innocence* out to publishers without effecting any of his suggested changes; Morag exploding in anger because Brooke refuses to accept her statement that she knows something about novels, gained from "something different from reading or teaching" (281NCL, 213UC). Morag's anger at Brooke, not Jules Tonnerre, causes the marriage to break down. Her reaction to Brooke's attempts to keep her dependent by speaking to her as if she were a child and by "correcting" her attempts at short story and novel writing, are all carefully emphasized before the reappearance of Tonnerre.

An outgrowth of the tension between career and female expectations seen in many novels featuring career women is the tendency on the part of the career woman heroine to try to separate her life as careerist from her life as woman. Some heroines actually leave the scene of their normal lives to practice their careers; Godwin's Violet Clay in her novel of that name and Lurie's Janet Belle Smith in *Real People* are examples. Others, though they do not leave physically, are constantly reminded of the difficulties of living in two different worlds. Laurence herself, in an interview with Rosemary Sullivan in 1983, spoke about the role conflict family and career posed for women:

The women writers--and there are many of them in this country who have chosen to marry and have children, as well as to do their own work--are really fairly heroic. Of course this is true of women in other professions as well. One thing I think that women writers are fortunate in is that they can do their work at home. Now if I had chosen to be a brain surgeon, I would have found it a great deal more difficult to bring up two children in the way that I wanted to bring them up, which was to be with them a lot of the time. So that I think that women writers are fortunate in that they can do their work at home. They are *not* fortunate in the sense that they are doing several full-time jobs. I used to laugh reading books of anthropology sometimes, because African chieftains who had been educated in England, say at Oxford, would go back to their villages, and would suffer from what was called "role conflict"--I thought: "Role conflict--I know exactly what *that* means. (73)

Unwittingly, she echoes the sentiments of many career women heroines.

Although, after her divorce from Brooke, Morag never deserts the world of womanhood for the world of the desexualized writer, she is often bothered by the disjunction between the two. The scene in which she cannot get "outside the novel" in time to welcome Brooke home to dinner reveals Laurence's attention to this theme (248NCL, 187UC); years later Morag is still trying to get "inside" the world of her writing in the morning and "outside" it in time to welcome Pique home from school (443NCL, 341UC). In Vancouver, without Brooke's interference, she is "too tired and lousy most evenings to do any writing at all" because of her pregnancy (316NCL, 242UC). In England, her writing is interrupted by Pique's illness and her affair with McRaith. In each instance, Laurence reminds us that these interruptions, stemming from Morag's feminine role of mother and mistress, *are* interruptions: "A month away from it, and getting back inside will be torture," she thinks after Pique begins to mend. And, she acknowledges, she "works much better when McRaith is not in London, . . . herself and her time then not being divided" (404NCL, 310UC). In the novel's present, the pattern continues, with Royland, the Smiths, and even Pique causing Morag to mark her annoyance when they interrupt her at work. "This had been the pattern of life for how long?" she thinks after one such interruption. "Morag at this table, working, and people arriving and saying in effect 'Please don't let me interrupt you.' But they *did* interrupt her, damn it" (372NCL, 286UC). But she goes on to indicate her allegiance to both worlds: "The only thing that could be said for it was that if no one ever entered that door, the situation would be infinitely worse" (372NCL, 286UC). In her wish to share in both the career world and the world of the traditionally feminine woman, Morag Gunn is at one with most contemporary fictional career heroines.

A fifth, and major, thematic concern in novels featuring career women as heroines is the search of the heroine for a romantic hero. The search itself presents a formal problem, since the romantic impulse and the career impulse of the heroine, or, to put it another way, the love plot and the career-development plot, are, as we have seen, often at odds. Novelists have dealt with this problem in various ways. Some--Phelps in her early short stories and Godwin in *Violet Clay* are the best examples--have simply eliminated heroes from their fiction. Others--Phelps in *A Silent Partner*, Atwood in *Lady Oracle*, Jong in *Fear of Flying*, Phelps in *Doctor Zay*, Cather in *The Song of the Lark*, French in *The Women's Room*--have had their career women heroines desert unworthy men or, even more tellingly, reject worthy ones for fear that love will interrupt their career plans. Only a few contemporary women novelists--Gordon in *Men and Angels* and Piercy in *Fly*

Away Home--have begun to allow their career heroines to have romantic relationships with men who help, rather than hinder, their careers. It is almost as if novelists who feature career women as heroines cannot imagine a romantic hero to go with the troublesome heroines they have created.

Laurence deals with the problem of love interest in *The Diviners* in two distinct ways. First, in relating the history of Morag's marriage to Brooke Skelton, she follows the pattern of allowing her heroine to desert a man who stands in the way of her career. Secondly, she creates, in the persons of Jules Tonnerre and Dan McRaith, alternative romantic heroes who do not interfere with the growth of Morag's career. Indeed, both help her to develop as a writer: Jules by teaching her about the relationship between history and invention in fiction as he relates his Tonnerre stories, and McRaith by sharing his work with her and allowing her to share hers. Beyond this, both men do not take up a good deal of the time Morag needs to spend on her career. Morag, although she hungers for male companionship throughout much of the novel, admits that perhaps this is best. "If he were here all the time," she thinks of Dan McRaith, "[I suspect I] would become impatient with him, resentful of anyone's constant presence. No doubt under those circumstances, too, [I] would be expected to make the meals and do the laundry for him as well as for [myself] and Pique" (404NCL, 310UC). Yet neither McRaith nor Jules Tonnerre ask these things of her, and so they do not pose major threats to her writing.

The last pages of *The Diviners* deal with the passing down of talents as Morag gazes after Pique, who has inherited her talent for story and Jules's talent for song. They speak of Morag's own talent and her allegiance to it. "The necessary doing of the thing," Laurence writes of her heroine's feeling for her life work at this point, "--that mattered" (477NCL, 369UC). It is no accident that the novel ends with the image of Morag writing, returning to her house, "to write the remaining private and fictional words, and to set down her title" (477NCL, 370UC). That, in a novel focusing on a writer's career, is how things should be.

NOTES

1. For discussions of the female *Kunstlerroman*, see Susan Gubar, "The Birth of the Artist as Heroine: (Re)production, the *Kunstlerroman* Tradition, and the Fiction of Katherine Mansfield," *The Representation of Women in Fiction*, Ed. Carolyn G. Heilbrun and Margaret Higonnet (Baltimore: Johns Hopkins University Press, 1983), pp. 19-59; and Grace Stewart, *A New Mythos: The Novel of the Artist as Heroine: 1877-1977* (St. Albans: Eden Press Women's Publications, 1979).

2. For two discussions of *The Diviners* as *Kunstlerroman*, see Michel Fabre, "Words and the World: The Diviners as an Explanation of the Book of Life," *A Place to Stand On: Essays By and About Margaret Laurence*, ed. George Woodcock (Edmonton, Alberta: NeWest Press, 1983), pp. 247-69; and Sherrill Grace, "A Portrait of the Artist as Laurence Hero," *Margaret Laurence: An Appreciation*, ed. Christl Verduyn (Peterborough, Ontario, Canada: Broadview Press, 1988), pp. 162-71.

WORKS CONSULTED

Du Plessis, Rachel Blau. *Writing Beyond the Ending: Narrative Strategies of Twentieth-century Women Writers*. Bloomington: Indiana University Press, 1985.

Fabre, Michel. "Words and the World": *The Diviners* as an Explanation of the Book of Life." *A Place To Stand On: Essays By and About Margaret Laurence*. Ed. George Woodcock. Edmonton, Alberta: NeWest Press, 1983, 247-69.

Grace, Sherrill, "A Portrait of the Artist as Laurence Hero." *Margaret Laurence: An Appreciation*. Ed. Christl Verduyn. Peterborough, Ontario, Canada: Broadview Press, 1988, 162-71.

Harris, Barbara. *Beyond Her Sphere: Women and the Professions in American History*. Westport, Conn.: Greenwood Press, 1981.

Kessler-Harris, Alice. *Out to Work: A History of Wage-Earning Women in the United States*. New York: Oxford University Press, 1982.

Laurence, Margaret. *The Diviners*. Toronto: McClelland and Stewart, New Canadian Library, (1974) 1995; Chicago: University of Chicago Press, 1993.

Nochlin, Linda. "Why Are There No Great Women Artists?" *Women in Sexist Society: Studies in Power and Powerlessness*. Ed. Vivian Gornick. New York: Basic Books, 1971, 344-66.

Roskowski, Susan J. "The Novel of Awakening." *The Voyage In: Fictions of Female Development*. Ed. Elizabeth Abel, Marianne Hirsch, and Elizabeth Langland. Hanover, Conn.: University Press of New England, 1983, 49-68.

Sullivan, Rosemary. "Interview with Margaret Laurence." *A Place to Stand On: Essays By and About Margaret Laurence*. Ed. George Woodcock. Edmonton, Alberta: NeWest Press, 1983, 61-79.

Chapter 17

Wordsmith and Woman: Morag Gunn's Triumph Through Language
Laurie Lindberg

Each of Margaret Laurence's Canadian-set novels features a female protagonist searching for her identity. Hagar in *The Stone Angel*, Rachel in *A Jest of God*, Stacey in *The Fire-Dwellers*, and Morag in *The Diviners*--each one, in her own style and with a different degree of success, attempts to discover exactly who she is and what her life means.

Like Laurence's other female heroes, Morag Gunn grows up in the stultifying atmosphere of the prairie town of Manawaka, Manitoba; like the others, she longs to escape. Morag, the adopted daughter of the town garbage collector and his wife, faces even more challenges than the others, for they are at least respectable, and she is only one step above the outcast Métis (half-breed Indians) in the eyes of the townspeople. Despite the odds against her, Morag somehow reaches a higher level of self-awareness and a greater measure of wisdom than any of the others. This major difference between the earlier characters and Morag is remarked by a number of critics, among them Barbara Hehner, who observes that Morag "is, for the first time, a woman who has already found a measure of fulfillment, whose present life is busy, and, by and large, satisfying" (48).

As *The Diviners* begins, Morag is already clearly self-aware and relatively contented with her life. The other protagonists must struggle at two levels, in their present lives and in the flashbacks that recreate their pasts, but Morag's struggles in the present are few. Leona Gom points out that Morag is "the most self-aware of any of Laurence's characters, and, in terms of character development, she changes little, if at all" (247). It is mainly from the flashbacks, called in this novel "Memorybank Movies," that the reader learns of Morag's difficult journey from frustration, fear, and ignorance to autonomy, fulfillment, and a kind of wisdom. Now, at the age of forty-seven, Morag writes to a friend, "I've worked out my major dilemmas as much as I'm likely to do in this life" (*The Diviners*, Toronto: McClelland and Stewart, New Canadian Library, 1995, 311; Chicago: University of Chicago Press, 1993, 238-39). All parenthetical references are to these works.

What most clearly distinguishes Morag from Laurence's previous heroines is the fact that she is a writer by profession. Whereas the others demonstrate considerable sensitivity to language and to a large extent achieve their "limited victories" by means of words and voice, Morag alone makes of language her life's work. Having discovered very young that she is a wordsmith, Morag never loses sight of this knowledge. Even through the years when her primary occupation is wife and mother, she continues to write. Morag's commitment to language plays a large part in her development both as a writer and as a person. She achieves through her success with language a sense of identity and fulfillment far beyond that of any of the earlier Manawaka heroines.

In all of the Laurence novels we find the theme of the power of language, but in *The Diviners* we find, according to Theo Dombrowski, "the fullest treatment of a concern central to much of Laurence's fiction" (Word and Fact 50). This theme of the power of language is expressed at both levels of the complex narrative structure of the novel. At one level, a third person, past-tense narrative follows Morag throughout the spring and summer of her forty-seventh year. At the second narrative level, Morag engages in the extensive reminiscences (written in the third person, present tense) which reveal her past. *The Diviners* traces the development of a writer from her earliest experiments with language through her impressive achievements as a mature novelist. *The Diviners* is not only the story of the making of an artist, however; it is also the story of a woman whose journey ends with self-realization.

Dombrowski points out that the matter of language and communication "has two aspects, the words of human interchange and the words of imaginative vision, but as Laurence makes clear in *The Diviners*, the two aspects are often closely allied" (Word and Fact 50). So interrelated are they, in fact, that it is virtually impossible to trace Morag's development in one area separately from her development in the other. Yet the division may give us a place at which to begin as we consider the ways in which Morag grows through language as a person and as a writer in the various stages of her life.

Morag's earliest memories reveal her as an imaginative and sensitive child, playing under the spruce trees "as tall as angels, dark angels perhaps" (19NCL, 9UC) with imaginary friends Peony, Rosa Picardy, and Blue-Sky Mother. These characters the adult Morag identifies as *"totally individuated persons (as the pretentious phrase has it, when describing okay fiction)"* (20NCL, 10UC), who provide a country child with her only playmates. Her early imaginative vision thus fulfills her need for interchange with others. When Morag's parents are stricken ill, however, the imaginary friends disappear. Morag's memories of this frightening and confusing time demonstrate her childhood awareness of words. Mrs. Pearl, who is staying to help out, must "chonk-chonk-chonk" the pump to start the flow of water. Dr. MacLeod's car comes "whamming" into Morag's yard, and the days of her parents' illness "snail along" for the anxious child. When terrified by her father's cries, Morag "scuttles back to the kitchen like a cockroach--she *is* a cockroach; she feels like one, running, scuttling" (24NCL and 13UC). The child's response to the loss of her parents is not one of inarticulate resignation; she wastes no time in verbalizing her response to this incomprehensible tragedy: "Morag is talking in her head. To God. Telling Him it was all His fault and this is why she is so mad at Him. Because He is no good, is why" (25NCL and 14UC).

Following the death of her parents and her adoption by Christie and Prin Logan, the Manawaka garbage collector and his wife, Morag becomes aware that words can be used as weapons. She is unwilling to ask Christie what the school children mean when they refer to him as "Scavenger," but she recognizes it as a term of derision. She also recognizes the malice in the nickname given to her next-door neighbor, incontinent Eva Winkler--"Eva Weakguts" (42NCL, 28UC). Morag's initial response to language used in this way by her classmates is to refrain from speaking at all, so that her first-grade teacher later describes her as "a timid little thing . . . well not exactly timid more well just very quiet never spoke to a soul except that poor little Eva Whatsername" (72NCL, 51UC).

In second grade, however, Morag at least inwardly defies her persecutors, and one reason for her bravery is her increasing dexterity with words. She thinks, "Seven is much older than six. A person knows a hell of a sight more. And can read. Some kids still can't read yet. But they are dumb, dumbbells, dumb bunnies. Morag can read like sixty. Sometimes she doesn't let on in school, though. Just depends on how she feels. So there" (42NCL and 28UC). Her skill in reading allows her to feel the equal of those children who laugh at her because of her homemade clothing and her disreputable adopted parents. Morag has the child's natural desire to identify with and admire her parents, but she also wishes to gain the respectability that her association with the Logans virtually precludes. Although she does not speak her criticism aloud, Morag cannot help but observe the way the Logans talk. When Prin, for instance, comments that she herself "wasn't none too bright," Morag thinks, "you were supposed to say wasn't any too bright but Prin didn't know that" (43NCL, 29UC). When Christie teases Morag by asking, "Did they *learn* you much today, then?" the child turns away, thinking, "He knows better. He says it like that on purpose. A joke. Prin would say it not on purpose" (44NCL, 29UC). Even at the age of seven, Morag is conscious not only of the role of standard word usage as a criterion of respectability but also of a speaker's intention.

Morag's growing understanding of words makes it possible for her to censor her own language and thus avoid the negative reactions that vulgar language can provoke in others. Although the colorful, casual oaths she hears from Christie appeal to her, she has sensibly decided to use them only in appropriate circumstances: "Morag loves to swear, but doesn't do it at school because you get the strap or else have to stand out in the hall by yourself where the coats are hung" (44NCL, 29UC). For her classmate Skinner Tonnerre, vulgar language confers power, but Morag, after a short-lived period of rebellion as a twelve-year-old, chooses to use language to win respectability, which means that she must reject the vulgarity of the Logans and the half-breed Tonnerres. She works hard to make her speech conform to that of the respectable townspeople, hoping to earn their acceptance:

But all this makes no difference. When church is over, and they're all filing out, . . . no one will say *Good Morning* to Morag and Prin. Not on your life. . . . They're a bunch of--well, a bunch of so-and-so's. Morag does not swear. If you swear at fourteen it only makes you look cheap, and she is not cheap, goddamn it. Gol-darn it. (121-22NCL, 89UC)

She imitates the language--if not the attitudes--of those around her whose respectability she envies.

While Morag is trying to refine her public language, the words of human interchange, she is also busy developing her private store of words, the words of imaginative vision. Along with delight in her growing vocabulary comes an increasing interest in accuracy and precision. When Eva Winkler has an "accident" in class and the janitor is called to clean up the mess, Morag muses about what she perceives as the incongruity between the object and its use: "Paris Green. What a music name for that poison stuff" (42NCL, 28UC). She also notices that blackboard is not an accurate name for what her myopic eyes scan with such difficulty; "Should be called the greyboard," she thinks, "always smudged with chalk" (75NCL, 53UC). At home she is similarly observant. She comments on the flies on the dirty kitchen table in this way: "The flies are blue-bottles--how come they got this nice name given to them? They're ugly" (49NCL, 33UC). The cushion that Christie has brought home from the dump Morag describes as "a blue plush (pl-uush--rich sounding, but it is really like velvet only cheaper and not so smoo-ooth on the fingers) cushion" (51NCL, 34UC).

Although it will be years before she learns the names for the figures she creates as a child, Morag's imaginative use of language continues to develop in the direction of metaphor. For example, Morag sees her first-grade teacher as "Tall, giant, like a big tree walking and waving its arms. A tree wearing spectacles" (40NCL, 26UC). Another time, driving with Christie in a nice neighborhood of town, Morag sees

red snapdragons like velvet, really *rich* velvet, and orange lilies with freckles on the throats. The blinds are pulled down over the front windows of the houses, to keep out the heat. Cream-colored blinds, all fringed with lace and tassels. The windows are the eyes, closed, and the blinds are the eyelids, all creamy, fringed with lacy lashes. Blinds make the houses to be blind. Ha ha. (46NCL, 31UC)

Using her imagination and her facility with words, Morag unconsciously practices the skills that will enable her eventually to achieve success as a writer. Fascinated as Morag is by individual words, she is even more impressed with groups of words artfully combined. Dombrowski comments that for Morag "the greatest power of words is achieved not by their effect in isolation or in phrases, but in the stylized forms of songs or fiction. Indeed, the talismanic power of words is especially felt by those who are able to go far beyond mere fact so that . . . they use whole configurations of words to establish an existence that is at once fictional and real" (Word 60). Although Morag has experimented with creating her own stories about the spruce-family, the first tales that she remembers hearing told are those that Christie relates to her about his mythic ancestors, Piper Gunn and his wife Morag. Inspired by Christie's tales, Morag writes her own in a notebook that she keeps hidden in a dresser drawer, thus beginning her own career as a teller of tales. Although she despises Christie's smelly clothing, his embarrassing behavior, his disreputable job, she respects him as a purveyor of stories and poems. When he notices her copying a poem by Wordsworth into her notebook for school, he introduces her to what he calls real poetry, the poems of the Gaelic poet Ossian about the mythic hero Cuchullin. Together they admire these poems by the man Christie insists was "the greatest song-maker of them all" (73NCL, 51UC).

Soon Morag is filling a scribbler with her own creative endeavor, a story she has invented about a character she calls Clowny Macpherson, one of Piper Gunn's crew:

> Morag, upstairs. Writing in her scribbler. This one is nearly full.... Morag is working on another story as well. In another scribbler. She does not know where it came from. It comes into your head, and when you write it down, it surprises you, because you never knew what was going to happen until you put it down. (97-98NCL, 70UC)

Although Morag's earliest stories were retellings of Christie's, Morag now creates her own characters and situations, the ideas for her writing appearing to her seemingly by magic.

Morag gains an important new perspective on her writing and herself from Miss Melrose, her high-school English teacher: "No one ever before has talked to Morag about what was good and bad in writing, and shown her why. It is amazing. And when you look at the composition again, you can see why. Some things work and other things don't work" (135NCL, 98-99UC). As she becomes more conscious of the process of artistic invention, she also begins the purposeful development of her craft as a writer. Although she does not yet have the confidence to publish her short story in the school paper, as Miss Melrose suggests, she does face the fact that writing seems to be her fate. Locked in a school restroom, "crying her eyes out" after hearing the teacher's praise of her work, Morag realizes:

> She is not sad. She has known for some time what she has to do, but never given the knowledge to any other person or thought that any person might suspect. Now it is as though a strong hand has been laid on her shoulders. Strong and friendly. But merciless. (136NCL, 99-100UC)

Morag does not choose to be a writer; her talent with language and her imagination have predetermined her course. From this point, Morag's consciousness of her identity as a writer plays an increasing part in her life, giving her confidence and a sense of purpose.

Working for the editor of the local paper provides valuable training for Morag once she has completed high school. At the newspaper office Morag receives practice not only in writing but also in placing her skill with language into perspective. When Morag, now confident about her facility with words, laughs at the homespun accounts of teas and meetings that are submitted to the paper, Editor MacLachlan rebukes her for her intolerance. "They are not very verbal people," he says, "but if you ever in your life presume to look down on them because you have the knack of words and they do not, then you do so at your eternal risk and peril" (170NCL, 126UC). So Morag struggles to place in proper perspective the undeniable talent that is hers, to reconcile her feeling that her linguistic gift makes her special and separate with the knowledge that she is in many other ways just like everyone else.

Morag's friendship with Ella Gerson, another fledgling writer whom she meets when both are first-year students at the university, confirms Morag in her ambition. Ella and Morag critique each other's writing and encourage each other to submit their work for publication. In talking with Ella, Morag realizes her ambivalence about her involvement with her work. When Ella inquires whether a character in one of Morag's stories is based on a real person, Morag at first replies that it is not. Then she hesitates, respecting words too much to settle for an easy answer:

And yet, in a way, it is. . . . No. Anyway, the child isn't her. She realizes almost with surprise that this is true. The child isn't her. Can the story child really exist separately? Can it be both her and not her? Ella is looking at her oddly.
"What's the matter, Morag?"
"I don't know. Sometimes I get--well, scared. I don't feel all that normal." (197NCL, 147UC)

In some ways, Morag's creative and verbal gifts do separate her from what is usually considered normal, and Morag is too sensitive not to be aware of this difference. Despite her talent with language and the enormous literary ambition that sets her apart from others, Morag experiences the normal desire for acceptance and love, perhaps even more intensely because of her childhood deprivation. With Ella and her family, the mother and sisters who come to treat her as their kin, Morag can be herself. She can share with them not only her ambitions for a literary career but also her hopes for a satisfying personal life: "I want to be glamorous and adored and get married and have kids. I still try to kid myself that I don't want that. But I do. I want all that. *As well*. All I want is everything" (198NCL, 147UC).

On the day that her first short story is published, Morag has her first real conversation with Brooke Skelton, professor of English at the university in Winnipeg where she is a student. When he congratulates her and offers to critique other stories she has written, Morag is thrilled by his recognition of her as a writer:

She goes to her room. Stays up all night writing another story. This story is totally unsentimental. Also, totally worthless. She perceives that not even for Dr. Skelton can she write a story which wasn't there to be written. A humbling thought, but not daunting.
Nothing will ever daunt her again. (207NCL, 154UC)

Publication of her work has confirmed Morag's belief in her skill with words and at the same time provided a bond with someone whom she respects for his verbal abilities.

Joyously, she enters into a love affair that soon leads to the proposal she has hoped for. Even at such an important moment in her life, however, Morag cannot dissociate herself from her identity as a wordsmith. She must clear her throat to accept his proposal, and this action begins a train of thought that reveals both Morag's fascination with words and her awareness that her verbal sensitivity can sometimes be a burden:

Frog in the throat? What a gruesome expression. Who could ever have thought that one up? Ugh. Those clammy clambering teeny saurian legs in your *gullet*, for God's sake? Worse, more hideous than crab-claws. . . . Words words words. Words haunt her, but she will become unhaunted now, forevermore. (219NCL, 163-4UC)

During the early years of the marriage, first in Winnipeg and then in Toronto, Morag works at altering her language in an effort to fit into Brooke's world. Although he enjoys her "idiomatic expressions," Morag struggles to prune them from her speech and leave only that which conforms to the language of the university, the "well-modulated grammatical voices, devoid of epithets, bland as tapioca pudding" (276NCL, 209UC). Without the least regret Morag abandons all vestiges of the working-class language of Manawaka for the language of academia, which is, according to Pamela McCallum, "not merely a more concise manner of speech: it suppresses any personal or emotional reaction within a formalized reply" (10). When Brooke offers Morag some sherry before dinner, Morag replies, "Please," "having recently learned to say, simply, *Please,* instead of *Oh yes thanks I'd just love some,* or worse, *Okay that'd be fine*" (214NCL, 160UC). The formalized replies that characterize Brooke's style of speech represent to Morag a way of identifying herself with the learned, cultured people whom she has always admired from afar.

Eventually, however, Morag realizes that her communication with Brooke is becoming increasingly superficial. He responds to her desire to hear about his childhood with a soothing reminder that they need their sleep, and he brushes aside her request to have a child with a glib comment on the unfortunate state of the world. When Morag temporarily abandons her academic objectivity and speaks with artistic passion at a seminar discussion, he is disturbed and she is embarrassed. Eventually their only real communication is during sex, and then only when Morag cooperates with her husband's peculiar ritual of demanding to know if she has been "a good girl" before they can make love.

During the first years of their marriage, Morag devotes herself happily to being the kind of wife Brooke wants: literate, well-dressed and coifed, an admirable cook. She pursues her writing in a desultory fashion, having temporarily suppressed her identity as a writer so that she may better play her role as professor's wife. Although she does not articulate her dissatisfaction with her life, Morag finds herself increasingly frustrated and begins to consider some alternatives--the child that she has wanted? A job? When Brooke inquires about her writing ("Have you given it up?"), Morag replies, "Everything I write seems bad" (241NCL, 182UC). His praise of her work does not thrill her as once it did, and we see that Morag is beginning to assume authority over her work: "'Brooke,' she says in a hard voice about the stories she has written, 'they aren't any good. They're trivial and superficial'" (241NCL, 182UC).

Nevertheless, Morag begins a novel. In resuming her writing, Morag also resumes her real identity. McCallum comments that, for Morag, "writing becomes the medium of a careful and sustained process of thought. It is essential to the communication of Morag's reflective development towards greater self-consciousness" (13). As Morag becomes increasingly self-aware, she moves further from Brooke, who takes her work very lightly. Although he encourages her to write, he assumes that her writing is nothing more than a pleasant pastime. At first Morag feels guilt because she resents Brooke's assumption that she will always place his needs before her need to write. When he suggests a movie, Morag agrees, although "[i]n fact, she would like to go back to Chapter Three. . . . Unfair to Brooke. Who is, after all, supporting her while she bashes away at the typewriter" (245NCL, 184UC). Because she feels that she must please Brooke, another time she agrees to dine out, despite the fact that she has spent an exhausting day in the company of her fictional creations and wants only to sleep. When Brooke's desires as a husband and Morag's needs as an artist clash, Morag continues to allow Brooke his way--but her resentment grows.

The failure of the marriage can be traced in terms of Morag's diminishing respect for Brooke's authority and increasing assumption of her own. When she finishes her first novel after three years of labor, Brooke requests to read the manuscript. Whereas once she would gratefully have accepted his judgment of her work, now Morag only reluctantly places her novel in his hands. She carefully weighs the suggestions he makes, saying little--and sends off the manuscript, unaltered, to a publisher. It is accepted for publication, provisionally, and Brooke is affronted when Morag refuses his help in making the necessary changes:

> "I'll take a quick run through it, if you like," Brooke says.
> "Well, thanks, but that's pretty well settled, the changes."
> "I see. My reactions aren't any longer welcome to you."
> "It's not that. It's--I know you know a lot about novels. But I know something, as well. Different from reading or teaching." (281NCL, 213UC)

In insisting upon the validity of her knowledge and judgment, Morag claims her authority as a writer. Her decision to publish *Spear of Innocence* under her maiden name rather than her married name is another unplanned but significant rejection of her husband's authority. Although she has not consciously decided to proclaim her independence in this manner, she realizes afterwards that perhaps she has been preparing for some time to leave Brooke.

The genteel, consciously proper and impersonal speech that Morag has cultivated since her marriage no longer seems adequate to her. She has long repressed the language she learned from Christie, but now this old language begins to work its way back into her consciousness. At first Morag resists: "Morag has experienced increasingly the mad and potentially releasing desire to speak sometimes as Christie used to speak. . . . But of course does no such thing" (276NCL, 209UC). Eventually, however, when Brooke once too often refers to her as his "little one," Morag suddenly reverts to the language familiar to her from childhood, the "stringy lean oaths with some protein in them, the Protean oaths upon which she was reared" (276NCL, 209UC). Brooke, who has steadfastly refused to recognize that Morag has changed since their first meeting, attributes her "hysterical" outburst to her monthly period. Morag, however, knows better. "That was, of course, an ill-considered outburst," she admits, "and it owes more to Christie's way of talking than mine, I guess. But it was meant" (277NCL, 210UC). Voicing the remembered language of her stepfather enables her to acknowledge the anger against Brooke that has been growing in her for some time, while her inability to defend her position in a calm and reasonable way makes her realize, *"I do not know the sound of my own voice. Not yet, anyhow"* (277NCL, 210UC). Cathy Davidson suggests that Morag's repudiation of Brooke's life and language grows out of her realization "that Christie's colorful, hyperbolic language is partly her language and that his half-comic stance of the court jester, the wise fool, must be the position from which she regards her own disordered life" (55).

As she learns to recognize who she is, Morag must come to what is for her the appalling realization of the end of her marriage. Eloquent as she has proven herself in terms of writing fiction, she is unable to articulate her feeling about the collapse of her relationship to Brooke. She cannot act; she cannot talk. A feeling of being separated from herself increases. Her desire to leave Brooke is blocked by her fear and guilt, and, unable to imagine a solution to her dilemma, she can resolve neither to leave nor to stay. As she aimlessly walks the Toronto streets, convinced that she is going "blind inside," Morag "is filled with the profound conviction that she will not write anything more, anyway. Big deal. Keel over with sorrow, world. As if it would matter" (284NCL, 215UC). But of course it would matter very much to Morag, who would be denying an essential part of herself if she were no longer to write. Her inability to find the words that will release her from a stifling and destructive relationship makes her doubt herself.

A chance encounter with her old friend from Manawaka, Jules "Skinner" Tonnerre, releases Morag from her paralysis. But she cannot follow Jules's advice to leave without seeing Brooke once more; she acknowledges that it may do no good, but nevertheless it is her way to try to explain what has happened. Morag's faith in the power of language remains, though when she confronts Brooke, she finds that "Words have lost meaning" (300NCL, 228UC). As she leaves the dubious security of her marriage and husband behind, Morag is still uncertain about herself. She knows, however, that she cannot remain with Brooke, who has stifled her growth as a writer and a person, not maliciously but because "Their voices [were] a million miles apart" (304NCL, 231UC). She takes with her as she enters the next stage of her life a wealth of experience with language and a tentative but growing sense of self.

Morag's years from twenty-eight to about forty-six are detailed in the section of the novel entitled "Rites of Passage." As the title makes clear, this is the period in her life when Morag comes of age. In terms of her private life and her career, she demonstrates heightened awareness and maturity. Her development as a novelist (she writes four successful novels during the time covered by the "Memorybank Movie[s]") contributes to her growth as a self-aware individual, for she is a writer who bases her imaginative worlds on the reality of her own experience. McCallum points out:

Writing is a means by which Morag can both formalize her denied past feelings and criticize them from the greater perception of present understanding. Each novel reworks her lived experience while simultaneously removing it from the limited particularity of a specific individual's experience. (13)

The first novel describes a naive young woman's effort to escape a restrictive small-town environment; the second a young wife's struggle against a domineering husband; the third a daughter's resentment of her disreputable father; and the fourth, from a semihistorical viewpoint, the experience of the early immigrants to Canada from Scotland, the land of Morag's ancestors. The fictional reworking of experiences somehow related to hers lends Morag increased insight into her own life. Her writing becomes, again according to McCallum, "the medium of a careful and sustained process of thought. . . . essential to the communication of Morag's reflective development towards greater self-consciousness" (13).

Also essential to Morag's growth is a resolution of her feelings about her stepfather. Only after Morag and her daughter Pique have moved to England does Morag begin to value Christie as he deserves. Now, when she relates the stories of Piper Gunn to Pique, she prefaces them with the "Tale of Christie Logan":

Now, when Christie told a tale, then, his voice would become different from the ordinary. It would be like the ranting of the pipe music, wild and stormy, until you could actually feel the things happening that he was telling you about. He had very blue eyes, Christie did, in those days, and when he was telling a tale, his eyes would be like the blue lightning and you would forget his small stature, for at those times he would seem a giant of a man. (391NCL, 300UC)

Thus Morag passes on to her daughter what she herself has learned of the history of her family, of the importance of myth, and, most significantly, of the power of language to preserve the past and to transform the ordinary into the extraordinary, to create beauty and express truth, lessons that Christie has taught her.

It is Christie's illness that brings Morag back to Manawaka after an absence of many years, and it is Christie with whom Morag must come to terms before she truly can know herself. She has always been troubled by her ambivalence towards her stepfather, but now she recognizes his strength and acknowledges her debt to him. They cannot talk together as in the old days, for Christie has suffered a stroke that has left this former teller of tales almost unable to speak. But Morag is able to say what needs to be said:

"Christie--I used to fight a lot with you, Christie, but you've been my father to me."
His responding words are slurred and whispered, but she hears them.
"Well--I'm blessed," Christie Logan says. Another way of indicating surprise would have been to say--Well, I'm damned. But that is not the phrase he has chosen. She sees from his eyes that the choice has been intentional. (420NCL, 323UC)

The legacy that he leaves to Morag is a love of storytelling and a gift for speaking the truth. She is, though an adopted daughter, very much his child. Once she has accepted her identity as Christie's daughter, she is able to settle down with Pique on a small place near McConnell's landing, a town quite similar to Manawaka.

The Morag that we see in the "Memorybank Movies" is a woman struggling to survive and to discover herself. The Morag of the present narrative is a woman who has already arrived at a level of stability and self-awareness that makes her struggles relatively minor within the context of a satisfying life. She has accepted her strengths and weaknesses as a writer and a woman.

Through her writing, Morag has come to terms with the limitations of language. By no means does she deny the power that words can have, but, like the other Manawaka heroines, she acknowledges that at times words are inadequate. Eventually she resigns herself to a reality that caused her alarm when, years earlier, she first found words inadequate to express her response to a Botticelli painting:

> *Lovely.* What a word. Like using a marshmallow to picture God. But *beautiful* is nearly as bad. How could you say? How can there be words for that face, for what lies behind those eyes? There have to be words. Maybe there are not. This thought is obscurely frightening. Like knowing that God does not actually see the little sparrow fall. (172NCL, 127UC)

At the age of twenty, she writes and rewrites her commentary on the painting, unwilling to give up her attempt to capture the exact words that will express her reaction. At the age of forty-seven, Morag still has the impulse to articulate her thoughts in precise, accurate language, but she accepts defeat calmly: *"I used to think words could do anything. Magic. Sorcery. Even miracle. But no, only occasionally"* (13NCL, 4UC).

Her acceptance of the limits, as well as the power, of language is an indication of Morag's wisdom and maturity. She has spent her life as a diviner, trying to discover the hidden truth and reveal it in her fiction just as her friend Royland has searched for water underground. Now she considers hers "A daft profession. Wordsmith. Liar, more likely. Weaving fabrications. Yet, with typical ambiguity, convinced that fiction was more true than fact. Or that fact was in fact fiction" (33NCL, 21UC). Her books have sold well, and she has established a considerable reputation for herself, yet Morag is not certain that she has been successful at her art, and Royland's announcement that he has lost his gift for divining causes Morag to wonder about her own:

> At least Royland knew he had been a true diviner. There were the wells, proof positive. Water. Real wet water. There to be felt and tasted. Morag's magic tricks were of a different order. She would never know whether they actually worked or not, or to what extent. That wasn't given to her to know. In a sense, it did not matter. The necessary doing of the thing--that mattered. (477NCL, 369UC)

Despite her loss of faith in the absolute power of the word, Morag has continued the "doing of the thing"--her effort to share with others through language the truth as she has found it. Ultimately, there are no certain answers, and Morag has understood that limitation. "It is perhaps," according to Dombrowski, "a token of the tone of acceptance which most characterizes Laurence's last novel, *The Diviners*, that the character who must remain baffled, cut off from intimate knowledge of any other human being, gains positive stature from that limitation" (Who Is This You? 22).

Like Rachel and Stacey, Morag learns that words are sometimes inadequate. When she returns to Manawaka for Prin's funeral, for instance, she spends a quiet time afterwards with her stepfather and finds to her dismay that he has forgotten the stories he once told her. In response to this loss, "Morag wants now to tell him, to tell him all the tales. But cannot. She can do nothing at all, except to reach her hand across the table and touch Christie's leathered lizardskin hand" (271NCL, 205UC). Her feelings of loss and compassion are too great for her to express in words; she can only keep silence in the face of her love and her grief. A feeling of awe provokes a similar response: when Morag observes a flock of Canada geese flying overhead, she finds it "A sound and a sight with such splendour in it that the only true response was silence" (436NCL, 336UC). Morag finds that silence is sometimes appropriate, even necessary.

Occasions when silence is the only true response seem to occur most often between Morag and Jules. When he visits her after a separation of years, there are no words: "She cannot say anything. She puts her arms out to him, and he holds her" (448NCL, 345UC). When he tells her that the town of Manawaka has refused to allow burial of his father, Morag is again speechless: "The Métis, once lord of the prairies. Now refused burial space in their own land. Morag cannot say anything. She has no right" (289NCL, 219UC). The burden of guilt that Morag bears by virtue of being one of the oppressors is so great that she feels that anything she might say would be presumptuous.

Again, when Morag is the only one who can describe for Jules the scene of his sister's death, she reluctantly dredges up the words to let him know the terrible facts but cannot express her sympathy: "There is nothing more can be said" (297NCL, 225UC). Finally, when Morag visits Jules, who is dying of cancer, she finds that the pattern remains the same. "No way of talking to him any differently, now, than she ever had," she thinks. "No way of saying everything she would like to say, either. Maybe none of it really needed saying, after all" (468NCL, 363UC). Each has been an important part of the other's life, though the actual time they have had together has been brief. Although they have not talked much, or often, they have spoken truly, and the bond between them is solid.

Usually a person who wants to talk everything through, Morag learns to tolerate silence. In fact, she realizes when she sees Jules and Pique together that silence can sometimes be a language of its own. Jules plays and sings a song he has written about his grandfather, and Pique listens closely. As Morag watches them both, Jules and Pique exchange a look that shows clearly that no words are needed: *"They do it in a different way, a way I can see, although it's not mine"* (452NCL, 348UC). Although sometimes frustrated because Pique does not share as many of her thoughts and experiences as her mother would like to know, Morag wisely understands that no rejection is intended.

Pique, like her father, is simply a person who relies less than does Morag on spoken words for communication. Despite her frequent doubts about the efficacy of verbal communication, Morag continues to rely on words as her primary medium for artistic expression and human interchange. At the conclusion of *The Diviners*, she walks into the house "to write the remaining private and fictional words, and to set down her title" (477NCL, 370UC), leaving the reader to assume that the novel we have watched her writing throughout the book has been the very novel we have been reading. Incidents that she relates in the book, as well as completion of the book itself, confirm Morag's faith in the power of words.

A very significant victory made possible by words is the reconciliation with Christie just before his death. Christie and Morag are both wordsmiths, in their different ways, and the fact that Christie at the end is unable to speak is a sorrow to them both. Her description of her stepfather's frustration over his speechlessness demonstrates how they both value language:

> He wants to speak desperately, but cannot. His mouth opens, and he strains. No words come. His eyes are filled with such pain and such knowing that Morag can scarcely endure the sight of them. What emerges from his mouth, then, is a squawk, a hoarse unverbal croaking like a bullfrog. He turns away from her, but not before she sees the shame in his eyes, at being thus diminished before her. (419NCL, 322UC)

For the old man who has prided himself upon his tales, the inability to speak represents a humiliating failure. (We are reminded of the "frog" in Morag's throat when she accepted Brooke's proposal.) But Morag is able to redeem his failure, and her own failure to let him know sooner how she appreciates him, by now finding the right words to let him know of her gratitude and love before he dies. She will never cease regretting her years of neglect, but the pain is eased by the knowledge of the closeness between them, made possible by the words in which she claims him as her father at the end of his life.

In a situation in Morag's present, words again serve to ease pain and promote closeness between speakers. Although for a time Morag is unable to voice the growing jealousy and frustration that she experiences in response to the relationship of Pique and her lover, Dan, who are staying with her, at least she can tell Royland how she has been feeling:

> "Look, it isn't that I don't want them to live together. I do want them to. It seems right. . . . But the plain fact is that I am forty-seven years old, and it seems fairly likely that I will be alone for the rest of my life, and in most ways this is really okay with me, and yet I am sometimes so goddam jealous of their youth and happiness and sex that I can't see straight. Horrible, eh?" (309NCL, 237UC)

Royland does not find it horrible but does remind Morag that Pique and Dan need to know how she is feeling. When Morag finally tells them, their response is unexpectedly gratifying:

> Silence. Then astonishment. Pique had taken one of her hands and Dan the other.
> "We thought that was what it was," Pique said, "but we couldn't say it unless you said it.

And, like, we're aware you're alone, Ma. But in other ways you aren't. You know?"
   True. Truer than Morag even yet knew? Perhaps.
   "I think it'll be okay, now," Morag said, when able to speak, "for you to stay here." (310NCL, 238UC)

Her willingness to express even those feelings that she finds discreditable results in increased closeness to the people she loves, and even in a new insight into her own thinking. Although Morag and Pique have experienced times of separation, the very real bond between them is deepened and strengthened by Morag's ability to put feelings into words.

Words have helped Morag come to terms with herself as well as with others. A book reviewer who refers to her once as an "older writer," for instance, initiates a chain of thought that leads to Morag's realization of the place which she has earned in the literary community: "Yes, older writer is the right phrase. Takes some mental adjustment, though. Meditation. Assimilation" (446NCL, 343UC). Language has provided an important means by which Morag has achieved self-awareness. She has frequently reminded herself of what she and others term her shortcomings--her unwillingness to learn to drive a car, her inability to stop smoking, her persistence in worrying about things that she cannot help. In a series of mental dialogues with the Canadian pioneer Catharine Parr Traill, Morag has repeatedly appealed for advice to this paragon of female virtue, diligence, and ingenuity. In the end, though, she dismisses Catharine, no longer needing the reminder of what she should be; she has decided that what she is is acceptable. She can tolerate her own foibles because she can appreciate her very considerable strengths.

Near the end of *The Diviners*, the Manawaka saga comes full circle when Morag receives from Jules the Scots plaid-pin which Hagar Shipley had given to her son John many years before. Upon the pin is written the motto which Hagar had especially loved: Gainsay Who Dare. Although John had valued the pin so little that he had traded it away, it comes in the end to someone who will treasure it as Hagar did. Reading the words on the pin, Morag thinks,

   My Hope Is Constant In Thee. It sounds like a voice from the past. Whose voice, though? Does it matter? It does not matter. What matters is that the voice is there, and that she has heard these words which have been given to her. And will not deny what has been given. *Gainsay Who Dare*. (458NCL, 353UC)

Unlike Hagar, who loved the motto but could not find the courage to live it, Morag has lived a life of true bravery, remaining steadfast, defying in a way Hagar never could the conventions that would have restricted her involvement in life. Largely because of the important role of language in her life, Morag achieves at the middle of her lifetime a measure of self-acceptance and wisdom that few female characters in literature ever achieve. Words have served as the medium which Morag has used to understand herself, to express her feelings, and to communicate her insights to others. In answer to the question that Pique once asked in a moment of anguish-- "Who cares about the right word?"--Morag's answer must be that she cares, very much. Her constant quest for the right word may be doomed to failure, but the quest itself must continue, for through language Morag has achieved success as a writer of insight and power, and success as a wise, independent, and loving human being. Unlike the other Manawaka heroines of Margaret Laurence, Morag Gunn is not just a survivor--she is a triumph.

WORKS CITED

Davidson, Cathy N. "Canadian Wry: Comic Vision in Atwood's *Lady Oracle* and Laurence's *The Diviners*." *Regionalism and the Female Imagination* 3.2-3 (1977/78): 50-55.
Dombrowski, Theo Quayle. "Who Is This You?: Margaret Laurence and Identity." *University of Windsor Review* 13.1 (1977): 21-38.
___. "Word and Fact: Laurence and the Problem of Language." *Canadian Literature* 80 (Spring 1979): 50-62.
Gom, Leona M. "Margaret Laurence and the First Person." *The Dalhousie Review* 55 (Summer 1975): 236-21.
Hehner, Barbara. "River of Now and Then: Margaret Laurence's Narratives." *Canadian Literature* 74 (Fall 1977): 40-57.
Laurence, Margaret. *The Diviners*. Toronto: McClelland and Stewart, New Canadian Library, (1974) 1995; Chicago: University of Chicago Press, 1993.
McCallum, Pamela. "Communication and History: Themes in Innis and Laurence." *Studies in Canadian Literature* 3.1 (Winter 1978): 5-16.

Chapter 18

Writing a Woman's Life: Celebration, Sorrow, and Pathos in Margaret Laurence's Memoir *Dance on the Earth*

Alexandra Pett

The writing of the story of a woman's life is not the same as the story itself, nor is remembering that story the same as living it. Paul de Man, in a well-known essay called "Autobiography as De-facement," raises an important theoretical issue in the form of a rhetorical question: "We assume that life produces the autobiography as an act produces its consequences, but can we not suggest, with equal justice, that the autobiographical project may itself produce and determine the life and that whatever the writer does is in fact governed by the technical demands of self-portraiture and thus determined, in all its aspects, by the resources of his medium?" (920) The metaphors used in enacting this autobiographical process vary, I believe, as the writer changes with the writing. Despite the flood of books about women's life writing, we are still in the infancy of our search for understanding of ways in which women have inscribed the self in their writing. As Sidonie Smith has explained, writing from the margins presents the woman autobiographer with many difficulties: "she resists participation in the fictions at the center of culture. Or, if she does not reject them, she self-reflexively appropriates bits and pieces of those fictions for her own purposes" (58). This description of the process of composing a woman's life story suggests a combining of disparate images to redesign what has at first seemed shapeless. In the case of Margaret Laurence's autobiography, *Dance on the Earth*, published posthumously in 1989, the design and reweaving of past experiences could be described as quilting; in fact, she tells us that she regrets a childhood rejection of her grandmother's quilts but feels her grandmother's artistry as a continuing part of her inheritance: "My grandmother's quilt may be irretrievably lost, but the patterns and colours are clear in my mind" (13). Writing autobiography can be a powerful tool in connecting with seemingly lost ancestral roots, what has been called "the continuum of ancestors, those who dance on the earth" (Coger 270). Since dancing is also an art form, the process of recovery involves reinventing the past. As a realist writer and careful researcher, Laurence distinguishes between fiction and autobiography in her memoir, providing readers with verifiable facts about the events of her life. More importantly, however, she invents images of self that transcend the need for referentiality. She seems aware that many readers will interpret the facts of her life and her reading of them differently from the ways she does; thus her creation of selves, often out of the void that loss of memory sustains, involves determination and skill. Inevitably, as Timothy Adams reminds us in *Telling Lies in Modern American Autobiography*, "what we choose to misrepresent is as telling as what really happened" (ix). Nancy Miller further defines the reading of autobiographies: "The classic move of the critic of autobiography is to track the places where the writer seems blind to the screen of his own self-disclosure; the cannier the writer the greater the desire on the part of the critic to uncover this spot" (31). Reading *Dance on the Earth*, I maintain, becomes a dance in itself, a competition between subject and readers in which connections emerge and dissolve.

In a recent study of Canadian women's autobiography, Helen Buss refers to mapping as joining "the activities of self-knowledge and knowledge of the world" (9). This metaphor of mapping works well, I believe, to describe Laurence's composing of the self in *Dance on the Earth*. I think that Laurence is feeling and recovering, half blind, the contours of a hidden past. That she wanted desperately as a young woman to escape from Neepawa and her family background is evident in her willingness and interest in spending her adult life away from Canada, first in Africa and then in England. In a letter to Adele Wiseman, written just after she was married, she refers to Neepawa as "nausea, real, not mental" (105). *Dance on the Earth* contains an introductory sentence that suggests the disgust she feels for other aspects of her world: "I have heard it said that war is for men what motherhood is for women. I find this appalling" (3). In writing about both her past and her present, then, Laurence is faced with the possibility of pain and disgust.

Where does this book begin? Perhaps the story of Margaret Laurence's adult life starts when she first lives away from her native country, her family, and her marriage. Recently separated from her husband and living with her children in a flat in Hampstead, England, Margaret Laurence reads about the life and death of another woman writer, Sylvia Plath; she has jokingly contemplated writing the story of her life (at age thirty-six), calling it *A Broken Reed*. She is appalled by Plath's suicide and concludes that, despite depression, she is a long way from taking her own life because she has been given "so much strength" by her mothers (*Dance on the Earth* 162). At this point in her life she refuses to participate in the desperation that would lead a woman writer to suicide. When she was questioned about the differences between her own life and that of Plath, she referred to her childhood as more positive than Plath's (Morley 30). Other commentators have stressed that Laurence points to Plath's mother as the area of difficulty in her life; Joan Givner, for example, tells us: "Thus, in a stroke she blames Plath's mother for the suicide and places on all mothers the burden of responsibility for their daughters' well being" (90). In *Dance on the Earth* she states clearly that Plath's incurable depression did not emerge from her life as a single parent: "Her situation had little to do with her death" (163).

Inevitably, *Dance on the Earth* raises more questions than it answers about

Laurence's biographies. If we believe Laurence that her relationship with her two children was a source of strength, must we also believe that her relationships with her mothers, which provide the organizing patterns of the book, gave her life-long nurturing? Does it matter that her stepmother/aunt, "Mum," died when she was only thirty-one, and that for most of her adult life she did not have a strong mother figure, except in imagination? Many readers of her memoir have found Laurence's perspective of her life disappointing, even dishonest, in its concealment of what was really at issue and in its seemingly intended silencing of readers' questions. However, Marlene Kadar, author of *Essays on Life Writing*, reminds us that life writing documents by literary women "do not necessarily simplify the questions we ask about the authors, nor do they present us with any one kind of life-writing document. If anything, they illustrate how complicated the genre of life writing can be as the subject of literary analysis" (19). For me, as reader of Laurence's memoir, the tributes to five mother figures work well to suggest the complexity of Laurence's personality and construction of the self; they also act to conceal the bitterness over the passing of creative life force in midlife, after the publication of her last novel, *The Diviners*. In this essay, I am using "Margaret" to refer to the identity of a private self, an identity that is suggestive rather than fully delineated, whereas I am using "Laurence" to refer to a consciously achieved public construct of self. I plan to survey the deaths of her four mothers, suggesting that the death of a mother figure is crucial to her creating of this book because in the writing she prefigures and comes to terms with her own imminent death. She also tries to shape what she believes will be the reactions of others to her death. Throughout my discussion, I am assuming that the death of the mother can be equated with the death of Margaret, who is the outstanding mother figure in this text. She is the fifth mother of her text.

At first I found it surprising that Laurence's memoir should be organized around mother figures because the powerful mothers in her fiction, such as Hagar Shipley, are negatively presented. The search for the effective good mother has almost become a cliche in women's writing, yet Laurence breathes life into the argument that women define meaningful selfhood in terms of connections and disconnections with the mother. She reminds us that "being a woman writer and a mother is very different from being a male writer and a father" (135). She creates a myth about herself as a woman writer: writing alone in her garden house in England, she is self-sacrificing and courageous, more concerned about the welfare of her children than her sexual fulfillment. Finally, success comes suddenly with the publication of *The Stone Angel*, and she achieves both national and international recognition. Her path to success is described in *Dance on the Earth* as linear, although not without setbacks. The appeal of this myth for other women writers, especially those who are housewives, mothers, and community workers is impossible to overstate; her success acts as a sign that other writing mothers can succeed. Yet she appears to have paid a heavy price for that success. Patricia Morley asks us to consider the shape of her life in the last thirteen years, when she was no longer able to write fiction: "What was she doing with her time during years which are for many artists their most productive ones?" (153). In her attempt to show herself triumphant, rather than victimized, Laurence must often resort to the creation of personal myths that are not ultimately persuasive.

What she does effectively, however, is to draw readers toward her emotionally. As women's life writing suggests, the death of mother is probably the most traumatic event in the life of a woman. Zora Neale Hurston foregrounds her mother's death as the beginning of her feelings of social estrangement in *Dust Tracks on the Road*; as both observer and participant, Simone de Beauvoir analyzes the events leading to her mother's death and her own reactions to them in *A Very Easy Death*.

The place to begin looking at Laurence's feelings about mothers is in the appendix, the additional essays and letters placed at the end of her text. I find it ironic but significant that she added the information about the death of Adele Wiseman's mother as a seeming afterthought; actually, the death of her friend's mother becomes central to understanding the myths of self which she composes as she writes and edits the story of her life. The key letter, addressed to her friend Budge Wilson, dated 17 January 1980, begins: "A very emotional and somehow kind of miraculous time here, during the period from Christmas until now." It goes on to chronicle the Christmas she spent with the Wisemens, referring specifically to the fact that Adele's mother, Chaika Wiseman, an elderly woman, is dying at home, surrounded by family and friends. She is an artist, the creator of dolls and other handcrafts. Laurence refers to *Old Woman at Play*, Adele's book about her mother and the development of creativity, published a decade earlier, in 1978. Photographs are taken of the dying woman with her embroidered tablecloths and a copy of Laurence's book, *The Olden Days Coat*. Laurence records that just as they were about to sit down to Christmas dinner, her daughter, Jocelyn, suddenly came up and put her arms around her. They wept together: "It seemed very natural; I guess a lot of us were crying, and yet it was not sad. . . . it was a kind of celebration of a woman whom we all loved so very much" (240). After Chaika's death, Laurence grieves, realizing that she was a mother figure to her for more than thirty years.

This letter encloses yet another letter, one that Adele finds in her mother's papers. It is a letter Laurence had written to Chaika in 1950, from England. Laurence rejoices in having the letter returned to her and plans to make copies for all of the children; she also asks that Budge eventually return the letter she is writing to her. The sense of wanting to have the messages of earlier years returned seems part of Laurence's preparation for death in the writing of *Dance on the Earth*. Certainly, in 1980, when she wrote the letter to Budge, and when she found again part of her earlier correspondence to Chaika, she was not anticipating an early death. But Laurence seems always to have had a need to possess her past and to integrate that past fully with the present. As many readers have observed, her creative sources were always in the past. Patricia Morley, for example, summarizes this point: "Laurence seems to have always worked retrospectively, drawing from the deep wells of remembered experience" (23). In some ways, then, the writing of her memoir is the last step in a process that was begun when she was still a young woman.

Laurence's book also forms an interesting contrast to Adele's *Old Woman at*

Play. Perhaps she wrote in response to it. The central question posed in Adele's book, which is both her own story and that of her mother, I believe, is why Chaika devoted much of her life to the creation of puppet dolls. Did she do it to console children or to give them pleasure? Adele does not answer this directly but she suggests that her mother wanted to deal with her own grief, to recognize the existence of both deformity and evil in the world. In a sense, this book allows the daughter, Adele, to comment on such family issues as the nature of her parents' marriage. Laurence may have learned a great deal from studying this book.

Adele Wiseman's relationship with her mother is a connecting of two artists; she knows that she has learned to be creative from watching and following her mother: "even as a child you knew you were being led, and as you grew older you sometimes suspected you were being taken, but who could resist? . . . You knew she was building a glittering web to contain you" (29). Adele recalls that, as a child, her mother's dolls spoke to her, and she wheedled the dolls out of her mother, hoping that there would be more of them for her than for her sister (111). For Laurence, it is the dance rather than the dolls, that gives shape and meaning to life. The figures of her past dance before her, as she introduces each in turn. She has even written a poem called "Old Women's Song" which contains this stanza: "I am one among them / dancing on the earth / mourning, grieving, raging, / yet jubilating birth" (*Dance* 19; cf. 228). How does her sense of death link to the sense of birth, and to the birth experiences that follow the accounts of the mothers dying? The circular form of *Dance on the Earth* suggests Laurence's concern for rebirth, for spiritual renewal as a possible benefit in the writing; in a sense, the writing may form her last hope for cure from the disease(s) that are destroying her body, perhaps also her mind. She returns in memory to what must have been a painful childhood.

Her first conscious memory is of visiting her mother as she lay dying: "My mother, lying in the grey-painted double bed, smiles at me. Her face is white and her dark hair is spread out across the white pillowcase. She touches my face, my hair" (24). She recalls a delay in finding out that her mother has died; she finds out from a friend, a day or so later. Although she does not express anger over this key incident for children, it is clear that being cut off from her birth mother at this early age has given her a nostalgia for all mothers. This craving for the maternal and sense of estrangement from it also affects her ambivalence toward the spiritual issues of her religious beliefs. Specifically, she views Christian religion as deficient in awareness of the female principle.

This part of Laurence's memoir first surprised me by the lack of anger directed toward her father and aunts. Why did they not tell her immediately and offer consolation? Laurence seems to avoid engaging in analysis that would lead to negative portraits of any of her parental figures. She prefers to idealize rather than face the pain of analytic thought. In fact, her mother, Verna, becomes a symbol of the hopefulness and self-sacrifice of many young mothers. She continues to grieve for her: "I mourn that young mother of mine still, and always will" (42). She concludes this account by saying that Verna passed her wordless dance on to her daughter. The death of this first mother establishes a pattern for the rest of the book: the mothers seem to die silently, wordlessly. Laurence herself can act out her emotions in dance, but she cannot find the words to write to describe them because the only language available to her is patrilinear. The language she needs is one that would uphold the passing of life from mother to daughter. She tells us she has not seen this dance but she now "knows" it (19). As readers, we can only imagine for ourselves what the steps of the mothers' dance of death might be. Laurence never states that her life's story defines the shape of most women's lives or even of many other women's lives, yet it is clear to me that she is in search of an essential design. Athough she would reject essentialist theories, I believe, she wants to use her life to illustrate a pattern in women's autobiography, the shape of a woman's life that often evades our closest reading. This is apparent to me in the focus on the death of her stepmother/aunt, the woman who was Mum. The dying of Mum provides one of the strongest focuses in the text for it anticipates her own death and provides her with a way of telling her readers that the conclusion to her life was planned. The writing of Mum's death is a prophecy of her own death.

Laurence returned to Canada from the Gold Coast in 1957 with her two young children because her Mum was dying. In *Into Africa with Margaret Laurence*, Fiona Sparrow concludes that this departure from Africa was highly significant in Laurence's life, especially in the development of her marriage: "It was perhaps an omen for the future because their happiest years together, those spent in Africa, were over" (13). Laurence herself records in her memoir that the illness and death of Mum marked a turning point: "I felt like my life had changed irrevocably. The fun was over" (113).

Mum's death is a protracted event with stages that become important to Margaret because they chart her own journey toward self-assertion; the memoir encodes part of her struggle for independence in terms of the creating of the basement bedroom, next to her children, but away from her aunt. Her delight in this separate place of sleep and work works also to anticipate her later separation from her husband. In helping her aunt to care for Mum, Margaret wants to be close to the two elderly women, but not too close. Moreover, she cannot talk to Mum directly about her death. Instead, Mum quotes from Walter Savage Landor's "On His Seventy-fifth Birthday": "I warmed both hands before the fire of life / It sinks and I am ready to depart" (116). She finds herself speechless as she watches her mother die; her brother, on the other hand, often speaks for them both: "My brother, who was not a very verbal person, was sometimes able to speak when I could not" (119).

For Margaret, the most important aspect of Mum's dying has to do with her parting legacy, the editing of *This Side Jordan*. The stepmother and daughter collaborate in planning to revise the characterization in the African novel. Since Mum views the European characters as too stereotypical, Margaret plans to rethink her presentation of characterization in her novel. In a sense, she is also rethinking her relationship with Mum, who is, after all, not her birth mother, but a substitute figure. She appears not to have had an antagonistic relationship with Mum, whose identity as stepmother she sees as potentially more independent than that of birth mother. In recording childhood memories, she questions society's determined efforts to assign a subordinate role to stepmothers: "is it perhaps to say that only a birth mother can really be brought under society's control because a stepmother may be a more independent woman?"(50). She is aware of feeling a debt to Mum, who sacrificed much of her independent adult life in education for her: "We were back, suddenly, to her critic-teacher, lover-of-literature self, and I, to my younger self. It was her final gift to me" (117). Mum has also perhaps warned her stepdaughter not to judge her in terms of stereotypes about women's lives. In creating her past, Margaret also learns that mothers differ; Mum is not a mother physically connected to her (her physical distance from Mum in the dying process reveals that); she is, rather, a kind of cognitive coach.

One of the ambiguities in Margaret's accounts of the way her mother dies of the same disease that is killing her, too, as she writes *Dance on the Earth*, is the continuous presence of the seemingly malevolent Aunt Ruby; actually, Aunt Ruby, rather than Margaret, is Mum's major caregiver throughout her final illness. When she arrives in Victoria, she is faced with Aunt Ruby's practical competency and determination to control the environment in which Mum dies. Aunt Ruby seems to prevent her from organizing the house to suit her needs; in fact, Margaret's cruel remark to her aunt--"You've never had children" (115)--can be explained by this other woman's criticisms. In Aunt Ruby's presence, Margaret sees herself as inept, resorting to gestures of defiance and anger.

In a way that is important in her preparation for death, Margaret allows herself to recall the physical changes in her mother's body as her cancer accelerates. Remarking on a strange beauty in her mother's skin color, she distances herself, even in the process of recollection: "her skin had turned very dark, almost an olive black, apparently something that can happen with terminal cancer. It was not frightening. There was even a strange beauty about it" (120). This description of her mother as turning into a Black woman as she dies recalls the birthing scenes in the African hospital where Margaret is attended by Black women.

Finally, she records that "Mum's death went on and on" (120). She records that Mum is not interested in suicide, that she seems to drift on morphine, and that she takes a farewell look at her grandchildren. Although Margarent does not view the naked body of her mother (as Simone de Beauvoir does with horror in *A Very Easy Death*), she describes her mother as child-like in her dying. She seems to want to nurture Mum as a child, but because Mum is not her biological mother, she sustains a distance, as if reserving that mothering impulse to her own children, who are biologically linked to her. Death is not viewed negatively; rather, it is Mum's last accomplishment: "Her sisters were there when she finally achieved her death" (120). She does not seem to feel guilt over her absence from Mum at the time of death. Although she clearly loved Mum, she could live happily at great distances from her. Looking ahead to her own death, she concludes: "I have the feeling that, when I die, I won't need my children to be there at the last moment" (120). Writing her mother's death is a form of mental rehearsal for her own. That she is also feeling her way toward a belief in spiritual continuity is apparent when she states: "No one can tell about that last voyage--the one truly solitary one, but in a sense, not solitary at all--in which the baggage of an entire lifetime is finally lightened, perhaps in both senses of the word" (120). Death, then, can be viewed as a lightening process. From the rehearsal of Mum's death she learns to face the reality of her own mortality.

During the months of Mum's dying, she is also distracted from her grieving by the support of her mother-in-law, Elsie Laurence, who also lives in Victoria. Her account of Elsie's death receives no direct narration; we are advised, however, that this last mother was important to her because she was a writer whose development was delayed because of the duties of being wife and mother. But Laurence's devotion to her mother-in-law, Elsie, is rather vaguely suggested. I find it odd the way Margaret stresses the publication of Elsie's first book without her knowledge; the image of the unconsciously successful writer suggests a sort of painless birth. Does Laurence mean to imply that women writers do best when they write and publish without conscious knowledge of their success? A first reading of this short section of *Dance on the Earth* left me feeling that Laurence was deliberately trying to focus readers' attention away from the events in her life which she is narrating, specifically the separation and divorce from her husband. The story of Elsie's life, however, provides another way of looking at Margaret's. Elsie spent two years as a single parent while her husband, John, was at war: "He went away to war leaving his young wife pregnant with their first child, John Fergus Laurence, my future husband and the father of my children. . . . The next few years for Elsie must have been difficult, despite the support she received from her mother. She worked in the Land Titles Office, looked after her young son, and wrote without knowing that her first novel had been published" (127). Margaret's last visit to Elsie is recorded in another section of *Dance on the Earth*. She recalls having a serious accident: "On the way home to Gran's, running late for a lunch she was holding for me and in a hurry to catch the departing bus, I ran smack into a power pole with a metal box attached to it and cut my face deeply, right next to my right eye. David probably thought I was wounded for life. I mostly worried about blood dripping onto my good beige linen dress" (191). Her sister-in-law then ran a yellow light to get them to her mother-in-law's house for lunch on time! Since the purpose of this trip is to tell her "beloved mother-in-law" that she is about to be divorced, it is likely that stress led to an accident that might have been fatal. If we read this incident metaphorically, it is clear that Margaret's view of her mother-in-law was threatened by what happened in this visit. Certainly, her relationship with Elsie must have contained elements of competition since Elsie also published a book at the same time as *The Stone Angel*. Moreover, she comments on Elsie's death at age eighty-seven with a strange note of envy: "When I leave life, if I am half as much loved as Elsie Fry Laurence was and continues to be, I will consider myself, as I think she was, blessed among women" (131).

The views of dying mothers are retrospective; throughout most of her adult life, Laurence did not have a living mother figure. Yet she seems to have imagined a nurturing other, perhaps also an ideal reader and a source of inspiration. Ruth Perry has identified the need which many artists have for a nurturing presence and a mothering process: "The functions of the 'mothering' figures included intercepting the world, conferring unconditional approval, regulating the environment, supplying missing psychic elements, and mirroring certain aspects of the self of the artist" (6). Although none of her mothers was present in Elm Cottage, the place where she did much of her life's work, she found the spirit of a former occupant, Lady Maclean, reassuring: "I never saw The Lady except in her portrait, but she gave me a certain kind of strength" (169).

As Helen Buss has stated, Laurence's views of the importance of the mother relationship do not suggest "infantile dependence"; instead, "every mature communal and political effort, including her writing, is seen as a communal extension of maternal or maternal-surrogate influence and example" (190). However, I believe that we must also recognize the extent to which Laurence shaped her life's story around the thesis that mothers are vital in their daughters' creativity. In a way which is classic in the history of autobiography, she reads the past in the light of present insights and conviction.

Moreover, she omits those negative self-images which balance the need for self-fulfillment. For example, when Mum enters the hospital for the last time, she and her brother find themselves going out together to bars after visits. Is she trying to suggest that the grieving over Mum's departure from her life led to addictions she could not control? What happened in her relationship with her brother in later stages of her life? Did she focus on mother figures because talking about her brother and father was more painful than she could bear? Answers to these and other questions do not come easily because of the many omissions. For example, Laurence's focus on birthing does not lead to much detail about child care or the difficulties of single parenting; she does not allude to conflicts with her children. Or does she? In subsequent readings of this autobiography, I have concluded that her accounts of the controversy created over the sexually explicit scenes in *The Diviners* can be read in many ways; her emotional reaction may well have triggered memories of other conflicts in her life, especially those involving her own sexual development and that of her children, perhaps in their teens. Unlike other autobiographers such as Mary Meigs, who, in her first book *Lily Briscoe: A Self Portrait*, reveals both her lesbian identity and her reluctance to tell her mother about the real shape of her life, Laurence has already drawn on many of her life's experiences in the writing of her other books.

Instead, she writes the nearly present experiences in the life of difficulties overcome. This book was written in her Lakefield home, the home she delightedly decorated and furnished, the place where she lived alone in the last stage of her life. Laurence's last book conveys the feeling of release and joy that comes to her in choosing this final destination:

I picked the day that I would move into the Lakefield house: May 1, 1974. I chose May 1 because I thought it was a propitious day, both politically, for a member of the Old Left, and magically, for a believer in magic. When I arrived, the dishes had been washed and stored in the cupboards, the beds made up, and there was food in the refrigerator. Seldom has anyone moved into a house with such a sense of grace and such help from friends. (210)

In the same month, *The Diviners* was published; she recalls the launching party, with the water-divining contest, and her later anxieties at book-signing sessions. In a sense, this is the climax of her search for success and recognition. Although Lakefield is much like Neepawa, it is far distanced from that other place. In fact, Laurence has moved beyond the humiliations of her youth yet managed to keep the best of her memories intact.

This smoothing over, even finding of serenity, conforms to what Carolyn Heilbrun has objected to in women's autobiographies published before 1973. Heilbrun denounces the attempt of some women writers to "find beauty even in pain and transform rage into spiritual acceptance" (12). She uses Eudora Welty's *One Writer's Beginnings* as an example of this. A reader of *Dance on the Earth*, too, could become frustrated by Laurence's tendency to revise too carefully, perhaps in anticipation of a male audience. In this way she seems to belong to an earlier generation of women writers; I am thinking, for example, of Edith Wharton's careful shaping of her past in *A Backward Glance*. But Laurence does tell us that she knows she is evading some truths about her life:

I knew I didn't want to write the entire story of my life, for numerous reasons, one of them being that *is* mine and from the start I recognized that there were areas I wasn't prepared even to try to set down. I wanted to write more about my feelings about my mothers and about my own life views. I realized finally that this could only be done by coming as close as I could bear to my own life, but in such a way that I could also deal with broader themes that interested and absorbed me. (7)

The essay materials, then, frame her life and allow her to deal with the pain of recalling the past. In a sense, she cannot tell us directly about ways in which she was victimized as a woman, but she can comment on the sculpture called "Crucified Woman" (15), and she can express anger about the exclusion of the female principle in faith (15). Moreover, Laurence describes her reactions to the singing of hymns as one of exclusion: "'I love these hymns; I love their music. Yet when I sing them I feel left out, deprived" (15). On subsequent readings of her autobiography, I have concluded that this is a clear comment on her feelings as a child on being socially excluded in the town of Neepawa. As a single parent, and as an aging single woman, she continues to feel cast in the role of outsider and to feel kinship with others who are marginalized in Canadian society.

The Diviners, her "spiritual autobiography" (208), probably comes closer to providing us with the secrets of Laurence's life than does *Dance on the Earth*. But she denies that this is so: "because I have written so much about women, I have often been told I write autobiographically. I have no objections to writers who do write straight out of their own lives, but apart from *A Bird in the House*, which is loosely based on my family and my childhood, I don't happen to be one of them" (209). However, we are still left with the case of unconscious self-revelation in both *The Diviners* and *Dance on the Earth*. The characterization of Morag provides some thought provoking ways of regarding Laurence in the last stages of her life: sipping a drink, smoking, thinking, reliving, dreaming, delighting in adult children but engaged in conflict with them, content with past achievements, and perhaps unable to imagine a future or enact change. Laurence suggests another possibility: what she wrote as fiction later became fact, as in the case of writing about the Métis peoples and then receiving a call from a Métis woman, Alice Williams, a quilter, who became her friend.

The writing of *Dance on the Earth* involves a collaboration between mother and daughter, Jocelyn, as well as the help of Joan Johnston. Jocelyn's preface records her views of the writing process as different from the composing of Laurence's other books because of the dictation into a tape recorder. Thus, her mother's voice was more closely recorded than in her other books. This writer's own reading of *Dance on the Earth* tells that Laurence made good use of the tape recorder; readers, in fact, have a palpable sense of her speaking voice; she comes alive as a speaking person. But that is only one dimension of the autobiography. Jocelyn's comments about her "superstitious feeling about the damn book" (xi) suggest that Laurence had a sense that her life was over long before she was diagnosed with lung cancer. She wanted to write her own last chapter, but in the end, Jocelyn wrote it. Her son, David, is also included; his photograph of her in the last year of her life provides the back cover of the book. Together, her children frame her life story.

Dance on the Earth is, however, a public document, written at a time when Laurence was concerned about maintaining her identity as a well-known and beloved public figure. She seems to strain at maintaining genial relations with potential readers, but her aim to comment assertively on public issues is clear. Her life writing is characterized by the determination to move from private to public spaces. As Carolyn Heilbrun states in *Writing a Woman's Life*, "Power is the ability to take one's place in whatever discourse is essential to action and the right to have one's part matter" (18). In fact, Laurence sums up her political and religious views more clearly than any of the other Canadian women autobiographers of her vintage. Her autobiography is much more a politicization of the personal than any of the following: Gabrielle Roy's *Enchantment and Sorrow* (1987), Dorothy Livesay's *Journey With My Selves* (1991) and Elizabeth Brewster's *The Invention of Truth* (1991). Laurence's difficulty seems to lie in moving easily from the private to the public and in linking the two in her daily life.

In conclusion, the deaths of the mothers in *Dance on the Earth* have both private and public meaning for Laurence; they chart her progress toward personal independence. It is significant that the first death recorded, that of her birth mother, has Victorian overtones, reflecting sentimental views of the role of woman in the household; the institutionalized death of the stepmother takes place outside the home, away from children and grandchildren; the death which Laurence favors is that of her friend's mother, an event in the home which leads to a celebration of life and mingling of families and customs. Laurence's own death was a solitary event; the acknowledgment of that event, however, was national and international. Her memoir does indeed draw attention to the passing of a public figure, whose body will be encased imaginatively in the quilt/ shroud which she has been weaving with words as she creates this text. The production of the book, then, acts as a ritualized celebration of her death.

Margaret Laurence's autobiography provides us, finally, with further understanding of the difficulties of Canadian writers in the mid-twentieth century.

Naively, she makes a courageous decision to take her children to England, as the ideal place to write; she believes that there she will find a community of other writers to sustain her: "I imagined, wrongly as it turned out, there would be a literary community that would receive me with open arms and I would at last have the company of other writers, members of my tribe" (157-58). Throughout the editing of this book, and, by implication, her life, she does not mention the deep disappointment she must have felt. Laurence's return to Canada, as she records it, is triumphant because she has achieved success. Read from another perspective, her life's events suggest the desperation that was involved in achieving that success; perhaps she felt she could not go home unless she was an acclaimed writer. Furthermore, in the myth of the Canadian woman writer which she creates, sexual relationships outside marriage have no place: "It was a foregone conclusion, in my mind, that I would never take a man to Elm Cottage. My children were more important than any sexual relationship could ever be. Anyhow, living out in the wilds of Buckinghamshire, where was I going to meet anyone? I used to wonder if I had deliberately isolated myself so that a relationship with a man would be all but impossible" (170). Having no other way to earn a living than writing, she must succeed or perish! Her return to Canada, however, did involve learning to teach, to speak in public, and to perform administrative duties.

A postcolonial who chose to spend her most productive years in the heart of the empire, a sensual woman who denied her own sensuality in midlife, and an outstanding feminist writer who worried that she had no career other than writing, Margaret Laurence still presents a series of contradictions. *Dance on the Earth* has no point of resolution or conclusion; Laurence's memoir fragments in the last pages as she breaks into a polyphony of many voices in prayer, speech, private discourse, and essay. The memoir seems, mysteriously, to suggest her hope for spiritual continuity, at least for readers who will turn again to the opening pages of the book.

WORKS CITED

Adams, Timothy Dow. *Telling Lies in Modern American Autobiography*. Chapel Hill and London: University of North Carolina Press, 1990.

Buss, Helen M. *Mapping Our Selves: Canadian Women's Autobiography in English*. Montreal and Kingston: McGill-Queen's University Press, 1993.

Coger, Greta M. K. McCormick. "Dance, Nurture, Write: Margaret Laurence's Memoir *Dance on the Earth*." *American Review of Canadian Studies* 22.2 (Summer 1992): 259-70.

de Man, Paul. "Autobiography as De-facement." *Modern Language Notes* 94.5 (December 1979): 919-30.

Givner, Joan. "'Thinking Back Through Our Mothers': Reading the Autobiography of Margaret Laurence." *A Room of One's Own* 15 (December 1992): 82-94.

Heilbrun, Carolyn. *Writing a Woman's Life*. New York: Norton, 1988.

Kadar, Marlene. *Essays on Life Writing*. Toronto: University of Toronto Press, 1992.

Landor, Walter Savage. "On His Seventy-fifth Birthday." *Oxford Anthology of English Literature*. Vol. 2. Ed. Frank Kermode and John Hollander. London: Oxford University Press, 1973, 585.

Laurence, Margaret. *Dance on the Earth: A Memoir*. Toronto: McClelland and Stewart, 1989.
Miller, Nancy. "Autobiographical Deaths." *Massachusetts Review* 33.1 (Spring 1992): 19-47.
Morley, Patricia. *Margaret Laurence: The Long Journey Home*. Reprint, with an Afterword. Montreal and Kingston: McGill-Queen's University Press, 1991.
Perry, Ruth, and Martine Watson Brownley. *Mothering the Mind: Twelve Studies of Writers and Their Silent Partners*. New York: Holmes Meier, 1984.
Smith, Sidonie. *A Poetics of Women's Autobiography: Marginality and the Fictions of Self-Representation*. Bloomington and Indianapolis: Indiana University Press, 1987.
Sparrow, Fiona. *Into Africa with Margaret Laurence*. Toronto: Educational Canadian Works (ECW), 1992.
Wiseman, Adele. *Old Woman at Play*. Toronto: Clarke, Irwin, 1978.

Selected Bibliography

Researchers should also consult the Works Cited included with individual chapters.

Baum, Rosalie Murphy. "'Unique and Irreplaceable': Margaret Laurence's Hagar." *Old Testament Women in Western Literature*. With an introduction by Raymond-Jean Frontain and Jan Wojcik. Conway, Arkansas: University of Central Arkansas Press, 1991.

Bell, Mark. "'Une economie de tendresse': Thematic Strand in the Manawaka Novels." *Margaret Laurence Review* 1.1 (1991): 25-28, 38-40.

Buss, Helen. *Mapping Ourselves: Canadian Women's Autobiography in English*. Montreal and Kingston: McGill-Queen's University Press, 1993.

___. "Margaret Laurence's Dark Lovers: Sexual Metaphor, and the Movement Toward Individualization, Hierogamy and Mythic Narrative in Four Manawaka Books." *Atlantis: A Women's Studies Journal (Journal d'etudes sur la femme)* 11.2 (Spring 1988): 97-107.

Chellappan, K. "Time and Place in Margaret Laurence's *The Stone Angel* and T. S. Eliot's *East Coker*: A Comparison." *Margaret Laurence Review* 2 (1992) and 3 (1993): 8-11.

Coger, Greta M. K. McCormick. "Interviews: Margaret Laurence Growing up in Neepawa. I. Virginia Shore Sanburn, Phyllis Ralph, Margaret Murray, Gerald Murray. II. Dorothy Campbell Henderson, Marlene Siatecki." *Margaret Laurence Review* 2 (1992) and 3 (1993): 31-51.

___. "Margaret Laurence. The Creation of Women Protagonists." *International Literature in English. The Major Writers*. Ed. Robert L. Ross. New York and London: Garland, 1991, 293-302.

___. "Review Essay: Dance, Nurture, Write: Margaret Laurence's Memoir." *American Review of Canadian Studies* 22.2 (Summer 1992): 259-70.

___. Ten Interviews recorded in July, 1984.

Givner, Joan. "Review Essay. A Broken Read: The Autobiography of Margaret Laurence's *Dance on the Earth*." *Margaret Laurence Review* 2 (1992) and 3 (1993): 26-30.

Godard, Barbara. "The Origin of Narrative / Narrative of Origins: *The Diviners* as Supplement." *Open Letter* Seventh Series 7 (Spring 1990): 26-73.

Greene, Gayle. *Changing the Story: Feminist Fiction and the Tradition*. Bloomington, Indiana: Indiana University Press, 1991.

Gubar, Susan M., and Sandra M. Gilbert, eds. *The Norton Anthology of Literature by Women:*

The Tradition in English. New York: W. W. Norton, 1985.
___. "Women and Aging and Death." *Margaret Laurence Review* 4 (1994) and 5 (1995).
Howells, Cora Ann. *Private and Fictional Worlds: Canadian Women Novelists of the 1970s and 1980s.* London: Methuen, 1987.
Irvine, Lorna. *Critical Spaces: Margaret Laurence and Janet Frame.* Columbia, South Carolina: Camden House, 1995.
Kertzer, Jon. *"That House in Neepawa": Margaret Laurence's "A Bird in the House."* Toronto: ECW Press, 1992.
Lane, Dorothy F. "'A Habitable Kingdom': The Canadian Crusoe Motif in Traill's *Canadian Crusoes* and Laurence's *The Diviners.*" *Margaret Laurence Review* 2 (1992) and 3 (1993): 1-7.
___. "Uncomfortable Tradition," review of *Silence Made Visible: Howard O'Hagan and Tay John,* Ed. by Margery Fee, and *Into Africa with Margaret Laurence,* by Fiona Sparrow. *Canadian Literature* 141 (Summer 1994): 116-17.
Laurence, Margaret. *A Bird in the House.* Toronto: McClelland and Stewart, New Canadian Library, (1970, 1989, 1991) 1994; Chicago: University of Chicago Press, 1993.
___. *The Christmas Birthday Story.* Toronto: McClelland and Stewart, 1982.
___. *Dance on the Earth. A Memoir.* Toronto: McClelland and Stewart, 1989.
___. *The Diviners.* Toronto: McClelland and Stewart, New Canadian Library, (1974, 1988) 1995; Chicago: University of Chicago Press, 1993.
___. *The Fire-Dwellers.* Toronto: McClelland and Stewart, New Canadian Library, (1969, 1988) 1991; Chicago: University of Chicago Press, 1993.
___. *Heart of a Stranger.* Toronto: McClelland and Stewart, 1976.
___. *Jason's Quest.* London: Macmillan; Toronto: McClelland and Stewart; New York: Knopf, 1970.
___. *A Jest of God.* Toronto: McClelland and Stewart, New Canadian Library, (1966, 1974, 1988) 1993; Chicago: University of Chicago Press, 1993.
___. *Long Drums and Cannons: Nigerian Novelists and Dramatists 1952-1966.* London: Macmillan, 1968; New York: Praeger, (1969) 1970.
___. *Margaret Laurence-Al Purdy: A Friendship in Letters 1966-1986.* Ed. John Lennox. Toronto: McClelland and Stewart, 1993.
___. *The Olden Days Coat.* Toronto: McClelland and Stewart, 1979.
___. *The Prophet's Camel Bell.* Toronto: McClelland and Stewart, New Canadian Library, (1963, 1988) 1989.
___. *This Side Jordan.* Toronto: McClelland and Stewart, New Canadian Library, (1960, 1989) 1995.
___. *Six Darn Cows.* Toronto: James Lorimer, 1979.
___. *The Stone Angel.* Toronto: McClelland and Stewart, New Canadian Library, (1964, 1968, 1988) 1995; Chicago: University of Chicago Press, 1995.
___. *The Tomorrow-Tamer and Other Stories.* Toronto: McClelland and Stewart, New Canadian Library, (1963) 1970.
___. *A Tree for Poverty.* Toronto: ECW Press, (1954) 1992.
Lemieux, Angelika Maeser. Review of *Changing the Story: Feminist Fction and the Tradition,* by Gayle Greene. *Margaret Laurence Review* 2 (1992) and 3 (1993): 31-32.
___. "The Theme of the Voyage in the Fiction of Margaret Laurence." *Voyages: Real and Imaginary, Personal and Collective.* Ed. John Lennox, Lucie Lequin, Michele Lacombe, Allen Saeger. Selected Proceedings of the 20th Conference of the Association for Canadian Studies at Carleton University, Ottawa, June 4 and 5, 1993, Montreal: Association for Canadian Studies, 1994, 89-98.

Lindberg, Laurie. Review of *The Diviners*, by Margaret Laurence. *Branching Out* 3.1 (Feb./ Mar. 1976): 39-40.
Lucking, David. "'And Strange Speech is in Your Mouth': Language and Alienation in Laurence's *This Side Jordan*." *Canadian Literature* 141 (Summer 1994): 57-74.
Margaret Laurence Review 1.1 (1991); 2 (1992) and 3 (1993).
Morley, Patricia. *Margaret Laurence. The Long Journey Home*. Reprint, with an Afterword. Montreal and Kingston: McGill-Queen's University Press, 1991.
Moss, John. *The Canadian Novel. Here and Now*. Vol. 1. Toronto: NC Press Limited, 1993.
Quigley, Theresia. *The Child Hero in the Canadian Novel*. Toronto: NC Press Limited, 1991.
Scott, James S. "Self-Writing, Self-Transcendence, Commemoration: Margaret Laurence's *A Bird in the House*." *Journal of the Short Story in English (Les Cahiers de la Nouvelle)* 12 (Spring 1989): 87-105.
Sparrow, Fiona. *Into Africa with Margaret Laurence*. Toronto: ECW Press, 1992.
Staines, David, ed. Papers from the University of Ottawa Margaret Laurence Symposium, April 30-May 2, 1994. University of Ottawa Press, forthcoming.
Stovel, Nora Foster. Review of *Dance on the Earth: A Memoir*, by Margaret Laurence. *Margaret Laurence Review* 2 (1992) and 3 (1993): 55-56.
___. *Rachel's Children: Margaret Laurence's "A Jest of God*.*"* Toronto: ECW Press, 1992.
___. *Stacey's Choice: Margaret Laurence's "The Fire-Dwellers*.*"* Toronto: ECW Press, 1993.
Tsutsumi, Toshika. "Canadian Literature and Nationalism: The Cases of Laurence and Atwood." *Obirin Studies in English Language and Literature* 30 (1990): 25-39.
___. "A Comparative Study of the 'Regions' in Laurence and Faulkner." *Obirin Studies in English Language and Literature* 33 (1993): 91-109.
___. "The Indian in Canadian Literature Through Margaret Laurence's Manawaka Stories." *Obirin Studies in English Language and Literature* 32 (1992): 31-46.
Verduyn, Christl, ed. "Contra / diction / s: Language in *The Diviners*." *Journal of Canadian Studies* 26.3 (Fall 1991): 52-67.
___. *Margaret Laurence: An Appreciation*. Peterborough, Ontario: Broadview Press, 1988.
Warwick, Susan J. *Margaret Laurence: An Annotated Bibliography*. Downsview, Ontario: ECW Press, 1979.
___. "A Laurence Log." *Margaret Laurence: An Appreciation*. Ed. Christl Verduyn. Peterborough, Ontario: Broadview Press, 1988.
Woodcock, George. "The Human Elements: Margaret Laurence's Fiction." *The World of Canadian Writing*. Vancouver: Douglas, 1980, 49-62.
___. *Introducing Margaret Laurence's "The Stone Angel*.*"* Toronto: ECW Press, 1989.
___, ed. *A Place to Stand On. Essays By and About Margaret Laurence*. Edmonton, Alberta: NeWest Press, 1983.
Xiaowei, Chen. "Towards Mother's Role: An Analysis of Change in Hagar's Character Reflected in the Language." *Margaret Laurence Review* 2 (1992) and 3(1993): 12-14.
Xiques, Donez. Introduction to *A Tree for Poverty*, by Margaret Laurence. Toronto: ECW Press and McMaster University Press, (1954) 1993, 7-15.
Zirker, Herbert. "Picaresque Subtexts and Contexts in Margaret Laurence's Narrative: A Generic and Socio-historical Approach." *Margaret Laurence Review* 2 (1992) and 3(1993): 15-21.

ARCHIVAL COLLECTIONS

Margaret Laurence Home, Inc., Neepawa, Manitoba.
McMaster University Archives, Hamilton, Ontario.
National Library of Canada, Literary Manuscript Collections, Ottawa, Ontario.
Trent University Archives, Peterborough, Ontario.
University of Manitoba Archives, Defoe Library, Winnipeg, Manitoba.
University of Winnipeg Archives. Winnipeg, Manitoba.
York University Archives, North York, Ontario.

Index

A-Okay Smith, 180
abortion, 181
Abraham, 6, 22; wife, 27
Abrahams, Cecil, xiv, xxvii, 137-142
Achebe, Chinua, 137-140
Adams, Timothy, 204
affair, 176, 183
African, xxiii, 14, 98, 127, 138, 208; Black women, 209; oral poetry, 130; stories, 108
African Child, The (Laye), xiv, xxii
Afrikaners, 127
Airforce, 95
Album, 103
Alcott, Louisa May, 179, 180
Allkirk, Moore & Bright, 7
Alther, Lisa, 179
American, 41, 179; separate origins, 44
Anastasia of the Hebrides, 127
ancestors, 11, 12, 18, 42-44, 63, 70, 127-28, 137-42, 190; creates, 144; MacInnes, 119
androgyny, 18, 19, 22; of angel, 27
Andrzejewski, B. W., 129-133
angel, 4, 5, 17-20, 22-26, 51-52, 71, 170; bird-man, 18; emblem of guilt, 165; fall of, all powerful, 21; mother as martyr, 166; pride, 27
Annals of the Parish, The (Galt), xxii
Anthology of Literature by Women, xx
antimacassared, 26
archangel, 20

Arlene, 7, 21, 57-58, 164
Asai, Akai, xiv
Atwood, Margaret, xxi, 44, 99, 179, 180, 183
August (Rossner), 180
Aurelius, Marcus, 45
Austin, Mary Hunter, 179
autobiography, 94, 203-15, 212. *See also* Laurence, *Dance on the Earth*
Awakening, The (Chopin), 167, 179

Backward Glance (A. E. Wharton). 212
Bader, 104
Badlands (Kroetsch), 44
Baez, Joan, 128
Bailey, Nancy, 107n
Baldwin, James, *The Fire Next Time*, 29
Barnard, Ann, xiv
Barren Ground (Glasgow), 179
Batoche, Battle of, 10, 100, 115, 121, 149
Baum, Rosalie Murphy, xiv-xv, xxvii, 51-62, 153-60
Bauman, Richard, 144
Bell, Alice, xiv, xxv, 51-62
Belloc, Hilaire, 3
belwo, 130-133
Bernini, 5, 19
Besner, Neil, xiv, xxv
Bible, 8, 26, 69, 73; and Esau, 27; Genesis, 27; Isaac and Jacob, Sarah, 27; Israelite, Joseph, 5; Jacob, 20-21, 71-

72; Jeremiah, 67; Jesus, 8; Job, 23, 73; Leah, 64; Moses, 6; New Testament, 69; Noah, 29
Bildungsroman, female, 180
Birney, Earle, 46
Black and Gold, xvii, 124
Blau du Plessis, Rachel, 180
Blewett, David, 8-9
blindness, 18, 20; stone blind, 18, 20
Bluejay Crescent, 75, 175
bohemians, 26-27
Bök, Christian, 104, 109
Bourlon Wood, Battle of, 149
Bram, 20, 21, 24-27, 52, 53, 57-59, 60-61, 163-66, 169; Bramble, 22, 26; at dance, 162; mark tomb for horse, 26
Branching Out, xxi
Brewster, Elizabeth, 213
Brick House, 85, 86, 91, 95
Bronte, Charlotte, 179
Brooke Skelton, 10, 42, 98, 126, 141, 180-84, 193-95
Browning, Robert, 19
Bryce, George, 99
Buckle Fennick, 69, 75, 78 n8
Burns, Robert, xxiii
Burton, Richard, 130
Buss, Helen, xiv, xxi, 39, 104, 107 n1, 167, 169, 170, 211

cage, bird in a, 20
Cahill, Kevin M., 131
Calla Mackie, 66-67, 70, 157; lily, 70
Ian Cameron, 11, 15; compliant, 154-57; May, 63, 71; Niall, 63
Cameron Funeral Home, 64, 67, 69, 71
Canada, xviii, xxi, 13, 196, 208, 214; Canadians, xix, 3, 42, 44, 137-40, 166, 213; foreshortened, 44; Scots-Presbyterian ancestry as distinctly, 63
Canfield, Dorothy, 179
canning factory, 20, 24, 27, 58, 61, 167
Capital (Marx), 145
career, 179-83; men hinder, growth, 184
Carrington, de Papp, 98, 107 n1
Cariboo country, 76
Cather, Willa, 179-83
Catherine wheel, 65
Caulfield, Dorothy, 97
cemetery, 8, 17, 20, 21, 27, 51-52, 70

centrifugal reading, 97-104, 107 n1
centripetal reading, 103-104, 106 n1
Chancellor of Trent University, xvii
Changing the Story (Greene), xx, 105
chicks, xx, xxi, 7, 24-25, 55-58
child, 8, 74; children, 63, 66-70, 176
Chopin, Kate, 168, 179
Chris, 95
Christ, 46; Christian, 18, 103, 207
Christ, Carol, 161, 164, 166
Christie Logan, xxii, 3, 42, 98-101, 146-48, 189-96; tales, 42, 99, 181-82
civilization, 18
clan, 6, 101, 144; Clanranald, 18
Clans and Tartans of Scotland, The, 99, 144, 149
C.P.T., 101-102. *See* Traill
Clark, Archibald, 10
Close Sesame (Farah), 134
clearances, 145
cloth, 7-8
clothes, 18; *decent*, 58
Coger, Greta McCormick, xiii-xv, 115-28
coherence, 195; *Bird in the House*, 95
Coleridge, 8, 15 n5
colonialism, 14, 138, 164
Coloreds, 127
communication, 69
communion, 177
Companion of Order of Canada, xvii
compassion, 63, 64
conflict, 17, 19, 182-83
Conroy, Pat, xxiii
constipation motif, 23
Cooper, Cheryl, 107 n2
Corinthians, 20
corruption, moral, 5
couchgrass, 18
Country Doctor, A (Jewett), 179
Cousins (Vernon), xxiv
cowslips, 52, 166
Critical Approaches to the Fiction of Margaret Laurence (Nicolson), xix
Culloden, Battle of, xxiii, 115, 119; Canadian, 120
culture, 18, 26; failure, 28; triumph, 21
Currie, 6, 20-23, 26, 57, 166; generosity, 26; petrifaction, 22. *See* Dan Currie; Matt Currie

Crucified Woman, 212

Daly, Mary, 176
Dan Currie, 7, 23-24, 54-60, 85-91, 162, 199
Danielson, Larry, 144
Davidson, Arnold, 91
Davidson, Cathy, 195
Davies, Robertson, 44
de Beauvoir, Simone, 206
de Man, Paul, 204
de Vane, Ursula, 181
death, 4, 18-25, 45, 52, 55-56, 58, 60, 67, 75, 171, 207-11; Angel of, Chapel of, 71; deceased, 19, 21; deprived, 24; John's, 7; joy at Hagar's, 27; mother's, 207-13; unmannerly, 70-71
Death of Ivan Iliych, The (Tolstoy), xix
Deeiye, 134-35
dhu, 119, 149
dialectic, 28
dialogue, 174, 181
Diamond Lake, 76, 83
Diehl-Jones, Charlene, xiv
Dieppe, 10, 87
displacement, 17
diversity, 42, 44, 46, 69
diviner, 102, 197, 199, 211; lost, 43-44
Divining Deep and Surfacing: Women Writers on Spiritual Quest, 161
divorce, 180, 182-83
Doctor Raven, 73
Doctor Zay (Phelps), 179
Dombrowski, Theo, 188-190
d*öppelganger*, 66
Doris, 21, 24, 26-27, 53-54, 56-58, 158, 164, 167, 169
Dorson, Richard, 143
Drabble, Margaret, 179
dreams, Stacey's, 67-69
Dumont, 11, 100, 121
Dunvegan Castle, 119
dust, 17
Dust Tracks on the Road (Z. N. Hurston), 206
dynasties, 17-18, 26-27, 52; Currie, 20

Eaton's, T., 20
Edusei, Victor, 8
eggs, 19-20, 24-27; egg custard, 19, 51, 56, 60; eggshell, 7, 24; motif, 27
Egypt, 5, 18; Egyptian, 26-27, 70, 85; salesman, 70
Eliot, T. S., xxi, 8, 37-38, 175
Ella Gerson, 99, 192
Elm Cottage, 211, 215
emblem, 17-19
Enchantment and Sorrow (Gabrielle Roy), 213
endurance, 176
England, xxi, 11, 13, 183, 214
epigraph, 15, 64, 70, 174
Essays on Life Writing (Kadar), 205
eternity, 17, 25
ethic, Protestant work, 22
ethnicity, 69
Eva Winkler, 180-81
exodus, 5
eyes, 4-5, 72, 75; blind, 165; eyeballs, 18

Fabre, Michel, xxv, 184
family, 182; extended, xxii
Fanon, Franz, xxvi, 129-132
fantasy, 69, 174
Farah, Nuruddin, 134-35
fate, 21
father, 25; founding, 18; Rachel's, 71-72
Faulkner, William, xix; Quentin Compson of *The Sound and the Fury*, 33; *Yoknapatawpha Fiction and Margaret Laurence's Manawaka Fiction*, 29, 38 n1, 39 n6
Fear of Flying (Jong), 183
feminine, 167, 170, 181-82
feminist, xxi, 103-106, 214; early essay, 181; movement, 175; writers, 176
Fetish for Love, A, 108
fiction, 181-82
Fifth Business (Davies), 44
Findley, Timothy, 44
Finishing School, The (Godwin), 181
Finnegan, Ruth, 131, 132, 133
fire, 12, 74-77, 174; of trials, 27
First Footsteps in East Africa (Burton), 130
First Lady of Manawaka, 129
Flamingo Dance Hall, 75
flashback, 64. *See* past
flora images, 17-18, 70; hyacinth, lily, crocuses, 70

Fly Away Home, (Piercy), 183
folklore, 129, 143
Forster, E. M., *Howards End*, 31, 64
Founder, 22, 26; John never, 27
framework, 174
freedom, 15, 64
French, Marilyn, 81, 179, 182-83
Frontain, Raymond-Jean, xix
Frost, Robert, 23
Frye, Northrop, 44
Fulton, Keith Louise, 109
funeral parlors, 23, 70-71

gabei, 130-132
Gainsay Who Dare, 162, 200
Galaal, Musa, 129, 132
Galloping Mountain, 9, 13, 83
Galt, John, xxii
garbage, 8, 15, 24, 102, 126, 141;
  collector, 3, 189; dump, 17, 190;
  Scavenger, 189; town refuse collector,
  180; town scavenger, 141
genre, 180
Gibbs, Robert, 85
gift of tongues, 66, 67
Gilbert, Sandra M., xx
Gissing, George, 179
Givner, Joan, 204
Glasgow, Ellen, 179, 180
God, 18, 20, 73
Godard, Barbara, 105, 108
goddess-mother, 25
Godfrey, David, xxii
Godwin, Gail, 179-83
Goldie, Terrie, 107 n1
Gordon, Mary, 179, 183
Governor-General's Award, xvii, 65
Grace, Sherrill, 81, 108 n2, 184 n2
Grandfather Connor, 82-96
Grandmother MacLeod, 82, 119
Greene, Gayle, xx, 105
Grisham, John, xvii
Gubar, Susan M., xx, 184
Gunn, 119; Colin, 101, 123; Robert,
  99. *See also* Morag Gunn
Gunnars, Kristjans, 77 n3, 105
gypsy, 26-27

Hades, 71-72
Hagar Shipley, xx, xxiii, 5-7, 17-28, 51-61, 126; aggressive, 153; anger, 24;
biblical, 27; Bram, 59-60; clothes, 58;
the Egyptian, 18; frozen rage, 170;
matrophobia, 165; motherless, 166;
nonconformist, 27; pride, 61, 163;
regeneration, 171; at six, 54; Stacey
and, 69; turning point, 72
half-breed, 9, 13, 17, 22, 138, 147-48
Hamovitch, Mitzi, xxiv, xxvii, 173
Hargeisa, 129
Harlow, Robert, 65
Harrison, Dr. D. H., premier, 1887, 121
Harrison, Dick, 107 n1
Hassan, Mohamed Abdullah, 131, 132
Hauge, Hans, 103
Healey, W. J., 146
Hector, Jonas, 71-72, 76; Trojan, 72
hegemonic, 104
Hehner, Barbara, 81, 107 n1, 187
Heidegger, Martin, 35
Heilbrun, Carolyn, 184 n1
Henderson, Dorothy Campbell, xiv,
  120-21
hero(s), 183-84; female, 187-201
heroine, xix, xxiv, 19, 21, 27, 41-44, 63-65. 176. 179. 187-197; artist as, 182;
  career woman, 179-84; search for
  romantic hero, 183, 184
Hersi, 133, 134
Highland heritage, 6, 115-24, 145-46
Hind-Smith, Joan, 168
Hiroshima, 175
Hjartarson, Paul, 105
Home-maker, The (Canfield), 179
Horney, Karen, xxvii, 154, 160
horses, 22, 59, 61, 84-86
Howard's End (Forster), 64; connect, 64
Howells, Cora Ann, 78, 105
humor, 3, 5, 19-20, 189; jest of God, 73
Hunter, James, 146
Hurston, Zora Neale, 206
husband, 180-82

ice, 24-27
identity, xxii-xxiv, 1, 3, 63-69, 127, 143,
  187-200
Idiom of Poetry, The (Pottle), 14
imagery, 7, 64, 168; bird, 20, 70-71;
  flora and fauna, 69-70; griffin, 71
imagination, 27, 41, 46, 181

imperialism, 14
independence, 180
Indian, 10, 17, 18, 52, 58, 83, 140, 141, 162-63, 175-76; Haida, 69
innerfilms, 42, 68, 69
intertextuality, xxi
Into Africa with Margaret Laurence (Sparrow), 208
Invention of Truth, The (Brewster), 213
irony, 19, 25, 27
Irving, John, 41, 44-46
Italy, 19, 69
"It Was Like the Book Says, But It Wasn't," 99

James Doherty, 67; Grace, 67
Jane Eyre (C. Bronte), 181
Japonica, Street, 66; Funeral Chapel, 71
Jason Currie, 21, 26-27, 52-55, 60, 161
Jason with Golden Fleece, 21
Jericho's Brick Battlements, 84-91
Jewett, Sarah Orne, 179
Joanna Godden (Kaye-Smith), 179
Jocelyn, xviii, 206, 213
John Shipley, 6-7, 19, 21-25, 53, 57-59, 163-64; death, 59; favorite, 27
Johnnie Kestoe, 7-9
Johnston, Joan, 213
Johnston, Lucille, xv
Jonah, 42, 64, 71-73, 102, 108, 181
Jong, Erica, 179, 183
Journey with My Selves (Dorothy Livesay), 213
Joyce, James, xxi, 105
Jules Tonnerre, xxiii, 9, 12, 13, 42, 99, 182, 184; shaman, 107, 195, 198; Tales, 100, 122-24, 138-41, 143-49. *See also* Skinner
Jung, 25

Kadar, Marlene, 205
Kamouraska, 106
Kaplan, Melissa, xiv
Kapteijns, Lidwein, xxviii
Kaye-Smith, Sheila, 179
Kazlik, Nick. *See* Nick Kazlik
Keats, 26, 167; Ode to a Nightengale, 34
Keith, W. J., 105
Kertzer, Jan, 94, 103
Killam, G. D., 78 n6, 137

Kinlochaline, castle of, 117, 159
knife, 13, 54, 149; sold, 59
Kogawa, Joy, 44
Kolodny, Annette, 166
Kroetsch, Robert, 44, 138
Kunstlerroman, female, xxi, xxviii, 104, 105, 179, 181, 184 n1

Lady Oracle (Atwood), 180, 183
Lady Strafford, 145; Bitch-Duchess, 145
Lady Sutherland, 145
Ladybird, 74, 77, 174
Laing, R. D., 65
Lakefield, xviii, 211-12
Lakoff, Robin, 173
Land Before Her, The (Kolodny), 166
Landor, Walter Savage, 208
language, 41, 68; improper, 3, 98, 193-95; Scottish reductive idiom, xxiii
Language and Women's Place, 173
Laurence, Elsie Fry, 210
Laurence, Margaret, *A Bird in the House,*, xxiii, 15, 81-97, 153, 212; *Dance on the Earth* (1989), xviii, xxi, xxiv, 90, 204-214, 100, 108 n5; *The Diviners*, (1974), xxi-xxiii, 3, 7, 9, 11, 15, 29, 34, 37-39; and Faulkner, 29, 38 n1, 39 n6; *The Fire-Dwellers*, (1969), xix, xxiv, 9, 15, 29-39; 63-79; *Heart of a Stranger* (1976), xviii, 4; *Jason's Quest*, xxvi; *A Jest of God* (1966), 11, 15, 29, 36, 37, 63-79, 154; *Long Drums and Cannons*, (1968), xviii, 137; *Margaret Laurence--Al Purdy Correspondence: A Friendship in Letters*, xix; *New Wind in a Dry Land*, (1963), xviii; *The Olden Days Coat*, (1979), 208; *The Prophet's Camel Bell*, (1963), xviii, 129, 132, 133, 137; "The Rain Child," 37; *The Stone Angel*, (1964), xviii, 5-7, 11, 13, 15, 17, 28, 51-56, 69, 103, 108, 157-58, 161-71, 210; *This Side Jordan* (1960), xviii, 7, 129, 137, 208; *The Tomorrow-Tamer and Other Stories*, (1963), xviii, 39, 82*; A Tree for Poverty*, (1954), xiv, xviii, 129-135
Laye, Camara, xiv, xxii
Layton, Irving, 138

Lazarus Tonnerre, 9-13, 42-43, 138, 140, 148
Lees, Murray, 20, 23-24, 53, 61, 168
Lemieux, Angelika Maeser, xxi
Lennox, John, xviii
Lessing, Doris, 179
letters, 64, 69; three as framework, 64
Lewis, I. M., 130-131
lifework, 4
Lilac Stonehouse, 42
Lily Briscoe: A Self Portrait, 211
Lindberg, Laurie, xxviii, 187-201
lineage, 18
Literatures in African Languages (Andrzejewski), 133
Livesay, Dorothy, 213
Lobodiak, John, 127
loons, 76, 83, 85, 88
Lord, 176
Losers (poem by Sandburg), 64, 74
Lottie Dreiser, 7, 21, 24-27, 55-58, 60
love, 59, 63, 67, 183-84; affair, 176
Luke Venturi, 69, 76, 176, 183
Lurie, Alison, 179, 180, 182

Mac (Clifford MacAindra), 3, 63, 68, 78 n7, 174-176; Duncan; near-drowning, 176; Ian, 174; Jen, 64, 68, 174, 176; Katie, 68, 174
MacDiarmid, Hugh, xxiii
MacDonalds, 18
MacEwan, Grant, 99
Macfarlane, Karen, xiv
MacInnes, 119
MacLachlan, editor, 128, 191
MacLeod, Grandmother, 82, 119, 153-59; Ewen, 123, 159, 188
MacLennan, Hugh, 44, 108 n6
Macpherson, James, xxii, 3, 10, 99
Maggie Tefler, 141
Man Made Language (Spender), 173
Manawaka, xviii, 8-12, 17, 43, 51-53, 58, 69, 81-95, 98, 102, 115, 138-41, 148, 175, 196; and Faulkner, 29, 38 n1, 39 n6; *Manawaka Banner*, 10, 122; *Manawaka World of Margaret Laurence, The* (Thomas), 37; titled founders of, 26-27
Manitoba, 5, 13, 18
Mapping Our Selves (Buss), xiv, xxi

marble, 19, 22, 23
Margaret Laurence Review, xiv, xxviii
Margaret Laurence: The Long Journey Home (Morley), xix
marriage, 27, 52, 176, 182-84, 193-95, 208
Marvin, 21, 27, 53, 56-58, 60, 126, 158, 160, 164, 167
Marx, Karl, 145
Maslow, Abraham, 154
matriarch, 101, 176
Matt Currie. *See* Dan Currie
Matthews, Lawrence, 105
McAmmond, Wes, xix, xxvi, 115, 120-23
McCallum, Pamela, 107, 193, 196
McClelland and Stewart, xxiv, xxviii
McConnell's Landing, 11, 43, 101, 197
McCullers, Carson, xx
McKee, Mrs., 3
McLean, Ken, xiv, xxv, 97, 108 n2
McMurtrie, Mrs. 26
Medusa, 170
Meg Merrilies, 167
Meigs, Mary, 211
Melrose, Miss, 191
memory, 41, 44, 64, 68, 98, 167
Memorybank Movies, xiii, 42, 97-102, 187-197
Men and Angels (Gordon), 183
Mensah, Jacob Abraham, 7
mentors, 181
metafiction, xxi, 41, 103
metamorphosis, 27,
metaphors, 188; blindness, 17, 62, 174; cockroach, 188; confinement, 176; egg as foetus, maternity, 25; functioning of, 8; ice, 23-24; metaphysicality, 28; rivers, 42, 103; silence, 174; traps, 176
Métis/ Métisse, xxiii, xxvi, 9, 11, 12, 15-16, 18, 20-21, 36, 38-39 n6; 42, 98-104, 116-21, 127, 139-41, 143, 146-49, 188, 198, 205, 211-13
Miller, Nancy, 204
Milne, Catherine Simpson, 116, 123
Milton, John, 105, 106
Mississippi, xxii
Mitchell, Joni, 128
Moby Dick, 71
modernist, 41, 105

monuments, 18, 25-26, 41
Morag Gunn, xx, 3, 9-11, 13, 41-46, 97-108, 128, 139-49, 179-84, 188-200; as a child, 182; identity, 187; like Margaret, 212; tales, 42; Venus, xxi, 66
Morley, Patricia, 78 n4, 81, 95, 107 n1, 205
Mortlock, Melanie, 106 n1
Morton, Desmond, 111, 147
Morton, W. L., 106 n1
mother, xviii, 18-19, 21, 23, 176; birth, 206-207; daughter, 107 n1, 166, 213; Hagar as, 167-71; mother-in-law, 210; step, 205, 208-10
Mother and Daughter Relationships in Manawaka Works of Margaret Laurence (Buss), 39, 182
Mother and Two Daughters, A (Godwin), xviii, 182
Mull, Isle of, 119
multiculturalism, xxi-xxiii, xxvi, 115, 122, 169
Munch, paintings by, 66
Murray, Gerald, 115, 123-25
Murray, Margaret, 124
My Hope Is Constant In Thee, 200
myth, xxi, xxii, 42, 98, 101

Nanuk, 88
Napoleon, 20
Narcissus, 30, 34
narrative, first-person, 65; third-person, 68, 69
Nathaniel Amegbe, 7-8
nationalism, 14
nature, 17-18; versus culture, 2, 28
Nero, 64, 74
neurotic, 65, 156-157, 160
New, W. H., 107 n1, 171
New Mythos: The Novel of the Artist as Heroine, 1877-1977, A, 182, 184
New Perspectives on Margaret Laurence (Coger), xix
Newman, Paul, 65
Niall Cameron, 63, 123, 127
Nick Kazlik, 65, 67, 71, 72, 156; Nestor the Jestor, 67; as snake, 71
Nicolson, Colin, xx, 78
nineteenth century, 179, 180
Nochlin, Linda, 181

Northwest Territories, 176
notebook (for scribbler), 181
nursery rhymes, 64, 70

O Pioneers! (Cather), 179
O'Casey, Sean, 9
O'Connor, Flannery, xxii
Oates, Joyce Carol, 179
Obasan (Kogawa), 44
Odd Woman, The (Gissing), 179, 180
Old Women at Play, 206
old, the, 15; old age, xix
Olmstead, Wendy, xiv
Olsen, Tillie, 173
On Lies, Secrets and Silence (Rich), 177
Onan, 30, 34
One Writer's Beginnings (Welty), 212
Ontario, 11, 13
opposites, 17, 27; structural, 27
oral tradition, 130, 137-40, 143-49
Orangemen, 120
order, 18, 23, 26
origins, 44, 46
orphan, 180
Ossian, xxii, 3, 10, 15 n2, 99, 149, 191
Our Inner Conflicts (Horney), 154-58
outcast, 15
Ozymandias, 18

paranoia, 66, 71, 74
Parton, Sara, 179, 180
past, 41-44, 46, 64- 69, 161, 166, 171
pastor, 19, 23
patriarchal, 19, 173, 175, 177
Paul, Saint, 27, 66, 73
Peace Corps, 130
Penguin Book of Oral Poetry, The (Finnegan), 131-33
peonies, 17, 26, 51, 58; Peony, 188
Persephone figure, 71
petrifaction, 20, 22-23
Pett, Alexandra, xiv, xxviii, 203-14
petunias, 26, 166
pharoahs, 17-19, 26, 70; father, 27; fledgling, 5; grass, 26
Phelps, Elizabeth Stewart, 179-83
Phelps, Henry Carr, 1
Piercy, Marge, 179, 182, 183
Pifer, Lynn, xxvii, 143-51
pin, Scottish Currie plaid, 59, 119, 149

228 Index

pioneers, 18, 21
Piper Gunn, 3, 42-43, 144, 146, 181, 190-95; Piper Gunn's Woman, 139, 181; and the Rebels, 100
Pique, xxiii, 9-12, 17, 97, 127, 141, 148, 180-82, 183-84, 196, 198
Piquette, 10, 12, 42-43, 74, 83, 86, 89, 140, 141, 148; right word, 200
place to stand on, 4; *A Place to Stand On*, 79, 96, 110, 185
Plath, Sylvia, 179, 204
plot, 181-82; love-plot, 183
poems, 3, 9, 11-14
poetry, 4-7, 9, 11, 14-15, 129; lyric, 14
Porter, Katherine Anne, xxii
Portrait of the Artist as a Young Man, A (Joyce), xxi
postcolonialism, xviii-xix, 215
postmodernist, 105
Pottle, Frederick A., 14, 15
Powe, B. W., 106
Powell, Barbara, xxvii
Powers, Lyall H., xxiv, xxv, 29-40; *Faulkner's Yoknapatawpha Comedy*, 38
prairie, 17, 69; bluffs, 4
Presbyterian religion, 6, 18, 24; work ethic, 22
Price, Reynolds, xxiii
pride, 6, 18, 27, 63
procreation, 25
Prometheus, 37
"The Prophet." *See* Riel, Louis
Prospero's Child, 42, 108, 181
Provost, The (Galt), xxii
Purdy, Al, 138

Queen's Own Cameron Highlanders, 10, 123, 126
Queen's University, xxii
Quigley, Theresia, xiv

Rachel, xix, 63-67, 68-79, 128, 154-60, 187, 198; biblical, 64, 67; as birdlike image, 71; and Stacey, 68-70; Thomasina, 70
Ralph, Phyllis, 126
Real People (Lurie), 180, 182
Rebellion of 1885, xxiii, 100, 122, 141, 147; Red River of 1870, 146-47
rebirth, 207
reconciliation, 21, 27
Redl, Carolyn Hlus, xiv
Regina Weese, 19, 21, 51, 56
Renaissance, 5, 19
Renault, Mary, 129
Representation of Women in Fiction, 184
resonance, 82
Rich, Adrienne, 165, 170, 175, 176
Richalife, 78 n7, 174, 175, 176
Ridge of Tears, 108 n6, 119
Riel, Louis, 11, 121, 147
ring, 170; sapphire, 119; seal-ring, 119
"Robin Mills" (2) (Purdy), 93
Roderick, 119, 123, 126
romantic, 26, 182-84
Rooke, Constance, 170
Roskowki, Susan, 180
Rossner, Judith, 179, 180
Roy, Gabrielle, 213
Royland, 43, 103, 140, 199
Ruth Hall (Parton), 179, 180

Salinger, J. D., xx
Sandburg, Carl, 64, 71, 74, 77 n2
schizophrenic, 65, 68
science fiction fantasies, 69
Scotland, xxii, 13, 104, 146, 149, 196
Scots-Presbyterian, 63, 67, 138, 140
Scott, Walter, 26
Scottish heritage, xxii, 13, 115
Selected Poems (Eliot), 175
Self Analysis (Horney), 154
self-alienation, 154
self-divided, 65-66
self-made, 21
Selkirk, Lord, 146
Sellar, Patrick, 145
Seven Oaks, Massacre of, 10, 120; of 1816, 100, 147
sex, 45, 68, 70-72, 176; initiation, 41; medieval, 18; sexism, 15
sexuality, 18, 22, 161-63
Shadow of Eden, 43, 108, 181
Shadow Point, 7, 26-27, 56-61, 167-68
Shakespeare, William, xxi, 105-106
Shinwell, Harvey, 92
Shipley, 17, 21; not modeled on biblical, 27; spontaneity of, 22

Index   229

Silent Partner, A (Phelps), 179-80, 183
Silverthreads, 24, 56, 164, 167
Simpson, Verna, 204; Ruby, 209
Skeen, Anita, xiv
Skinner, 10, 11, 13, 100, 181-82; Tales, 100. *See* Jules Tonnerre
slavery, 27
Small Changes (Piercy), 182
snapshots, 42, 67, 98, 181
Somali Poetry, 130, 131
Somalia: A Perspective (Cahill), 131
song, 9, 19, 11, 70-71, 149, 184
Song of the Lark, The (Cather), 179-83
Southerners, xxii
Soyinka, Wole, xiv, xxii
Sparrow, Fiona, xiv, xviii, xxvi, 137-42
Spear of Innocence, 42, 102, 108, 180, 181, 182
Spencer, Elizabeth, xiii, xiv, xxii
Spender, Stephen, 173
Stacey MacAindra, xx, 3, 9, 63-79, 173, 188, 198; self-aware, 63, 67, 174-76
Staines, David, xx
statue, 21, 22, 25
stepmother, xviii, xxi, 208. *See also* mother
Stevens, Wallace, Sunday Morning, 33
Stewart, Grace, 182, 184
Story of Avis, The (Phelps), 179, 182
storytellers, xix
Stovel, Nora Foster, xiv, xxv, 63-79
Stovel, Bruce, xiv, xxiv, xxv, 81-95
stranger, 68
strength of conviction, 144
strategies, 174, 180
subversive, 97
Sullivan, Rosemary, 182
Summons to Memphis, A (Taylor), xxiii
Susan Spray (Kaye-Smith), 179
Sutherland, Isles of, 119; Lady, 145, 147; Clearances of 1806 to 1820, 145
Swamp Angel, The, 77
Swayze, Walter, xxiv, xxv, 3-16, 103
symbol, 28, 51; characters of birds and animals, 71; of a destiny, 18; duality, 22; egg, 25; fire and snow, 12; golden city, 70; goldfish, 75; landscape and seasonal, 70; living, redemptive water, 23, 24; money, 180; purgatorial flames, 74; settings as, 70; sun-king, 8; water, 75-77; whale's belly, 72; womb as tomb,71
symbolism, 64, 65, 70

Tabernacle of the Risen and Reborn, 66
talent, 180, 181, 185
tales, 182; bear-stories, 45; Christie, 181; Piper Gunn, 181; Jules Tonnerre, 184
tale-telling, 134, 138-141, 181
Taylor, Cynthia, xxvii, 161-71
Taylor, Peter, xxiii
teachers, 66, 67, 181, 190
technology, 176
Telling Lies in Modern American Autobiography (T. Adams), 204
Tempest, The, xxi, 71, 105
terror, a holy, 21, 171
Tess Shipley, 75, 176
textiles, 7
Thayer, Cora, 7
themes, 182-84; communication, 68; identity, 180; Judgement, 74; living water and free flight, of ice, of petrifaction, 27; money, 180; opposition, 17; place, 4, 6; reading, 98; role of teachers, 181; snow, 12; sun-king, 8; talent, 180, 181; thirst for survival, 28; writer's life and art, 41
Things Fall Apart (Achebe), 138, 139
Thomas, Clara, 65, 101, 106 n1, 108 n2, 137; *Manawaka World of Margaret Laurence, The*, 37
Thomas, Dylan, 35, 37, 38, 56
Thompson, Kent, 81
Thor Thorlakson, 3, 9, 175
time, 4, 41-42, 44, 70, 117
Tolstoy, Leo, xix
Tonnerre family, 10, 13, 74, 181, 184
tradition, 180-82
Traill, Catherine Parr, 101, 181
Tsutsumi, Toshiko, xiv
tumor, 73
Tutankhuman's tomb, 26
Twain, Mark, *Tom Sawyer*, 30
Two Solitudes (MacLennan), xxvii
Tyler, Anne, xxiii, 1

Ukrainians, xix, 67, 127
United College, 4
University of Brandon, 77

University of Sierra Leone, xxii

Vancouver, xviii, 6, 10, 13, 42, 43, 63, 123, 141, 174, 176, 183
Vanessa, xx, 82-95, 154, 158-59
Vauthier, Simone, 108
Venus, Venusians, xxi, 66
Venturi, Luke. *See* Luke Venturi
Verduyn, Christl, 105, 184 n2
Verna, xvii, 207
Vernon, Judy, xxiv
Very Easy Death, A (de Beauvoir), 206
Vilette (C. Bronte), 179
Violet Clay (Godwin), 180, 182-85
viper, psychological, 24
voices, two, 66-67; protest, subversive, 173-77; voice, 71, 76, 123, 173-74
Voices in Time (MacLennan), 44
Vox, xvii, 4

Wachakwa River, 23, 67, 140-41
war, 6, 7, 14; Civil War, xxiii; World War I and II, 33, 115, 119-23, 126-27, 148, 159
Ward, Susan, xxviii, 179-86
Ware, Tracy, xiv
Wars, The (Findley), 44
WASP (white Anglo-Saxon Protestant), 98
Waste Land, The (Eliot), xxi, 8
water-diviner, 15, 24; tears, 27
Welty, Eudora, xxii, 212
Wemyss, John, 120; Peggy, xvii, 4; Robert, xvii, 115, 208, 211

Westkott, Marcia, 153-55
Wharton, A. Edith, 212
Wilson, Ethel, 77
Winnipeg Citizen, xviii, xxvi
Winnipeg, 10, 42, 63, 67, 82, 92
Wiseman, Adele, 204; Chaika, 204-207
Wojcik, Jan, xix
woman, 170; career, 179-82; indignant, old, 28; middle class, 179; motherless, 166; novelists, 183; writers, 181-83
Woman of Genius, A (Austin), 179
women, elderly, 153-59; language of, 173-176; life-writing, women-story, 206, 208
Women of the Red River (Healey), 146
Women's Room, The (French), 182, 183
Woodcock, George, 39, 78 n, 100, 184 n2
Woodward, Joanne, 65
wordsmith, 187-201; Christmas, 199
Work (Alcott), 179
World According to Garp, The, 41-47
writerly text, 97-98
writing, 45, 103, 180-86, 206-209; death, 209; as divining, 197; novel of awakening, 161-71
Writing a Woman's Life (Heilbrun), 184
writer, 3, 15, 44-46, 180, 184, 191-200, 203-214; desexualized, 183; Elsie Laurence, 210; feminist, success, 216; insight, power, a triumph, 201; lifework, 4; major, xxi; older, 200

About the Editor and Contributors

GRETA MARGARET KAY MCCORMICK COGER has studied postcolonial literatures since teaching at the University of Sierra Leone; published *Index of Subjects, Proverbs, and Themes in the Writings of Wole Soyinka* (Greenwood 1988), *"Ake. The Years of Childhood"* (Salem 1989), and "Religion in the Literature of Wole Soyinka" (Rodopi, forthcoming); initiated and was president of the Margaret Laurence Society; edits the *Margaret Laurence Review* and *Margaret Laurence Newsletter*, and has published on Margaret Laurence in *International Literature in English: The Major Writers* (Garland 1991), *The American Review of Canadian Studies*, and *Crosscurrent*.

CECIL ABRAHAMS is vice president at Acadia University, Nova Scotia, and has published books on William Blake, South African writers, and postcolonial literatures.

ROSALIE MURPHY BAUM is associate professor, University of South Florida, and has published books and essays on contemporary poets and novelists in Britain, America, and Canada.

ALICE BELL has taught at the University of Wisconsin and Heidelberg College, Triffin, Ohio. Formerly senior editor for a custom education firm, she now freelances in California. She has published on Willa Cather and other American women writers.

NEIL BESNER, chair of Department of English, University of Winnipeg, is past president of the Manitoba Writers' Guild, and has published on Mavis Gallant.

MICHEL FABRE, University of the Sorbonne, a world authority on Richard Wright, has interviewed and published on Margaret Laurence.

MITZI HAMOVITCH was assistant professor, Queen's College, New York, teaching contemporary women's literature.

LAURIE LINDBERG is assistant professor, Pikeville College, Pikeville, Kentucky, taught at the University of Manitoba, published in newspapers and literary journals, and founded and edited *A Room of One's Own*.

KEN MCLEAN is professor, Bishop's University, Quebec, and is working on a biography of Laurence.

ALEXANDRA PETT teaches contemporary literature at Mount Royal College, Calgary.

LYNN PIFER is assistant professor, Mansfield University, Pennsylvania, and critiques North American folk history methods in *The Diviners*.

LYALL H. POWERS has published on William Faulkner and Henry James and in *PMLA*, *American Literature*, *Texas Studies in Language and Literature*, and *University of Toronto Quarterly*. He attended college with Margaret Laurence and is writing a biography of her.

FIONA SPARROW is author of *Into Africa with Margaret Laurence* (1992). She has lived in Somalia and Ghana where she became interested in African oral literature.

BRUCE STOVEL, Department of English, University of Alberta, was chair of English, Dalhousie University, and has published on Jane Austen, Fielding, Sterne, Richardson, Scott, Evelyn Waugh, Kingsley Amis, Brian Moore, and Canadian novelists.

NORA FOSTER STOVEL, associate professor, Department of English, University of Alberta, teaches twentieth-century English and Canadian literature. She has published on twentieth-century writers Margaret Drabble, D. H. Lawrence, Margaret Laurence, and on other Canadian literature. She is writing a comprehensive biography of Margaret Laurence and a critical study of all of Laurence's writing.

WALTER E. SWAYZE is emeritus professor and former chair of English, University of Winnipeg, Manitoba, Canada.

CYNTHIA TAYLOR is assistant professor, University of Southern Colorado, and teaches courses on American-Canadian women writers.

SUSAN WARD is associate professor, St. Lawrence University, and is a founding member of the Gender Studies Program. She has published on Elizabeth Stuart Phelps, Mary Gordon, and Margaret Laurence, and is at work on a book about career women in American fiction.